THE
MENNONITE
HYMNAL

FAITH AND LIFE PRESS, NEWTON, KANSAS
HERALD PRESS, SCOTTDALE, PENNSYLVANIA

THE MENNONITE HYMNAL

Acknowledgments

The publishers wish to acknowledge with grateful appreciation the cooperation and support of individuals,
trusts, and publishers who have granted permission for the
use of copyrighted songs.

We have earnestly and carefully endeavored to ascer-
tain the copyright status of each song. If any songs have
been included without proper permission or credit, the
publishers will upon notification gladly make necessary
corrections. For a detailed listing of acknowledgments for
both the Hymns and Worship Resources sections, see pages
608-611.

Preface

Music has a significant place in the life of the Christian church, especially the church at worship. The stream of church music, springing from its Judaic origins almost two thousand years ago, has been a constant and vital force in the life and faith of the church. Indeed one cannot imagine Christianity without the "psalms and hymns and spiritual songs" already an important part of worship in the Apostolic Church.

Moreover, this stream of music is as something alive, discarding the unusable, adaptive to new circumstances, creative in meeting needs as they may exist. Church music has not been contained in rigid, unyielding forms or patterns, but in different ways has supplied musical expression for the church in its developing life and worship. Hymnology, too, as a significant part of the musical heritage of the church, has not been locked in the closed canon of an ancient and unchanging tradition, but has been alive and growing, dynamically ministering to a living and growing Christendom.

Church music has also been important in the Anabaptist-Mennonite family of the church, ever since its birth in the Reformation. And here, too, church music by and large has been living rather than static, as may be attested by the many hymnals used or published at various times and places during the past four centuries.

Thus it was to be expected when two of the Mennonite brotherhoods, the (Old) Mennonite Church and the General Conference Mennonite Church, independently decided the hymnbook each was using, the *Church Hymnal* (1927) and *The Mennonite Hymnary* (1940) respectively, needed to be brought up to date. The delegates at the 1953 triennial session of the General Conference Mennonite Church discussed the need for revising *The Mennonite Hymnary* and a committee was appointed by the Conference's Board of Education and Publication to work on a revision. Similarly in 1957 the Music Committee of the Mennonite Church began work on revision of the *Church Hymnal*.

For several years each of the two music committees carefully examined its own and other hymnals, trying to determine to what extent its hymnal should be revised and developing a list of hymns it would like to include in a revision. The two committees were conscious of each other's work, shared the minutes of their meetings, and occasionally met jointly to compare notes and discuss the results of their work. Two convictions seemed to emerge from this period of independent work and informal sharing: each group believed a major revision of its hymnbook was necessary and each believed the attempt should be made to publish one rather than two hymnbooks.

Upon approval of a joint hymnal project by the two conferences, a joint hymnal committee was appointed in 1961 from the membership of the two music committees: Lester Hostetler, J. Harold Moyer, and George Wiebe of the General Conference; and Chester K. Lehman, Mary Oyer, and Walter E. Yoder of the (Old) Mennonite Church. Vernon H. Neufeld, who had convened the earlier exploratory sessions, was asked to continue as chairman of the Committee. Edward Stoltzfus joined the group in 1964 upon the death of Walter E. Yoder. The publishers were represented at meetings of the Committee by Ellrose Zook of Herald Press and Willard Claassen of Faith and Life Press.

PREFACE

The Joint Hymnal Committee subsequently became the principal working group in carrying the responsibility for producing one hymnal for the two brotherhoods. The Committee considered and synthesized the work of the separate music committees, using the results to develop a basic list of hymns for the collection. The Committee, through its members and specially appointed subcommittees, gave careful attention to the hymn texts and the available tunes, making appropriate selections and editing and arranging where it believed this necessary. The Introduction to *The Mennonite Hymnal* provides greater detail of the Committee's work with the texts and tunes.

Included in *The Mennonite Hymnal* is also a section entitled "Additional Worship Resources" to provide for greater congregational participation in Christian worship. Along with the singing of hymns this section will provide worshipers with opportunities for additional worship experiences.

There were many who in various ways contributed to the publication of the hymnal, but it is not possible to name them all. The following committees, however, and the members who served at various times are recognized for their participation and assistance in the project:

Joint Hymnal Committee

Vernon H. Neufeld, Chairman	Chester K. Lehman
J. Harold Moyer, Vice-chairman	Edward Stoltzfus
Mary Oyer, Executive Secretary	George Wiebe (Walter Thiessen, alternate)
Lester Hostetler, Coeditor	Willard Claassen, Publisher's Representative
Walter E. Yoder, Coeditor	Ellrose Zook, Publisher's Representative

General Conference Music Committee

Marvin Dirks
John Gaeddert
Walter H. Hohmann
Lester Hostetler
William Klassen
  (Chairman, 1965-   )
Russell Lantz
J. Harold Moyer
Vernon H. Neufeld
  (Chairman, 1960-65)
George Wiebe

(Old) Mennonite Music Committee

John Duerksen
Chester K. Lehman
Earl M. Maust
Mary Oyer
Roy D. Roth
J. Mark Stauffer
Edward Stoltzfus
  (Chairman, 1964-   )
Dwight Weldy
Walter E. Yoder
  (Chairman until 1964)

Text Committee

Marvin Dirks	Chester K. Lehman, Chairman
Paul Erb	John Ruth
Walter Klaassen	Edward Stoltzfus
William Klassen	

Tune Committee

J. Harold Moyer, Chairman	J. Mark Stauffer
Mary Oyer	Dwight Weldy
Orlando Schmidt	George Wiebe

Worship Aids Section Committee

William Klassen	Orlando Schmidt
John H. Mosemann, Chairman	Howard Zehr

PREFACE

In addition to the committee members, Arlene Hartzler served as consultant for the hymns for children and J. P. Classen provided valuable information on the chorales. Special recognition is given to Erik Routley, British hymnologist, who served generously as resource consultant.

Those who worked on the hymnal project sincerely believe that *The Mennonite Hymnal* will increase and deepen an appreciation among the churches for the rich hymnody of the Christian church; that through singing the hymns of the church members in the congregations will find themselves drawn together, with Christians everywhere, in oneness in Christ; and above all that through the singing of these hymns all will render their prayer and praise to God the Father and His Son Jesus Christ.

"Let the word of Christ dwell in you richly, as you teach and admonish one another in all wisdom, and as you sing psalms and hymns and spiritual songs with thankfulness in your hearts to God" (Colossians 3:16).

Vernon H. Neufeld
Chairman
Joint Hymnal Committee

Introduction

The Mennonite Hymnal is the successor to two Mennonite hymnbooks, the *Church Hymnal*, 1927, of the (Old) Mennonite Church and *The Mennonite Hymnary*, 1940, of the General Conference Mennonite Church. The committees responsible for its compilation began their work with these books. From these each congregation has developed a collection of its own familiar hymns which express its own situation and around which it builds valuable associations. The committees tried to select those hymns and tunes which are indispensable to the present life of Mennonite congregations. To these they added a large number of works from a wide variety of sources with the conviction that each congregation's experience would be invigorated by new expressions from Christians of other places and times.

They examined the texts for their theological appropriateness, clarity of expression, quality and durability, as well as for their present pertinence. Tunes were judged for their suitability for the text, quality and interest, ease of singing, and congregational usefulness—bearing in mind that most congregations would sing in four parts and frequently without accompaniment.

The *Church Hymnal*, 1927, and *The Mennonite Hymnary*, 1940, hold many hymns in common. However, details of text often differ, from one or two words to several stanzas. Means for reconciling these differences had to be found. The committees agreed to start with the author's original wording and to use it whenever possible. John Wesley, in his Preface to *A Collection of Hymns for the . . . People Called Methodists*, 1779, articulated a grievance of many hymn writers:

Many gentlemen have done my brother and me . . . the honour to reprint many of our hymns. Now they are perfectly welcome so to do, provided they print them just as they are. But I desire they would not attempt to mend them; for they are really not able. None of them is able to mend either the sense or the verse. Therefore I must beg of them one of these two favours: either to let them stand just as they are, to take them for better for worse; or to add the true reading in the margin, or at the bottom of the page; that we may no longer be accountable either for the nonsense or for the doggerel of other men.

However, Wesley himself changed Watts' first stanza of Psalm 100:

Sing to the Lord with joyful Voice;
Let ev'ry Land his Name adore;
The British Isles shall send the Noise
Across the Ocean to the Shore.

to our present hymn, "Before Jehovah's Aweful Throne" (48) ; and the committees for this hymnal found other changes desirable. Watts' "Alas and Did My Savior Bleed" has one line, "When God, the mighty Maker died," which is altered almost universally—as it is in this hymnal (170). John Cennick's "Lo! He Comes, with Clouds Descending" of 1752 (192) was rewritten by two other eighteenth-century authors.

The Text Committee tried to maintain the integrity of the author's statement. Alterations made for theological, linguistic, or traditional reasons are indicated immediately after the author's name, as follows:

† a slight change—generally one word
‡ alteration extends to several words or one line
"and Others" indicates extensive alterations; if possible the "Others" are identified.

Examination of the original texts, which often consist of many stanzas, yielded previously unused stanzas and even new hymns. The Text Committee discovered, for example, that the last four stanzas of the nine for "Praise to God, Immortal Praise" had a particular contribution to make; out of this poem came two hymns (524 and 525). The Committee selected five from thirteen stanzas for "There's a Wideness in God's Mercy" (78); several of these are new to Mennonite hymnals. The Committee members tried to include more complete sections and continuous versions of metrical Psalms and moved rather frequently beyond a four-stanza norm in order to enlarge the content of the hymn chosen.

The Tune Committee examined the original form of the music in most cases. Frequently the tune appeared originally as a single-line melody only, or as the tenor voice in a four-part version. Here it seemed appropriate to follow the standard procedure in hymnal editing—that of adjusting the musical arrangement to the needs of the text and the possibilities for congregational use. Music for *The Mennonite Hymnal* has been arranged for four-part singing, with the melody in the soprano voice. Only rarely is unison required, although any congregation may choose to sing many of the tunes in unison.

The *Church Hymnal* and *The Mennonite Hymnary* frequently differ in the choice of tunes used with texts they hold in common. The Joint Hymnal Committee was responsible for decisions on combinations of texts with tunes for *The Mennonite Hymnal*. For these judgments they considered common usage in Christendom, effectiveness for four-part singing, and vitality of expression for the twentieth century. *Stephanos* was chosen over *Bullinger* for "Art Thou Weary" (230), for example, because it seemed to be the more direct, congregational vehicle. *Warrington* was judged better for the structure of the Psalm setting, "Give to Our God Immortal Praise" (34), than *Lasst uns erfreuen*, which was used in a more suitable combination (51); furthermore, *Warrington* seemed the more appropriate companion to a Watts' Psalm because it is an English Psalm tune. For "Christ for the World We Sing" *Kirby Bedon* was replaced by *Malvern* and a new, dynamic setting, *Milton Abbas* (424 and 425). Occasionally a tune used by both groups seemed too worn to perpetuate further. The combination of "O Happy Day" with *Rockingham New* (398) from Joseph Funk's *Harmonia Sacra* replaces the more familiar setting. Only rarely did the attempt to reconcile differences between hymnals result in the use of a text twice to accommodate the version from each book.

Rhythm is more varied here than in previous Mennonite hymnals. Time signatures are used when the meter is regular and the song leader can be assured of one basic pattern. Signatures are omitted if measures differ in length or character. In some of these cases the result is simpler for the congregation, if not for the song leader. The music seems to flow more naturally in *Dundee*, for example (258), if the note lengths are varied rather than uniform. In other cases the character of the melody depends largely upon rhythmic interest. The rhythms of some of the Reformation tunes have been restored for variety and vitality (91, 118, 284). Fermatas ($\frown$) have been used sparingly—only where they seem helpful to group participation or where, as in certain Gospel Songs, they function as an integral part of the style.

Dynamics are not indicated unless permission for the use of the music called for their inclusion.

Amens are not always used; rather, they appear with hymns of prayer and praise. The congregation is free to use or omit them as they wish.

Some of the more difficult numbers are placed in the Choral Section near the end of the book. However, even these can be congregational.

Dates of composition for text and music are indicated immediately after the author's and composer's name. The specific date is in most cases that of the first appearance in print, unless the actual date of writing is certain. The latter, however, is not so designated.

The Mennonite Hymnal will be published in both round- and shape-note editions. The first Mennonite singing-school book, *Genuine Church Music,* by Joseph Funk, 1832, used the American system of four shape-notes (mi, fa, sol, la) to facilitate reading. These expanded to seven shapes in his 1851 edition. Since that time most (Old) Mennonite hymnals have been available in shape-note editions—usually with the Jesse B. Aiken shapes, which are used in the shape-note edition of *The Mennonite Hymnal.*

The Mennonite Hymnal is a testimony to the richness of the Christian tradition of singing and to Mennonites' indebtedness to the church of all times and places. It draws on various cultural backgrounds of Mennonites. Their most distinctive book, the *Ausbund* of 1564, which is still in use, is represented by brief portions of three texts joined with tunes that the sixteenth-century Anabaptists might have known (40, 344, 384). Mennonites who have remained close to their German background still sing Lutheran chorales; chorale texts and tunes are well represented. Those who spoke English in the early nineteenth century absorbed the American tradition of Watts' texts—along with authors such as Wesley and Newton—and replaced their Germanic past with American tunes and folk hymns from the singing-school tradition. These strands—German and American—join in this book to enrich the resources of each. The Mennonites' use of the more recent Gospel Songs is perpetuated in this book with a collection in a separate section.

To the major emphases of previous books this hymnal adds a variety of materials. The number of Greek and Latin texts in translation has been enlarged. These were chosen on the basis of their timelessness and durability through centuries of use. Six non-Western hymns (55, 209, and 362, for example) express, at least in token, the committees' interest in being a part of the worldwide church. A search for works in contemporary idiom yielded only a few which seemed usable and singable for Mennonite congregations (Text examples: 295 and 457; Tunes: 172, 207, 228, and 353).

The Mennonite Hymnal offers a more varied group of tunes than previous books. Latin chants (92, for example), Welsh tunes (62, 253, 459), French Calvinist Psalm tunes (70 and 121), French church melodies from the seventeenth and eighteenth centuries (44 and 456), and French Psalm tunes from the past few decades (617 and 618) are included. Folk tunes from various countries—England (71), Denmark (218), Sweden (335)—supplement the larger number of American folk hymns (112, 147, 273, and 322, to mention a few).

The Mennonite Hymnal, thus, is a collection of widely varied hymns and tunes. It represents a number of approaches to taste and to the function of hymns in worship. All of the persons who have had a part in its preparation hope that each congregation can draw from the whole of over six hundred hymns a collection of its own which will be appropriate to its character and size, its musical experience, and its spiritual needs.

Mary Oyer
Executive Secretary
Joint Hymnal Committee

Contents

THE HYMNS

CONTENTS

ADDITIONAL WORSHIP RESOURCES

ACKNOWLEDGMENTS

INDEXES

HOLY GOD, WE PRAISE THY NAME 1

GROSSER GOTT, WIR LOBEN DICH 7.8.7.8.7.7.

Late 4th century
Te Deum laudamus
Tr. Clarence Augustus Walworth†, 1853

Katholisches Gesangbuch, Vienna, 1776

1 Ho - ly God, we praise Thy name; Lord of all, we bow be - fore Thee;
2 Hark, the loud ce - les - tial hymn, An - gel choirs a - bove are rais - ing;
3 Lo! the ap - os - tol - ic train Join Thy sa - cred name to hal - low;
4 Ho - ly Fa - ther, Ho - ly Son, Ho - ly Spir - it, three we name Thee;

All on earth Thy scep - ter claim, All in heav'n a - bove a - dore Thee.
Cher - u - bim and ser - a - phim, In un - ceas - ing cho - rus prais - ing,
Proph-ets swell the glad re - frain, And the white-robed mar - tyrs fol - low;
Though in es - sence on - ly one, Un - di - vid - ed God we claim Thee,

In - fi - nite Thy vast do - main, Ev - er - last - ing is Thy reign.
Fill the heav'ns with sweet ac-cord: Ho - ly, ho - ly, ho - ly Lord.
And, from morn till set of sun, Through the church the song goes on.
And a - dor - ing bend the knee, While we own the mys - ter - y. A - men.

Tr. Ignaz Franz, 1771

1 Grosser Gott, wir loben dich!
  Herr, wir preisen deine Stärke!
Vor dir neigt die Erde sich
  und bewundert deine Werke.
Wie du warst vor aller Zeit,
  so bleibst du in Ewigkeit.

2 Alles, was dich preisen kann,
  Cherubim und Seraphinen,
stimmen dir ein Loblied an,
  alle Engel, die dir dienen,
rufen dir stets ohne Ruh:
  Heilig, heilig, heilig zu.

3 Auf dem ganzen Erdenkreis
  loben Grosse und auch Kleine
dich, Gott Vater; dir zum Preis
  singt die heilige Gemeine,
sie verehrt auf seinem Thron
  deinen eingebornen Sohn.

4 Stehe denn, o Herr, uns bei,
  die wir dich in Demut bitten,
die dein Blut dort machte frei,
  als du für uns hast gelitten.
Nimm uns nach vollbrachtem Lauf
  zu dir in den Himmel auf.

GOD: ADORATION AND PRAISE

2 ALL PEOPLE THAT ON EARTH DO DWELL

OLD HUNDREDTH L.M.

William Kethe, 1561
Version of the *Scottish Psalter*, 1650

Pseaumes octante trois. . . , Geneva, 1551

1 All   peo-ple that on earth do dwell, Sing to the Lord with cheer-ful voice.
2 Know that the Lord is God in - deed, With-out our aid He did us make:
3 O   en - ter then His gates with praise, Ap-proach with joy His courts un - to:
4 For why? the Lord our God is good, His mer-cy is for - ev - er sure:

Him serve with mirth, His praise forth tell, Come ye be - fore Him and re - joice.
We   are His flock, He doth us feed, And for His sheep He doth us take.
Praise, laud, and bless His name al-ways, For it is seem-ly so to do.
His   truth at all times firm-ly stood, And shall from age to age en - dure. A-men.

3 ALL PEOPLE THAT ON EARTH DO DWELL

OLD HUNDREDTH L.M.

William Kethe, 1561
Version of the *Scottish Psalter*, 1650

MELODY IN TENOR

Pseaumes octante trois . . . , Geneva, 1551
Setting by Claude Goudimel, 1565

1 All   peo-ple that on earth do dwell, Sing to the Lord with cheer-ful voice.
2 Know that the Lord is God in - deed, With-out our aid He did us make:
3 O   en - ter then His gates with praise, Ap-proach with joy His courts un - to:
4 For why? the Lord our God is good, His mer-cy is for - ev - er sure:

Him serve with mirth, His praise forth tell, Come ye be - fore Him and re - joice.
We   are His flock, He doth us feed, And for His sheep He doth us take.
Praise, laud, and bless His name al - ways, For it is seem-ly so to do.
His   truth at all times firm-ly stood, And shall from age to age en - dure.

GOD: ADORATION AND PRAISE

COME, THOU ALMIGHTY KING 4

ITALIAN HYMN 6.6.4.6.6.6.4.

Anonymous, c. 1757

Felice de Giardini, 1769

1 Come, Thou Al - might - y King, Help us Thy
2 Come, Thou In - car - nate Word, Gird on Thy
3 Come, Ho - ly Com - fort - er, Thy sa - cred
4 To the great One in Three E - ter - nal

name to sing, Help us to praise: Fa - ther, all -
might - y sword, Our prayer at - tend: Come, and Thy
wit - ness bear In this glad hour: Thou who al -
prais - es be Hence ev - er - more. His sov - ereign

glo - ri - ous, O'er all vic - to - ri - ous, Come, and reign
peo - ple bless, And give Thy Word suc - cess; Spir - it of
might - y art, Now rule in ev - ery heart, And ne'er from
maj - es - ty May we in glo - ry see, And to e -

o - ver us, An - cient of Days.
ho - li - ness On us de - scend.
us de - part, Spir - it of power.
ter - ni - ty Love and a - dore. A - men.

GOD: ADORATION AND PRAISE

5 HOLY, HOLY, HOLY, LORD GOD ALMIGHTY

NICAEA 11.12.12.10.

Reginald Heber, 1826

John Bacchus Dykes, 1861

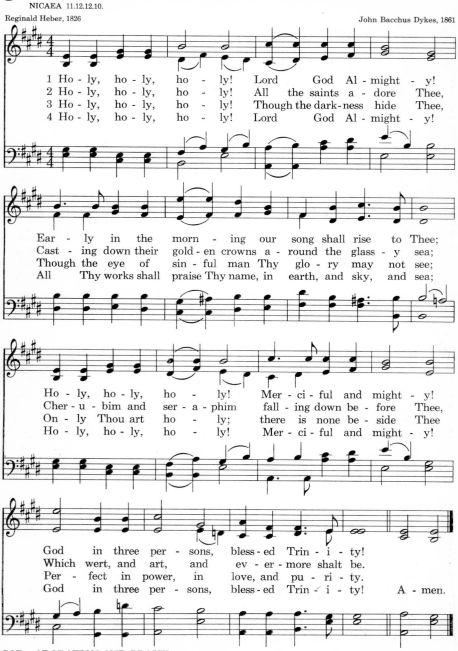

1 Ho - ly, ho - ly, ho - ly! Lord God Al - might - y!
2 Ho - ly, ho - ly, ho - ly! All the saints a - dore Thee;
3 Ho - ly, ho - ly, ho - ly! Though the dark-ness hide Thee,
4 Ho - ly, ho - ly, ho - ly! Lord God Al - might - y!

Ear - ly in the morn - ing our song shall rise to Thee;
Cast - ing down their gold - en crowns a - round the glass - y sea;
Though the eye of sin - ful man Thy glo - ry may not see;
All Thy works shall praise Thy name, in earth, and sky, and sea;

Ho - ly, ho - ly, ho - ly! Mer - ci - ful and might - y!
Cher - u - bim and ser - a - phim fall - ing down be - fore Thee,
On - ly Thou art ho - ly; there is none be - side Thee
Ho - ly, ho - ly, ho - ly! Mer - ci - ful and might - y!

God in three per - sons, bless - ed Trin - i - ty!
Which wert, and art, and ev - er - more shalt be.
Per - fect in power, in love, and pu - ri - ty.
God in three per - sons, bless - ed Trin - i - ty! A - men.

GOD: ADORATION AND PRAISE

OPEN NOW THY GATES OF BEAUTY 6

UNSER HERRSCHER 8.7.8.7.7.7.

Benjamin Schmolck, 1732
Tut mir auf die schöne Pforte
Tr. Catherine Winkworth†, 1863

Joachim Neander, 1680

1 O - pen now thy gates of beau - ty, Zi - on,
2 Gra - cious God, I come be - fore Thee, Come Thou
3 Speak, O God, and I will hear Thee, Let Thy

let me en - ter there, Where my soul, in joy - ful du - ty,
al - so down to me; Where we find Thee, and a - dore Thee,
will be done in - deed; May I un - dis - turbed draw near Thee

Waits for Him who an - swers prayer; O how bless - ed
There a heav'n on earth must be. To my heart O
While Thou dost Thy peo - ple feed. Here of life the

is this place, Filled with sol - ace, light, and grace!
en - ter Thou, Let it be Thy tem - ple now.
foun - tain flows, Here is balm for all our woes. A - men.

GOD: ADORATION AND PRAISE

7 GOD HIMSELF IS WITH US

WUNDERBARER KÖNIG 6.6.8.6.6.8.3.3.6.6.

Gerhard Tersteegen, 1729
Gott ist gegenwärtig
Tr. *Hymnal 1940*

A und Ω, Glaub-und Liebesübung
Bremen, **1680**

1 God Him-self is with us; Let us all a - dore Him, And with awe ap -
2 Come, a-bide with - in me; Let my soul, like Ma - ry, Be Thine earth-ly
3 Glad-ly we sur - ren - der Earth's de-ceit-ful trea - sures, Pride of life, and

pear be - fore Him. God is here with - in us; Soul, in si - lence
sanc - tu - ar - y. Come, in-dwell-ing Spir - it, With trans-fig - ured
sin - ful plea - sures: Glad - ly, Lord, we of - fer Thine to be for -

fear Him, Hum-bly, fer-vent-ly draw near Him. Now His own Who have known
splen-dor; Love and hon-or will I ren - der. Where I go Here be - low,
ev - er, Soul and life and each en-deav - or. Thou a - lone Shalt be known

God, in wor-ship low - ly, Yield their spir-its whol - ly.
Let me bow be - fore Thee, Know Thee, and a - dore Thee.
Lord of all our be - ing, Life's true way de - cree - ing. A - men.

GOD: ADORATION AND PRAISE

JEHOVAH, LET ME NOW ADORE THEE 8

DIR, DIR, JEHOVAH   9.10.9.10.10.10.

Bartholomäus Crasselius, 1695
Dir, Dir Jehovah
Tr. Catherine Winkworth†, 1863

J. A. Freylinghausen's *Neues*
Geistreiches Gesangbuch, 1704

1 Je - ho - vah, let me now a - dore Thee, For where is there a God, such,
2 O Fa - ther, draw me to my Sav - ior That Thy dear Son may draw me
3 O joy! our hope and trust are found - ed On His sure Word, and wit - ness
4 O joy! In His name we draw near Thee, Who ev - er plead - eth for the

Lord, as Thou? With songs I fain would come be - fore Thee; O let Thy
un - to Thee; Thy Spir - it guide my whole be - hav - ior And rule both
in the heart; I know Thy mer - cies are un - bound - ed, And all good
sons of men; I ask in faith and Thou wilt hear me, In Him Thy

Ho - ly Spir - it teach me now To praise Thee in His name through whom a -
sense and rea - son thus in me, That, Lord, Thy peace I taste may ne'er de -
gifts Thou free - ly wilt im - part, Nay, more is lav - ished by Thy boun - teous
prom - is - es are all A - men. O joy for me! and praise be ev - er

lone Our songs can please Thee, through Thy bless - ed Son.
part, But wake sweet mel - o - dies with - in my heart.
hand, Than we can ask or seek or un - der - stand.
Thine, Whose won-drous love has made such bless - ings mine! A - men.

GOD: ADORATION AND PRAISE

9 PRAISE TO THE LORD, THE ALMIGHTY

LOBE DEN HERREN 14.14.4.7.8.

Joachim Neander, 1680
Lobe den Herren, den mächtigen König der Ehren
Tr. Catherine Winkworth, 1863

Gesangbuch, Stralsund, 1665

1 Praise to the Lord! the Al-might-y, the King of cre - a - tion!
2 Praise to the Lord! who o'er all things so won-drous-ly reign - eth,
3 Praise to the Lord! who doth pros-per thy work and de - fend thee,
4 Praise to the Lord! O let all that is in me a - dore Him!

O my soul, praise Him, for He is thy health and sal - va - tion!
Shel - ters thee un - der His wings, yea, so gen - tly sus - tain - eth;
Sure - ly His good - ness and mer - cy here dai - ly at - tend thee;
All that hath life and breath, come now with prais - es be - fore Him!

All ye who hear, Now to His tem - ple draw near,
Hast thou not seen How thy de - sires have been
Pon - der a - new What the Al - might - y can do,
Let the A - men Sound from His peo - ple a - gain,

Join me in glad a - do - ra - tion!
Grant - ed in what He or - dain - eth?
If with His love He be - friend thee!
Glad - ly for aye we a - dore Him! A - men.

GOD: ADORATION AND PRAISE

1 Lobe den Herren, den mächtigen König der Ehren!
Meine geliebete Seele, das ist mein Begehren.
Kommet zu Hauf!
Psalter und Harfe, wacht auf!
Lasset den Lobgesang hören!

2 Lobe den Herren, der alles so herrlich regieret,
der dich auf Flügeln des Adelers sicher geführet,
der dich erhält,
wie es dir selber gefällt.
Hast du nicht dieses verspüret?

O THAT I HAD A THOUSAND VOICES 10

O DASS ICH TAUSEND ZUNGEN 9.8.9.8.8.8.

Johann Mentzer, 1704
O dass ich tausend Zungen hätte
Tr. Catherine Winkworth, 1863, and Others

Johann Balthasar König, 1738

1 O that I had a thou-sand voi - ces And with a thou-sand tongues could tell
2 Ye for-est leaves, so green and ten - der, That dance for joy in sum-mer air;
3 Ye crea-tures that have breath and motion, That fill with life, earth, sea and sky,
4 O Fa-ther, deign Thou, I be-seech Thee, To lis - ten to my earth-ly lays;

Of Him in whom the earth re-joi - ces Who all things wise-ly does and well!
Ye mea-dow grass-es, bright and slen-der, Ye flowers, so won-drous sweet and fair,
O join me in my heart's de-vo - tion, As I ex - alt the Lord most high:
A nob-ler strain in heav'n shall reach Thee When I with angels hymn Thy praise,

My grate-ful heart would then be free To tell what God has done for me.
That live to show His praise a - lone, Help me to make His glo - ry known.
My ut-most powers can ne'er a-right De - clare the won-ders of His might.
And learn a - mid their choirs to sing Loud hal - le - lu - jahs to my King.

GOD: ADORATION AND PRAISE

11 THE GOD OF ABRAHAM PRAISE

LEONI 6.6.8.4.D.

Jewish Doxology
yigdal 'elōhīm ḥay wᵉ yištabbaḥ
Paraphrase by Thomas Olivers, 1770

Hebrew Melody
Adapted by Meyer Leoni, c. 1770

1 The God of A-brah'm praise, Who reigns en-throned a-bove,
2 The God of A-brah'm praise, At whose su-preme com-mand
3 He by Him-self hath sworn, I on His oath de-pend;
4 The whole tri-um-phant host Give thanks to God on high;

An-cient of ev-er-last-ing days, And God of love:
From earth I rise and seek the joys At His right hand:
I shall, on ea-gle's wings up-borne, To heav'n as-cend:
"Hail, Fa-ther, Son, and Ho-ly Ghost!" They ev-er cry:

Je-ho-vah! Great I AM! By earth and heav'n con-fessed;
I all on earth for-sake, Its wis-dom, fame, and power;
I shall be-hold His face, I shall His power a-dore,
Hail, A-brah'm's God and mine! (I join the heav'n-ly lays;)

I bow and bless the sa-cred name, For-ev-er blessed.
And Him my on-ly por-tion make, My shield and tower.
And sing the won-ders of His grace For-ev-er-more.
All might and maj-es-ty are Thine, And end-less praise. A-men.

WE PRAISE THEE, O GOD, OUR REDEEMER 12

KREMSER 12.11.12.11.

Julia Bulkey Cady Cory, 1902

Dutch Folk Song in
Nederlandtsch Gedenekelanck, 1626

1 We praise Thee, O God, our Re - deem - er, Cre - a - tor,
2 We wor - ship Thee, God of our fa - thers, we bless Thee;
3 With voic - es u - nit - ed our prais - es we of - fer,

In grate - ful de - vo - tion our trib - ute we bring.
Through life's storm and tem - pest our guide hast Thou been.
To Thee, great Je - ho - vah, glad an - thems we raise.

We lay it be - fore Thee, we kneel and a - dore Thee,
When per - ils o'er - take us, es - cape Thou wilt make us,
Thy strong arm will guide us, our God is be - side us,

We bless Thy ho - ly name, glad prais - es we sing.
And with Thy help, O Lord, our bat - tles we win.
To Thee, our great Re - deem - er, for - ev - er be praise. A - men.

GOD: ADORATION AND PRAISE

13 JOYFUL, JOYFUL, WE ADORE THEE

HYMN TO JOY 8.7.8.7.D.

Henry van Dyke, 1908

Arranged from
Ludwig van Beethoven, 1823

1 Joy - ful, joy - ful, we a - dore Thee, God of glo - ry, Lord of love;
2 All Thy works with joy sur-round Thee, Earth and heav'n re - flect Thy rays,
3 Thou art giv - ing and for - giv - ing, Ev - er bless-ing, ev - er blest,
4 Mor-tals, join the might-y cho - rus Which the morn-ing stars be - gan;

Hearts un - fold like flowers be - fore Thee, Prais-ing Thee their sun a - bove.
Stars and an - gels sing a-round Thee, Cen - ter of un - bro - ken praise;
Well-spring of the joy of liv - ing, O - cean-depth of hap - py rest!
Fa - ther-love is reign-ing o'er us, Broth-er - love binds man to man.

Melt the clouds of sin and sad - ness; Drive the dark of doubt a - way;
Field and for - est, vale and moun-tain, Bloom-ing mead-ow, flash - ing sea,
Thou our Fa - ther, Christ our Broth-er, All who live in love are Thine:
Ev - er sing-ing, march we on - ward, Vic - tors in the midst of strife;

Giv - er of im - mor - tal glad-ness, Fill us with the light of day!
Chant-ing bird and flow-ing foun-tain, Call us to re - joice in Thee.
Teach us how to love each oth - er, Lift us to the joy di - vine.
Joy - ful mu - sic lifts us sun-ward In the tri - umph song of life.

GOD: ADORATION AND PRAISE

O COME, LOUD ANTHEMS LET US SING 14

SALISBURY L.M. with Refrain

Based on Psalm 95
Tate and Brady's *New Version*
   of the Psalms†, 1696
Refrain added

"Haydn" in Lowell Mason's
Boston Handel and Haydn Society
   Collection . . . , 1822

1 O come, loud an - thems let us sing, Loud thanks to our Al -
2 In - to His pres - ence let us haste, To thank Him for His
3 The depths of earth are in His hand, Her se - cret wealth at
4 O let us to His courts re - pair, And bow with ad - o -

might - y King; For we our voic - es high should raise, When
fa - vors past; To Him ad - dress, in joy - ful songs, The
His com - mand; The strength of hills that reach the skies, Sub -
ra - tion there; Down on our knees, de - vout - ly all, Be -

REFRAIN

our sal - va - tion's Rock we praise.
praise that to His name be - longs.
ject - ed to His em - pire lies.   Great is the Lord! what
fore the Lord, our Ma - ker, fall.

tongue can frame An e - qual hon - or to His name. A - men.

GOD: ADORATION AND PRAISE

15 O WORSHIP THE KING

LYONS 10.10.11.11.

Based on Psalm 104
Robert H. Grant, 1833

W. Gardiner's *Sacred Melodies*, 1815

1 O wor - ship the King all glo - rious a - bove,
2 O tell of His might, O sing of His grace,
3 Thy boun - ti - ful care, what tongue can re - cite?
4 Frail chil - dren of dust, and fee - ble as frail,

O grate - ful - ly sing His power and His love;
Whose robe is the light, whose can - o - py space;
It breathes in the air, it shines in the light,
In Thee do we trust, nor find Thee to fail;

Our Shield and De - fend - er, the An - cient of Days,
His char - iots of wrath the deep thun - der - clouds form,
It streams from the hills, it de - scends to the plain,
Thy mer - cies how ten - der, how firm to the end!

Pa - vil - ioned in splen-dor, and gird - ed with praise.
And dark is His path on the wings of the storm.
And sweet - ly dis - tils in the dew and the rain.
Our Mak - er, De - fend - er, Re - deem - er and Friend. A - men.

GOD: ADORATION AND PRAISE

PRAISE, MY SOUL, THE KING OF HEAVEN 16

BENEDIC ANIMA 8.7.8.7.8.7.

Henry Frances Lyte, 1834

John Goss, 1869

1 Praise, my soul, the King of heav - en; To His feet thy
2 Praise Him for His grace and fa - vor To our fa - thers
3 Fa - ther - like, He tends and spares us; Well our fee - ble
4 An - gels, help us to a - dore Him; Ye be - hold Him

trib - ute bring; Ran - somed, healed, re - stored, for - giv - en,
in dis - tress; Praise Him, still the same for - ev - er,
frame He knows; In His hands He gen - tly bears us,
face to face; Sun and moon, bow down be - fore Him;

Who, like me, His praise should sing? Praise Him, praise Him,
Slow to chide, and swift to bless; Praise Him, praise Him,
Res - cues us from all our foes; Praise Him, praise Him,
Dwell - ers all in time and space, Praise Him, praise Him,

praise Him, praise Him, Praise the ev - er - last - ing King.
praise Him, praise Him, Glo - rious in His faith - ful - ness.
praise Him, praise Him, Wide - ly as His mer - cy goes.
praise Him, praise Him, Praise with us the God of grace. A - men.

GOD: ADORATION AND PRAISE

17 MY SOUL, AWAKE AND RENDER

WACH AUF, MEIN HERZ 7.7.7.7.

Paul Gerhardt, 1648
Wach auf, mein Herz, und singe
Tr. Johann Christian Jacobi, 1720, and Others

N. Selnecker's
Christliche Psalmen . . . , 1587

1 My soul, a - wake and ren - der To
2 O Lord, be Thou my trea - sure, Ful -
3 Thy love be my sal - va - tion, My

God, thy great de - fend - er, Thy prayer and thy thanks-
fill in me Thy plea - sure, And let Thy Spir - it
heart Thy hab - i - ta - tion, Thy Word my food and

giv - ing For all the joys of liv - ing.
guide me Lest e - vil should be - tide me.
glad - ness Till heaven dis - pels all sad - ness.

18 MY GOD, HOW ENDLESS IS THY LOVE

WARD L.M.

Isaac Watts, 1709

"Scotch Tune"
Arranged by Lowell Mason, 1830

1 My God, how end - less is Thy love! Thy gifts are ev - 'ry eve - ning new;
2 Thou spread'st the cur - tains of the night, Great Guard-ian of my sleep - ing hours;
3 I yield my pow'rs to Thy com-mand; To Thee I con - se - crate my days;

GOD: ADORATION AND PRAISE

And morn-ing mer-cies from a-bove Gen-tly dis - til like ear-ly dew.
Thy sov-'reign word re-stores the light, And quick-ens all my drow-sy pow'rs.
Per - pet-ual bless-ings from Thine hand De-mand per - pet - ual songs of praise.

ERE THE BLUE HEAVENS 19

GERMANY L.M.

Isaac Watts, 1707

W. Gardiner's *Sacred Melodies*, 1815

1 Ere the blue heav'ns were stretched a - broad, From ev - er -
2 By His own power were all things made; By Him sup -
3 Mor - tals with joy be - held His face, Th' e - ter - nal
4 Arch - an - gels leave their high a - bode To learn new

last - ing was the Word; With God He was; the
port - ed, all things stand; He is the whole cre -
Fa - ther's on - ly Son; How full of truth! how
mys - t'ries here, and tell The loves of our de -

Word was God, And must di - vine - ly be a - dored.
a - tion's head, And an - gels fly at His com - mand.
full of grace! When through His eyes the God - head shone.
scend - ing God, The glo - ries of Em - man - u - el.

GOD: ADORATION AND PRAISE

20 PRAISE THOU THE LORD, O MY SOUL

LOBE DEN HERREN, O MEINE SEELE 10.8.10.8.8.8.8.

Based on Psalm 146
Johann Daniel Herrnschmidt, 1714
Lobe den Herren, o meine Seele
Tr. Lester Hostetler, 1938

New-vermehrte Christliche Seelenharf
Ansbach, 1664

1 Praise thou the Lord, O my soul, sing prais-es! Him let me bless in
2 Praise, all ye peo-ple, His name all-glo-rious, Him who in heav'n and

life and death. All through my days His great love a-maz-es,
earth doth reign. All that hath life and breath, sound the cho-rus,

Him let me praise with ev-ery breath, Who life and light hath giv'n to me.
Sing ye His praise with glad re-frain. Ye chil-dren of our ho-ly God,

Bless, O my soul, e-ter-nal-ly. Hal-le-lu-jah! Hal-le-lu-jah!
Fa-ther and Son, and Spir-it, laud. Hal-le-lu-jah! Hal-le-lu-jah! A-men.

GOD: ADORATION AND PRAISE

SING PRAISE TO GOD 21

MIT FREUDEN ZART 8.7.8.7.8.8.7.

Johann Jacob Schütz, 1675
Sei Lob und Ehr dem höchsten Gut
Tr. Frances Elizabeth Cox, 1864

Adapted from *Geneva 138, Pseaulmes . . .* , Lyon, 1547
Bohemian Brethren's *Kirchengeseng . . .* ,
Berlin, 1566

1 Sing praise to God who reigns a-bove, The God of all cre - a - tion,
2 What God's al-might-y power hath made His gra-cious mer - cy keep - eth;
3 The Lord is nev - er far a - way, Through-out all grief dis - tress - ing
4 Then all my glad-some way a - long, I sing a - loud Thy prais - es,

The God of power, the God of love, The God of our sal - va - tion;
By morn-ing glow or eve-ning shade, His watch-ful eye ne'er sleep - eth,
An ev - er-pres-ent help and stay, Our peace, and joy, and bless - ing.
That men may hear the grate-ful song My voice un - wear - ied rais - es:

With heal - ing balm my soul He fills, And ev - ery faith - less
With - in the king - dom of His might, Lo! all is just, and
As with a moth - er's ten - der hand, He leads His own, His
Be joy - ful in the Lord, my heart! Both soul and bod - y

mur-mur stills; To God all praise and glo - ry!
all is right: To God all praise and glo - ry!
cho - sen band; To God all praise and glo - ry!
bear your part! To God all praise and glo - ry! A - men.

GOD: ADORATION AND PRAISE

22 LET ALL THE WORLD

LUCKINGTON 10.4.6.6.6.6.10.4.

George Herbert, 1633

Basil Harwood, 1908

1 Let all the world in ev-ery corn-er sing "My God and King!"
2 Let all the world in ev-ery corn-er sing "My God and King!"

The heavens are not too high; His praise may thith-er fly:
The church with psalms must shout, No door can keep them out:

The earth is not too low; His prais-es there may grow,
But, a-bove all, the heart Must bear the long-est part.

Let all the world in ev-ery corn-er sing "My God and King!"
Let all the world in ev-ery corn-er sing "My God and King!"

GOD: ADORATION AND PRAISE

WE WOULD EXTOL THEE 23

GENEVA 124 (OLD 124th) 10.10.10.10.10.

Based on Psalm 145
Nichol Grieve, 1940

Pseaumes octante trois . . . , Geneva, 1551
Harmony adapted from Claude Goudimel, 1565

1 We would ex - tol Thee, ev - er - bless - ed Lord; Thy ho - ly
2 Age shall to age pass on the end - less song, Tell - ing the
3 Thou, Lord, art gra - cious, mer - ci - ful to all, Nigh to Thy

name for ev - er be a - dored; Each day we live to
won - ders which to Thee be - long, Thy might - y acts with
chil - dren when on Thee they call; Slow un - to an - ger,

Thee our psalm we raise: Thou, God and King, art wor - thy of our
joy and fear re - late; Laud we Thy glo - ry while on Thee we
pit - i - ful and kind, Thou to com - pas - sion ev - er art in-

praise, Great and un - search - a - ble in all Thy ways.
wait, Glad in the knowl - edge of Thy love so great.
clined: We love Thee with our heart and strength and mind.

GOD: ADORATION AND PRAISE

24 HOLY LORD, HOLY LORD

FAHRE FORT 6.7.8.7.8.9.6.

Christian Gregor, 1778
Heiliger, Heiliger, Heiliger, Herr Zebaoth
Tr. F. W. Foster, C. G. Clemens, J. Swertner‡, 1789

J. A. Freylinghausen's *Neues
Geistreiches Gesangbuch*,
1704

1 Ho - ly Lord, ho - ly Lord, Ho - ly and al - might - y Lord,
2 Thanks and praise, thanks and praise, Thanks and praise be ev - er Thine,
3 Lord, our God, Lord, our God, May Thy pre - cious sav - ing Word,

Thou, who, as the great Cre - a - tor, Art by all Thy works a - dored;
That Thy Word to us is giv - en, Teach-ing us with pow'r di - vine,
Till our race is here com - plet - ed, Light un - to our path af - ford;

Source of u - ni - ver - sal na - ture, And to man re -
That the Lord of earth and heav - en, Ev - er - last - ing
And, when in Thy pres - ence seat - ed, We to Thee will

deemed by Je - sus' blood, Lord, our God! Lord, our God!
life for us to gain, Once was slain, once was slain.
ren - der for Thy grace Cease-less praise, cease - less praise. A - men.

GOD: ADORATION AND PRAISE

I'LL PRAISE MY MAKER 25

NASHVILLE 8.8.8.8.8.8.

Based on Psalm 146
Isaac Watts, 1719

Lowell Mason, 1832

1 I'll praise my Mak - er with my breath, And when my voice is
2 Hap - py the man whose hopes re - ly On Is - rael's God; He
3 The Lord hath eyes to give the blind; The Lord sup - ports the
4 I'll praise Him while He lends me breath, And when my voice is

lost in death, Praise shall em - ploy my no - bler powers; My
made the sky And earth and seas, with all their train: His
sink - ing mind; He sends the la - b'ring con - science peace; He
lost in death, Praise shall em - ploy my no - bler powers; My

days of praise shall ne'er be past, While life, and thought, and
truth for - ev - er stands se - cure; He saves th'op - pressed, He
helps the stran - ger in dis - tress, The wid - ow and the
days of praise shall ne'er be past, While life, and thought, and

be - ing last, Or im - mor - tal - i - ty en - dures.
feeds the poor, And none shall find His prom - ise vain.
fa - ther - less, And grants the pris - 'ner sweet re - lease.
be - ing last, Or im - mor - tal - i - ty en - dures. A - men.

GOD: ADORATION AND PRAISE

26 LORD, WHO CAN BE WITH THEE COMPARED

HERR, DIR IST NIEMAND 9.9.8.9.9.8.9.8.9.8.

Johann A. Cramer, 1763
Herr, Dir ist Niemand zu vergleichen
Tr. Harriett R. Spaeth, 1913

Justin Heinrich Knecht, 1793

1 Lord, who can be with Thee com-par-ed? Or who Thy great-ness
Praise, hon-or, maj-es-ty re-ceiv-ing, Thou Source and Life of
2 Ex-alt, my soul, ex-alt the glo-ry Of my Cre-a-tor,
Sing thy tri-um-phant songs be-fore Him, Re-peat them, all His

hath de-clar-ed? What ar-dent thought dis-cerned a-right?
all the liv-ing, Thy daz-zling vest-ment is the light! Fur-ther than
tell the sto-ry That all the earth may un-der-stand!
saints, a-dore Him Who holds us by His might-y hand! Re-joice in

our poor reck-'ning stretch-es, Be-yond the ken of mor-tal eye, Or bound-less
Him, ye hosts of heav-en, To Him a-lone your voic-es raise; Wor-thy is

depths of star-ry reach-es, There hast Thou set Thy throne on high.
He, to whom be giv-en Hon-or and wor-ship, thanks and praise. A-men.

GOD: ADORATION AND PRAISE

PRAISE THE LORD, YE HEAVENS 27

FABEN 8.7.8.7.D.

Based on Psalm 148
Foundling Hospital Collection, c. 1796, St. 1 and 2
Edward Osler, 1836, St. 3

John H. Wilcox, 1849

1 Praise the Lord: ye heav'ns, a - dore Him; Praise Him, an - gels in the height;
2 Praise the Lord, for He is glo - rious; Nev - er shall His prom - ise fail:
3 Wor - ship, hon - or, glo - ry, bless - ing, Lord, we of - fer un - to Thee;

Sun and moon, re - joice be - fore Him, Praise Him, all ye stars of light.
God hath made His saints vic - to - rious; Sin and death shall not pre - vail.
Young and old, Thy praise ex - press - ing, In glad hom - age bend the knee.

Praise the Lord, for He hath spo - ken; Worlds His might - y voice o - beyed;
Praise the God of our sal - va - tion; Hosts on high, His power pro - claim;
All the saints in heav'n a - dore Thee; We would bow be - fore Thy throne:

Laws which nev - er shall be bro - ken For their guid-ance He hath made.
Heav'n and earth and all cre - a - tion, Laud and mag-ni - fy His name.
As Thine an - gels serve be-fore Thee, So on earth Thy will be done. A - men.

28 O GOD, WE PRAISE THEE

TALLIS' ORDINAL C.M.

Based on *Te Deum laudamus*.
Tate and Brady's
Supplement to the New Version . . . , 1700

Thomas Tallis, c. 1567

1 O God, we praise Thee, and con-fess That Thou the on - ly Lord
2 To Thee all an - gels cry a - loud; To Thee the powers on high,
3 O ho - ly, ho - ly, ho - ly Lord, Whom heav'n-ly hosts o - bey,
4 Th'a - pos - tles, glo - rious com-pan - y, And proph-ets crowned with light,
5 The ho - ly church through-out the world, O Lord, con - fess - es Thee,

And ev - er - last - ing Fa-ther art, By all the earth a - dored.
Both cher - u - bim and ser - a-phim, Con - tin - ual - ly do cry:
The world is with the glo - ry filled Of Thy ma - jes - tic ray.
With all the mar-tyrs, no - ble host, Thy con-stant praise re - cite.
That Thou e - ter - nal Fa-ther art, Of bound-less maj - es - ty. A - men.

29 SONGS OF PRAISE THE ANGELS SANG

MONKLAND 7.7.7.7.

James Montgomery†, 1819

Hymn Tunes of the United Brethren, 1824
Arranged by John Bernard Wilkes, 1861

1 Songs of praise the an - gels sang, Heav'n with al - le - lu - ias rang,
2 Songs of praise a - woke the morn When the Prince of Peace was born;
3 Heav'n and earth must pass a - way, Songs of praise shall crown that day;
4 Saints be - low with heart and voice Still in songs of praise re - joice.

GOD: ADORATION AND PRAISE

When cre - a - tion was be - gun, When God spake and it was done.
Songs of praise a - rose when He Cap - tive led cap - tiv - i - ty.
God will make new heav'ns and earth, Songs of praise shall hail their birth.
Learn - ing here, by faith and love, Songs of praise to sing a - bove. A - men.

ANGELS HOLY, HIGH AND LOWLY 30
WINDERMERE 8.7.8.8.7.

Based on *Benedicite*.
John Stuart Blackie, 1845

Frederick Charles Maker, 1891

1 An - gels ho - ly, High and low - ly, Sing the prais - es
2 Bond and free man, Land and sea man, Earth, with peo - ples
3 Praise Him ev - er, Boun - teous Giv - er; Praise Him, Fa - ther,

of the Lord! Earth and sky, all liv - ing na - ture, Man, the
wide - ly stored, Wan - d'rer lone o'er prai - ries am - ple, Full - voiced
Friend, and Lord! Each glad soul its free course wing-ing, Each glad

stamp of thy Cre - a - tor, Praise ye, praise ye, God the Lord!
choir, in cost - ly tem-ple, Praise ye, praise ye, God the Lord!
voice its free song sing-ing, Praise the great and might-y Lord! A-men.

GOD: ADORATION AND PRAISE

31 NOW THANK WE ALL OUR GOD

NUN DANKET ALLE GOTT 6.7.6.7.6.6.6.6.

Martin Rinckart, 1636
Nun danket alle Gott
Tr. Catherine Winkworth, 1858

Johann Crüger, 1647

1 Now thank we all our God With heart and hands and voic - es,
2 O may this boun-teous God Through all our life be near us,
3 All praise and thanks to God, The Fa - ther, now be giv - en,

Who won- drous things hath done, In whom His world re - joic - es;
With ev - er joy - ful hearts And bless - ed peace to cheer us;
The Son, and Him who reigns With Them in high - est heav - en,

Who, from our moth - ers' arms Hath blessed us on our way
And keep us in His grace, And guide us when per - plexed,
The one e - ter - nal God, Whom earth and heav'n a - dore;

With count-less gifts of love, And still is ours to - day.
And free us from all ills In this world and the next.
For thus it was, is now, And shall be ev - er - more. A - men.

GOD: ADORATION AND PRAISE

1 Nun danket alle Gott
mit Herzen, Mund und Händen,
der grosse Dinge tut
an uns und allen Enden;
der uns an Leib und Seel
von früher Kindheit an
unzählig viel zu gut
bis hieher hat getan.

2 Der ewig reiche Gott
woll uns in unserm Leben
ein immer fröhlich Herz
und edlen Frieden geben,
und uns in seiner Gnad
erhalten fort und fort
und uns aus aller Not
erlösen hier und dort.

3 Lob, Ehr und Preis sei Gott,
dem Vater und dem Sohne
und dem, der beiden gleich
im höchsten Himmelsthrone,
dem dreimal einen Gott,
wie er ursprünglich war
und ist und bleiben wird
jetzund und immerdar!

ALL PRAISE TO HIM WHO REIGNS ABOVE 32

RICHMOND C.M.

W. H. Clark, c. 1888

Thomas Haweis, 1792

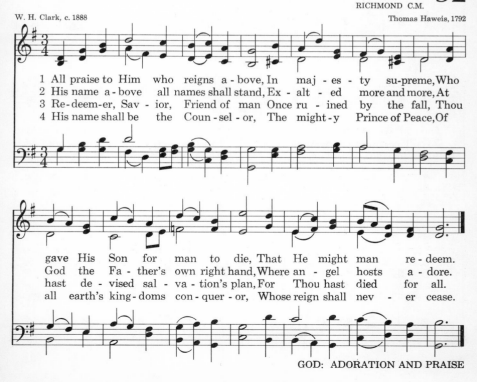

1 All praise to Him who reigns a-bove, In maj-es-ty su-preme, Who
2 His name a-bove all names shall stand, Ex-alt-ed more and more, At
3 Re-deem-er, Sav-ior, Friend of man Once ru-ined by the fall, Thou
4 His name shall be the Coun-sel-or, The might-y Prince of Peace, Of

gave His Son for man to die, That He might man re-deem.
God the Fa-ther's own right hand, Where an-gel hosts a-dore.
hast de-vised sal-va-tion's plan, For Thou hast died for all.
all earth's king-doms con-quer-or, Whose reign shall nev-er cease.

GOD: ADORATION AND PRAISE

33 I WILL EVER SING THY PRAISES

WOMIT SOLL ICH 8.7.8.7.8.8.7.7.

Ludwig Andreas Gotter, 1697
Womit soll ich dich wohl loben
Tr. Rudolph A. John, 1912

Justin Heinrich Knecht, 1797

1 I will ev - er sing Thy prais - es, Might-y God and gra - cious King;
2 All the peo - ple shall pro-claim Thee, Sing Thy praise from shore to shore;
3 When at last my feet have found Thee, When at last I am Thine own;

Glad my heart its trib - ute rais - es, And to Thee my psalms I'll sing;
Ev - ery hu-man heart shall name Thee God and King for ev - er - more;
When the ran-somed hosts sur-round Thee, On Thy great e - ter - nal throne;

Thou art King of all cre - a - tion, Ev - ery land and ev - ery na - tion,
On Thy throne in heav-en vault-ed, In Thy maj - es - ty ex - alt - ed,
When in yon - der land of glo - ry, An - gels tell re-demp-tion's sto - ry,

"Thou-sand, thou-sand thanks to Thee, Might-y God," my song shall be! A - men.

GOD: ADORATION AND PRAISE

GIVE TO OUR GOD IMMORTAL PRAISE 34

WARRINGTON L.M.

Based on Psalm 136
Isaac Watts, 1719

Ralph Harrison, 1784

1 Give to our God im - mor - tal praise; Mer - cy and truth are
2 Give to the Lord of lords re - nown; The King of kings with
3 He built the earth, He spread the sky, And fixed the star - ry
4 He fills the sun with morn - ing light; He bids the moon di -

all His ways: Won - ders of grace to God be - long;
glo - ry crown; His mer - cies ev - er shall en - dure,
lights on high: Won - ders of grace to God be - long;
rect the night: His mer - cies ev - er shall en - dure,

Re - peat His mer - cies in your song.
When lords and kings are known no more.
Re - peat His mer - cies in your song.
When suns and moons shall shine no more. A - men.

5 He sent His Son with power to save
From guilt, and darkness, and the grave:
Wonders of grace to God belong;
Repeat His mercies in your song.

6 Through this vain world He guides our feet,
And leads us to His heav'nly seat:
His mercies ever shall endure,
When this vain world shall be no more.

GOD: ADORATION AND PRAISE

35 GREAT GOD, INDULGE MY HUMBLE CLAIM

HAGERSTOWN L.M.

Based on Psalm 63
Isaac Watts, 1719

John David Brunk, 1902

1 Great God, in - dulge my hum - ble claim, Thou art my hope, my joy, my rest; The glo - ries that com - pose Thy name Stand all en - gaged to make me blest.

2 Thou great and good, Thou just and wise; Thou art my Fa - ther and my God; And I am Thine by sa - cred ties, Thy son, Thy serv - ant, bought with blood.

3 With ear - ly feet I love t'ap - pear A - mong Thy saints, and seek Thy face; Oft have I seen Thy glo - ry there, And felt the pow'r of sov - 'reign grace.

4 I'll lift my hands, I'll raise my voice, While I have breath to pray or praise; This work shall make my heart re - joice, And spend the rem - nant of my days. A - men.

36 FROM ALL THAT DWELL BELOW

DEUS TUORUM MILITUM L.M.

Based on Psalm 117
Isaac Watts, 1719

Grenoble Antiphoner, 1753

1 From all that dwell be - low the skies Let the Cre - a - tor's praise a - rise;

2 E - ter - nal are Thy mer - cies, Lord; E - ter - nal truth at - tends Thy Word;

GOD: ADORATION AND PRAISE

Let the Redeem-er's name be sung Through ev-ery land, by ev-ery tongue.
Thy praise shall sound from shore to shore Till suns shall rise and set no more. A-men.

ETERNAL FATHER, WHEN TO THEE 37

WAREHAM L.M.

Hervey Doddridge Ganse, c. 1870

William Knapp, 1738

1 E - ter - nal Fa - ther, when to Thee, Be - yond all
2 But, Sav - ior, Thou art by my side; Thy voice I
3 And Thou, great Spir - it, in my heart Dost make Thy
4 Blest Trin - i - ty, in whom a - lone All things cre -

worlds, by faith I soar, Be - fore Thy bound - less
hear, Thy face I see: Thou art my Friend, my
tem - ple day by day; The Ho - ly Ghost of
a - ted move or rest, High in the heav'ns Thou

maj - es - ty I stand in si - lence, and a - dore.
dai - ly Guide; God o - ver all, yet God with me.
God Thou art, Yet dwell - est in this house of clay.
hast Thy throne; Thou hast Thy throne with - in my breast. A - men.

GOD: ADORATION AND PRAISE

38 ALL GLORY BE TO GOD ON HIGH

ALLEIN GOTT IN DER HÖH 8.7.8.7.8.8.7.

Based on *Gloria in Excelsis*
Nicolaus Decius, 1522
Allein Gott in der Höh
Tr. Catherine Winkworth†, 1863

Nicolaus Decius, 1522

1 All glo-ry be to God on high, Who hath our race be-friend-ed!
2 We praise, we wor-ship Thee, we trust, And give Thee thanks for ev - er,
3 O Je-sus Christ, our God and Lord, Son of Thy heav'n-ly Fa - ther,
4 O Ho-ly Spir-it, pre-cious Gift, Thou Com-fort-er un-fail - ing,

To us no harm shall now come nigh, The strife at last is end - ed;
O Fa-ther, that Thy rule is just And wise, and chang-es nev - er:
O Thou who hast our peace re-stored And the lost sheep dost gath - er,
O'er Sa-tan's snares our souls up-lift, And let Thy power a - vail - ing

God show-eth His good-will toward men, And peace shall dwell
Thy bound-less power o'er all things reigns, Done is what-e'er
Thou Lamb of God, to Thee on high From out our depths
A - vert our woes and calm our dread, For us the Sav -

on earth a - gain; O thank Him for His good - ness.
Thy will or-dains; Well for us that Thou rul - est!
we sin - ners cry, Have mer - cy on us, Je - sus!
ior's blood was shed; We trust in Thee to save us! A - men.

GOD: ADORATION AND PRAISE

1 Allein Gott in der Höh sei Ehr
   und Dank fuer seine Gnade,
darum, dass nun und nimmermehr
   uns rühren kann ein Schade.
Ein Wohlgefalln Gott an uns hat;
nun ist gross Fried ohn Unterlass.
   All Fehd hat nun ein Ende.

2 Wir beten an und loben dich,
   wir bringen Ehr und danken,
dass du, Gott Vater, ewiglich
   regierst ohn alles Wanken.
Ganz unbegrenzt ist deine Macht;
allzeit geschieht, was du bedacht.
   Wohl uns solch eines Herren!

3 O Jesu Christe, Gottes Sohn,
   für uns ein Mensch geboren,
gesandt von deines Vaters Thron
   zu retten, was verloren;
Lamm Gottes, heilger Herr und Gott,
nimm an die Bitt von unsrer Not:
   Erbarm dich unser aller!

4 O heilger Geist, du höchstes Gut,
   mit deinem Heil uns tröste;
vor Satans Macht nimm uns in Hut,
   die Jesus Christ erlöste
durch Marter gross und bittern Tod.
Wend ab all unser Leid und Not!
   Auf dich wir uns verlassen.

HIGH IN THE HEAVENS, ETERNAL GOD 39

TRURO L.M.

Based on Psalm 36
Isaac Watts, 1719

Thomas Williams' *Psalmodia Evangelica*, 1789

1 High in the heav'ns, E - ter - nal God, Thy good - ness
2 For - ev - er firm Thy jus - tice stands, As moun - tains
3 My God, how ex - cel - lent Thy grace, Whence all our
4 Life, like a foun - tain, rich and free, Springs from the

in full glo - ry shines; Thy truth shall break through
their foun - da - tions keep; Wise are the won - ders
hope and com - fort springs! The sons of Ad - am
pres - ence of my Lord; And in Thy light our

ev - ery cloud That veils and dark - ens Thy de - signs.
of Thy hands; Thy judg-ments are a might - y deep.
in dis - tress Fly to the shad - ow of Thy wings.
souls shall see The glo - ries prom - ised in Thy Word. A - men.

GOD: ADORATION AND PRAISE

40 I SING WITH EXULTATION

NUN WEND IHR HÖREN SAGEN   7.5.7.5.7.6.7.6.

Felix Manz, c. 1526
Mit Lust so will ich singen
Tr. Marion Wenger, 1966

"Bentzenauer Ton," Nürnberg, 1540

1 I   sing with ex - ul - ta - tion,   All   my heart de - lights
2 Whom God sent as   ex - am - ple,   Light my feet to   guide.
3 Sing   praise to Christ our Sav - ior, Who   in grace in - clined
4 Christ bids us, none com - pel - ling, To   His glo - rious throne.

In   God, who brings sal - va - tion, Frees from death's dread might.
Be - fore my end He   bade me   In   His realm a - bide.
To   us   re - veals His   na - ture, Pa - tient, lov - ing,   kind.
He   on - ly who is   will - ing   Christ as Lord to   own,

I   praise Thee, Christ of heav - en, Who   ev - er shall en - dure,
That   I   might love and cher - ish His   right-eous-ness di - vine;
His   love di - vine out - pour - ing He   shows to ev - ery - one,
He   is   as-sured of heav - en   Who   will right faith pur - sue,

Who takes a - way my   sor - row, Keeps me safe and se - cure.
That   I   with Him for - ev - er   Bliss   e - ter - nal might find.
Un-feigned and like His   Fa - ther's, As   no oth - er has done.
With heart made pure do pen - ance, Seal'd with bap - tism true.

GOD: ADORATION AND PRAISE

THROUGH ALL THE CHANGING SCENES 41

IRISH C.M.

Based on Psalm 34
Tate and Brady's *New Version*
of the Psalms, 1696 and 1698

*A Collection of Hymns and
Sacred Poems*, Dublin, 1749

1 Through all the chang - ing scenes of life, In
2 O mag - ni - fy the Lord with me, With
3 The hosts of God en - camp a - round The
4 O make but tri - al of His love; Ex -

trou - ble and in joy, The prais - es of my
me ex - alt His name; When in dis - tress to
dwell - ings of the just; De - liv - 'rance He af -
pe - rience will de - cide How blest are they, and

God shall still My heart and tongue em - ploy.
Him I called, He to my res - cue came.
fords to all Who on His suc - cor trust.
on - ly they, Who in His truth con - fide. A - men.

5 Fear Him, ye saints, and you will then
   Have nothing else to fear;
Make you His service your delight;
   Your wants shall be His care.

6 For God preserves the souls of those
   Who on His truth depend;
To them and their posterity
   His blessings shall descend.

GOD: ADORATION AND PRAISE

42 O GOD, THE ROCK OF AGES

GREENLAND 7.6.7.6.D.

Edward Henry Bickersteth, 1880

Johann Michael Haydn, 1806

1 O God, the Rock of A - ges, Who ev - er - more hast been,
2 Our years are like the shad - ows On sun - ny hills that lie,
3 O Thou, who canst not slum - ber, Whose light grows nev - er pale,
4 Lord, crown our faith's en - deav - or With beau - ty and with grace,

What time the tem - pest ra - ges, Our dwell - ing place se - rene;
Or grass - es in the mead - ows That blos - som but to die:
Teach us a - right to num - ber Our years be - fore they fail.
Till, clothed in light for - ev - er, We see Thee face to face:

Be - fore Thy first cre - a - tions, O Lord, the same as now,
A sleep, a dream, a sto - ry By stran - gers quick - ly told,
On us Thy mer - cy light - en, On us Thy good - ness rest,
A joy no lan - guage mea - sures; A foun - tain brim - ming o'er;

To end - less gen - er - a - tions The ev - er - last - ing Thou!
An un - re - main - ing glo - ry Of things that soon are old.
And let Thy Spir - it bright - en The hearts Thy - self hast blessed.
An end - less flow of plea - sures; An o - cean with - out shore. A - men.

GOD: MAJESTY AND HOLINESS

IMMORTAL, INVISIBLE, GOD 43

ST. DENIO 11.11.11.11.

Walter Chalmers Smith†, 1867

Welsh Hymn Melody, 1839

1 Im - mor - tal, in - vis - i - ble, God on - ly wise,
2 Un - rest - ing, un - hast - ing, and si - lent as light,
3 To all, life Thou giv - est to both great and small;
4 Great Fa - ther of glo - ry, pure Fa - ther of light,

In light in - ac - ces - si - ble hid from our eyes,
Nor want - ing, nor wast - ing, Thou rul - est in might;
In all life Thou liv - est, the true life of all;
Thine an - gels a - dore Thee, all veil - ing their sight;

Most bless - ed, most glo - rious, the An - cient of Days,
Thy jus - tice like moun-tains high soar - ing a - bove
We blos - som and flour - ish as leaves on the tree,
All praise we would ren - der; O help us to see

Al - might - y, vic - to - rious, Thy great name we praise.
Thy clouds which are foun-tains of good - ness and love.
And with - er and per - ish, but naught chang-eth Thee.
'Tis on - ly the splen-dor of light hid - eth Thee. A - men.

GOD: MAJESTY AND HOLINESS

44 O SPLENDOR OF GOD'S GLORY

SOLEMNIS HAEC FESTIVITAS L.M.

Ambrose of Milan, d. 397
Splendor paternae gloriae
Tr. Louis F. Benson, 1910

Paris Gradual, 1689

1 O Splen - dor of God's glo - ry bright, From light e -
2 Come, ver - y Sun of heav - en's love, In last - ing
3 Con - firm our will to do the right, And keep our
4 Dawn's glo - ry gilds the earth and skies, Let Him, our

ter - nal bring - ing light, Thou Light of light, light's
ra - diance from a - bove, And pour the Ho - ly
hearts from en - vy's blight; Let faith her ea - ger
per - fect Morn, a - rise, The Word in God the

liv - ing Spring, True Day, all days il - lu - min - ing:
Spir - it's ray On all we think or do to - day.
fires re - new And hate the false, and love the true.
Fa - ther One, The Fa - ther im - aged in the Son.

O SPLENDOR OF GOD'S GLORY 45

SPLENDOR PATERNAE L.M.

Ambrose of Milan, d. 397
Splendor paternae gloriae
Tr. Louis F. Benson, 1910

Sarum Plainsong

1 O Splen-dor of God's glo-ry bright, From light e-ter-nal
2 Come, ver-y Sun of heav-en's love, In last-ing ra-diance
3 Con-firm our will to do the right, And keep our hearts from
4 Dawn's glo-ry gilds the earth and skies, Let Him, our per-fect

bring-ing light, Thou Light of light, light's liv-ing Spring,
from a-bove, And pour the Ho-ly Spir-it's ray
en-vy's blight; Let faith her ea-ger fires re-new
Morn, a-rise, The Word in God the Fa-ther One,

True Day, all days il-lu-min-ing:
On all we think or do to-day.
And hate the false, and love the true.
The Fa-ther im-aged in the Son. A-men.

GOD: MAJESTY AND HOLINESS

46 GREAT GOD, HOW INFINITE ART THOU

WINDSOR C.M.

Isaac Watts†, 1707

W. Damon's *Booke of Musicke*, 1591

1, 5 Great God, how in - fi - nite art Thou! How
2 Thy throne e - ter - nal a - ges stood, Ere
3 E - ter - ni - ty, with all its years, Stands
4 Our lives through var - ious scenes are drawn, And

poor and weak are we! Let the whole race of
seas or stars were made: Thou art the ev - er -
pres - ent in Thy view; To Thee there's noth - ing
vexed with tri - fling cares, While Thine e - ter - nal

crea - tures bow, And pay their praise to Thee.
liv - ing God, Were all the na - tions dead.
old ap - pears; Great God, there's noth - ing new.
thought moves on Thine un - dis - turbed af - fairs. A - men.

47 O LORD, OUR LORD, IN ALL THE EARTH

DUNFERMLINE C.M.

Based on Psalm 8
Psalter, 1912

Scottish Psalter, 1615

1 O Lord, our Lord, in all the earth How ex - cel - lent Thy name!
2 When I re - gard the won-drous heav'ns, Thy hand - i - work on high,
3 O what is man, in Thy re - gard To hold so large a place!
4 On man Thy wis - dom hath be-stowed A power well nigh di - vine;
5 Thy might - y works and won-drous grace Thy glo - ry, Lord, pro - claim.

GOD: MAJESTY AND HOLINESS

Thy glo - ry Thou hast spread a - far In all the star - ry frame.
The moon and stars or-dained by Thee, O what is man! I cry.
And what the son of man, that Thou Dost vis - it him in grace!
With hon-or Thou hast crowned his head With glo - ry like to Thine.
O Lord, our Lord, in all the earth How ex - cel - lent Thy name! A - men.

BEFORE JEHOVAH'S AWEFUL THRONE 48

WATTS L.M.

Based on Psalm 100
Isaac Watts, 1719
Altered by John Wesley, 1736

John D. Brunk, 1910

1 Be - fore Je - ho - vah's awe - ful throne, Ye na - tions,
2 His sov - 'reign power with - out our aid, Made us of
3 We are His peo - ple, we His care, Our souls, and
4 We'll crowd Thy gates with thank - ful songs, High as the
5 Wide as the world is Thy com - mand, Vast as e -

bow with sa - cred joy: Know that the Lord is God
clay, and formed us men; And when like wan - d'ring sheep
all our mor - tal frame; What last ing hon - ors shall
heav'ns our voic - es raise; And earth, with her ten thou -
ter - ni - ty Thy love; Firm as a rock Thy truth

a - lone: He can cre - ate, and He de - stroy.
we strayed, He brought us to His fold a - gain.
we rear, Al - might - y Mak - er, to Thy name?
sand tongues, Shall fill Thy courts with sound - ing praise.
must stand, When roll - ing years shall cease to move. A - men.

GOD: MAJESTY AND HOLINESS

49 THIS IS MY FATHER'S WORLD

TERRA BEATA S.M.D.

Maltbie D. Babcock, 1901

Franklin L. Sheppard, 1915

1 This is my Fa-ther's world, And to my list'-ning ears, All na - ture sings, and round me rings The mu - sic of the spheres. This is my Fa-ther's world: I rest me in the thought Of rocks and trees, of skies and seas; His hand the won - ders wrought.

2 This is my Fa-ther's world, The birds their car - ols raise, The morn - ing light, the lil - y white, De - clare their Mak - er's praise. This is my Fa-ther's world: He shines in all that's fair; In the rus - tling grass I hear Him pass, He speaks to me ev-ery-where.

3 This is my Fa-ther's world, O let me ne'er for - get That though the wrong seems oft so strong, God is the Rul - er yet. This is my Fa-ther's world: The bat - tle is not done, Je - sus, who died shall be sat - is - fied, And heav'n and earth be one. A - men.

GOD: CREATOR OF HEAVEN AND EARTH

I SING THE MIGHTY POWER OF GOD 50

ELLACOMBE C.M.D.

Isaac Watts‡, 1715

Adapted from
Gesangbuch . . . , Württemberg, 1784

1 I sing the might-y power of God, That made the moun-tains rise;
2 I sing the good-ness of the Lord, That filled the earth with food;
3 There's not a plant or flower be-low, But makes Thy glo-ries known;

That spread the flow-ing seas a-broad, And built the loft-y skies.
He formed the crea-tures with His word, And then pro-nounced them good.
And clouds a-rise, and tem-pests blow, By or-der from Thy throne;

I sing the wis-dom that or-dained The sun to rule the day;
Lord, how Thy won-ders are dis-played, Wher-e'er I turn my eye:
While all that bor-rows life from Thee Is ev-er in Thy care,

The moon shines full at His com-mand, And all the stars o-bey.
If I sur-vey the ground I tread, Or gaze up-on the sky!
And ev-ery-where that man can be, Thou, God, art pres-ent there. A-men.

GOD: CREATOR OF HEAVEN AND EARTH

51 ALL CREATURES OF OUR GOD AND KING

LASST UNS ERFREUEN L.M. with Alleluias

Francis of Assisi, d. 1226
Laudato sia Dio mio Signore
Tr. William Henry Draper, 1931

Kirchengesangbuch, Köln, 1623
Harmonized and arranged
by Ralph Vaughan Williams, 1906
Arrangement altered

1 All crea-tures of our God and King, Lift up your voice and with us sing
2 Thou rush-ing wind that art so strong, Ye clouds that sail in heav'n a - long,
3 Thou flow-ing wa-ter, pure and clear, Make mu-sic for thy Lord to hear,
4 And all ye men of ten-der heart, For - giv-ing oth-ers, take your part,
5 Let all things their Cre-a-tor bless, And wor-ship Him in hum-ble - ness,

Al - le - lu - ia, Al - le - lu - ia! Thou burn-ing sun with gold-en beam,
O praise Him, Al - le - lu - ia! Thou ris - ing morn in praise re - joice,
Al - le - lu - ia! Al - le - lu - ia! Thou fire so mas-ter - ful and bright,
O sing ye, Al - le - lu - ia! Ye who long pain and sor-row bear,
O praise Him, Al - le - lu - ia! Praise, praise the Fa-ther, praise the Son,

Thou sil - ver moon with soft - er gleam, O praise Him, O praise Him,
Ye lights of eve - ning, find a voice, O praise Him, O praise Him,
That giv - est man both warmth and light, O praise Him, O praise Him,
Praise God and on Him cast your care, O praise Him, O praise Him,
And praise the Spir - it, three in one, O praise Him, O praise Him,

Al - le - lu - ia, al - le - lu - ia, al - le - lu - ia!
Al - le - lu - ia, al - le - lu - ia, al - le - lu - ia!
Al - le - lu - ia, al - le - lu - ia, al - le - lu - ia!
Al - le - lu - ia, al - le - lu - ia, al - le - lu - ia!
Al - le - lu - ia, al - le - lu - ia, al - le - lu - ia! A - men.

GOD: CREATOR OF HEAVEN AND EARTH

ALL CREATURES OF OUR GOD AND KING 52

LASST UNS ERFREUEN L.M. with Alleluias

Francis of Assisi, d. 1226
Laudato sia Dio mio Signore
Tr. William Henry Draper, 1931

Kirchengesangbuch, Köln, 1623
Original form of melody

1 All crea-tures of our God and King, Al - le - lu - ia! Lift up your voice
2 Thou rush-ing wind that art so strong, Al - le - lu - ia! Ye clouds that sail
3 Thou flow-ing wa - ter, pure and clear, Al - le - lu - ia! Make mu - sic for
4 And all ye men of ten-der heart, Al - le - lu - ia! For - giv-ing oth-
5 Let all things their Cre-a - tor bless, Al - le - lu - ia! And wor-ship Him

and with us sing Al - le - lu - ia! Thou burn-ing sun with gold - en
in heav'n a - long, Al - le - lu - ia! Thou ris - ing morn, in praise re -
thy Lord to hear, Al - le - lu - ia! Thou fire so mas - ter - ful and
ers, take your part, Al - le - lu - ia! Ye who long pain and sor - row
in hum-ble - ness, Al - le - lu - ia! Praise, praise the Fa - ther, praise the

beam, O praise Him! Thou sil - ver moon with soft - er gleam,
joice, O praise Him! Ye lights of eve - ning, find a voice,
bright, O praise Him! That giv - est man both warmth and light,
bear, O praise Him! Praise God and on Him cast your care,
Son, O praise Him! And praise the Spir - it, three in one,

O praise Him! Al - le - lu - ia, al - le - lu - ia, al - le - lu - ia!
O praise Him! Al - le - lu - ia, al - le - lu - ia, al - le - lu - ia!
O praise Him! Al - le - lu - ia, al - le - lu - ia, al - le - lu - ia!
O praise Him! Al - le - lu - ia, al - le - lu - ia, al - le - lu - ia!
O praise Him! Al - le - lu - ia, al - le - lu - ia, al - le - lu - ia! A-men.

GOD: CREATOR OF HEAVEN AND EARTH

53 COME, O MY SOUL, IN SACRED LAYS

PARK STREET L.M.

Author Unknown
Sometimes attributed to
Thomas Blacklock, d. 1791

Frederick M. A. Venua, c. 1810

1 Come, O my soul, in sa - cred lays, At-tempt thy great Cre -
2 En - throned a - mid the ra - diant spheres, He glo - ry like a
3 In all our Mak - er's grand de - signs, Al - might - y power with
4 Raised on de - vo - tion's loft - y wing, Do thou, my soul, His

a - tor's praise: But O what tongue can speak His fame? What mor - tal
gar - ment wears; To form a robe of light di - vine, Ten thou-sand
wis - dom, shines; His works, through all this won-drous frame, De - clare the
glo - ries sing; And let His praise em - ploy thy tongue, Till lis-t'ning

verse can reach the theme? What mor - tal verse can reach the theme?
suns a - round Him shine, Ten thou-sand suns a - round Him shine.
glo - ry of His name, De - clare the glo - ry of His name.
worlds shall join the song, Till lis - t'ning worlds shall join the song.

54 GOD OF THE EARTH, THE SKY, THE SEA

SHELTERING WING L.M.

Samuel Longfellow, 1864

Joseph Barnby, 1872

1 God of the earth, the sky, the sea, Mak-er of all a - bove, be - low,
2 Thy love is in the sunshine's glow, Thy life is in the quick-ening air;
3 We feel Thy calm at eve-ning's hour, Thy grand-eur in the march of night;
4 But high-er far, and far more clear, Thee in man's spir-it we be-hold:

GOD: CREATOR OF HEAVEN AND EARTH

Cre - a - tion lives and moves in Thee, Thy pres -ent life through all doth flow.
When lightnings flash and·stormwinds blow,There is Thy power; Thy law is there.
And when the morn-ing breaks with power,We hear Thy word,"Let there be light!"
Thine im-age and Thy-self are there, Th'in-dwell-ing God, pro-claimed of old.

GOD, THE LORD OMNIPOTENT 55

TOASIA 7.8.7.9.

Taiwan
Tr. Boris and Clare Anderson, 1961

Toasia
Pepuhoan

1 God, the Lord om - nip- o -tent, To His will cre - a - tion He bent,
2 Sun that fills the sky with light, Moon and stars that shine in the night,
3 Ev- ery grain which earth doth yield, Fruit and flower, and grass in the field,
4 Birds that fly a - bove our head, By the hands of God they are fed.

There-fore, to His name we raise Glo - ry, hon- or, maj - es - ty and praise.
Hill and val - ley, moun-tain peak, Of His power in - ef - fa - ble they speak.
Fish that swim in stream and sea, God made them all ver - y cun - ning - ly.
In - sects crawl-ing at our feet Share God's prov-i-dence to them com - plete.

5 People too in every land
  Live out of His bountiful hand.
  He alone their needs provides,
  His the will that all their way decides.

6 God is God, and only He,
  Idols are merely vanity.
  He alone to men can be
  Life that springs to all eternity.

GOD: CREATOR OF HEAVEN AND EARTH

56 THE SPACIOUS FIRMAMENT ON HIGH

CREATION L.M.D.

Joseph Addison†, 1712

Arranged from Franz Joseph Haydn, 1798

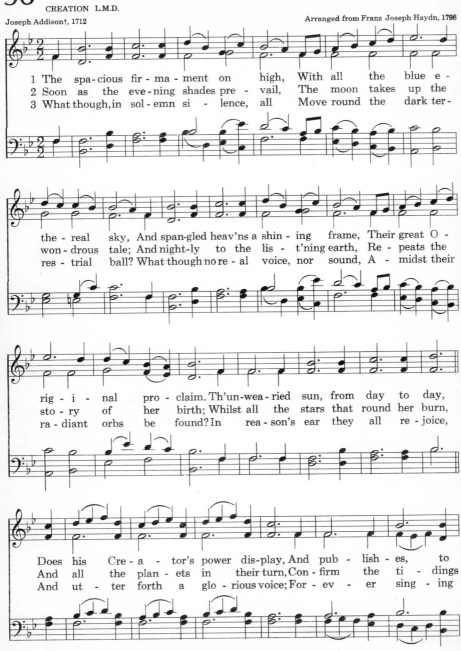

1 The spa-cious fir-ma-ment on high, With all the blue e-
2 Soon as the eve-ning shades pre-vail, The moon takes up the
3 What though,in sol-emn si-lence, all Move round the dark ter-

the-real sky, And span-gled heav'ns a shin-ing frame, Their great O-
won-drous tale; And night-ly to the lis-t'ning earth, Re-peats the
res-trial ball? What though no re-al voice, nor sound, A-midst their

rig-i-nal pro-claim. Th'un-wea-ried sun, from day to day,
sto-ry of her birth; Whilst all the stars that round her burn,
ra-diant orbs be found? In rea-son's ear they all re-joice,

Does his Cre-a-tor's power dis-play, And pub-lish-es, to
And all the plan-ets in their turn, Con-firm the ti-dings
And ut-ter forth a glo-rious voice; For-ev-er sing-ing

GOD: CREATOR OF HEAVEN AND EARTH

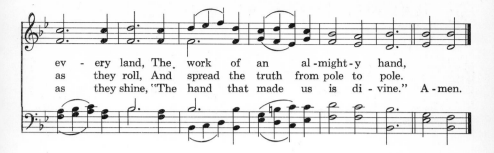

ev - ery land, The work of an al - might - y hand,
as they roll, And spread the truth from pole to pole.
as they shine, "The hand that made us is di - vine." A - men.

LORD OF ALL BEING, THRONED AFAR 57

LOUVAN L.M.

Oliver Wendell Holmes, 1848

Virgil C. Taylor, 1846

1 Lord of all be - ing, throned a - far, Thy glo - ry
2 Sun of our life, Thy wak - ening ray Sheds on our
3 Our mid - night is Thy smile with-drawn; Our noon - tide
4 Grant us Thy truth to make us free, And kin - dling

flames from sun and star; Cen - ter and soul of ev - ery
path the glow of day; Star of our hope, Thy sof - tened
is Thy gra - cious dawn; Our rain - bow arch, Thy mer - cy's
hearts that burn for Thee; Till all Thy liv - ing al - tars

sphere, Yet to each lov - ing heart how near!
light Cheers the long watch - es of the night.
sign; All, save the clouds of sin, are Thine.
claim One ho - ly light, one heav'n - ly flame. A - men.

GOD: CREATOR OF HEAVEN AND EARTH

58 FOR THE BEAUTY OF THE EARTH

DIX 7.7.7.7.7.7.

Folliott Sandford Pierpoint‡, 1864

Arranged from Conrad Kocher
by William Henry Monk, 1861

1 For the beau-ty of the earth, For the beau-ty of the skies,
2 For the beau-ty of each hour Of the day and of the night,
3 For the joy of hu-man love, Broth-er, sis-ter, par-ent, child,
4 For Thy church, that ev-er-more Lift-eth ho-ly hands a-bove,

For the love which from our birth O-ver and a-round us lies:
Hill and vale, and tree and flower, Sun and moon, and stars of light:
Friends on earth, and friends a-bove; For all gen-tle thoughts and mild:
Of-fering up on ev-ery shore Her pure sac-ri-fice of love:

Lord of all, to Thee we raise This our hymn of grate-ful praise. A-men.

59 HEAVEN AND EARTH, THE SEA AND AIR

GOTT SEI DANK 7.7.7.7.

Joachim Neander, 1680
Himmel, Erde, Luft und Meer
Tr. Catherine Winkworth, 1858
and Frances Elizabeth Cox, 1841

J. A. Freylinghausen's *Neues*
Geistreiches Gesangbuch, 1704

1 Heav'n and earth, the sea and air, All their Mak-er's praise de-clare;
2 See the sun, with glo-rious ray, Pierce the clouds at ope-ning day;
3 See how He hath ev-ery-where Made this earth so rich and fair;
4 Lord, great won-ders work-est Thou! To Thy sway all crea-tures bow;

GOD: CREATOR OF HEAVEN AND EARTH

Wake, my soul, a-wake and sing; Now thy grate-ful prais-es bring.
Moon and stars, in splen-dor bright. Praise their God through si-lent night.
Hill and vale and fruit-ful land, All things liv-ing show His hand.
Write Thou deep-ly in my heart What I am, and what Thou art. A-men.

GOD, WHO MADEST EARTH AND HEAVEN 60

GOTT DES HIMMELS 8.7.8.7.7.7.

Heinrich Albert, 1642
Gott des Himmels und der Erde
Tr. Richard Massie, 1857, and Catherine Winkworth, 1855

Heinrich Albert, 1642

1 God, who mad-est earth and heav-en, Fa-ther, Son, and Ho-ly Ghost,
2 Help me, that I may this morn-ing In the Spir-it al-so rise;
3 Lead me, and di-rect my do-ings By Thy ho-ly Word and will;

Who the day and night hast giv-en, Sun, and moon, and star-ry host;
And my soul with grace a-dorn-ing, Lord, pre-pare it in such wise,
Or-der all my ways and go-ings, Keep me, Lord, this day, from ill;

Whose strong hand the world sus-tains, And what-ev-er it con-tains;
That I may, with-out dis-may, Look for Thy great judg-ment day.
No-where else, ex-cept with Thee, Can I safe-ly guard-ed be. A-men.

GOD: CREATOR OF HEAVEN AND EARTH

61 PRAISE THE LORD, HIS GLORIES SHOW

GWALCHMAI 7.7.7.7. with Alleluias

Based on Psalm 150
Henry Francis Lyte, 1834

Joseph David Jones, 1868

1 Praise the Lord, His glo-ries show, Al - le - lu - ia!
2 Earth to heav'n, and heav'n to earth, Al - le - lu - ia!
3 Praise the Lord, His mer-cies trace, Al - le - lu - ia!

Saints with - in His courts be - low, Al - le - lu - ia!
Tell His won - ders, sing His worth, Al - le - lu - ia!
Praise His prov - i - dence and grace, Al - le - lu - ia!

An - gels round His throne a - bove, Al - le - lu - ia!
Age to age and shore to shore, Al - le - lu - ia!
All that He for man hath done, Al - le - lu - ia!

All that see and share His love. Al - le - lu - ia!
Praise Him, praise Him ev - er - more! Al - le - lu - ia!
All He sends us through His Son. Al - le - lu - ia! A - men.

GOD: CREATOR OF HEAVEN AND EARTH

LET THE WHOLE CREATION CRY 62

LLANFAIR 7.7.7.7. with Alleluias

Based on Psalm 148
Stopford A. Brooke†, 1881

Robert Williams, 1817

1 Let the whole cre - a - tion cry Al - le - lu - ia!
2 Praise Him, all ye hosts a - bove, Al - le - lu - ia!
3 War - riors fight - ing for the Lord, Al - le - lu - ia!
4 Men and wom - en, young and old, Al - le - lu - ia!

Glo - ry to the Lord on high! Al - le - lu - ia!
Ev - er bright and fair in love! Al - le - lu - ia!
Pro - phets burn - ing with His word, Al - le - lu - ia!
Raise the an - them man - i - fold; Al - le - lu - ia!

Heav'n and earth, a - wake and sing, Al - le - lu - ia!
Sun and moon, up - lift your voice, Al - le - lu - ia!
Those to whom the arts be - long, Al - le - lu - ia!
And let chil - dren's hap - py hearts, Al - le - lu - ia!

"God is God and there - fore King," Al - le - lu - ia!
Night and stars in God re - joice, Al - le - lu - ia!
Join the rush - ing of the song, Al - le - lu - ia!
In this wor - ship bear their parts: Al - le - lu - ia!

GOD: CREATOR OF HEAVEN AND EARTH

63 MY SHEPHERD WILL SUPPLY MY NEED

RESIGNATION C.M.D.

Based on Psalm 23
Isaac Watts, 1719

Folk Hymn.
F. Lewis' *Beauties of Harmony*, c. 1828
Version from Joseph Funk's *Genuine Church Music*, 1832

1 My Shep - herd will sup - ply my need; Je - ho - vah
2 When I walk through the shades of death Thy pres - ence
3 The sure pro - vi - sions of my God At - tend me

is His name: In pas - tures fresh He makes me feed, Be -
is my stay; One word of Thy sup - port - ing breath Drives
all my days; O may Thy house be my a - bode, And

side the liv - ing stream. He brings my wan - d'ring spir - it
all my fears a - way. Thy hand, in sight of all my
all my work be praise. There would I find a set - tled

back, When I for - sake His ways; And leads me,
foes, Doth still my ta - ble spread; My cup with
rest, While oth - ers go and come; No more a

GOD: HIS LOVE AND MERCY

for His mer - cy's sake, In paths of truth and grace.
bless - ings o - ver - flows, Thine oil a - noints my head.
stran - ger, nor a guest, But like a child at home.

O LOVE OF GOD, HOW STRONG 64

ALFRETON L.M.

Horatius Bonar, 1864

William Beastall, c. 1818

1 O love of God, how strong and true! E - ter - nal
2 O wide - em - brac - ing, won - drous love, We read thee
3 We read thee best in Him who came, To bear for
4 We read thy power to bless and save, E'en in the
5 O love of God, our shield and stay, Through all the

and yet ev - er new, Un - com - pre - hend - ed
in the sky a - bove, We read thee in the
us the cross of shame; Sent by the Fa - ther
dark - ness of the grave; Still more in res - ur -
per - ils of our way; E - ter - nal love, in

and un - bought, Be - yond all knowl - edge and all thought.
earth be - low, In seas that swell and streams that flow.
from on high, Our life to live, our death to die.
rec - tion light, We read the full - ness of thy might.
thee we rest, For - ev - er safe, for - ev - er blest!

GOD: HIS LOVE AND MERCY

65 THE KING OF LOVE MY SHEPHERD IS

DOMINUS REGIT ME 8.7.8.7.

Based on Psalm 23
Henry Williams Baker, 1868

John Bacchus Dykes, 1868

1 The King of love my Shep-herd is, Whose good-ness fail-eth nev - er;
2 Where streams of liv - ing wa - ter flow My ran-somed soul He lead - eth,
3 Per - verse and fool - ish oft I strayed, But yet in love He sought me,
4 In death's dark vale I fear no ill With Thee, dear Lord, be - side me;

I noth - ing lack if I am His And He is mine for - ev - er.
And, where the ver-dant pas-tures grow, With food ce - les - tial feed - eth.
And on His shoul-der gent - ly laid, And home, re-joic - ing, brought me.
Thy rod and staff my com - fort still, Thy cross be-fore to guide me. A-men.

5 Thou spread'st a table in my sight,
Thy unction grace bestoweth,
And O what transport of delight
From Thy pure chalice floweth.

6 And so through all the length of days
Thy goodness faileth never;
Good Shepherd, may I sing Thy praise
Within Thy house forever.

66 THE LORD MY SHEPHERD IS

SWEET DAY S.M.

Based on Psalm 23
Isaac Watts, 1719

Benjamin Carl Unseld, 1878

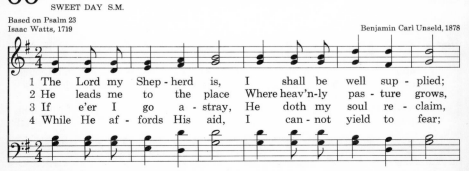

1 The Lord my Shep - herd is, I shall be well sup - plied;
2 He leads me to the place Where heav'n-ly pas - ture grows,
3 If e'er I go a - stray, He doth my soul re - claim,
4 While He af - fords His aid, I can - not yield to fear;

GOD: HIS LOVE AND MERCY

Since He is mine and I am His, What can I want be - side?
Where liv-ing wa - ters gen - tly pass, And full sal - va - tion flows.
And guides me in His own right way, For His most ho - ly name.
Tho' I should walk thro' death's dark shade, My Shep-herd's with me there. A - men.

5 In spite of all my foes
   Thou dost my table spread,
   My cup with blessings overflows,
   And joy exalts my head.

6 The bounties of Thy love
   Shall crown my following days;
   Nor from Thy house will I remove
   Nor cease to speak Thy praise.

THE LORD'S MY SHEPHERD 67

CRIMOND C.M.

Based on Psalm 23
Scottish Psalter, 1650

Jessie Seymour Irvine, 1872

1 The Lord's my Shep-herd, I'll not want. He makes me down to lie
2 My soul He doth re - store a - gain; And me to walk doth make
3 Yea, though I walk in death's dark vale, Yet will I fear none ill:
4 My ta - ble Thou hast fur - nish - ed In pres - ence of my foes;
5 Good-ness and mer - cy all my life Shall sure - ly fol - low me:

In pas - tures green; He lead-eth me The qui - et wa - ters by.
With - in the paths of right-eous-ness, Ev'n for His own name's sake.
For Thou art with me; and Thy rod And staff me com-fort still.
My head Thou dost with oil a - noint, And my cup o - ver-flows.
And in God's house for - ev - er-more My dwell-ing place shall be. A - men.

GOD: HIS LOVE AND MERCY

68 WHAT MERCY AND DIVINE COMPASSION

MIR IST ERBARMUNG 9.8.9.8.8.8.

Philipp Friedrich Hiller, 1767
Mir ist Erbarmung widerfahren
Tr. Frieda Kaufman, 1938

J. G. Schicht's
Allgemeines Choral-Buch . . . , 1819

1 What mer - cy and di - vine com - pas - sion Has God in
2 E - ter - nal wrath should be my por - tion: The Lamb of
3 Great God, ac - cept my ad - o - ra - tion; Help me Thy
4 Thy boun-teous grace is my as - sur - ance, The blood of

Christ re - vealed to me! My haugh - ty spir - it would not
God, for sin - ners slain, Re - moved the curse and con - dem -
mer - cy to con - fess, In Je - sus Christ is my sal -
Christ my on - ly plea, Thy heart of love my con - so -

ask it, Yet He be - stowed it, full and free. In God my
na - tion, His blood a - toned for ev - ery stain. God's love in
va - tion; He is my hope in life and death; His blood, His
la - tion Un - til Thy glo - rious face I see; My theme, through

heart doth now re - joice: I praise His grace with
Christ on Cal - v'ry's tree From guilt and shame has
right - eous - ness a - lone I claim be - fore Thy
nev - er - end - ing days, Shall be Thy great re -

GOD: HIS LOVE AND MERCY

grate - ful voice. I praise His grace with grate - ful voice.
set me free. From guilt and shame has set me free.
judg - ment throne. I claim be - fore Thy judg - ment throne.
deem - ing grace. Shall be Thy great re - deem - ing grace.

AWAKE, MY SOUL, AWAKE MY TONGUE 69

DUKE STREET L.M.

H. Boyd's *Psalm and Hymn Tunes*, 1793
Attributed to John Hatton, d. 1793

Anne Steele†, 1760

1 A - wake, my soul, a - wake my tongue, My God de -
2 Di - vine - ly free His mer - cy flows, For - gives my
3 His mer - cy, with un - chang - ing rays, For - ev - er
4 While all His works His praise pro - claim, And men and

mands the grate - ful song; Let all my in - most powers re -
sins, al - lays my woes, And bids ap - proach-ing death re -
shines, while time de - cays: And chil-dren's chil - dren shall re -
an - gels bless His name, O let my heart, my life, my

cord The won-drous mer - cy of the Lord.
move, And crowns me with in - dul - gent love.
cord The truth and good - ness of the Lord.
tongue At - tend, and join the bliss - ful song! A - men.

GOD: HIS LOVE AND MERCY

70 LET US, WITH A GLADSOME MIND

GENEVA 136 7.7.7.7.

Based on Psalm 136
John Milton‡, 1623

Les cent cinquante pseaumes . . ., Geneva, 1562
Harmony adapted from Claude Goudimel, 1565

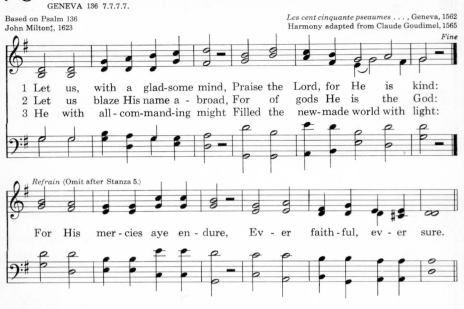

1 Let us, with a glad-some mind, Praise the Lord, for He is kind:
2 Let us blaze His name a - broad, For of gods He is the God:
3 He with all - com-mand-ing might Filled the new-made world with light:

Refrain (Omit after Stanza 5.)

For His mer - cies aye en - dure, Ev - er faith - ful, ev - er sure.

4 All things living He doth feed,
His full hand supplies their need:
Refrain

5 Let us, with a gladsome mind,
Praise the Lord, for He is kind.

71 GOD IS LOVE, HIS MERCY BRIGHTENS

SUSSEX 8.7.8.7.

John Bowring, 1825

From an English Traditional Melody
Ralph Vaughan Williams, 1906

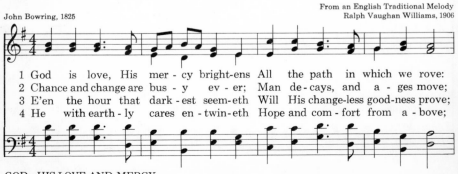

1 God is love, His mer - cy bright-ens All the path in which we rove:
2 Chance and change are bus - y ev - er; Man de - cays, and a - ges move;
3 E'en the hour that dark - est seem-eth Will His change-less good-ness prove;
4 He with earth - ly cares en - twin-eth Hope and com - fort from a - bove;

GOD: HIS LOVE AND MERCY

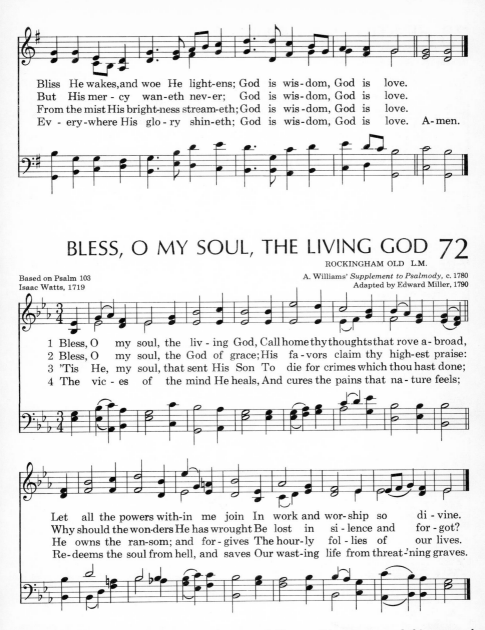

Bliss He wakes, and woe He light-ens; God is wis-dom, God is love.
But His mer - cy wan-eth nev-er; God is wis-dom, God is love.
From the mist His bright-ness stream-eth; God is wis-dom, God is love.
Ev - ery-where His glo - ry shin-eth; God is wis-dom, God is love. A-men.

BLESS, O MY SOUL, THE LIVING GOD 72

ROCKINGHAM OLD L.M.

Based on Psalm 103
Isaac Watts, 1719

A. Williams' *Supplement to Psalmody*, c. 1780
Adapted by Edward Miller, 1790

1 Bless, O my soul, the liv - ing God, Call home thy thoughts that rove a - broad,
2 Bless, O my soul, the God of grace; His fa - vors claim thy high-est praise:
3 'Tis He, my soul, that sent His Son To die for crimes which thou hast done;
4 The vic - es of the mind He heals, And cures the pains that na - ture feels;

Let all the powers with-in me join In work and wor-ship so di - vine.
Why should the won-ders He has wrought Be lost in si - lence and for - got?
He owns the ran-som; and for - gives The hour-ly fol - lies of our lives.
Re-deems the soul from hell, and saves Our wast-ing life from threat-'ning graves.

5 Our youth decayed His power repairs;
His mercy crowns our growing years:
He satisfies our mouth with good,
And fills our hopes with heav'nly food.

6 He sees th' oppressor and th' oppressed,
And often gives the sufferers rest:
But will His justice more display
In the last great rewarding day.

GOD: HIS LOVE AND MERCY

73 BE STILL, MY SOUL

FINLANDIA 10.10.10.10.10.10.

Catharina A. D. von Schlegel, 1752
Stille, mein Wille
Tr. Jane Laurie Borthwick, 1855

From Jean Sibelius, 1899
Arranged for *The Hymnal*, 1933 (Presbyterian)

1 Be still, my soul! the Lord is on thy side;
2 Be still, my soul! thy God doth un - der - take
3 Be still, my soul! the hour is has-t'ning on

Bear pa-tient-ly the
To guide the fu - ture
When we shall be for-

cross of grief or pain; Leave to thy God to or - der and pro - vide,
as He has the past. Thy hope, thy con - fi - dence, let noth-ing shake;
ev - er with the Lord, When dis-ap - point-ment, grief, and fear are gone,

In ev - ery change He faith-ful will re - main. Be still, my soul! thy
All now mys - te - rious shall be bright at last. Be still, my soul! the
Sor-row for - got, love's pur-est joys re - stored. Be still, my soul! when

best, thy heav'n-ly Friend Through thorn-y ways leads to a joy - ful end.
waves and winds still know His voice who ruled them while He dwelt be-low.
change and tears are past, All safe and bless - ed we shall meet at last. A-men.

GOD: HIS LOVE AND MERCY

WHEN ALL THY MERCIES, O MY GOD 74

GENEVA C.M.

John Cole, 1805
Version from Joseph Funk's *Harmonia Sacra.*

Joseph Addison, 1712

1 When all Thy mer - cies, O my God, My
2 Ten thou - sand thou - sand pre - cious gifts My
3 Through ev - ery per - iod of my life Thy

1 When all Thy mer-cies, O my God,
2 Ten thou - sand thou-sand pre - cious gifts
3 Through ev - ery per - iod of my life

1 When all Thy mer-cies, O my God,
2 Ten thou-sand thou-sand pre-cious gifts
3 Through ev - 'ry per-iod of my life

ris - ing soul sur - veys, Trans-port - ed with the
dai - ly thanks em - ploy; Nor is the least a
good - ness I'll pur - sue; And af - ter death, in

Trans - port-ed with the
Nor is the least a
And af - ter death, in

view, I'm lost In won - der, love and praise.
cheer - ful heart, That tastes those gifts with joy.
dis - tant worlds, The glo - rious theme re - new.

view, I'm lost
cheer - ful heart,
dis - tant worlds,

4 Through all eternity, to Thee
A joyful song I'll raise;
But O eternity's too short
To utter all Thy praise!

Soprano and Tenor parts have been exchanged.

GOD: HIS LOVE AND MERCY

75 LOVE DIVINE, ALL LOVES EXCELLING

BEECHER   8.7.8.7.D.

Charles Wesley‡, 1747

John Zundel, 1870

1 Love di-vine, all loves ex-cell-ing, Joy of heav'n, to earth come down;
2 Breathe, O breathe Thy lov-ing Spir-it In-to ev-ery trou-bled breast;
3 Come, Al-might-y to de-liv-er, Let us all Thy grace re-ceive;
4 Fin-ish, then, Thy new cre-a-tion; Pure and spot-less let us be;

Fix in us Thy hum-ble dwell-ing, All Thy faith-ful mer-cies crown.
Let us all in Thee in-her-it, Let us find the prom-ised rest;
Sud-den-ly re-turn, and nev-er, Nev-er-more Thy tem-ples leave.
Let us see Thy great sal-va-tion Per-fect-ly re-stored in Thee;

Je-sus, Thou art all com-pas-sion, Pure, un-bound-ed love Thou art;
Take a-way the love of sin-ning; Al-pha and O-me-ga be;
Thee we would be al-ways bless-ing, Serve Thee as Thy hosts a-bove,
Changed from glo-ry in-to glo-ry, Till in heav'n we take our place,

Vis-it us with Thy sal-va-tion, En-ter ev-ery trem-bling heart.
End of faith, as its be-gin-ning, Set our hearts at lib-er-ty.
Pray, and praise Thee with-out ceas-ing, Glo-ry in Thy per-fect love.
Till we cast our crowns be-fore Thee, Lost in won-der, love, and praise. A-men.

GOD: HIS LOVE AND MERCY

LOVE DIVINE, ALL LOVES EXCELLING 76

BLAENWERN 8.7.8.7.D.

Charles Wesley‡, 1747

William Penfro Rowlands, 1915

1 Love di - vine, all loves ex - cell -ing, Joy of heav'n, to earth come down,
2 Breathe, O breathe Thy lov - ing Spir- it In - to ev - ery trou - bled breast;
3 Come, Al - might-y to de - liv - er, Let us all Thy grace re - ceive;
4 Fin - ish, then, Thy new cre - a - tion: Pure and spot - less let us be;

Fix in us Thy hum - ble dwell-ing, All Thy faith - ful mer - cies crown:
Let us all in Thee in - her - it, Let us find the prom-ised rest;
Sud - den - ly re - turn, and nev - er, Nev - er - more Thy tem - ples leave.
Let us see Thy great sal - va -tion, Per - fect - ly re - stored in Thee,

Je - sus, Thou art all com - pas-sion, Pure, un - bound-ed love Thou art;
Take a - way the love of sin-ning, Al - pha and O - me - ga be;
Thee we would be al - ways bless-ing, Serve Thee as Thy hosts a - bove,
Changed from glo - ry in - to glo-ry, Till in heav'n, we take our place,

Vis - it us with Thy sal - va-tion, En - ter ev - ery trem-bling heart.
End of faith, as its be - gin-ning, Set our hearts at lib - er - ty.
Pray, and praise Thee with-out ceas-ing, Glo - ry in Thy per - fect love.
Till we cast our crowns be-fore Thee, Lost in won - der, love, and praise. A-men.

GOD: HIS LOVE AND MERCY

77 WHAT GOD HATH DONE IS DONE ARIGHT

WAS GOTT TUT DAS IST WOHLGETAN   8.7.8.7.4.4.7.7.

Benjamin Schmolck, 1720
Was Gott tut das ist wohlgetan
Tr. Frances Elizabeth Cox, 1864

Severus Gastorius, 1681

1 What God hath done is done a-right, So think all true be - liev - ers;
2 What God hath done is done a-right, In gifts with - held or sent us;
3 What God hath done is done a-right, May He sub - mis - sive make us!

They feel His love, they own His might, Though fond hopes prove de - ceiv - ers:
And what suf - fic - eth in His sight, Should al - ways well con - tent us:
His gra - cious prom - ise He doth plight, That He will ne'er for - sake us:

Mid seem - ing ill God loves them still, And, e'en by sor -
'Tis for our sakes He gives or takes; Then, hum - bly bowed
Our Sav - ior knows Our wants and woes, And all we need

row's leav - en, Would raise their hearts to heav - en.
be - fore Him, In si - lence we a - dore Him.
pro - vid - eth: Praise God, what - e'er be - tid - eth! A - men.

GOD: HIS LOVE AND MERCY

1 Was Gott tut, das ist wohlgetan,
   so denken Gottes Kinder.
Er sieht sie oft gar strenge an
   und liebt sie doch nicht minder;
er zieht ihr Herz nur himmelwärts,
   wenn er sie lässt auf Erden
ein Ziel der Plagen werden.

2 Was Gott tut, das ist wohlgetan.
   Gibt er, so kann man nehmen;
Nimmt er, wir sind nicht übler dran,
   wenn wir uns nur bequemen.
Die Linke schmerzt, die Rechte herzt,
   und beide Hände müssen
wir doch in Demut küssen.

3 Was Gott tut, das ist wohlgetan.
   Er weist uns oft den Segen,
und eh er noch gedeihen kann,
   muss sich die Hoffnung legen.
Weil er allein der Schatz will sein,
   so macht er andre Güter
durch den Verlust uns bitter.

THERE'S A WIDENESS IN GOD'S MERCY 78

WELLESLEY 8.7.8.7.

Frederick William Faber, 1862

Lizzie Shove Tourjée, 1878

1 There's a wide-ness in God's mer-cy, Like the
2 There is wel-come for the sin-ner, And more
3 There is grace e-nough for thou-sands Of new
4 For the love of God is broad-er Than the
5 But we make His love too nar-row By false

wide-ness of the sea: There's a kind-ness in
grac-es for the good; There is mer-cy with
worlds as great as this; There is room for fresh
mea-sures of man's mind; And the heart of the
lim-its of our own; And we mag-ni-fy

His jus-tice, Which is more than lib-er-ty.
the Sav-ior; There is heal-ing in His blood.
cre-a-tions In that up-per home of bliss.
E-ter-nal Is most won-der-ful-ly kind.
His strict-ness With a zeal He will not own. A-men.

GOD: HIS LOVE AND MERCY

79 LORD, THOU HAST SEARCHED AND SEEN

BERA L.M.

Based on Psalm 139
Isaac Watts, 1719

John Edgar Gould, 1849

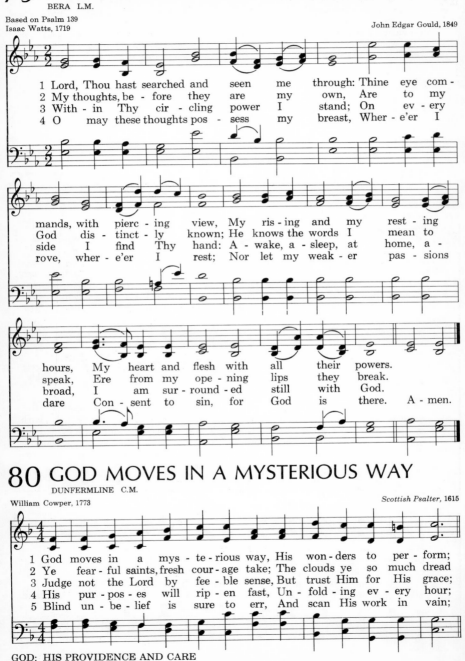

1 Lord, Thou hast searched and seen me through: Thine eye com-
2 My thoughts, be - fore they are my own, Are to my
3 With - in Thy cir - cling power I stand; On ev - ery
4 O may these thoughts pos - sess my breast, Wher - e'er I

mands, with pierc - ing view, My ris - ing and my rest - ing
God dis - tinct - ly known; He knows the words I mean to
side I find Thy hand: A - wake, a - sleep, at home, a -
rove, wher - e'er I rest; Nor let my weak - er pas - sions

hours, My heart and flesh with all their powers.
speak, Ere from my ope - ning lips they break.
broad, I am sur - round - ed still with God.
dare Con - sent to sin, for God is there. A - men.

80 GOD MOVES IN A MYSTERIOUS WAY

DUNFERMLINE C.M.

William Cowper, 1773

Scottish Psalter, 1615

1 God moves in a mys - te - rious way, His won - ders to per - form;
2 Ye fear - ful saints, fresh cour - age take; The clouds ye so much dread
3 Judge not the Lord by fee - ble sense, But trust Him for His grace;
4 His pur - pos - es will rip - en fast, Un - fold - ing ev - ery hour;
5 Blind un - be - lief is sure to err, And scan His work in vain;

GOD: HIS PROVIDENCE AND CARE

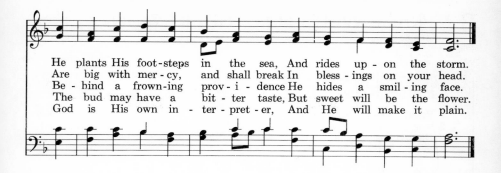

He plants His foot-steps in the sea, And rides up-on the storm.
Are big with mer-cy, and shall break In bless-ings on your head.
Be-hind a frown-ing prov-i-dence He hides a smil-ing face.
The bud may have a bit-ter taste, But sweet will be the flower.
God is His own in-ter-pret-er, And He will make it plain.

HAST THOU NOT KNOWN 81

ST. MAGNUS C.M.

Based on Isaiah 40: 28-31
Isaac Watts, 1707
Altered in *Scottish Paraphrases*, 1781

Jeremiah Clark, 1707

1 Hast thou not known, hast thou not heard That firm re-mains on high
2 Art thou a-fraid His power shall fail When comes thy e-vil day?
3 Su-preme in wis-dom as in power The Rock of A-ges stands;
4 He gives the con-quest to the weak, Sup-ports the faint-ing heart;

The ev-er-last-ing throne of Him Who formed the earth and sky?
And can an all-cre-a-ting arm Grow wea-ry or de-cay?
Though Him thou canst not see, nor trace The work-ing of His hands.
And cour-age in the e-vil hour His heav'n-ly aids im-part. A-men.

5 Mere human power shall fast decay,
   And youthful vigor cease;
But they who wait upon the Lord
   In strength shall still increase.

6 They with unwearied feet shall tread
   The path of life divine,
With growing ardor onward move,
   With growing brightness shine.

GOD: HIS PROVIDENCE AND CARE

82 PRAISE WAITS FOR THEE IN ZION

ABRIDGE C.M.

Based on Psalm 65
Scottish Psalter, 1650
Altered by Nichol Grieve, 1940

Isaac Smith, c. 1780

1 Praise waits for Thee in Zi - on, Lord; To Thee
2 Our sins have proved too strong for us And led
3 Blessed is the man whom Thou didst choose And mak'st
4 We sure - ly shall be sat - is - fied With Thy

vows paid shall be; O Thou that hear - er art
us far a - stray. Our man - i - fold in - iq -
ap - proach to Thee, That he with - in Thy tem -
a - bun - dant grace, And with the good - ness of

of prayer, All flesh shall come to Thee.
ui - ties We pray Thee purge a - way.
ple courts May still a dwell - er be.
Thy house, Ev'n of Thy ho - ly place. A - men.

83 O GOD OF BETHEL

SALZBURG C.M.

Based on Genesis 28: 19-21
Philip Doddridge, d. 1751 and John Logan, d. 1788
Altered in *Scottish Paraphrases*, 1781

Johann Michael Haydn, 1806

1 O God of Beth - el, by whose hand Thy peo - ple still are fed;
2 Our vows, our prayers, we now pre - sent Be - fore Thy throne of grace;
3 Through each per - plex - ing path of life Our wan - d'ring foot - steps guide;
4 O spread Thy cov - 'ring wings a - round, Till all our wan - d'rings cease,
5 Such bless-ings from Thy gra - cious hand Our hum - ble prayers im - plore;

GOD: HIS PROVIDENCE AND CARE

Who through this wea - ry pil-grim-age Hast all our fa - thers led:
God of our fa - thers, be the God Of their suc - ceed - ing race.
Give us each day our dai - ly bread,And rai - ment fit pro - vide.
And at our Fa - ther's loved a - bode Our souls ar - rive in peace.
And Thou shalt be our cho-sen God,And por - tion ev - er - more. A-men.

O GOD, OUR HELP IN AGES PAST 84

ST. ANNE C.M.

Based on Psalm 90
Isaac Watts †, 1719

William Croft (?), 1708

1 O God, our help in a - ges past, Our hope for years to come,
2 Un - der the shad - ow of Thy throne Thy saints have dwelt se - cure;
3 Be - fore the hills in or - der stood, Or earth re - ceived her frame,
4 A thou-sand a - ges in Thy sight Are like an eve - ning gone;

Our shel - ter from the storm - y blast, And our e - ter - nal home.
Suf - fi - cient is Thine arm a - lone, And our de - fense is sure.
From ev - er - last - ing Thou art God, To end - less years the same.
Short as the watch that ends the night Be - fore the ris - ing sun. A - men.

5 Time, like an ever-rolling stream,
   Bears all its sons away;
   They fly forgotten, as a dream
   Dies at the opening day.

6 O God, our help in ages past,
   Our hope for years to come,
   Be Thou our guard while troubles last,
   And our eternal home.

GOD: HIS PROVIDENCE AND CARE

85 GOD IS MY LIGHT

GOTT IST GETREU   4.6.6.4.6.6.9.9.4.

Johann Heinrich Karl Hengstenberg, 1825
Gott ist mein Licht
Tr. Ernst William Hengstenberg, c. 1835

Johann Rudolph Ahle, c. 1661

1 God is my light! My soul, do not de-spair In hours of thy dis-tress!
2 God is my trust! My soul, be not a-fraid, Thy help-er will a-bide;
3 The king-dom His! Thro'out the earth He reigns With wis-dom, grace, and might;

The sun with-draws, And earth is dark and drear: My light will nev-er cease.
"I'll not for-sake thee!" He has kind-ly said, He's ev-er at thy side;
The stars go on, And time its course main-tains Be-neath His watch-ful sight;

On days of joy with splen-dor beam-ing, Through nights of
In fee-ble age will yet stand by thee, No re-al
In si-lence on-ward still pro-ceed-ing, The u-ni-

grief its rays are gleam-ing; God is my light!
good will He de-ny thee: God is my trust!
verse o-beys His lead-ing, The king-dom His!   A-men.

GOD: HIS PROVIDENCE AND CARE

GOD THE OMNIPOTENT 86

RUSSIAN HYMN 11.10.11.9.

Henry Fothergill Chorley‡, 1842, St. 1 and 2
John Ellerton‡, 1870, St. 3 and 4

Alexis Lvov, 1833

1 God the om - nip - o - tent! King, who or - dain - est
2 God the all - mer - ci - ful! Earth hath for - sak - en
3 God the all - right - eous one! Man hath de - fied Thee;
4 God the all - prov - i - dent! Earth by Thy chas - t'ning

Thun - der Thy clar - ion, the light - ning Thy sword,
Thy ways all ho - ly, and slight - ed Thy Word;
Yet to e - ter - ni - ty stand - eth Thy Word;
Yet shall to free - dom and truth be re - stored;

Show forth Thy pit - y on high where Thou reign - est:
Bid not Thy wrath in its ter - rors a - wak - en:
False - hood and wrong shall not tar - ry be - side Thee:
Through the thick dark - ness Thy king - dom is has - t'ning:

Give to us peace in our time, O Lord.
Give to us peace in our time, O Lord.
Give to us peace in our time, O Lord.
Thou wilt give peace in Thy time, O Lord. A - men.

GOD: HIS LAWS AND JUDGMENT

87 THAT DAY OF WRATH

WINDHAM L.M.

Thomas of Celano, 13th century
Dies irae, dies illa
Tr. Walter Scott‡, 1805

Daniel Read, 1785

1 That day of wrath, that dread-ful day, When heav'n and earth shall pass a - way!
2 When, shriv-'ling like a parch-ed scroll, The flam-ing heav'ns to - geth-er roll,
3 O on that day, that wrath-ful day, When man to judg - ment wakes from clay,

What power shall be the sin-ner's stay? How shall he meet that dread-ful day?
And loud - er yet, and yet more dread, Swells the high trump that wakes the dead?
Be Thou, O Christ, the sin-ner's stay, Tho' heav'n and earth shall pass a - way. A-men.

88 O DAY OF GOD, DRAW NIGH

BELLWOODS S.M.

Robert B. Y. Scott‡, 1937

James Hopkirk, 1938

1 O day of God, draw nigh In beau - ty and in power;
2 Bring to our trou - bled minds, Un - cer - tain and a - fraid,
3 Bring jus - tice to our land, That all may dwell se - cure,
4 Bring to our world of strife Thy sov - ereign word of peace,
5 O day of God, draw nigh, As at cre - a - tion's birth,

Come with Thy time-less judg-ment now To match our pres-ent hour.
The qui - et of a stead-fast faith, Calm of a call o - beyed.
And fine - ly build for days to come Foun-da - tions that en - dure.
That war may haunt the earth no more And des - o - la - tion cease.
Let there be light a - gain, and set Thy judg-ments in the earth. A - men.

GOD: HIS LAWS AND JUDGMENT

THE LORD IS KING, O PRAISE HIS NAME 89

SO LANGE JESUS BLEIBT L.M.

Nicolaus Ludwig von Zinzendorf, 1742
So lange Jesus bleibt der Herr
Tr. Esther Bergen, 1959

Choralbuch der Mennoniten
Gemeinden Russlands, Halbstadt, 1914

1 The Lord is King, O praise His name, O'er all the
2 O see the might - y hand of God, His love and
3 This shall the song for - ev - er be Of saints be -
4 O star that lights the pil - grim's way! Our Lord of

earth His grace pro - claim! From age to age, from day to
mer - cy chang-eth not! His blood and right - eous-ness a -
fore the crys - tal sea: O Christ, that on the cross hath
lords, our hope and stay! The head to whom we hom-age

day, His won- ders grow more glo - rious - ly.
vail; His grace and par - don nev - er fail!
bled, Hast safe - ly through life's val - ley led.
bring, The rock to which our faith may cling! A - men.

1 So lange Jesus bleibt der Herr,
wird's alle Tage herrlicher.
So war's, so ist's, so wird es sein
bei seiner gläubigen Gemein.

2 Es bleibt bei dem bekannten Wort
von Zeit zu Zeit, von Ort zu Ort:
Christi Blut und Gerechtigkeit
bleibt der Gemeine Schmuck und Kleid.

3 Das Psalmlied am krystallnen Meer,
das Losungswort vom kleinen Heer
ist: "Eines hat uns durchgebracht,
Lamm Gottes, dass du warst geschlacht."

4 Du bist und bleibest unser Herr,
der Leitstern deiner Wanderer,
der Deinen teures Oberhaupt,
dem keiner Feinde Macht sie raubt.

JESUS CHRIST: PRAISE AND GLORY

90 IN THEE IS GLADNESS

IN DIR IST FREUDE 5.5.7.D.5.5.5.5.9.D.

Johann Lindemann, c. 1595
In Dir ist Freude
Tr. Catherine Winkworth, 1858 and 1863

Adapted from Giovanni Giacomo
Gastoldi, 1591

1 In Thee is glad-ness A-mid all sad-ness, Je - sus, sun-shine of my heart!
2 If He is ours We fear no pow-ers, Nor of earth, nor sin, nor death;

By Thee are giv - en The gifts of heav-en, Thou the true Re-deem-er art!
He sees and bless-es In worst dis-tress-es, He can change them with a breath!

Our souls Thou wak-est, Our bonds Thou break-est, Who trusts Thee sure - ly
Where-fore the sto - ry Tell of His glo - ry With heart and voic - es;

Hath built se - cure - ly, He stands for - ev - er: Hal - le - lu - jah!
All heav'n re - joic - es In Him for - ev - er: Hal - le - lu - jah!

Our hearts are pin - ing To see Thy shin-ing, Dy - ing or liv - ing
We shout for glad-ness. Tri-umph o'er sad - ness, Love Thee and praise Thee,

To Thee are cleav - ing, Naught can us sev - er: Hal - le - lu - jah!
And still shall raise Thee Glad hymns for - ev - er: Hal - le - lu - jah!

LORD JESUS CHRIST, BE PRESENT NOW 91

HERR JESU CHRIST, DICH ZU UNS WEND L.M.

Pensum sacrum, Altenberg, 1648, St. 1-3
Cantionale sacrum, Gotha, 1651, St. 4
Herr Jesu Christ, dich zu uns wend
Tr. Catherine Winkworth‡, 1863

Cantionale Germanicum, Gochsheim, 1628

1 Lord Je - sus Christ, be pres - ent now, Our
2 Un - seal our lips to sing Thy praise, Our
3 Till we with saints in glad ac - cord Sing
4 All glo - ry to the Fa - ther, Son, And

hearts in true de - vo - tion bow, Thy Spir - it send with
souls to Thee in wor - ship raise, Make strong our faith, in -
"Ho - ly, ho - ly is the Lord!" And in the light of
Ho - ly Spir - it, three in one! To Thee, O bless - ed

grace di - vine, And let Thy truth with - in us shine.
crease our light That we may know Thy name a - right,
heav'n a - bove Shall see Thy face and know Thy love.
Trin - i - ty, Be praise through-out e - ter - ni - ty! A - men.

JESUS CHRIST: PRAISE AND GLORY

92 OF THE FATHER'S LOVE BEGOTTEN

DIVINUM MYSTERIUM 8.7.8.7.8.7.7.

Aurelius Clemens Prudentius, d. 413
Cordus natus ex Parentis
Tr. John Mason Neale and Henry W. Baker, 1861

13th-century Plainsong
Harmony by Winfred Douglas, 1940

1 Of   the Fa-ther's love be - got - ten, Ere the worlds be - gan   to be,
2 O   ye heights of heav'n, a - dore Him; An - gel hosts, His prais - es sing;
3 Thee   let old men, Thee let   young men, Thee let boys in   cho - rus sing;
4 Christ, to Thee with God the Fa - ther, And, O Ho - ly   Ghost, to Thee,

He   is Al - pha and O - me - ga, He the source, the end - ing He,
Powers, do-min-ions, bow be - fore Him, And ex - tol our God   and King;
Ma - trons, vir - gins, lit - tle maid - ens, With glad voic - es an - swer-ing;
Hymn and chant and high thanks-giv-ing, And un - wear-ied prais - es be:

Of   the things that are, that   have - - - been, And that
Let   no tongue on earth be   si - - - lent, Ev - ery
Let   their guile-less songs re - ech - - - o, And the
Hon - or, glo - ry, and do - min - - - ion, And e -

JESUS CHRIST: PRAISE AND GLORY

fu - ture years shall see, Ev - er-more and ev - er - more!
voice in con - cert ring, Ev - er-more and ev - er - more!
heart its mu - sic bring, Ev - er-more and ev - er - more!
ter - nal vic - to - ry, Ev - er-more and ev - er - more! A - men.

COME, LET US TUNE OUR LOFTIEST SONG 93

MOZART L.M.

Robert Athow West, 1849

Arranged from a *Kyrie*, published in Mainz, 1821

1 Come, let us tune our loft - iest song, And raise to
2 His sov - 'reign power our bod - ies made; Our souls are
3 Burn ev - ery breast with Je - sus' love; Bound ev - ery
4 Ex - tol the Lamb with loft - iest song; As - cend for

Christ our joy - ful strain; Wor - ship and thanks to
His im - mor - tal breath; And when His crea - tures
heart with rap - turous joy; And saints on earth, with
Him our cheer - ful strain; Wor - ship and thanks to

Him be - long, Who reigns, and shall for - ev - er reign.
sinned, He bled, To save us from e - ter - nal death.
saints a - bove, Your voic - es in His praise em - ploy.
Him be - long, Who reigns, and shall for - ev - er reign.

JESUS CHRIST: PRAISE AND GLORY

94 AT THE NAME OF JESUS

KING'S WESTON 6.5.6.5.D.

Caroline Maria Noel, 1875

Ralph Vaughan Williams, 1925
Arranged for *The Hymnbook*, 1955, (Presbyterian)

1 At the name of Je - sus Ev - ery knee shall bow,
2 At His voice cre - a - tion Sprang at once to sight,
3 Hum - bled for a sea - son, To re - ceive a name
4 In your hearts en - throne Him; There let Him sub - due
5 Broth - ers, this Lord Je - sus Shall re - turn a - gain,

Ev - ery tongue con - fess Him King of glo - ry now;
All the an - gel fac - es, All the hosts of light,
From the lips of sin - ners Un - to whom He came,
All that is not ho - ly, All that is not true:
With His Fa - ther's glo - ry, With His an - gel train;

'Tis the Fa - ther's plea - sure We should call Him Lord,
Thrones and dom - i - na - tions, Stars up - on their way,
Faith - ful - ly He bore it Spot - less to the last,
Crown Him as your Cap - tain In temp - ta - tion's hour;
For all wreaths of em - pire Meet up - on His brow,

Who from the be - gin - ning Was the might - y Word.
All the heav'n - ly or - ders, In their great ar - ray.
Brought it back vic - to - rious, When from death He passed;
Let His will en - fold you In its light and power.
And our hearts con - fess Him King of glo - ry now. A - men.

JESUS CHRIST: PRAISE AND GLORY

ALL HAIL THE POWER OF JESUS' NAME 95

CORONATION C.M.

Edward Perronet, 1779 and 1780
Altered by John Rippon

Oliver Holden, 1792

1 All hail the power of Je - sus' name! Let an - gels pros-trate fall;
2 Ye cho - sen seed of Is - rael's race, Ye ran-somed of the fall,
3 Let ev - ery kin - dred, ev - ery tribe, On this ter - res - trial ball,
4 O that with yon - der sa - cred throng We at His feet may fall!

Bring forth the roy - al di - a - dem,
Hail Him who saves you by His grace,
To Him all maj - es - ty as - cribe,
We'll join the ev - er - last - ing song,

And crown Him Lord of all; Bring forth the roy - al
And crown Him Lord of all; Hail Him who saves you
And crown Him Lord of all; To Him all maj - es -
And crown Him Lord of all; We'll join the ev - er -

di - a - dem, And crown Him Lord of all!
by His grace, And crown Him Lord of all!
ty as - cribe, And crown Him Lord of all!
last - ing song, And crown Him Lord of all! A - men.

Another setting of this hymn may be found at No. 601

JESUS CHRIST: PRAISE AND GLORY

96 JESUS, THOU MIGHTY LORD

DOANE 6.4.6,4.D.

Fanny Crosby, c. 1883

William Howard Doane, 1883

1 Je - sus, Thou might-y Lord, Great is Thy name; Still through e -
2 Je - sus, Thou might-y Lord, Je - sus, our King, Praise for Thy
3 Sought by Thy mer-cy, Lord, Saved by Thy power, Led by Thy

ter - nal years, Thou art the same; Change-less Thy ho - ly Word,
won-drous love Glad - ly we sing. Love in Thy di - a - dem
gra - cious hand, Kept ev - er - y hour. Thine shall the hon - or be,

True ev - er - more; Thy name we glo - ri-fy, Thy name a - dore.
Shines ev - er - more; Thy name we glo - ri-fy, Thy name a - dore.
Thine ev - er - more; Thy name we glo - ri-fy, Thy name a - dore. A - men.

97 FAIREST LORD JESUS

CRUSADERS' HYMN 5.6.8.5.5.8.

Gesangbuch, Münster, 1677, St. 1 and 3
Heinrich August Hoffmann von Fallersleben, 1842, St. 2
  Schönster Herr Jesu!
Tr. R. S. Willis' Church-Chorals... †, 1850

H. A. Hoffmann von Fallersleben's,
Schlesische Volkslieder, 1842
Harmony by Richard Storrs Willis, 1850

1 Fair-est Lord Je - sus, Rul - er of all na - ture, O Thou of God and man the Son;
2 Fair are the mead-ows, Fair-er still the wood-lands, Robed in the bloom-ing garb of spring;
3 Fair is the sun-shine, Fair-er still the moon-light, And all the twin-kling, star-ry host;

JESUS CHRIST: PRAISE AND GLORY

Thee will I cher - ish, Thee will I hon - or, Thou, my soul's glo-ry, joy and crown.
Je - sus is fair - er, Je - sus is pur - er, Who makes the woe-ful heart to sing.
Je - sus shines bright-er, Je - sus shines pur - er Than all the an-gels heav'n can boast.

JESUS, THOU JOY OF LOVING HEARTS 98

SHELTERING WING L.M.

Bernard of Clairvaux? c. 1150
Jesu dulcis memoria
Tr. Ray Palmer, 1858

Joseph Barnby, 1872

1 Je - sus, Thou joy of lov - ing hearts! Thou fount of
2 Thy truth un - changed hath ev - er stood; Thou sav - est
3 We taste Thee, O Thou liv - ing bread, And long to
4 Our rest - less spir - its yearn for Thee, Wher - e'er our
5 O Je - sus, ev - er with us stay; Make all our

life! Thou light of men! From the best bliss that
those that on Thee call; To them that seek Thee,
feast up - on Thee still; We drink of Thee, the
change - ful lot is cast; Glad, when Thy gra - cious
mo - ments calm and bright; Chase the dark night of

earth im - parts, We turn un - filled to Thee a - gain.
Thou art good, To them that find Thee, all in all.
foun - tain head, And thirst our souls from Thee to fill!
smile we see, Blest, when our faith can hold Thee fast.
sin a - way, Shed o'er the world Thy ho - ly light! A - men.

JESUS CHRIST: PRAISE AND GLORY

99 O COULD I SPEAK

ARIEL 8.8.6.8.8.6.

Samuel Medley†, 1789

From Wolfgang Amadeus Mozart, 1791
Arranged by Lowell Mason, 1836

1 O could I speak the match-less worth, O could I sound the
2 I'd sing the pre-cious blood He spilt, My ran-som from the
3 I'd sing the char-ac-ters He bears, And all the forms of
4 Well, the de-light-ful day will come When my dear Lord will

glo-ries forth, Which in my Sav-ior shine! I'd soar and
dread-ful guilt, Of sin, and wrath di-vine; I'd sing His
love He wears, Ex-alt-ed on His throne; In loft-iest
bring me home, And I shall see His face; Then with my

touch the heav'n-ly strings, And vie with Ga-briel while he sings
glo-rious right-eous-ness, In which all-per-fect heav'n-ly dress
songs of sweet-est praise, I would to ev-er-last-ing days
Sav-ior, Broth-er, Friend A blest e-ter-ni-ty I'll spend,

In tones al-most di-vine, In tones al-most di-vine.
My soul shall ev-er shine, My soul shall ev-er shine.
Make all His glo-ries known, Make all His glo-ries known.
Tri-um-phant in His grace, Tri-um-phant in His grace.

JESUS CHRIST: PRAISE AND GLORY

YE SERVANTS OF GOD 100

HANOVER 10.10.11.11.

Charles Wesley†, 1744

William Croft(?), 1708

1 Ye serv - ants of God, your Mas - ter pro - claim,
2 God rul - eth on high, al - might - y to save;
3 "Sal - va - tion to God, who sits on the throne!"
4 Then let us a - dore, and give Him His right,

And pub - lish a - broad His won - der - ful name;
And still He is nigh, His pres - ence we have.
Let all cry a - loud, and hon - or the Son:
All glo - ry and power and wis - dom and might,

The name all - vic - to - rious, of Je - sus ex - tol;
The great con - gre - ga - tion His tri - umphs shall sing,
The prais - es of Je - sus the an - gels pro - claim,
All hon - or and bless - ing, with an - gels a - bove,

His king - dom is glo - rious, And rules o - ver all.
As - crib - ing sal - va - tion to Je - sus, our King.
Fall down on their fac - es, and wor - ship the Lamb.
And thanks nev - er ceas - ing for in - fi - nite love. A - men.

JESUS CHRIST: PRAISE AND GLORY

101 GLORY TO GOD ON HIGH

ITALIAN HYMN 6.6.4.6.6.6.4.

James Allen, 1761, and Others

Felice de Giardini, 1769

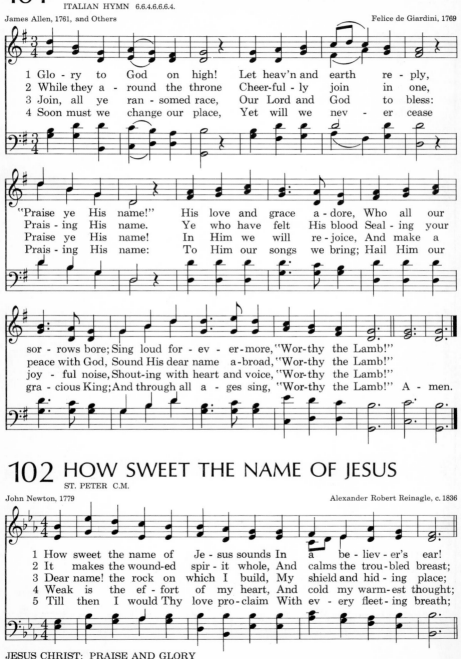

1 Glo-ry to God on high! Let heav'n and earth re-ply,
2 While they a-round the throne Cheer-ful-ly join in one,
3 Join, all ye ran-somed race, Our Lord and God to bless:
4 Soon must we change our place, Yet will we nev-er cease

"Praise ye His name!" His love and grace a-dore, Who all our
Prais-ing His name. Ye who have felt His blood Seal-ing your
Praise ye His name! In Him we will re-joice, And make a
Prais-ing His name: To Him our songs we bring; Hail Him our

sor-rows bore; Sing loud for-ev-er-more, "Wor-thy the Lamb!"
peace with God, Sound His dear name a-broad, "Wor-thy the Lamb!"
joy-ful noise, Shout-ing with heart and voice, "Wor-thy the Lamb!"
gra-cious King; And through all a-ges sing, "Wor-thy the Lamb!" A-men.

102 HOW SWEET THE NAME OF JESUS

ST. PETER C.M.

John Newton, 1779

Alexander Robert Reinagle, c. 1836

1 How sweet the name of Je-sus sounds In a be-liev-er's ear!
2 It makes the wound-ed spir-it whole, And calms the trou-bled breast;
3 Dear name! the rock on which I build, My shield and hid-ing place;
4 Weak is the ef-fort of my heart, And cold my warm-est thought;
5 Till then I would Thy love pro-claim With ev-ery fleet-ing breath;

JESUS CHRIST: PRAISE AND GLORY

It soothes his sor-rows, heals his wounds, And drives a - way his fear.
'Tis man - na to the hun-gry soul, And to the wea - ry rest.
My nev - er - fail - ing trea-sury filled With bound-less stores of grace.
But when I see Thee as Thou art, I'll praise Thee as I ought.
And may the mu - sic of Thy name Re-fresh my soul in death. A - men.

HOW BEAUTEOUS WERE THE MARKS 103

MARYTON L.M.

Arthur Cleveland Coxe†, 1840

Henry Percy Smith, 1874

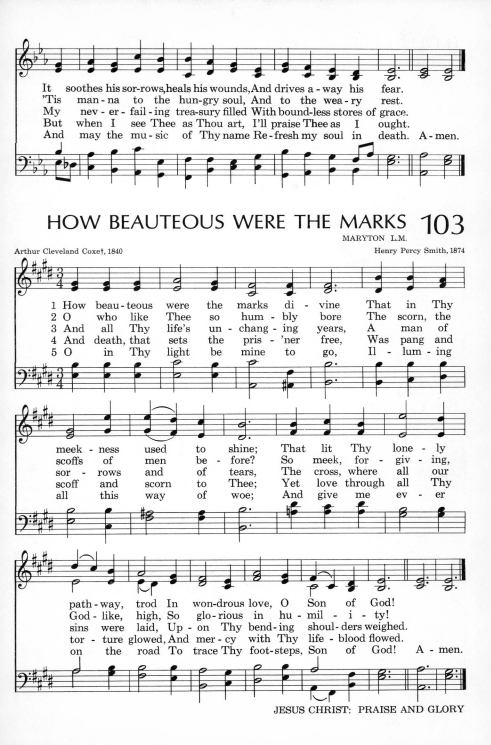

1 How beau - teous were the marks di - vine That in Thy
2 O who like Thee so hum - bly bore The scorn, the
3 And all Thy life's un - chang - ing years, A man of
4 And death, that sets the pris - 'ner free, Was pang and
5 O in Thy light be mine to go, Il - lum - ing

meek - ness used to shine; That lit Thy lone - ly
scoffs of men be - fore? So meek, for - giv - ing,
sor - rows and of tears, The cross, where all our
scoff and scorn to Thee; Yet love through all Thy
all this way of woe; And give me ev - er

path - way, trod In won-drous love, O Son of God!
God - like, high, So glo - rious in hu - mil - i - ty!
sins were laid, Up - on Thy bend-ing shoul - ders weighed.
tor - ture glowed, And mer - cy with Thy life - blood flowed.
on the road To trace Thy foot-steps, Son of God! A - men.

JESUS CHRIST: PRAISE AND GLORY

104 O FOR A THOUSAND TONGUES

AZMON C.M.

Charles Wesley, 1739

Carl Gotthelf Gläser, d. 1829
Arranged by Lowell Mason, 1839

1 O   for   a   thou-sand tongues to sing My great Re-deem-er's praise,
2 My   gra-cious Mas-ter   and my God, As - sist   me   to   pro-claim,
3 Je - sus! the name that charms our fears,That bids our sor-rows cease,
4 He   breaks the power of   can-celed sin, He   sets the pris-on-er free;
5 Glo - ry   to   God and praise and love Be   ev - er, ev - er   given

The glo-ries of my God and King, The tri-umphs of His grace.
To spread through all the earth a-broad The hon-ors of Thy name.
'Tis mu-sic in   the sin-ner's ears, 'Tis life, and health,and peace.
His blood can make the foul-est clean; His blood a-vailed for me.
By saints be-low and saints a-bove, The church in earth and heav'n. A-men.

105 COME, LET US JOIN

NEWBOLD C.M.

Isaac Watts, 1707

George Kingsley, 1847

1 Come, let us join our cheer-ful songs With an-gels round the throne; Ten thou-sand
2 "Wor - thy the Lamb that died,"they cry, "To be ex - alt - ed thus!" "Wor-thy the
3 Je - sus is wor-thy to re-ceive Hon-or and power di-vine; And bless-ings
4 The whole cre-a-tion join in one, To bless the sa - cred name Of Him that

thou-sand are their tongues,But all their joys are one, But all their joys are one.
Lamb!"our lips re-ply, "For He was slain for us, For He was slain for us."
more than we can give, Be,Lord,for-ev - er Thine, Be, Lord, for-ev - er Thine.
sits   up-on the throne,And to a - dore the Lamb,And to a - dore the Lamb.

JESUS CHRIST: PRAISE AND GLORY

O POWER OF LOVE 106

ST. PETERSBURG   9.8.9.8.9.9.

Gerhard Tersteegen, 1757
Ich bete an die Macht der Liebe
Tr. Herman Brückner‡, d. 1942

Dimitri S. Bortniansky, 1825

1 O power of love, all else tran-scend-ing In Je - sus
2 Thou art my rest, no earth - ly treas - ure Can sat - is -
3 To Thee my heart and life be giv - en, Thou art in

pres - ent ev - er - more, I wor-ship Thee, in hom - age bend-ing,
fy my yearn-ing heart, And naught can give to me the pleas-ure
truth my high - est good; For me Thy sa - cred side was riv - en,

Thy name to hon - or and a - dore: Yea, let my soul, in deep de -
I find in Thee, my cho - sen part, Thy love, so ten - der, so pos -
For me ·was shed Thy pre - cious blood. O Thou who art the world's sal -

vo - tion, Bathe in love's might-y bound-less o - cean.
sess - ing, Is joy to me, and ev - ery bless - ing.
va - tion, Be Thine my love and ad - o - ra - tion. A - men.

JESUS CHRIST: PRAISE AND GLORY

107 WHEN MORNING GILDS THE SKIES

LAUDES DOMINI 6.6.6.6.6.6.

Katholisches Gesangbuch, Würzburg, 1828
Beim frühen Morgenlicht
Tr. Edward Caswall†, 1854

Joseph Barnby, 1868

1 When morn-ing gilds the skies, My heart a-wak-ing cries:
2 Does sad-ness fill my mind, A sol-ace here I find:
3 The night be-comes as day, When from the heart we say:
4 Be this, while life is mine, My can-ti-cle di-vine,

May Je-sus Christ be praised! A-like at work or prayer
May Je-sus Christ be praised! Or fades my earth-ly bliss,
May Je-sus Christ be praised! In heav'n's e-ter-nal bliss,
May Je-sus Christ be praised! Be this th'e-ter-nal song,

To Je-sus I re-pair: May Je-sus Christ be praised!
My com-fort still is this: May Je-sus Christ be praised!
The love-liest strain is this: May Je-sus Christ be praised!
Through all the a-ges on: May Je-sus Christ be praised! A-men.

108 JESUS, THE VERY THOUGHT OF THEE

ST. AGNES C.M.

Bernard of Clairvaux?, c. 1150
Jesu dulcis memoria
Tr. Edward Caswall†, 1849

John Bacchus Dykes, 1866

1 Je-sus, the ver-y thought of Thee With sweet-ness fills my breast;
2 Nor voice can sing, nor heart can frame, Nor can the mem-'ry find
3 O hope of ev-ery con-trite heart! O joy of all the meek!
4 But what to those who find? Ah this Nor tongue nor pen can show;
5 Je-sus! our on-ly joy be Thou, As Thou our prize wilt be;

JESUS CHRIST: PRAISE AND GLORY

But sweet-er far Thy face to see, And in Thy pres-ence rest.
A sweet-er sound than Thy blest name, O Sav-ior of man-kind!
To those who fall, how kind Thou art! How good to those who seek!
The love of Je - sus, what it is, None but His loved ones know.
Je - sus! be Thou our glo - ry now, And through e-ter - ni - ty. A-men.

BEHOLD THE GLORIES OF THE LAMB 109

ST. MARTIN'S C.M.

Isaac Watts†, c. 1696

William Tans'ur, c. 1755

1 Be - hold the glo - ries of the Lamb, A - mid the Fa-ther's throne,
2 Let eld - ers wor - ship at His feet, The church a - dore a - round,
3 Those are the prayers of all the saints, And these the hymns they raise.
4 Now, to the Lamb that once was slain, Be end - less bless-ings paid;
5 Thou hast re - deemed our souls with blood, Hast set the pris -'ners free,

Pre - pare new hon - ors for His name, And songs be - fore un-known.
With vi - als full of o - dors sweet, And harps of sweet-er sound.
Je - sus is kind to our com-plaints, He loves to hear our praise.
Sal - va - tion, glo - ry, joy, re - main For-ev - er on Thy head.
Hast made us kings and priests to God, And we shall reign with Thee.

JESUS CHRIST: PRAISE AND GLORY

110 AWAKE, MY SOUL, IN JOYFUL LAYS

LOVING KINDNESS L.M. with Refrain

Samuel Medley, 1782

Folk Hymn
Joshua Leavitt's *Christian Lyre*, 1831

1 A - wake, my soul, in joy - ful lays, And sing thy great Re-
2 He saw me ru - ined in the fall, Yet loved me not - with-
3 Though nu - m'rous hosts of might - y foes, Though earth and hell my
4 When trou - ble, like a gloom - y cloud, Has gath - ered thick, and

deem - er's praise; He just - ly claims a song from me,
stand - ing all; He saved me from my lost es - tate,
way op - pose, He safe - ly leads my soul a - long,
thun - dered loud, He near my soul has al - ways stood,

His lov - ing - kind - ness, O how free! Lov - ing - kind - ness,
His lov - ing - kind - ness, O how great! Lov - ing - kind - ness,
His lov - ing - kind - ness, O how strong! Lov - ing - kind - ness,
His lov - ing - kind - ness, O how good! Lov - ing - kind - ness,

lov - ing - kind - ness, His lov - ing - kind - ness, O how free!
lov - ing - kind - ness, His lov - ing - kind - ness, O how great!
lov - ing - kind - ness, His lov - ing - kind - ness, O how strong!
lov - ing - kind - ness, His lov - ing - kind - ness, O how good!

JESUS CHRIST: PRAISE AND GLORY

O COME, O COME, EMMANUEL 111

VENI EMMANUEL   L.M. with Refrain

Anonymous
Veni, veni Emmanuel
Tr. John Mason Neale, 1851,
and Compilers of *Hymns Ancient and Modern*, 1861

Fifteenth Century Trope Melody
The Hymnal Noted, Part II, 1854

1. O come, O come, Em-man-u-el, And ran-som cap-tive
2. O come, Thou Rod of Jes-se, free Thine own from Sa-tan's
3. O come, Thou Day-spring, come and cheer Our spir-its by Thine
4. O come, Thou Key of Da-vid, come, And o-pen wide our
5. O come, O come, Thou Lord of might, Who to Thy tribes, on

Is-ra-el, That mourns in lone-ly ex-ile here,
tyr-an-ny; From depths of hell Thy peo-ple save,
ad-vent here; Dis-perse the gloom-y clouds of night,
heav'n-ly home; Make safe the way that leads on high,
Si-nai's height, In an-cient times didst give the law

Un-til the Son of God ap-pear.
And give them vic-tory o'er the grave.
And death's dark shad-ows put to flight. Re-joice! Re-joice! Em-
And close the path to mis-er-y.
In cloud and maj-es-ty and awe.

man-u-el Shall come to thee, O Is-ra-el! A-men.

JESUS CHRIST: ADVENT

112 HARK, THE GLAD SOUND

COMMUNION C.M.D.

Folk Hymn
"Robison" in J. Wyeth's *Repository
of Sacred Music, Part Second*, 1813

Philip Doddridge, 1755

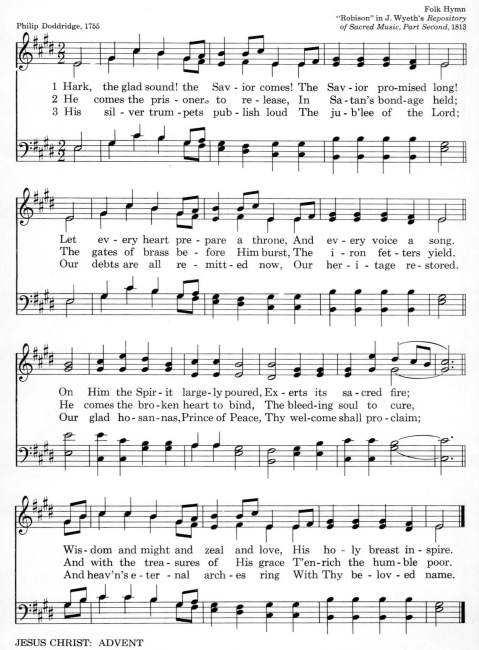

1 Hark, the glad sound! the Sav-ior comes! The Sav-ior pro-mised long!
2 He comes the pris-oners to re-lease, In Sa-tan's bond-age held;
3 His sil-ver trum-pets pub-lish loud The ju-b'lee of the Lord;

Let ev-ery heart pre-pare a throne, And ev-ery voice a song.
The gates of brass be-fore Him burst, The i-ron fet-ters yield.
Our debts are all re-mitt-ed now, Our her-i-tage re-stored.

On Him the Spir-it large-ly poured, Ex-erts its sa-cred fire;
He comes the bro-ken heart to bind, The bleed-ing soul to cure,
Our glad ho-san-nas, Prince of Peace, Thy wel-come shall pro-claim;

Wis-dom and might and zeal and love, His ho-ly breast in-spire.
And with the trea-sures of His grace T'en-rich the hum-ble poor.
And heav'n's e-ter-nal arch-es ring With Thy be-lov-ed name.

JESUS CHRIST: ADVENT

HAIL TO THE LORD'S ANOINTED

113

CRÜGER 7.6.7.6.D.

Johann Crüger, 1640
Adapted by William Henry Monk, 1861

James Montgomery†, 1821

1 Hail to the Lord's a-noint-ed, Great Da-vid's great-er Son! Hail to the time ap-point-ed, His reign on earth be-gun! He comes to break op-pres-sion, To set the cap-tive free, To take a-way trans-gres-sion, And rule in eq-ui-ty.

2 He comes with suc-cor speed-y To those who suf-fer wrong; To help the poor and need-y, And bid the weak be strong; To give them songs for sigh-ing, Their dark-ness turn to light, Whose souls, con-demned and dy-ing, Were pre-cious in His sight.

3 He shall come down like show-ers Up-on the fruit-ful earth; And love, joy, hope like flow-ers, Spring in His path to birth. Be-fore Him, on the moun-tains Shall peace, the her-ald, go; And right-eous-ness, in foun-tains, From hill to val-ley flow.

4 O'er ev-ery foe vic-to-rious, He on His throne shall rest, From age to age more glo-rious, All bless-ing and all blest. The tide of time shall nev-er His cov-e-nant re-move; His name shall stand for-ev-er; That name to us is Love. A-men.

JESUS CHRIST: ADVENT

114 VEILED IN DARKNESS JUDAH LAY

EBELING 7.7.7.7.7.7.

Douglas LeTell Rights, 1915

Johann Georg Ebeling, 1666

1 Veiled in dark - ness Ju - dah lay, Wait - ing for the
2 Still the earth in dark - ness lies. Up from death's dark
3 Light of light, we hum - bly pray, Shine up - on Thy

prom - ised day, While a - cross the shad - owy night
vale a - rise Voic - es of a world in grief,
world to - day; Break the gloom of our dark night,

Streamed a flood of glo - rious light, Heav'n - ly voic - es
Prayers of men who seek re - lief; Now our dark - ness
Fill our souls with love and light, Send Thy bless - ed

chant - ing then, "Peace on earth, good - will to men."
pierce a - gain, "Peace on earth, good - will to men."
word a - gain, "Peace on earth, good - will to men." A - men.

JESUS CHRIST: ADVENT

COME, THOU LONG-EXPECTED JESUS 115

HYFRYDOL 8.7.8.7.D.

Rowland Hugh Prichard, c. 1830
Harmonized by Ralph Vaughan Williams, 1951

Charles Wesley, 1745

1 Come, Thou long-ex-pect-ed Je-sus! Born to set Thy peo-ple free,
2 Born Thy peo-ple to de-liv-er, Born a child, and yet a King,

From our fears and sins re-lease us, Let us find our rest in Thee.
Born to reign in us for-ev-er, Now Thy gra-cious king-dom bring,

Is-rael's strength and con-so-la-tion, Hope of all the earth Thou art;
By Thy own e-ter-nal Spir-it, Rule in all our hearts a-lone;

Dear De-sire of ev-ery na-tion, Joy of ev-ery long-ing heart.
By Thy all suf-fi-cient mer-it, Raise us to Thy glo-rious throne. A-men.

JESUS CHRIST: ADVENT

116 O SAVIOR, REND THE HEAVENS WIDE

O HEILAND, REISS DIE HIMMEL AUF L.M.

Friedrich von Spee, 1623
O Heiland, reiss die Himmel auf
Tr. Martin L. Seltz, 1965

Gesangbuch, Augsburg, 1666
Harmony by Esther Wiebe, 1964

1 O Sav - ior, rend the heav - ens wide;
2 O Fa - ther, dew from heav - en send;
3 O earth, in flow - 'ring bud be seen;
4 Here dread - ful doom up - on us lies;
5 There will we all our prais - es bring

Come down, come down with might - y stride.
As gen - tle dew, O Son, de - scend.
Clothe hill and dale in garb of green.
Death looms so grim be - fore our eyes.
Ev - er to Thee, our Sav - ior King;

Un - bar the gates, the doors break down;
Drop down, you clouds, and tor - rents bring;
O earth, bring forth this Blos - som rare;
O come, lead us with might - y hand
There will we laud Thee and a - dore

Un - bar the way to heav - en's crown.
To Ja - cob's line rain down a King.
O Sav - ior, rise from mead - ow fair.
From ex - ile to our fa - ther - land.
For ev - er and for ev - er - more. A - men.

JESUS CHRIST: ADVENT

LET ALL MORTAL FLESH KEEP SILENCE 117

PICARDY 8.7.8.7.8.7.

Liturgy of St. James
Σιγησάτω πᾶσα σὰρξ βροτεία
Tr. Gerard Moultrie, 1864

French Carol Melody

In Unison

1 Let all mor - tal flesh keep si - lence, And with fear and
2 King of kings, yet born of Ma - ry, As of old on
3 Rank on rank the host of heav - en Spreads its van-guard
4 At His feet the six - winged ser - aph; Cher - u - bim with

trem - bling stand; Pon - der noth - ing earth - ly mind - ed,
earth He stood, Lord of lords, in hu - man ves - ture,
on the way, As the Light of light de - scend - eth
sleep - less eye, Veil their fac - es to the pres - ence,

For with bless - ing in His hand, Christ our God to
In the bod - y and the blood, He will give to
From the realms of end - less day, That the powers of
As with cease - less voice they cry, Al - le - lu - ia,

earth de - scend - eth, Our full hom - age to de - mand.
all the faith - ful His own self for heav'n - ly food.
hell may van - ish As the dark-ness clears a - way.
al - le - lu - ia, Al - le - lu - ia, Lord most high.

JESUS CHRIST: ADVENT

118 WAKE, AWAKE, FOR NIGHT IS FLYING

WACHET AUF, RUFT UNS DIE STIMME   8.9.8.8.9.8.6.6.4.8.8.

Philipp Nicolai, 1599
Wachet auf, ruft uns die Stimme
Tr. Catherine Winkworth, 1858

Philipp Nicolai, 1599

1 Wake, a - wake, for night is fly - ing, The watch-men on
2 Zi - on hears the watch-men sing - ing, And all her heart

the heights are cry - ing; A - wake, Je - ru - sa - lem, at last!
with joy is spring - ing, She wakes, she ris - es from her gloom;

Mid - night hears the wel - come voic - es, And at the thrill-
For her Lord comes down all - glo - rious, The strong in grace,

ing cry re - joic - es: Come forth, ye vir - gins, night is past!
in truth vic - to - rious, Her Star is risen, her Light is come!

JESUS CHRIST: ADVENT

The Bride-groom comes, a - wake, Your lamps with glad - ness take;
Ah come, Thou bless - ed Lord, O Je - sus, Son of God,

Al - le - lu - ia! And for His mar - riage feast pre - pare,
Al - le - lu - ia! We fol - low till the halls we see

For ye must go to meet Him there.
Where Thou hast bid us sup with Thee. A - men.

3 Now let all the heav'ns adore Thee,
  And men and angels sing before Thee,
    With harp and cymbal's clearest tone;
  Of one pearl each shining portal,
  Where we are with the choir immortal
    Of angels round Thy dazzling throne;
      Nor eye hath seen, nor ear
      Hath yet attain'd to hear
        What there is ours,
  But we rejoice, and sing to Thee
  Our hymns of joy eternally.

119 O HOW SHALL I RECEIVE THEE

VALET WILL ICH DIR GEBEN 7.6.7.6.D.

Paul Gerhardt, 1653
Wie soll ich dich empfangen
Tr. Arthur Tozer Russell, 1851, and Others

Melchior Teschner, 1613

1 O how shall I re - ceive Thee, How meet Thee on Thy way,
2 Thy Zi - on palms is strew - ing, And branch - es fresh and fair;
3 Love caused Thy in - car - na - tion; Love brought Thee down to me.
4 Thou com - est, Lord, with glad - ness, In mer - cy and good will,

Blest hope of ev - ery na - tion, My soul's de - light and stay?
My soul, to praise a - wak - ing, Her an - them shall pre - pare.
Thy thirst for my sal - va - tion Pro - cured my lib - er - ty.
To bring an end to sad - ness And bid our fears be still.

O Je - sus, Je - sus, give me Now by Thy own pure light
Un - end - ing thanks and prais - es From my glad heart shall spring;
O love be - yond all tell - ing, That led Thee to em - brace,
We wel - come Thee, our Sav - ior; Come gath - er us to Thee,

To know what-e'er is pleas - ing And wel - come in Thy sight.
And to Thy name the serv - ice Of all my powers I bring.
In love all love ex - cell - ing, Our lost and trou - bled race.
That in Thy light e - ter - nal Our joy - ous home may be.

JESUS CHRIST: ADVENT

LIFT UP YOUR HEADS, YE MIGHTY GATES 120

MACHT HOCH DIE TÜR 8.8.8.8.8.8.8.6.6.

Based on Psalm 24
Georg Weissel, 1642
Macht hoch die Tür, die Tor macht weit
Tr. Catherine Winkworth, 1863

J. A. Freylinghausen's *Neues*
Geistreiches Gesangbuch, 1704

1 Lift up your heads, ye might-y gates, Be-hold the King of glo-ry waits;
2 The Lord is just, a Help-er tried, Mer-cy is ev-er at His side,
3 O blest the land, the cit-y blest, Where Christ the Rul-er is con-fessed!
4 Re-deem-er, come! I o-pen wide My heart to Thee; here, Lord, a-bide!

The King of kings is draw-ing near, The Sav-ior of the world is here;
His king-ly crown is hol-i-ness, His scept-er, pit-y in dis-tress,
O hap-py hearts and hap-py homes To whom this King in tri-umph comes!
Let me Thy in-ner pres-ence feel, Thy grace and love in me re-veal,

Life and sal-va-tion doth He bring, Where-fore re-joice and glad-ly sing:
The end of all our woes He brings; Where-fore the earth is glad and sings:
The cloud-less Sun of joy He is, Who bring-eth pure de-light and bliss:
Thy Ho-ly Spir-it guide us on Un-til our glo-rious goal is won!

We praise Thee, Fa-ther, now! Cre-a-tor, wise art Thou!
We praise Thee, Sav-ior, now, Might-y in deed art Thou!
O Com-fort-er di-vine, What bound-less grace is Thine!
E-ter-nal praise and fame We of-fer to Thy name. A-men.

JESUS CHRIST: ADVENT

121 COMFORT, COMFORT YE MY PEOPLE

GENEVA 42 8.7.8.7.7.7.8.8.

Based on Isaiah 40
Johann Olearius
Tröstet, tröstet meine Lieben
Tr. Catherine Winkwortht, 1863

Pseaumes octante trois . . . , Geneva, 1551
Harmony adapted from Claude Goudimel, 1565

1 Com - fort, com-fort ye My peo - ple, Speak ye peace, thus saith our God;
2 Yea, her sins our God will par - don, Blot - ting out each dark mis - deed;
3 Hark, the voice of one that cri - eth In the des - ert far and near,
4 Make ye straight what long was crook-ed, Make the rough-er plac - es plain;

Com - fort those who sit in dark-ness, Mourn-ing 'neath their sor - rows' load.
All that well de-served His an - ger He no more will see or heed.
Bid - ding all men to re - pent-ance Since the king-dom now is here.
Let your hearts be true and hum - ble, As be - fits His ho - ly reign.

Speak ye to Je - ru - sa - lem Of the peace that waits for them;
She hath suf - fered man - y a day, Now her griefs have passed a - way;
O that warn - ing cry o - bey! Now pre - pare for God a way;
For the glo - ry of the Lord Now o'er earth is shed a - broad,

Tell her that her sins I cov - er, And her war-fare now is o - ver.
God will change her pin-ing sad-ness In - to ev - er-spring-ing glad-ness.
Let the val-leys rise to meet Him And the hills bow down to greet Him.
And all flesh shall see the to - ken That His Word is nev - er bro - ken. A-men.

JESUS CHRIST: ADVENT

JOY TO THE WORLD 122

ANTIOCH C.M.

Based on Psalm 98
Isaac Watts, 1719

"From Handel"
Lowell Mason, 1836

1 Joy to the world! the Lord is come; Let earth re-ceive her King;
2 Joy to the earth; the Sav-ior reigns; Let men their songs em-ploy;
3 No more let sins and sor-rows grow, Nor thorns in-fest the ground,
4 He rules the world with truth and grace, And makes the na-tions prove

Let ev-ery heart pre-pare Him room,
While fields and floods, rocks, hills, and plains,
He comes to make His bless-ings flow
The glo-ries of His right-eous-ness,

And heav'n and na-ture sing, And heav'n and na-ture sing,
Re-peat the sound-ing joy, Re-peat the sound-ing joy,
Far as the curse is found, Far as the curse is found,
And won-ders of His love, And won-ders of His love,

And heav'n and na-ture sing,

And heav'n and na-ture sing, And heav'n and na-

And heav'n, and heav'n and na-ture sing.
Re-peat, re-peat the sound-ing joy.
Far as, far as the curse is found.
And won-ders, won-ders of His love.

ture sing.

JESUS CHRIST: BIRTH

123 CHRISTIANS, AWAKE

YORKSHIRE 10.10.10.10.10.10.

John Byrom‡, c. 1749

John Wainwright, c. 1749

1 Chris-tians, a-wake! sa-lute the hap-py morn Where-on the
2 Then to the watch-ful shep-herds it was told, Who heard th'an-
3 He spake; and straight-way the ce-les-tial choir In hymns of
4 Then may we hope, th'an-gel-ic hosts a-mong, To sing, re-

Sav-ior of the world was born; Rise to a-dore the
gel-ic her-ald's voice, "Be-hold, I bring good ti-dings
joy, un-known be-fore, con-spire; The prais-es of redeemed, a glad tri-um-phal song; He that was born up-

mys-ter-y of love, Which hosts of an-gels chant-ed
of a Sav-ior's birth To you and all the na-tions
deem-ing love they sang, And heav'n's whole orb with al-le-
on this joy-ful day A-round us all His glo-ry

from a-bove; With them the joy-ful ti-dings first be-
up-on earth; This day hath God ful-filled His prom-ised
lu-ias rang; God's high-est glo-ry was their an-them
shall dis-play; Saved by His love, for-ev-er we shall

JESUS CHRIST: BIRTH

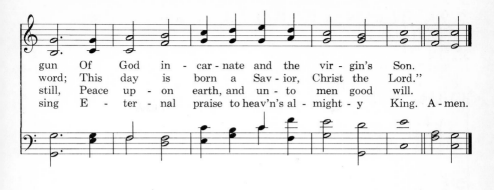

gun Of God in - car - nate and the vir - gin's Son.
word; This day is born a Sav - ior, Christ the Lord."
still, Peace up - on earth, and un - to men good will.
sing E - ter - nal praise to heav'n's al - might - y King. A - men.

ALL MY HEART THIS NIGHT REJOICES 124

WARUM SOLLT ICH MICH DENN GRÄMEN 8.3.3.6.D.

Paul Gerhardt, 1653
Fröhlich soll mein Herze springen
Tr. Catherine Winkworth, 1855

Johann Georg Ebeling, 1666

1 All my heart this night re - joic - es. As I hear, Far and
2 Come then, let us has - ten yon - der; Here let all, Great and

near, Sweet-est an - gel voic - es. "Christ is born," their choirs are
small, Kneel in awe and won - der! Love Him who with love is

sing - ing, Till the air Ev - ery - where Now with joy is ring - ing.
yearn-ing! Hail the star That from far Bright with hope is burn - ing!

JESUS CHRIST: BIRTH

125 TO US A CHILD OF HOPE IS BORN

ZERAH C.M.

Based on Isaiah 9: 6-7
John Morison in
Scottish Paraphrases, 1781

Lowell Mason, 1837

1 To us a Child of hope is born, To us
2 His name shall be the Prince of Peace, For ev -
3 His power, in - creas - ing, still shall spread; His reign

a Son is giv'n; Him shall the tribes of earth o - bey,
er - more a - dored, The Won - der - ful, the Coun - sel - or,
no end shall know; Jus - tice shall guard His throne a - bove,

Him all the hosts of heaven, Him shall the tribes
The great and might - y Lord, The Won - der - ful,
And peace a - bound be - low, Jus - tice shall guard

of earth o - bey, Him all the hosts of heaven.
the Coun - sel - or, The great and might - y Lord.
His throne a - bove, And peace a - bound be - low.

JESUS CHRIST: BIRTH

IT CAME UPON THE MIDNIGHT CLEAR 126

CAROL C.M.D.

Edmund Hamilton Sears†, 1849

Richard Storrs Willis, 1850

1 It came up - on the mid-night clear, That glo - rious song of old,
2 Still through the clo - ven skies they come, With peace-ful wings un - furled,
3 And ye, be - neath life's crush-ing load, Whose forms are bend-ing low,
4 For lo, the days are has-t'ning on, By proph-et bards fore - told,

From an - gels bend - ing near the earth To touch their harps of gold:
And still their heav'n-ly mu - sic floats O'er all the wea - ry world:
Who toil a - long the climb-ing way With pain - ful steps and slow:
When with the ev - er - cir - cling years Comes round the age of gold;

"Peace on the earth, good will to men, From heav'n's all-gra - cious King."
A - bove its sad and low - ly plains They bend on hov -'ring wing,
Look now! for glad and gold - en hours Come swift - ly on the wing:
When peace shall o - ver all the earth Its an - cient splen-dors fling,

The world in sol - emn still - ness lay, To hear the an - gels sing.
And ev - er o'er its Ba-bel-sounds The bless - ed an - gels sing.
O rest be - side the wea - ry road, And hear the an - gels sing.
And the whole world give back the song Which now the an - gels sing.

JESUS CHRIST: BIRTH

127 ANGELS WE HAVE HEARD ON HIGH

GLORIA   7.7.7.7. with Refrain

Traditional French Carol
Altered by Earl Marlatt, b. 1892

French Carol

1 An - gels we have heard on high, Sing - ing sweet-ly through the night,
2 Shep-herds, why this ju - bi - lee? Why these songs of hap - py cheer?
3 Come to Beth - le - hem and see Him whose birth the an - gels sing;
4 See Him in a man - ger laid Whom the an - gels praise a - bove;

And the moun-tains in re - ply Ech - o - ing their brave de - light.
What great bright-ness did you see? What glad ti - dings did you hear?
Come, a - dore on bend - ed knee Christ, the Lord, the new - born King.
Ma - ry, Jo - seph, lend your aid, While we raise our hearts in love.

REFRAIN

Glo - - - ri - a in ex-cel-sis De - o,

Glo - - - ri - a in ex-cel-sis De - o.

JESUS CHRIST: BIRTH

ANGELS FROM THE REALMS OF GLORY 128

REGENT SQUARE 8.7.8.7.8.7.

James Montgomery, 1816

Henry Smart, 1867

1 An - gels, from the realms of glo - ry, Wing your flight o'er
2 Shep - herds, in the field a - bid - ing, Watch - ing o'er your
3 Sa - ges, leave your con - tem - pla - tions, Bright - er vi - sions
4 Saints, be - fore the al - tar bend - ing, Watch - ing long in
5 Sin - ners, wrung with true re - pent - ance, Doom'd for guilt to

all the earth, Ye who sang cre - a - tion's sto - ry,
flocks by night, God with man is now re - sid - ing,
beam a - far; Seek the great de - sire of na - tions;
hope and fear, Sud - den - ly the Lord de - scend - ing
end - less pains, Jus - tice now re - vokes the sen - tence,

Now pro - claim Mes - si - ah's birth; Come and wor - ship,
Yon - der shines the in - fant - light; Come and wor - ship,
Ye have seen His na - tal star; Come and wor - ship,
In His tem - ple shall ap - pear; Come and wor - ship,
Mer - cy calls you, break your chains; Come and wor - ship,

Come and wor - ship, Wor - ship Christ the new - born King.
Come and wor - ship, Wor - ship Christ the new - born King.
Come and wor - ship, Wor - ship Christ the new - born King.
Come and wor - ship, Wor - ship Christ the new - born King.
Come and wor - ship, Wor - ship Christ the new - born King.

JESUS CHRIST: BIRTH

129 WHAT CHILD IS THIS

GREENSLEEVES 8.7.8.7. with Refrain

William Chatterton Dix, c. 1865

English Traditional Melody

1 What child is this, who, laid to rest, On Ma-ry's lap is sleep-ing?
2 Why lies He in such mean es-tate Where ox and ass are feed-ing?
3 So bring Him in-cense, gold, and myrrh, Come, peas-ant, king, to own Him,

Whom an-gels greet with an-thems sweet, While shep-herds watch are keep-ing?
Good Chris-tian, fear: for sin-ners here The si-lent Word is plead-ing.
The King of kings sal-va-tion brings, Let lov-ing hearts en-throne Him.

REFRAIN

This, this is Christ the King, Whom shep-herds guard and an-gels sing:

Haste, haste to bring Him laud, The babe, the son of Ma-ry.

JESUS CHRIST: BIRTH

SILENT NIGHT, HOLY NIGHT 130

SILENT NIGHT Irregular

Joseph Mohr, 1818
Stille Nacht, Heilige Nacht
Tr. John Freeman Young, 1863

Franz Grüber, 1818

1 Si - lent night, ho - ly night, All is calm, all is bright
2 Si - lent night, ho - ly night, Shep-herds quake at the sight,
3 Si - lent night, ho - ly night, Son of God, love's pure light

Round yon vir - gin moth-er and child. Ho - ly in-fant so ten-der and mild,
Glo - ries stream from heav-en a - far, Heaven-ly hosts sing al - le - lu - ia;
Ra - diant beams from Thy ho-ly face, With the dawn of re - deem - ing grace,

Sleep in heav-en-ly peace, Sleep in heav-en-ly peace.
Christ, the Sav - ior is born! Christ, the Sav-ior is born!
Je - sus, Lord, at Thy birth, Je - sus, Lord, at Thy birth.

1 Stille Nacht, heilige Nacht!
Alles schläft, einsam wacht
nur das traute, hochheilige Paar,
das im Stalle zu Bethlehem war
bei dem himmlischen Kind,
bei dem himmlischen Kind.

2 Stille Nacht, heilige Nacht!
Hirten erst kund gemacht;
durch der Engel Hallelujah
tönt es laut von fern und nah:
Christ, der Retter, ist da!
Christ, der Retter, ist da!

3 Stille Nacht, heilige Nacht!
Gottes Sohn, o wie lacht
Lieb aus deinem holdseligen Mund,
da uns schlägt die rettende Stund,
Christ, in deiner Geburt!
Christ, in deiner Geburt!

JESUS CHRIST: BIRTH

131 LO, HOW A ROSE E'ER BLOOMING

ES IST EIN ROS' 7.6.7.6.6.7.6.

Köln, 1599, St. 1 and 2; Berlin, 1844, St. 3
Es ist ein Ros' entsprungen
Tr. Theodore Baker, 1894, St. 1 and 2
and Harriet R. Spaeth, 1875, St. 3

Alte Catholische Geistliche Kirchengeseng,
Köln, 1599
Harmony by Michael Praetorius, 1609

1 Lo, how a rose e'er bloom-ing From ten-der stem hath sprung,
2 I - sai - ah 'twas fore-told it, The rose I have in mind,
3 This flower,whose fra-grance ten-der With sweet-ness fills the air,

Of Jes-se's lin-eage com-ing, As men of old have sung.
With Ma-ry we be-hold it. The Vir-gin moth-er kind.
Dis-pels with glo-rious splen-dor The dark-ness ev-ery-where.

It came, a flow-'ret bright, A-mid the cold
To show God's love a-right. She bore to them
True Man, yet ver-y God, From sin and death

of win-ter, When half-spent was the night.
a Sav-ior, When half-spent was the night.
He saves us And light-ens ev-ery load.

JESUS CHRIST: BIRTH

O COME, ALL YE FAITHFUL 132

ADESTE FIDELES Irregular

Anonymous, 18th c.
Adeste fideles laeti triumphantes
Tr. Frederick Oakeley, 1842, and Others, St. 1, 3, 4
and William Mercer†, 1854, St. 2

John Francis Wade? c. 1740-43

1 O come, all ye faith-ful, Joy-ful and tri-um-phant, O come ye, O come
2 True God of true God, Light of light e - ter - nal, Our low-ly na -
3 Sing, choirs of an - gels, Sing in ex - ul - ta - tion, Sing, all ye cit-i-
4 Yea, Lord, we greet Thee, Born this hap-py morn-ing, Je - sus, to Thee

ye to Beth - le -hem; Come and be - hold Him, Born the King of an - gels;
ture He hath not ab-horred; Son of the Fa-ther, Be-got-ten, not cre - a - ted;
zens of heav'n a -bove; Glo - ry to God... In... the... high-est;
be . . . glo - ry giv'n; Word of the Fa-ther, Now in flesh ap-pear-ing:

REFRAIN

O come, let us a - dore Him, O come, let us a - dore Him,

O come, let us a - dore Him, Christ the Lord.

JESUS CHRIST: BIRTH

133 O LITTLE TOWN OF BETHLEHEM

ST. LOUIS 8.6.8.6.7.6.8.6.

Phillips Brooks, 1868

Lewis Henry Redner, 1868

1 O little town of Beth-le-hem, How still we see thee lie!
2 For Christ is born of Ma - ry, And gath-ered all a - bove,
3 How si - lent - ly, how si - lent - ly, The won-drous gift is giv'n!
4 O ho - ly Child of Beth-le-hem! De - scend to us, we pray;

A - bove thy deep and dream-less sleep The si - lent stars go by;
While mor - tals sleep, the an - gels keep Their watch of won-d'ring love.
So God im - parts to hu-man hearts The bless - ings of His heav'n.
Cast out our sin, and en - ter in: Be born in us to - day.

Yet in thy dark streets shin - eth The ev - er - last - ing Light;
O morn - ing stars, to - geth - er Pro - claim the ho - ly birth!
No ear may hear His com - ing, But in this world of sin,
We hear the Christ-mas an - gels The great glad ti - dings tell;

The hopes and fears of all the years Are met in thee to - night.
And prais-es sing to God the King, And peace to men on earth.
Where meek souls will re-ceive Him still, The dear Christ en - ters in.
O come to us, a - bide with us, Our Lord Em-man - u - el. A - men.

JESUS CHRIST: BIRTH

FROM HEAVEN ABOVE TO EARTH 134

VOM HIMMEL HOCH L.M.

Martin Luther, 1535
Vom Himmel hoch, da komm' ich her
Tr. Catherine Winkworth†, 1855

V. Schumann's *Geistliche*
Lieder, 1539

1 From heav'n a - bove to earth I come To
2 To you this night is born a child Of
3 Now let us all with glad - some cheer Fol -
4 Wel - come to earth, Thou no - ble Guest, Through

bear good news to ev - ery home; Glad ti - dings of great
Ma - ry, cho - sen moth - er mild; This lit - tle child, of
low the shep - herds and draw near To see this won - drous
whom e'en wick - ed men are blest! Thou com'st to share our

joy I bring, Where - of I now will say and sing:
low - ly birth, Shall be the joy of all your earth.
gift of God, Who hath His on - ly Son be - stowed.
mis - er - y; What can we ren - der, Lord, to Thee?

5 My heart for very joy doth leap,
My lips no more can silence keep;
I, too, must raise with joyful tongue
That sweetest ancient cradle-song:

6 Glory to God in highest heaven,
Who unto us His Son hath given!
While angels sing with joyful mirth
A glad new year to all the earth.

JESUS CHRIST: BIRTH

135 HARK! THE HERALD ANGELS SING

MENDELSSOHN 7.7.7.7.D. with Refrain

Charles Wesley, 1739, and Others

Arranged from Felix Mendelssohn, 1840

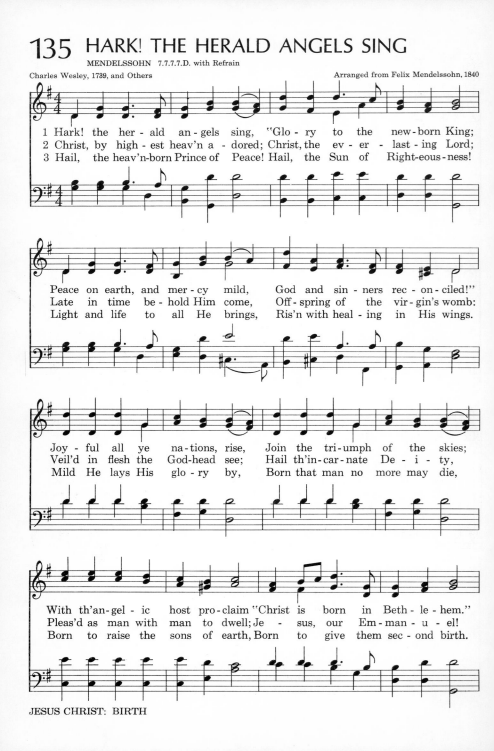

1 Hark! the her - ald an - gels sing, "Glo - ry to the new-born King;
2 Christ, by high - est heav'n a - dored; Christ, the ev - er - last - ing Lord;
3 Hail, the heav'n-born Prince of Peace! Hail, the Sun of Right-eous-ness!

Peace on earth, and mer - cy mild, God and sin - ners rec - on - ciled!"
Late in time be - hold Him come, Off - spring of the vir - gin's womb:
Light and life to all He brings, Ris'n with heal - ing in His wings.

Joy - ful all ye na - tions, rise, Join the tri - umph of the skies;
Veil'd in flesh the God-head see; Hail th'in - car - nate De - i - ty,
Mild He lays His glo - ry by, Born that man no more may die,

With th'an - gel - ic host pro - claim "Christ is born in Beth - le - hem."
Pleas'd as man with man to dwell; Je - sus, our Em - man - u - el!
Born to raise the sons of earth, Born to give them sec - ond birth.

JESUS CHRIST: BIRTH

Hark! the her-ald an-gels sing, "Glo-ry to the new-born King." A-men.

LET ALL TOGETHER PRAISE OUR GOD 136

LOBT GOTT, IHR CHRISTEN C.M.

Nicolaus Herman, c. 1554
Lobt Gott, ihr Christen alle gleich
Tr. Arthur Tozer Russell†, 1851

Nicolaus Herman, 1554
Harmony by Johann Sebastian Bach, c. 1735-1740

1 Let all to-geth-er praise our God Up-on His loft-y throne; For He un-clos-es heav'n to-day And gives to us His Son, And gives to us His Son.

2 He lays a-side His maj-es-ty And seems as noth-ing worth, And takes on Him a serv-ant's form, Who made the heav'n and earth, Who made the heav'n and earth.

3 Be-hold the won-der-ful ex-change Our Lord with us doth make! Lo, He as-sumes our flesh and blood, And we of heav'n par-take, And we of heav'n par-take.

4 The glo-rious gates of par-a-dise The an-gel guards no more; This day a-gain those gates un-fold. With praise our God a-dore, With praise our God a-dore! A-men.

JESUS CHRIST: BIRTH

137 THE FIRST NOEL THE ANGEL DID SAY

THE FIRST NOEL Irregular

Traditional Carol

English Carol, published 1833

1 The first No - el the an - gel did say
2 They look - ed up and saw a star
3 And by the light of that same star,
4 This star drew nigh to the north - west,
5 Then en - tered in those wise men three,

Was to cer - tain poor shep - herds in fields as they lay;
Shin - ing in the east, be - yond them far,
Three wise men came from coun - try far;
O'er Beth - le - hem it took its rest,
Full rev - er - ent - ly up - on their knee,

In fields where they lay keep - ing their sheep,
And to the earth it gave great light,
To seek for a king was their in - tent
And there it did both stop and stay,
And of - fered there, in His pres - ence,

On a cold win - ter's night that was so deep.
And so it con - tin - ued both day and night.
And to fol - low the star wher - ev - er it went.
Right o - ver the place where Je - sus lay.
Their gold, and myrrh, and frank - in - cense.

JESUS CHRIST: BIRTH

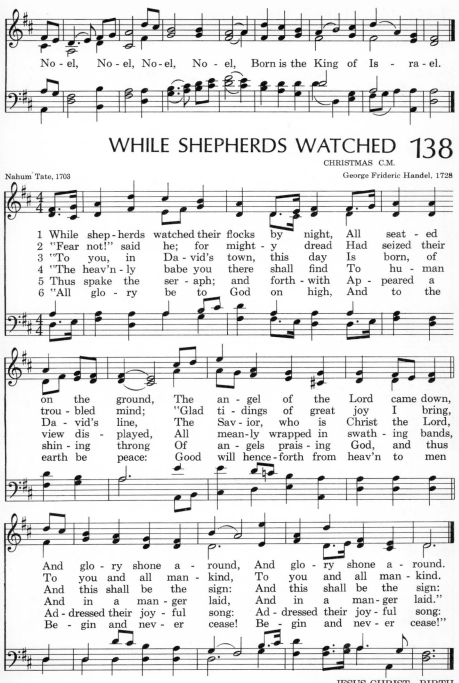

No - el, No - el, No - el, No - el, Born is the King of Is - ra - el.

WHILE SHEPHERDS WATCHED 138

CHRISTMAS C.M.

Nahum Tate, 1703

George Frideric Handel, 1728

1 While shep - herds watched their flocks by night, All seat - ed
2 "Fear not!" said he; for might - y dread Had seized their
3 "To you, in Da - vid's town, this day Is born, of
4 "The heav'n - ly babe you there shall find To hu - man
5 Thus spake the ser - aph; and forth - with Ap - peared a
6 "All glo - ry be to God on high, And to the

on the ground, The an - gel of the Lord came down,
trou - bled mind; "Glad ti - dings of great joy I bring,
Da - vid's line, The Sav - ior, who is Christ the Lord,
view dis - played, All mean - ly wrapped in swath - ing bands,
shin - ing throng Of an - gels prais - ing God, and thus
earth be peace: Good will hence - forth from heav'n to men

And glo - ry shone a - round, And glo - ry shone a - round.
To you and all man - kind, To you and all man - kind.
And this shall be the sign: And this shall be the sign:
And in a man - ger laid, And in a man - ger laid."
Ad - dressed their joy - ful song: Ad - dressed their joy - ful song:
Be - gin and nev - er cease! Be - gin and nev - er cease!"

JESUS CHRIST: BIRTH

139 WORSHIP THE LORD

WAS LEBET, WAS SCHWEBET 12.10.12.10.

John Samuel Bewley Monsell†, 1863

Manuscript Chorale Book, Üttingen, 1754

1 Wor - ship the Lord in the beau - ty of hol - i - ness,
2 Low at His feet lay thy bur - den of care - ful - ness,
3 Fear not to en - ter His courts in the slen - der - ness
4 These, though we bring them in trem - bling and fear - ful - ness,
5 Wor - ship the Lord in the beau - ty of hol - i - ness,

Bow down be - fore Him, His glo - ry pro - claim;
High on His heart He will bear it for thee,
Of the poor wealth thou wouldst reck - on as thine;
He will ac - cept for the name that is dear;
Bow down be - fore Him, His glo - ry pro - claim;

Gold of o - be - dience and in - cense of low - li - ness
Com - fort thy sor - rows, and an - swer thy prayer - ful - ness,
Truth in its beau - ty, and love in its ten - der - ness,
Morn - ings of joy give for eve - nings of tear - ful - ness,
Gold of o - be - dience and in - cense of low - li - ness

Bring and a - dore Him; the Lord is His name!
Guid - ing thy steps as may best for thee be.
These are the of - ferings to lay on His shrine.
Trust for our trem - bling, and hope for our fear.
Bring and a - dore Him; the Lord is His name!

JESUS CHRIST: EPIPHANY

FROM THE EASTERN MOUNTAINS 140

PRINCETHORPE 6.5.6.5.D.

Godfrey Thring†, 1873

William Pitts, 1871

1 From the east - ern moun - tains Press - ing on they come,
2 There their Lord and Sav - ior Meek and low - ly lay,
3 Thou who in a man - ger Once hast low - ly lain,
4 Gath - er in the out - casts, All who've gone a - stray,
5 On - ward through the dark - ness Of the lone - ly night,

Wise men in their wis - dom, To His hum - ble home;
Won - drous light that led them On - ward on their way,
Who dost now in glo - ry O'er all king - doms reign,
Throw Thy ra - diance o'er them, Guide them on their way:
Shin - ing still be - fore them With Thy kind - ly light,

Stirred by deep de - vo - tion, Hast - ing from a - far,
Ev - er now to light - en Na - tions from a - far,
Gath - er in the hea - then, Who in lands a - far
Those who've nev - er known Thee, Those who've wan - dered far,
Guide them, Jew and Gen - tile, Home-ward from a - far,

Ev - er jour-ney-ing on - ward, Guid - ed by a star.
As they jour - ney home - ward By that guid - ing star.
Ne'er have seen the bright - ness Of Thy guid - ing star,
Guide them by the bright - ness Of Thy guid - ing star.
Young and old to - geth - er, By Thy guid - ing star. A - men.

JESUS CHRIST: EPIPHANY

141 HOW BRIGHT APPEARS THE MORNING STAR

WIE SCHÖN LEUCHTET DER MORGENSTERN 8.8.7.8.8.7.4.12.8.

Philipp Nicolai, 1599
Wie schön leuchtet der Morgenstern
William Mercer, 1859

Philipp Nicolai, 1599

1 How bright ap - pears the morn-ing star, With mer-cy beam - ing from a - far!
2 Re-joice, ye heav'ns, thou earth, re-ply! With praise, ye sin - ners, fill the sky!

The host of heav'n re - joic - es! O right-eous branch! O Jes-se's rod!
For this His in - car - na - tion! In - car-nate God, put forth Thy power,

Thou Son of man, and Son of God! We too will lift our voic - es.
Ride on, ride on, great Con-quer-or, Till all know Thy sal - va - tion.

Je - sus! Je - sus! Ho - ly, ho - ly! yet most low - ly!
A - men, a - men! Al - le - lu - ia, al - le - lu - ia!

JESUS CHRIST: EPIPHANY

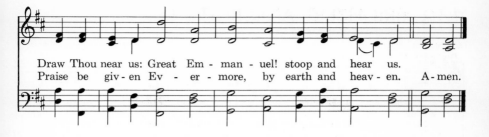

Draw Thou near us: Great Em - man - uel! stoop and hear us.
Praise be giv - en Ev - er - more, by earth and heav - en. A - men.

AS WITH GLADNESS MEN OF OLD 142

DIX 7.7.7.7.7.7.

From Conrad Kocher, 1838
Adapted by William Henry Monk, 1861

William C. Dix, c. 1858

1 As with glad-ness men of old Did the guid-ing star be-hold;
2 As with joy-ful steps they sped To that low-ly man-ger-bed,
3 As they of-fered gifts most rare, At that man-ger rude and bare,
4 Ho - ly Je - sus, ev - ery day Keep us in the nar - row way;

As with joy they hailed its light, Lead-ing on-ward, beam-ing bright;
There to bend the knee be-fore Him whom heav'n and earth a - dore;
So may we with ho - ly joy, Pure and free from sin's al - loy,
And, when earth-ly things are past, Bring our ran-somed souls at last

So, most gra-cious Lord, may we Ev - er-more be led to Thee.
So may we with will - ing feet Ev - er seek Thy mer - cy seat.
All our cost-liest treas-ures bring, Christ, to Thee, our heav'n-ly King.
Where they need no star to guide, Where no clouds Thy glo - ry hide. A - men.

JESUS CHRIST: EPIPHANY

143 BRIGHTEST AND BEST

MORNING STAR 11.10.11.10.

Reginald Heber, 1811

James Prockter Harding, 1892

1 Bright - est and best of the sons of the morn - ing,
2 Cold on His cra - dle the dew - drops are shin - ing,
3 Say, shall we yield Him, in cost - ly de - vo - tion,
4 Vain - ly we of - fer each am - ple ob - la - tion,
5 Bright - est and best of the sons of the morn - ing,

Dawn on our dark - ness, and lend us Thine aid;
Low lies His head with the beasts of the stall;
O - dors of E - dom and of - f'rings di - vine,
Vain - ly with gifts would His fa - vor se - cure;
Dawn on our dark - ness, and lend us Thine aid;

Star of the east, the ho - ri - zon a - dorn - ing,
An - gels a - dore Him in slum - ber re - clin - ing,
Gems of the moun - tain and pearls of the o - cean,
Rich - er by far is the heart's ad - o - ra - tion,
Star of the east, the ho - ri - zon a - dorn - ing,

Guide where our in - fant Re - deem - er is laid.
Mak - er, and Mon - arch, and Sav - ior of all.
Myrrh from the for - est, or gold from the mine?
Dear - er to God are the prayers of the poor.
Guide where our in - fant Re - deem - er is laid. A - men.

JESUS CHRIST: EPIPHANY

FORTY DAYS AND FORTY NIGHTS 144

AUS DER TIEFE 7.7.7.7.

George Hunt Smyttan, 1856
Altered by Francis Pott and Others, 1861

Gesangbuch, Nürnberg, 1676

1 For - ty days and for - ty nights Thou wast fast - ing in the wild;
2 Shall not we Thy watch-ings share, And from earth-ly joys ab - stain,
3 And if Sa - tan, vex - ing sore, Flesh or spir - it should as - sail,
4 Keep, O keep us, Sav - ior dear, Ev - er con-stant by Thy side;

For - ty days and for - ty nights Tempt-ed, and yet un - de - filed.
Fast - ing with un - ceas-ing prayer, Glad with Thee to suf - fer pain?
Thou, his van-quish - er be - fore, Grant we may not faint nor fail.
That with Thee we may ap - pear At the e-ter - nal Eas-ter-tide. A - men.

O MASTER OF THE LOVING HEART 145

ABRIDGE C.M.

Calvin W. Laufer, 1927

Isaac Smith, c. 1780

1 O Mas - ter of the lov - ing heart, The Friend of all in need,
2 Thy days were full of kind - ly acts, Thy speech was true and plain;
3 Thy face was warm with sym - pa - thy, Thy hand God's strength re-vealed;
4 O grant us hearts like Thine, dear Lord, So joy - ous, true, and free,

We pray that we may be like Thee, In thought and word and deed.
And no one ev - er sought Thee, Lord, Who came to Thee in vain.
Who saw Thy face, or felt Thy touch, Were com-fort - ed and healed.
That all Thy chil-dren ev - ery - where Be drawn by us to Thee. A-men.

JESUS CHRIST: LIFE AND MINISTRY

146 YE FAIR GREEN HILLS OF GALILEE

STELLA   8.8.8.8.8.8.

Eustace R. Conder, 1887

Easy Tunes for Catholic Schools, 1852

1 Ye fair green hills of Gal - i - lee, That gir - dle
2 "We saw no glo - ry crown His head As child - hood
3 Je - sus! my Sav - ior, Mas - ter, King, Who didst for

qui - et Naz - a - reth, What glo - rious vi - sion did ye see,
rip - ened in - to youth; No an - gels on His er - rands sped;
me the bur - den bear, While saints in heav'n Thy glo - ry sing,

When He who con - quered sin and death Your flow - 'ry
He wrought no sign; but meek - ness, truth, And du - ty
Let me on earth Thy like - ness wear; Mine be the

slopes and sum - mits trod, And grew in grace with man and God?
marked each step He trod, And love to man, and love to God."
path Thy feet have trod, Du - ty, and love to man and God. A-men.

JESUS CHRIST: LIFE AND MINISTRY

MY DEAR REDEEMER AND MY LORD 147

SOCIAL BAND L.M.D.

Isaac Watts, 1707-1709

Folk Hymn
J. Ingalls' *Christian Harmony*, 1805

1 My dear Re-deem-er and my Lord, I read my du - ty in Thy Word;
2 Cold moun-tains and the mid-night air Wit-nessed the fer - vor of Thy prayer;

But in Thy life the law ap - pears Drawn out in liv - ing char - ac - ters.
The des-ert Thy temp-ta-tions knew, Thy con - flict and Thy vic - t'ry too.

Such was Thy truth, and such Thy zeal, Such def-erence to Thy Fa-ther's will,
Be Thou my pat-tern; make me bear More of Thy gra - cious im - age here;

Such love, and meek-ness so di - vine, I would tran-scribe and make them mine.
Then God the Judge shall own my name A - mong the fol - l'wers of the Lamb.

JESUS CHRIST: LIFE AND MINISTRY

148 FIERCE RAGED THE TEMPEST

ST. AËLRED 8.8.8.3.

Godfrey Thring, 1861

John Bacchus Dykes, 1862

1 Fierce raged the tem - pest o'er the deep,
2 "Save, Lord, we per - ish!" was their cry,
3 The wild winds hushed; the an - gry deep
4 So, when our life is cloud - ed o'er,

Watch did Thine anx - ious serv - ants keep;
"O save us in our ag - o - ny!"
Sank, like a lit - tle child, to sleep;
And storm - winds drift us from the shore,

But Thou wast wrapped in guile - less sleep, Calm and still.
Thy word a - bove the storm rose high, "Peace! be still."
The sul - len bil - lows ceased to leap, At Thy will.
Say, lest we sink to rise no more, "Peace! be still."

149 THOU ART THE WAY

RICHMOND C.M.

George Washington Doane†, 1824

Thomas Haweis, 1792

1 Thou art the Way: to Thee a - lone From sin and death we flee;
2 Thou art the Truth: Thy Word a - lone True wis - dom can im - part;
3 Thou art the Life: the rend - ing tomb Pro - claims Thy con-qu'ring arm;
4 Thou art the Way, the Truth, the Life: Grant us that way to know,

JESUS CHRIST: LIFE AND MINISTRY

And he who would the Fa - ther seek, Must seek Him, Lord, by Thee.
Thou on - ly canst in - form the mind And pu - ri - fy the heart.
And those who put their trust in Thee Nor death nor hell shall harm.
That truth to keep, that life to win, Whose joys e - ter - nal flow.

IMMORTAL LOVE, FOREVER FULL 150

SERENITY C.M.

John Greenleaf Whittier, 1866

William V. Wallace, 1856

1 Im - mor - tal love, for - ev - er full, For - ev -
2 Our out - ward lips con - fess the name All oth -
3 We may not climb the heav'n - ly steeps To bring
4 The heal - ing of His seam - less dress Is by
5 O Lord and Mas - ter of us all, What - e'er

er flow - ing free, For - ev - er shared, for - ev - er
er names a - bove; Love on - ly know - eth whence it
the Lord Christ down, In vain we search the low - est
our beds of pain; We touch Him in life's throng and
our name or sign, We own Thy sway, we hear Thy

whole, A nev - er - ebb - ing sea!
came, And com - pre - hend - eth love.
deeps, For Him no depths can drown.
press, And we are whole a - gain.
call, We test our lives by Thine. A - men.

JESUS CHRIST: LIFE AND MINISTRY

151 THOU TO WHOM THE SICK AND DYING

JESUS, JESUS, NICHTS ALS JESUS 8.7.8.7.7.7.

Godfrey Thring, 1870

Bonner's *Vollkommenes* . . . *Choral-Buch*, 1715

1 Thou to whom the sick and dy - ing Ev - er
2 Still the wea - ry, sick, and dy - ing Need a
3 May each child of Thine be will - ing, Will - ing
4 So may sick - ness, sin, and sad - ness, To Thy

came, nor came in vain, Still with heal - ing words re - ply - ing
broth-er's, sis - ter's care; On Thy high - er help re - ly - ing
both in hand and heart, All the law of love ful - fill - ing,
heal - ing pow - er yield, Till the sick and sad, in glad - ness,

To the wea - ried cry of pain, Hear us, Je - sus,
May we now their bur - den share, Bring - ing all our
Ev - er com - fort to im - part; Ev - er bring - ing
Res - cued, ran - som'd, cleansed and healed, One in Thee to -

as we meet Sup - pliants at Thy mer - cy seat.
of - f'rings meet, Sup - pliants at Thy mer - cy seat.
of - f'rings meet, Sup - pliant to Thy mer - cy seat.
geth - er meet, Par - don'd at Thy judg - ment seat. A - men.

JESUS CHRIST: LIFE AND MINISTRY

THINE ARM, O LORD, IN DAYS OF OLD 152

ST. MATTHEW C.M.D.

Edward Hayes Plumptre, 1864

William Croft? 1708

1 Thine arm, O Lord, in days of old, Was strong to heal and save;
2 And lo! Thy touch brought life and health, Gave speech, and strength, and sight;
3 Be Thou our great De - liv - 'rer still, Thou Lord of life and death,

It tri-umphed o'er dis - ease and death, O'er dark-ness and the grave.
And youth re-newed and fren - zy calmed Owned Thee, the Lord of light.
Re - store and quick-en, soothe and bless, With Thine al - might - y breath;

To Thee they went: the blind, the dumb, The pal - sied, and the lame,
And now, O Lord, be near to bless, Al - might-y as of yore,
To hands that work and eyes that see Give wis - dom's heav'n-ly lore,

The lep - er and his taint-ed life, The sick with fe - vered frame:
In crowd-ed street, by rest-less couch, As by Gen - nes-aret's shore.
That whole and sick, and weak and strong, May praise Thee ev - er-more. A-men.

JESUS CHRIST: LIFE AND MINISTRY

153 NOT ALWAYS ON THE MOUNT

LOB SEI DEM ALLMÄCHTIGEN L.M.

Frederick L. Hosmer, 1882

Johann Crüger, 1640

1 Not al - ways on the mount may we Rapt in
2 "Lord, it is good, a - bid - ing here," We cry,
3 Yet, hath one such ex - alt - ed hour Up - on
4 Till all the low - ly vale grows bright, Trans - fig -

the heav'n - ly vi - sion be: The shores of thought and
the heav'n - ly pres - ence near; The vi - sion van - ish -
the soul re - deem - ing power, And in its strength through
ured in re - mem - bered light, And in un - tir - ing

feel - ing know The Spir - it's tid - al ebb and flow.
es, our eyes Are lift - ed in - to va - cant skies.
af - ter days We trav - el our ap - point - ed ways.
souls we bear The fresh - ness of the up - per air.

5 The mount for vision: but below
The paths of daily duty go,
And nobler life therein shall own
The pattern on the mountain shown.

JESUS CHRIST: LIFE AND MINISTRY

ALL GLORY, LAUD, AND HONOR 154

VALET WILL ICH DIR GEBEN 7.6.7.6. with Refrain

Theodulph of Orleans, c. 820
Gloria laus et honor
Tr. John Mason Neale†, 1851

Melchior Teschner, 1613

REFRAIN (Sing after each stanza)

All glo-ry, laud, and hon - or To Thee, Re-deem-er, King,

To whom the lips of chil - dren Made sweet ho-san-nas ring.

1 Thou art the King of Is - rael, Thou Da-vid's roy-al Son,
2 The com-pa-ny of an - gels Are prais-ing Thee on high,
3 The peo-ple of the He - brews With palms be-fore Thee went;
4 To Thee, be-fore Thy pas - sion, They sang their hymns of praise;
5 Thou didst ac-cept their prais - es; Ac - cept the prayers we bring,

Who in the Lord's name com - est, The King and bless-ed one.
And mor-tal men, and all things Cre - at - ed, make re - ply.
Our praise and prayer and an - thems Be - fore Thee we pre - sent.
To Thee, now high ex - alt - ed, Our mel-o-dy we raise.
Who in all good de - light - est, Thou good and gra-cious King.

JESUS CHRIST: TRIUMPHAL ENTRY

155 HOSANNA, LOUD HOSANNA

ELLACOMBE C.M.D.

Jennette Threlfall, d. 1880

Adapted from *Gesangbuch* . . . ,
Württemberg, 1784

1 Ho - san - na, loud ho - san - na The lit - tle chil - dren sang;
2 From Ol - i - vet they fol - lowed 'Mid an ex - ult - ant crowd,
3 "Ho - san - na in the high - est!" That an - cient song we sing,

Through pil - lared court and tem - ple The love - ly an - them rang;
The vic - tor palm-branch wav - ing, And chant - ing clear and loud;
For Christ is our Re - deem - er, The Lord of heav'n our King.

To Je - sus, who had blessed them Close fold - ed to His breast,
The Lord of men and an - gels Rode on in low - ly state,
O may we ev - er praise Him With heart and life and voice,

The chil - dren sang their prais - es, The sim - plest and the best.
Nor scorned that lit - tle chil - dren Should on His bid - ding wait.
And in His bliss - ful pres - ence E - ter - nal - ly re - joice! A - men.

JESUS CHRIST: TRIUMPHAL ENTRY

RIDE ON, RIDE ON IN MAJESTY 156

WINCHESTER NEW L.M.

Henry Hart Milman, 1827

From *Musicalisch Hand-buch*, published
by George Rebelein's Widow, 1690
Arranged by William Henry Havergal, 1847

1 Ride on, ride on in maj-es-ty; Hark, all the tribes ho-san-na cry;
2 Ride on, ride on in maj-es-ty, In low-ly pomp ride on to die;
3 Ride on, ride on in maj-es-ty; Thy last and fierc-est strife is nigh;
4 Ride on, ride on in maj-es-ty, In low-ly pomp ride on to die;

Thy hum-ble beast pur-sues his road With palms and scattered garments strowed.
O Christ, Thy tri-umphs now be-gin O'er cap-tive death and con-quered sin.
The Fa-ther, on His sap-phire throne, Ex-pects His own a-noint-ed Son.
Bow Thy meek head to mor-tal pain, Then take, O God, Thy power, and reign. A-men.

JESUS CHRIST: TRIUMPHAL ENTRY

O THOU, WHO THROUGH THIS HOLY 157

WETHERBY C.M.

John Mason Neale, 1842

Samuel Sebastian Wesley, 1872

1 O Thou, who through this ho-ly week, Didst suf-fer for us all;
2 We can-not un-der-stand the woe Thy love was pleased to bear:
3 Thy feet the path of suf-f'ring trod, Thy hand the vic-t'ry won:

The sick to heal, the lost to seek, To raise up them that fall:
O Lamb of God, we on-ly know That all our hopes are there.
What shall we ren-der to our God For all that He hath done? A-men.

JESUS CHRIST: PASSION

158 AH, HOLY JESUS

HERZLIEBSTER JESU 11.11.11.5.

Johann Heermann, c. 1630
Herzliebster Jesu
Tr. Robert Bridges, 1899
St. 3 omitted with permission

Johann Crüger, 1640

1 Ah, ho - ly Je - sus, how hast Thou of - fend - ed, That man to judge Thee hath in hate pre - tend - ed? By foes de - rid - ed, by Thine own re - ject - ed, O most af - flict - ed.

2 Who was the guilt - y? Who brought this up - on Thee? A - las, my trea - son, Je - sus, hath un - done Thee. 'Twas I, Lord Je - sus, I it was de - nied Thee: I cru - ci - fied Thee.

3 For me, kind Je - sus, was Thy in - car - na - tion, Thy mor - tal sor - row, and Thy life's ob - la - tion: Thy death of an - guish and Thy bit - ter pas - sion, For my sal - va - tion.

4 There - fore, kind Je - sus, since I can - not pay Thee, I do a - dore Thee, and will ev - er pray Thee Think on Thy pit - y and Thy love un - swerv - ing, Not my de - serv - ing. A - men.

JESUS CHRIST: PASSION

O SACRED HEAD, NOW WOUNDED 159

HERZLICH TUT MICH VERLANGEN 7.6.7.6.D.

Based on *Salve caput cruentatum*
Paul Gerhardt, 1656

O Haupt voll Blut und Wunden
Tr. James Waddell Alexander†, 1830

Hans Leo Hassler, 1601
Harmony by Johann Sebastian Bach, 1729

1 O sa-cred Head, now wound-ed, With grief and shame weighed down!
2 O no-blest brow and dear-est, In oth-er days the world
3 What Thou, my Lord, hast suf-fered Was all for sin-ners' gain:
4 What lan-guage shall I bor-row To thank Thee, dear-est Friend,
5 Be near when I am dy-ing, O show Thy cross to me;

Now scorn-ful-ly sur-round-ed With thorns, Thy on-ly crown:
All feared when Thou ap-pear-edst; What shame on Thee is hurled!
Mine, mine was the trans-gres-sion, But Thine the dead-ly pain.
For this Thy dy-ing sor-row, Thy pit-y with-out end?
And for my suc-cor fly-ing, Come, Lord, and set me free;

O sa-cred Head, what glo-ry, What bliss till now was Thine!
How art Thou pale with an-guish, With sore a-buse and scorn;
Lo, here I fall, my Sav-ior! 'Tis I de-serve Thy place;
O make me Thine for-ev-er; And should I faint-ing be,
These eyes, new faith re-ceiv-ing, From Je-sus shall not move;

Yet, though de-spised and gor-y, I joy to call Thee mine.
How does that vis-age lan-guish, Which once was bright as morn!
Look on me with Thy fa-vor, Vouch-safe to me Thy grace.
Lord, let me nev-er, nev-er, Out-live my love to Thee.
For he who dies be-liev-ing, Dies safe-ly, through Thy love. A-men.

JESUS CHRIST: PASSION

160 GO TO DARK GETHSEMANE

REDHEAD NO. 76 (AJALON) 7.7.7.7.7.7.

James Montgomery, 1820

Richard Redhead, 1853

1 Go to dark Geth - sem - a - ne, Ye that feel the tempt-er's power,
2 Fol - low to the judg-ment hall; View the Lord of life ar - raigned.
3 Cal-v'ry's mourn-ful moun-tain climb; There, a - dor - ing at His feet,
4 Ear - ly has - ten to the tomb Where they laid His breath-less clay:

Your Re-deem-er's con-flict see; Watch with Him one bit - ter hour:
O the worm-wood and the gall! O the pangs His soul sus - tained!
Mark that mir - a - cle of time, God's own sac - ri - fice com - plete:
All is sol - i - tude and gloom; Who hath tak - en Him a - way?

Turn not from His griefs a-way; Learn of Je - sus Christ to pray.
Shun not suf-f'ring, shame, or loss; Learn of Him to bear the cross.
"It is fin-ished!" hear the cry; Learn of Je - sus Christ to die.
Christ is ris'n! He meets our eyes. Sav - ior, teach us so to rise. A - men.

161 'TIS MIDNIGHT, AND ON OLIVE'S BROW

OLIVE'S BROW L.M.

William Bingham Tappan, 1822

William Batchelder Bradbury, 1853

1 'Tis mid-night, and on Ol - ive's brow The star is dimmed that late - ly shone;
2 'Tis mid-night, and from all re-moved Em-man-uel wres-tles lone with fears;
3 'Tis mid-night, and for oth-ers' guilt The Man of Sor-rows weeps in blood;
4 'Tis mid-night, and from e - ther-plains Is borne the song that an - gels know;

JESUS CHRIST: PASSION

'Tis mid-night, in the gar-den now The suf-f'ring Sav-ior prays a - lone.
E'en the dis - ci - ple whom He loved Heeds not his Mas-ter's grief and tears.
Yet He who hath in an-guish knelt Is not for-sak-en by His God.
Un-heard by mor-tals are the strains That sweet-ly soothe the Sav-ior's woe. A-men.

THRONED UPON THE AWFUL TREE 162

SPANISH HYMN 7.7.7.7.7.7.

John Ellerton, 1875

Arranged by Benjamin Carr, 1824

1 Throned up - on the aw - ful tree, King of grief, I watch with Thee:
2 Si - lent thro' those three dread hours, Wres-tling with the e - vil powers,
3 Hark that cry that peals a - loud Up - ward thro' the whelm-ing cloud!
4 Lord, should fear and an - guish roll Dark - ly o'er my sin - ful soul,

Dark - ness veils Thine an-guished face, None its lines of woe can trace,
Left a - lone with hu - man sin, Gloom a-round Thee and with - in,
Thou, the Fa - ther's on - ly Son, Thou, His own a - noint - ed one,
Thou, who once was thus be - reft That Thine own might ne'er be left,

None can tell what pangs un-known Hold Thee si - lent and a - lone.
Till th'ap-point-ed time is nigh, Till the Lamb of God may die.
Thou dost ask Him, can it be? "Why hast Thou for-sak - en Me?"
Teach me by that bit - ter cry In the gloom to know Thee nigh. A - men.

JESUS CHRIST: PASSION

163 WHAT WONDROUS LOVE IS THIS

WONDROUS LOVE Irregular

Folk text
J. Mercer's *Cluster of Spiritual Songs*, 1836

Folk Hymn
"Christopher" in W. Hauser's *Hesperian Harp*, 1848
Harmony by Alice Parker, 1966

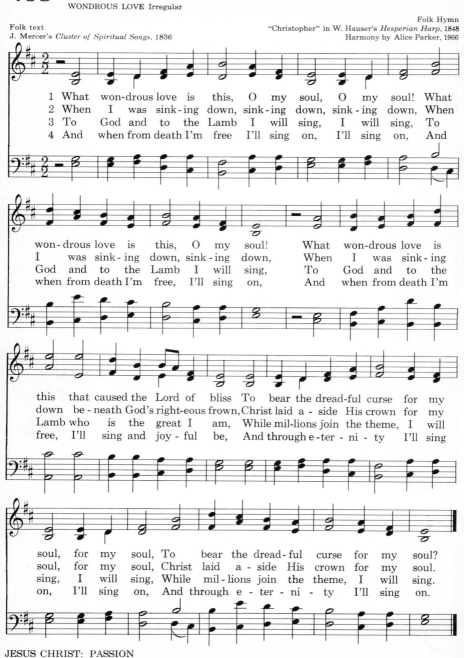

1 What won-drous love is this, O my soul, O my soul! What
2 When I was sink-ing down, sink-ing down, sink-ing down, When
3 To God and to the Lamb I will sing, I will sing, To
4 And when from death I'm free I'll sing on, I'll sing on, And

won-drous love is this, O my soul! What won-drous love is
I was sink-ing down, sink-ing down, When I was sink-ing
God and to the Lamb I will sing, To God and to the
when from death I'm free, I'll sing on, And when from death I'm

this that caused the Lord of bliss To bear the dread-ful curse for my
down be-neath God's right-eous frown, Christ laid a-side His crown for my
Lamb who is the great I am, While mil-lions join the theme, I will
free, I'll sing and joy-ful be, And through e-ter-ni-ty I'll sing

soul, for my soul, To bear the dread-ful curse for my soul?
soul, for my soul, Christ laid a-side His crown for my soul.
sing, I will sing, While mil-lions join the theme, I will sing.
on, I'll sing on, And through e-ter-ni-ty I'll sing on.

JESUS CHRIST: PASSION

WERE YOU THERE 164

WERE YOU THERE Irregular

Negro Spiritual

Traditional Negro Melody

1 Were you there when they cru - ci - fied my Lord?
2 Were you there when they nailed Him to the tree?
3 Were you there when they laid Him in the tomb?
4 Were you there when He rose up from the dead?

Were you there when they cru - ci - fied my Lord?
Were you there when they nailed Him to the tree? O!
Were you there when they laid Him in the tomb?
Were you there when He rose up from the dead?

Some-times it caus - es me to trem - ble, trem - ble, trem - ble.

Were you there when they cru - ci - fied my Lord?
Were you there when they nailed Him to the tree?
Were you there when they laid Him in the tomb?
Were you there when He rose up from the dead?

JESUS CHRIST: PASSION

165 WHEN I SURVEY

ROCKINGHAM OLD L.M.

A. Williams' *Supplement to Psalmody* . . . , c. 1780
Adapted by Edward Miller, 1790

Isaac Watts†, 1707

1 When I sur - vey the won - drous cross, On which the
2 For - bid it, Lord, that I should boast, Save in the
3 See, from His head, His hands, His feet, Sor - row and
4 Were the whole realm of na - ture mine, That were a

Prince of glo - ry died, My rich - est gain I count but
death of Christ my God; All the vain things that charm me
love flow min - gled down; Did e'er such love and sor - row
pres - ent far too small; Love so a - maz - ing, so di -

loss, And pour con - tempt on all my pride.
most, I sac - ri - fice them to His blood.
meet, Or thorns com - pose so rich a crown?
vine, De - mands my soul, my life, my all.

166 CROSS OF JESUS, CROSS OF SORROW

CROSS OF JESUS 8.7.8.7.

William John Sparrow Simpson†, 1887

John Stainer, 1887

1 Cross of Je - sus, cross of sor - row, Where the blood of Christ was shed,
2 Here the King of all the a - ges, Thron'd in light ere worlds could be,
3 O mys - te - rious con - de - scend - ing! O a - ban - don - ment sub - lime!
4 Ev - er - more for hu - man fail - ure By His pas - sion we can plead;

JESUS CHRIST: PASSION

Per - fect man on thee did suf - fer, Per - fect God on thee has bled!
Robed in mor-tal flesh is dy - ing, Cru - ci - fied by sin for me.
Ver - y God Him-self is bear-ing All the suf - fer - ings of time!
God has borne all mor-tal an-guish, Sure-ly He will know our need. A - men.

WHEN I SURVEY 167

HAMBURG L.M.

Isaac Wattst, 1707

Lowell Mason, 1824

1 When I sur - vey the won - drous cross, On which the
2 For - bid it, Lord, that I should boast, Save in the
3 See, from His head, His hands, His feet, Sor - row and
4 Were the whole realm of na - ture mine, That were a

Prince of glo - ry died, My rich - est gain I
death of Christ my God; All the vain things that
love flow min - gled down; Did e'er such love and
pres - ent far too small; Love so a - maz - ing,

count but loss, And pour con-tempt on all my pride.
charm me most, I sac - ri - fice them to His blood.
sor - row meet, Or thorns com-pose so rich a crown?
so di - vine, De-mands my soul, my life, my all. A - men.

JESUS CHRIST: PASSION

168 CHRIST, THE LIFE OF ALL THE LIVING

ALLE MENSCHEN MÜSSEN STERBEN 8.7.8.7.7.7.7.7.

Ernst Christoph Homburg, 1659
Jesu, meines Lebens Leben
Tr. Catherine Winkworth†, 1863

Christoph Anton, c. 1642

1 Christ, the life of all the liv - ing, Christ, the death of death our foe,
2 Thou, ah Thou, hast tak-en on Thee Bit - ter strokes, a cru - el rod;
3 Then for all that wrought our par-don, For Thy sor - rows deep and sore,

Who Thy - self for us once giv - ing To the dark - est depths of woe,
Pain and scorn were heaped up-on Thee, O Thou sin - less Son of God;
For Thine an - guish in the gar - den, I will thank Thee ev - er - more;

Pa - tient - ly didst yield Thy breath But to save my soul from death;
On - ly thus for me to win Res - cue from the bonds of sin;
Thank Thee with my lat - est breath For Thy sad and cru - el death,

Thousand, thousand thanks shall be, Bless - ed Je-sus, brought to Thee.
Thousand, thousand thanks shall be, Bless - ed Je-sus, brought to Thee.
For that last and bit - ter cry, And shall praise Thee, Lord, on high. A - men.

JESUS CHRIST: PASSION

IN THE CROSS OF CHRIST I GLORY 169

RATHBUN 8.7.8.7.

John Bowring, 1825

Ithamar Conkey, 1849

1 In the cross of Christ I glo-ry, Tow-'ring o'er the wrecks of time;
2 When the woes of life o'er-take me; Hopes de-ceive and fears an-noy,
3 When the sun of bliss is beam-ing Light and love up-on my way,
4 Bane and bless-ing, pain and plea-sure, By the cross are sanc-ti-fied;

All the light of sa-cred sto-ry, Gath-ers round its head sub-lime.
Nev-er shall the cross for-sake me; Lo! it glows with peace and joy.
From the cross the ra-diance stream-ing, Adds more lus-ter to the day.
Peace is there that knows no mea-sure, Joys that through all time a-bide.

ALAS! AND DID MY SAVIOR BLEED 170

MARTYRDOM C.M.

Hugh Wilson, late 18th century
Adapted by Robert Archibald Smith, 1825

Isaac Watts‡, 1707

1 A-las! and did my Sav-ior bleed? And did my Sov-ereign die?
2 Was it for crimes that I have done He groaned up-on the tree?
3 Well might the sun in dark-ness hide, And shut his glo-ries in,
4 But drops of grief can ne'er re-pay The debt of love I owe;

Would He de-vote that sa-cred head, For sin-ners such as I?
A-maz-ing pit-y! grace un-known! And love be-yond de-gree!
When Christ, the might-y Mak-er, died For man, the crea-ture's sin.
Here, Lord, I give my-self a-way, 'Tis all that I can do.

JESUS CHRIST: PASSION

171 BENEATH THE CROSS OF JESUS

ST. CHRISTOPHER 7.6.8.6.8.6.8.6.

Elizabeth C. Clephane, 1872

Frederick Charles Maker, 1881

1 Be - neath the cross of Je - sus I fain would take my stand,
2 Up - on that cross of Je - sus My eye at times can see
3 I take, O cross, thy shad - ow For my a - bid - ing place;

The shad - ow of a might - y rock With - in a wea - ry land;
The ver - y dy - ing form of One Who suf - fered there for me;
I ask no oth - er sun-shine than The sun-shine of His face,

A home with-in the wil - der-ness, A rest up - on the way,
And from my smit - ten heart with tears Two won - ders I con - fess,
Con - tent to let the world go by, To know no gain nor loss,

From the burn - ing of the noon-tide heat, And the bur - den of the day.
The won-ders of His glo-rious love And my un-wor - thi - ness.
My sin - ful self my on - ly shame, My glo - ry all the cross.

JESUS CHRIST: PASSION

MY SONG IS LOVE UNKNOWN 172

LOVE UNKNOWN 6.6.6.6.4.4.4.4.

Samuel Crossman, 1664

John Ireland, 1925

1 My song is love un-known, My Sav-ior's love to me, Love
2 He came from His blest throne, Sal - va-tion to be - stow; But
3 Some-times they strew His way, And His sweet prais-es sing; Re -
4 Here might I stay and sing, No sto-ry so di - vine; Nev-

to the love - less shown, That they might love - ly be.
men made strange, and none The longed-for Christ would know.
sound-ing all the day Ho - san - nas to their king.
er was love, dear King, Nev - er was grief like Thine.

O who am I, That for my sake
But O, my friend, My friend in - deed,
Then "Cru - ci - fy!" Is all their breath,
This is my friend, In whose sweet praise

My Lord should take Frail flesh, and die?
Who at my need His life did spend!
And for His death They thirst and cry.
I all my days Could glad - ly spend.

JESUS CHRIST: PASSION

173 O LAMB OF GOD ALL HOLY

O LAMM GOTTES 7.7.7.7.7.7.7.8.

Based on *Agnus Dei*
Nicolaus Decius, **1522** or **1523**
O Lamm Gottes unschuldig
Tr. Arthur Tozer Russell, 1851

Nicolaus Decius, 1542

1 O Lamb of God all ho - ly! Who on the cross didst suf - fer,
2 O Lamb of God all ho - ly! Who on the cross didst suf - fer,
3 O Lamb of God all ho - ly! Who on the cross didst suf - fer,

And pa - tient still and low - ly, Thy - self to scorn didst of - fer;
And pa - tient still and low - ly, Thy - self to scorn didst of - fer;
And pa - tient still and low - ly, Thy - self to scorn didst of - fer;

Our sins by Thee were tak - en, Or hope had us for -
Our sins by Thee were tak - en, Or hope had us for -
Our sins by Thee were tak - en, Or hope had us for -

sak - en: Have mer - cy on us, O Je - sus!
sak - en: Have mer - cy on us, O Je - sus!
sak - en: Thy peace be with us, O Je - sus! A - men.

JESUS CHRIST: PASSION

THE DAY OF RESURRECTION 174

LANCASHIRE 7.6.7.6.D.

John of Damascus, d. c. 750
Ἀναστάσεως ἡμέρα
Tr. John Mason Neale‡, 1862

Henry Thomas Smart, 1835

1 The day of res-ur-rec-tion! Earth, tell it out a-broad;
2 Our hearts be pure from e-vil, That we may see a-right
3 Now let the heav'ns be joy-ful, Let earth her song be-gin;

The pass-o-ver of glad-ness, The pass-o-ver of God.
The Lord in rays e-ter-nal Of res-ur-rec-tion light;
Let the round world keep tri-umph, And all that is there-in;

From death to life e-ter-nal, From this world to the sky,
And, lis-t'ning to His ac-cents, May hear, so calm and plain,
In-vis-i-ble and vis-i-ble, Their notes let all things blend,

Our Christ hath brought us o-ver With hymns of vic-to-ry.
His own "All hail!" and hear-ing, May raise the vic-tor strain.
For Christ the Lord hath ris-en, Our joy that hath no end.

JESUS CHRIST: RESURRECTION

175 LIFT YOUR GLAD VOICES

RESURRECTION Irregular

Henry Waret, 1817

John Edgar Gould, c. 1879

1 Lift your glad voic-es in tri-umph on high, For Je-sus hath
2 He burst from the fet-ters of dark-ness that bound Him, Re-splend-ent in
3 Glo-ry to God, in full an-thems of joy; The be-ing He
4 But Je-sus hath cheered the dark val-ley of sor-row, And bade us, im-

ris-en, and man shall not die; Vain were the ter-rors that gath-ered a-
glo-ry, to live and to save: Loud was the cho-rus of an-gels on
gave us death can-not de-stroy: Sad were the life we may part with to-
mor-tal, to heav-en as-cend: Lift then your voic-es in tri-umph on

round Him, And short the do-min-ion of death and the grave.
high, The Sav-ior hath ris-en, and man shall not die.
mor-row, If tears were our birth-right, and death were our end.
high, For Je-sus hath ris-en, and man shall not die.

176 THE LORD IS RISEN INDEED

BENJAMIN S.M.

Thomas Kelly, 1802

Arranged from Franz Joseph Haydn, 1798

1 "The Lord is ris'n in-deed," And are the ti-dings true? Yes, they be-held
2 "The Lord is ris'n in-deed," Then jus-tice asks no more; Mer-cy and truth
3 "The Lord is ris'n in-deed," Then is His work per-formed; The cap-tive sure-
4 "The Lord is ris'n in-deed," At-tend-ing an-gels hear; Up to the courts
5 Then take your gold-en lyres, And strike each cheer-ful chord, Join all the bright

JESUS CHRIST: RESURRECTION

the Sav - ior bleed, And saw Him liv - ing too, And saw Him liv - ing too.
are now a - greed, Who stood op-posed be - fore, Who stood op-posed be - fore.
ty now is freed, And death, our foe, dis-armed, And death, our foe, dis-armed.
of heav'n, with speed, The joy-ful ti - dings bear, The joy-ful ti - dings bear.
ce - les - tial choirs, To sing our ris - en Lord, To sing our ris - en Lord.

CHRIST THE LORD IS RISEN AGAIN 177

STRAF MICH NICHT IN DEINEM ZORN 7.7.7.7. with Refrain

Michael Weisse, 1531
Christus ist erstanden
Tr. Catherine Winkworth, 1858

Hundert . . . geistliche Arien, Dresden, 1694

1 Christ the Lord is risen a - gain! Christ hath bro - ken ev - ery chain!
2 He who gave for us His life, Who for us en - dured the strife,
3 He who bore all pain and loss Com - fort-less up - on the cross,
4 He who slum-ber'd in the grave, Is ex - alt - ed now to save;

Hark, the an - gels shout for joy, Sing - ing ev - er - more on high,
Is our Pas - chal Lamb to - day! We too sing for joy, and say:
Lives in glo - ry now on high, Pleads for us and hears our cry:
Now through Chris-ten-dom it rings That the Lamb is King of kings!

REFRAIN

Christ the Lord, Christ the Lord, Christ the Lord is ris - en! Al - le - lu - ia!

5 Now He bids us tell abroad,
How the lost may be restored,
How the penitent forgiven,
How we too may enter heav'n.
(REFRAIN)

6 Thou our Paschal Lamb indeed,
Christ, today Thy people feed;
Take our sins and guilt away,
That we all may sing for aye,
(REFRAIN)

JESUS CHRIST: RESURRECTION

178 COME, YE FAITHFUL, RAISE THE STRAIN

AVE VIRGO VIRGINUM (GAUDEAMUS PARITER) 7.6.7.6.D.

John of Damascus, d. c. 750
Αισωμεν πάντες λαοί
Tr. John Mason Neale, 1859

Johann Horn, 1544

1 Come, ye faith - ful, raise the strain Of tri - um - phant glad - ness;
2 'Tis the spring of souls to - day; Christ hath burst His pris - on,
3 Now the queen of sea - sons, bright With the day of splen - dor,
4 Nei - ther might the gates of death, Nor the tomb's dark por - tal,

God hath brought His Is - ra - el In - to joy from sad - ness;
And from three days' sleep in death As a sun hath ris - en;
With the roy - al feast of feasts, Comes its joy to ren - der;
Nor the watch - ers, nor the seal Hold Thee as a mor - tal:

Loosed from Pha - raoh's bit - ter yoke Ja - cob's sons and daugh - ters;
All the win - ter of our sins, Long and dark, is fly - ing
Comes to glad Je - ru - sa - lem, Who with true af - fec - tion
But to - day a - midst the Twelve Thou didst stand, be - stow - ing

Led them with un - mois-tened foot Through the Red Sea wa - ters.
From His light, to whom we give Laud and praise un - dy - ing.
Wel - comes in un - wea - ried strains Je - sus' res - ur - rec - tion.
That Thy peace which ev - er - more Pass - eth hu - man know - ing.

JESUS CHRIST: RESURRECTION

CHRIST THE LORD IS RISEN TODAY 179

EASTER HYMN 7.7.7.7. with Alleluias

Charles Wesley, 1739

Lyra Davidica, 1708

1 "Christ the Lord is ris'n to - day,"
2 Lives a - gain our glo - rious King,
3 Love's re - deem - ing work is done,
4 Soar we now, where Christ has led?

Al - le - lu - ia!

Sons of men and an - gels say,
Where, O death, is now thy sting?
Fought the fight, the bat - tle won,
Fol - l'wing our ex - alt - ed Head,

Al - le - lu - ia!

Raise your joys and tri - umphs high,
Dy - ing once He all doth save,
Death in vain for - bids His rise:
Made like Him, like Him we rise,

Al - le - lu - ia!

Sing ye heav'ns, and earth re - ply.
Where thy vic - to - ry, O grave?
Christ has o - pened par - a - dise!
Ours the cross, the grave, the skies!

Al - le - lu - ia!

JESUS CHRIST: RESURRECTION

180 THINE IS THE GLORY

JUDAS MACCABEUS   10.11.11.11. with Refrain

Edmond Bundry, 1884
A toi la gloire, ô Ressuscité
Tr. R. Birch Hoyle‡, 1923

Arranged from George Frideric Handel, 1746

1 Thine is the glo - ry, Ris - en, con-quering Son; End - less is the
2 Lo! Je - sus meets us. Ris - en from the tomb, Lov - ing - ly He
3 No more we doubt Thee, Glo - rious Prince of life! Life is nought with-

vic - tory Thou o'er death hast won. An - gels in bright rai - ment
greets us, Scat-ters fear and gloom; Let the church with glad - ness
out Thee; Aid us in our strife; Make us more than con-querors,

Rolled the stone a - way, Kept the fold - ed grave-clothes
Hymns of tri - umph sing, For our Lord now liv - eth;
Through Thy death-less love; Bring us safe through Jor - dan

Refrain

Where Thy bod - y lay.
Death hath lost its sting. Thine is the glo - ry, Ris - en, con-quering Son;
To Thy home a - bove.

JESUS CHRIST: RESURRECTION

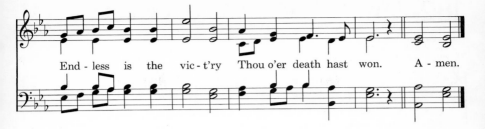

Endless is the vic-t'ry Thou o'er death hast won. A - men.

JOY DAWNED AGAIN ON EASTER DAY 181

PUER NOBIS NASCITUR L.M.

Anonymous 4th or 5th century
Aurora lucis rutilat. Pt. III. *Claro Paschali gaudio*
Tr. *The Hymnary,* 1872

Piae Cantiones, 1582

1 Joy dawned a - gain on Eas - ter day, The sun shone
2 His ris - en flesh with ra - diance glow'd; His wound-ed
3 O Je - sus, King of gen - tle - ness, Do Thou our
4 Je - sus, who art the Lord of all, In this our
5 All praise, O ris - en Lord, we give To Thee, who,

out with fair - er ray, When, to their long - ing eyes re-stored,
hands and side He showed: Those scars their si - lent wit - ness gave
in - most hearts pos - sess; And we to Thee will ev - er raise
Eas - ter fes - ti - val, From ev - ery weap - on death can wield
dead, a - gain dost live; To God the Fa - ther e - qual praise,

Th' a - pos - tles saw their ris - en Lord.
That Christ was ris - en from the grave.
The trib - ute of our grate - ful praise.
Thine own re - deemed, Thy peo - ple, shield.
And God the Ho - ly Ghost, we raise. A - men.

JESUS CHRIST: RESURRECTION

182 JESUS CHRIST, MY SURE DEFENSE

JESUS, MEINE ZUVERSICHT 7.8.7.8.7.7.

C. Runge's *Praxis pietatis melica*, 1653
Jesus, meine Zuversicht
Tr. Catherine Winkworth‡, 1863

C. Runge's *Praxis pietatis melica*, 1653

1 Je - sus Christ, my sure de-fense And my Sav - ior, ev - er
2 Je - sus, my Re - deem - er, lives! I, too, un - to life must
3 Nay, too close - ly am I bound Un - to Him by hope for
4 Sav - ior, draw a - way our heart Now from plea-sures base and

liv - eth; Know - ing this, my con - fi - dence Rests up -
wak - en; He will have me where He is. Shall my
ev - er; Faith's strong hand the rock hath found, Grasped it,
hol - low, Let us there with Thee have part, Here on

on the hope it giv - eth, Though the night of death
cour - age then be shak - en? Shall I fear? Or could
and will leave it nev - er; Not the ban of death
earth Thy foot - steps fol - low. Fix our hearts be - yond

be fraught Still with many an anx - ious thought.
the Head Rise and leave His mem - bers dead?
can part From its Lord the trust - ing heart.
the skies, Whith - er we our - selves would rise. A - men.

JESUS CHRIST: RESURRECTION

ALLELUIA! THE STRIFE IS O'ER 183

VICTORY 8.8.8. with Alleluias

Anonymous, Köln, 1695
Finita jam sunt praelia
Tr. Francis Pott, 1861

Giovanni Pierluigi da Palestrina, 1591
Adapted by William Henry Monk, 1861

Al - le - lu - ia! Al - le - lu - ia! Al - le - lu - ia!

1 The strife is o'er, the bat - tle done;
2 The powers of death have done their worst,
3 The three sad days have quick - ly sped;
4 Lord, by the stripes which wound - ed Thee,

The vic - to - ry of life is won;
But Christ their le - gions hath dis - persed;
He ris - es glo - rious from the dead;
From death's dread sting Thy ser - vants free,

The song of tri - umph has be - gun. Al - le - lu - ia!
Let shout of ho - ly joy out - burst. Al - le - lu - ia!
All glo - ry to our ris - en Head! Al - le - lu - ia!
That we may live and sing to Thee, Al - le - lu - ia! A - men.

JESUS CHRIST: RESURRECTION

184 REJOICE, THE LORD IS KING

ARTHUR'S SEAT   6.6.6.6. with Refrain

Charles Wesley, 1746

From John Goss, d. 1880
Arranged in *Hymns and Songs of Praise*, 1874

1 Re - joice, the Lord is King: Your Lord and King
2 Je - sus, the Sav - ior, reigns, The God of truth
3 His king - dom can - not fail, He rules o'er earth
4 He sits at God's right hand Till all His foes

a - dore; Mor - tals, give thanks and sing, And
and love; When He had purged our stains, He
and heav'n; The keys of death and hell Are
sub - mit, And bow to His com - mand, And

REFRAIN

tri - umph ev - er - more:
took His seat a - bove: Lift up your heart, lift
to our Je - sus giv'n:
fall be - neath His feet:

up your voice; Re - joice, a - gain I say, re - joice. A - men.

JESUS CHRIST: ASCENSION

HAIL THE DAY THAT SEES HIM RISE 185

LLANFAIR 7.7.7.7. with Alleluias

Charles Wesley‡, 1739   Robert Williams, 1817

1 Hail the day that sees Him rise, Al - le - lu - ia!
2 There the glo - rious tri - umph waits; Al - le - lu - ia!
3 See, He lifts His hands a - bove! Al - le - lu - ia!
4 Lord, be - yond our mor - tal sight, Al - le - lu - ia!

Glo - rious to His na - tive skies; Al - le - lu - ia!
Lift your heads, e - ter - nal gates, Al - le - lu - ia!
See, He shows the prints of love! Al - le - lu - ia!
Raise our hearts to reach Thy height, Al - le - lu - ia!

Christ, a - while to mor - tals giv'n, Al - le - lu - ia!
Wide un - fold the ra - diant scene, Al - le - lu - ia!
Hark! His gra - cious lips be - stow, Al - le - lu - ia!
There Thy face un - cloud - ed see, Al - le - lu - ia!

En - ters now the high - est heav'n. Al - le - lu - ia!
Take the King of glo - ry in! Al - le - lu - ia!
Bless - ings on His church be - low. Al - le - lu - ia!
Find our heav'n of heav'ns in Thee! Al - le - lu - ia! A - men.

JESUS CHRIST: ASCENSION

186 LOOK, YE SAINTS

CORONAE 8.7.8.7.4.7.

Thomas Kelly, 1809

William Henry Monk, 1871

1 Look, ye saints, the sight is glo-rious: See the "Man of Sor-rows" now;
2 Crown the Sav-ior, an-gels, crown Him; Rich the tro-phies Je-sus brings;
3 Sin-ners in de-ri-sion crowned Him, Mock-ing thus the Sav-ior's claim;
4 Hark, those bursts of ac-cla-ma-tion! Hark, those loud tri-um-phant chords!

From the fight re-turned vic-to-rious, Ev-ery knee to Him shall bow;
In the seat of pow'r en-throne Him, While the vault of heav-en rings:
Saints and an-gels crowd a-round Him, Own His ti-tle, praise His name:
Je-sus takes the high-est sta-tion; O what joy the sight af-fords:

Crown Him! Crown Him! Crowns be-come the Vic-tor's brow.
Crown Him! Crown Him! Crown the Sav-ior "King of kings."
Crown Him! Crown Him! Spread a-broad the Vic-tor's fame.
Crown Him! Crown Him! "King of kings, and Lord of lords." A-men.

187 MAJESTIC SWEETNESS SITS ENTHRONED

ORTONVILLE C.M.

Samuel Stennett†, 1787

Thomas Hastings, 1837

1 Ma-jes-tic sweet-ness sits en-throned Up-on the Sav-ior's brow; His head with ra-diant
2 No mor-tal can with Him com-pare A-mong the sons of men; Fair-er is He than
3 To Him I owe my life and breath, And all the joys I have; He makes me tri-umph
4 To heav'n, the place of His a-bode, He brings my wea-ry feet; Shows me the glo-ries
5 Since from His boun-ty I re-ceive Such proofs of love di-vine, Had I a thou-sand

JESUS CHRIST: ASCENSION

glo-ries crowned, His lips with grace o'er-flow, His lips with grace o'er-flow.
all   the fair   That fill the heav'n-ly   train,   That fill the heav'n-ly   train.
o - ver death, And saves me from the   grave,   And saves me from the   grave.
of   my God,   And makes my joys com-plete,   And makes my joys com-plete.
hearts to give,   Lord, they should all be   Thine,   Lord, they should all be   Thine. A-men.

RISE, GLORIOUS CONQUEROR 188

DORT 6.6.4.6.6.6.4.

Matthew Bridges, 1848

Lowell Mason, 1832

1 Rise,   glo - rious   Con - qu'ror, rise   In - to   Thy   na - tive skies;
2 Vic - tor   o'er   death   and hell,   Che - ru - bic   le - gions swell
3 En - ter,   in - car - nate God!   No   feet   but   Thine   have trod
4 Li - on   of   Ju - dah, hail!   And   let   Thy   name   pre - vail

As - sume Thy   right;   And where in   many   a   fold   The clouds are
The   ra - diant   train: Prais - es   all   heav'n in - spire;   Each an - gel
The   ser - pent   down: Blow the   full   trum - pets, blow,   Wid - er   yon
From   age   to   age: Lord of   the   roll - ing years,   Claim for Thine

back-ward rolled, Pass through those gates of gold, And reign   in   light.
sweeps his lyre,   And claps his   wings   of   fire,   Thou Lamb once slain!
por - tals throw,   Sav - ior,   tri - um-phant, go,   And take Thy   crown!
own the spheres,   For Thou hast bought with tears   Thy   her - it - age.   A - men.

JESUS CHRIST: ASCENSION

189 THE HEAD THAT ONCE WAS CROWNED

ST. MAGNUS C.M.

Thomas Kelly, 1820

Jeremiah Clark, 1707

1 The head that once was crowned with thorns Is crowned with glo - ry now;
2 The high-est place that heav'n af - fords Is His, is His by right,
3 The joy of all who dwell a - bove; The joy of all be - low,
4 The cross He bore is life and health, Through shame and death to Him:

A roy - al di - a - dem a - dorns The might - y Vic - tor's brow.
The King of kings, and Lord of lords, And heav'n's e - ter - nal Light.
To whom He man - i - fests His love, And grants His name to know.
His peo-ple's hope, His peo-ple's wealth, Their ev - er - last - ing theme.

190 SING WE TRIUMPHANT HYMNS

DEO GRACIAS L.M.

The Venerable Bede, d. 735
Hymnum canamus Domino
Tr. Benjamin Webb, 1854

English Melody, 15th century

1 Sing we tri-um-phant hymns of praise, New hymns to heav'n ex - ult - ing raise:
2 O grant us thith - er - ward to tend, And with un - wear - ied hearts as - cend
3 Be Thou our joy and strong de-fense, Who art our fu - ture re - com-pense:
4 O ris - en Christ, as-cend-ed Lord, All praise to Thee let earth ac - cord,

Christ, by a road be-fore un - trod, As-cend-eth to the throne of God.
To-ward Thy king-dom's throne, where Thou, As is our faith, art seat-ed now.
So shall the light that springs from Thee Be ours through all e - ter - ni - ty.
Who art, while end-less a - ges run, With Fa-ther and with Spir-it one. A-men.

JESUS CHRIST: ASCENSION

CROWN HIM WITH MANY CROWNS 191

DIADEMATA S.M.D.

Matthew Bridges, 1851

George Job Elvey, 1868

1 Crown Him with man-y crowns, The Lamb up-on His throne;
2 Crown Him the Lord of love: Be-hold His hands and side,
3 Crown Him the Lord of peace; Whose pow'r a scep-ter sways
4 Crown Him the Lord of years, The Po-ten-tate of time;

Hark! how the heav'n-ly an-them drowns All mu-sic but its own:
Rich wounds, yet vis-i-ble a-bove, In beau-ty glo-ri-fied:
From pole to pole, that wars may cease, Ab-sorbed in prayer and praise:
Cre-a-tor of the roll-ing spheres, In-ef-fa-bly sub-lime:

A - wake, my soul, and sing Of Him who died for thee,
No an-gel in the sky Can ful-ly bear that sight,
His reign shall know no end; And round His pierc-ed feet
All hail, Re-deem-er, hail! For Thou hast died for me:

And hail Him as thy match-less King Through all e-ter-ni-ty.
But down-ward bends his burn-ing eye At mys-ter-ies so bright.
Fair flow'rs of par-a-dise ex-tend Their fra-grance ev-er sweet.
Thy praise shall nev-er, nev-er fail Through-out e-ter-ni-ty. A-men.

JESUS CHRIST: ASCENSION

192 LO! HE COMES

ST. THOMAS (HOLYWOOD) 8.7.8.7.8.7.

John Cennick, 1752
and Charles Wesley, 1758
Alt. by Martin Madan, 1760

John Francis Wade, c. 1743

1 Lo! He comes, with clouds de-scend-ing Once for our sal-
2 Ev - ery eye shall now be-hold Him Robed in dread-ful
3 Ev - ery is - land, sea and moun-tain, Heav'n and earth shall
4 Now re-demp-tion, long ex-pect-ed, See in sol - emn
5 Yea, a - men! let all a - dore Thee, High on Thine e -

va - tion slain; Thou - sand, thou - sand saints at - tend - ing
maj - es - ty; Those who set at naught and sold Him,
flee a - way; All who hate Him must, con - found - ed,
pomp ap - pear; All His saints, by man re - ject - ed,
ter - nal throne; Sav - ior, take the pow'r and glo - ry,

Swell the tri - umph of His train; Al - le - lu - ia!
Pierced, and nailed Him to the tree, Deep - ly wail - ing,
Hear the trump pro - claim the day: Come to judg - ment!
Now shall meet Him in the air: Al - le - lu - ia!
Claim the king - dom for Thine own: Al - le - lu - ia!

Al - le - lu - ia! God ap - pears on earth to reign.
Deep - ly wail - ing, Shall the true Mes - si - ah see.
Come to judg - ment! Come to judg - ment! Come a - way!
Al - le - lu - ia! See the day of God ap - pear.
Al - le - lu - ia! Thou shalt reign, and Thou a - lone.

JESUS CHRIST: SECOND COMING

CHRIST IS COMING! LET CREATION 193

UNSER HERRSCHER 8.7.8.7.8.7.

John Ross MacDuff†, 1853

Joachim Neander, 1680

1 Christ is com - ing! let cre - a - tion From her groans and
2 Earth can now but tell the sto - ry Of Thy bit - ter
3 Long Thine ex - iles have been pin - ing, Far from rest, and
4 With that bless - ed hope be - fore us, Let no harp re -

trav - ail cease; Let the glo - rious proc - la - ma - tion
cross and pain; She shall yet be - hold Thy glo - ry,
home, and Thee: But, in heav'n - ly ves - tures shin - ing,
main un - strung; Let the might - y ad - vent cho - rus

Hope re - store and faith in - crease: Christ is com - ing!
When Thou com - est back to reign: Christ is com - ing!
Soon they shall Thy glo - ry see! Christ is com - ing!
On - ward roll from tongue to tongue: "Christ is com - ing!

Christ is com - ing! Come, Thou bless - ed Prince of Peace.
Christ is com - ing! Let each heart re - peat the strain.
Christ is com - ing! Haste the joy - ous ju - bi - lee.
Christ is com - ing! Come, Lord Je - sus, quick - ly come!" A - men.

JESUS CHRIST: SECOND COMING

194 REJOICE, ALL YE BELIEVERS

GREENLAND 7.6.7.6.D.

Laurentius Laurenti, 1700
Ermuntert euch, ihr Frommen
Tr. Sarah Borthwick Findlater†, 1854

Johann Michael Haydn, 1806

1 Re - joice, all ye be - liev - ers! And let your lights ap - pear;
2 See that your lamps are burn - ing; Re - plen - ish them with oil;
3 Ye saints, who here in pa - tience Your cross and suf - f'rings bore,
4 Our hope and ex - pec - ta - tion, O Je - sus, now ap - pear;

The eve - ning is ad - vanc - ing, A dark - er night is near.
And wait for your sal - va - tion, The end of earth - ly toil.
Shall live and reign for - ev - er, When sor - row is no more:
A - rise, Thou Sun so longed for, O'er this be - night - ed sphere.

The Bride-groom is a - ris - ing, And soon He will draw nigh;
The watch - ers on the moun - tain Pro - claim the Bride-groom near,
A - round the throne of glo - ry The Lamb ye shall be - hold,
With hearts and hands up - lift - ed, We plead, O Lord, to see

Up! pray, and watch, and wres - tle! At mid-night comes the cry.
Go meet Him as He com - eth, With Al - le - lu - ias clear.
In tri - umph cast be - fore Him Your di - a - dems of gold.
The day of earth's re - demp - tion That brings us home to Thee. A - men.

JESUS CHRIST: SECOND COMING

THE BRIDEGROOM SOON WILL CALL US 195

FREUT EUCH, IHR LIEBEN 7.6.7.6.D.

Johann Walther, 1552
Der Bräutgam wir bald rufen
Tr. Matthias Loy, 1880

Leonhart Schröter, 1587

1 The Bride-groom soon will call us, Come, all ye wed-ding guests!
2 There shall we see de-light-ed Our dear Re-deem-er's face,
3 They will not blush to own us As broth-ers, sis-ters dear,
4 In yon-der home shall nev-er Be si-lent mus-ic's voice;
5 In man-sions fair and spa-cious Will God the feast pre-pare,

May not His voice ap-pall us, While slum-ber binds our breasts;
Who leads our souls be-night-ed To glo-ry by His grace;
Love ev-er will be shown us When we with them ap-pear;
With hearts and lips for-ev-er We shall in God re-joice;
And ev-er kind and gra-cious, Bid us its rich-es share;

May all our lamps be burn-ing, And oil be found in store,
The pa-tri-archs shall meet us, The proph-ets' ho-ly band,
We all shall come be-fore Him, Who for us Man be-came,
The an-gels shall a-dore Him, All saints shall sing His praise,
There bliss that knows no mea-sure From springs of love shall flow,

That we, with Him re-turn-ing, May o-pen find the door.
A-pos-tles, mar-tyrs, greet us In that ce-les-tial land.
As Lord and God a-dore Him, And ev-er bless His name.
And bring with joy be-fore Him Their sweet-est heav'n-ly lays.
And nev-er chang-ing plea-sure His boun-ty will be-stow.

JESUS CHRIST: SECOND COMING

196 THE KING SHALL COME

ST. MICHEL'S C.M.D.

Based on a Greek text
John Brownlie, 1907

W. Gawler's *Hymns and Psalms*, 1785 to 1788

1 The King shall come when morn-ing dawns, And light tri-um-phant breaks;
2 O bright-er than the ris-ing morn, When He, vic-to-rious, rose,
3 The King shall come when morn-ing dawns, And earth's dark night is past;

When beau-ty gilds the east-ern hills, And life to joy a-wakes.
And left the lone-some place of death, De-spite the rage of foes;
O haste the ris-ing of that morn, That day that aye shall last.

Not as of old, a lit-tle child To bear, and fight, and die;
O bright-er than that glo-rious morn, Shall this fair morn-ing be,
The King shall come when morn-ing dawns, And light and beau-ty brings;

But crowned with glo-ry like the sun, That lights that morn-ing sky.
When Christ, our King, in beau-ty comes, And we His face shall see.
Hail! Christ the Lord; Thy peo-ple pray Come quick-ly, King of kings. A-men.

JESUS CHRIST: SECOND COMING

JESUS CAME, THE HEAVENS ADORING 197

BENEDIC ANIMA 8.7.8.7.8.7.

Godfrey Thring, 1864

John Goss, 1869

1 Je - sus came, the heav'ns a - dor - ing, Came with peace from realms on high; Je - sus came for man's re - demp-tion, Low - ly came on earth to die; Al - le - lu - ia! Al - le - lu - ia! Came in deep hu - mil - i - ty.

2 Je - sus comes a - gain in mer - cy, When our hearts are bowed with care; Je - sus comes a - gain in an - swer To an ear - nest, heart-felt prayer; Al - le - lu - ia! Al - le - lu - ia! Comes to save us from de - spair.

3 Je - sus comes to hearts re - joic - ing, Bring - ing news of sins for - given; Je - sus comes in sounds of glad - ness, Lead - ing souls re - deemed to heav'n; Al - le - lu - ia! Al - le - lu - ia! Now the gate of death is riv'n.

4 Je - sus comes in joy and sor - row, Shares a - like our hopes and fears; Je - sus comes, what - e'er be - falls us, Glads our hearts, and dries our tears; Al - le - lu - ia! Al - le - lu - ia! Cheer-ing e'en our fail - ing years.

5 Je - sus comes on clouds tri - um - phant, When the heav'ns shall pass a - way; Je - sus comes a - gain in glo - ry; Let us then our hom - age pay, Al - le - lu - ia! ev - er sing - ing Till the dawn of end - less day.

JESUS CHRIST: SECOND COMING

198 CHRIST IS THE WORLD'S TRUE LIGHT

O GOTT, DU FROMMER GOTT   6.7.6.7.6.6.6.6.

George Wallace Briggs, 1931

A. Fritsch's *Himmels-Lust*, 1679
Harmony by Johann Sebastian Bach, c. 1740

1 Christ is the world's true light, Its cap-tain of sal-va-tion,
2 In Christ all ra-ces meet, Their an-cient feuds for-get-ting,
3 One Lord, in one great name U-nite us all who own Thee;

The day-star clear and bright Of ev-ery man and na-tion;
The whole round world com-plete, From sun-rise to its set-ting,
Cast out our pride and shame That hin-der to en-throne Thee;

New life, new hope a-wakes, Wher-e'er men own His sway:
When Christ is throned as Lord, Men shall for-sake their fear,
The world has wait-ed long, Has trav-ailed long in pain;

Free-dom her bond-age breaks, And night is turned to day.
To plow-share beat the sword, To prun-ing hook the spear.
To heal its an-cient wrong, Come, Prince of Peace, and reign. A-men.

JESUS CHRIST: REIGN AND KINGDOM

WAKE THE SONG OF JUBILEE 199

AMBOY 7.7.7.7.D.

Leonard Bacon, 1823

Lowell Mason, 1845

1 Wake the song of ju - bi - lee, Let it ech - o o'er the sea!
2 Now the des - ert lands re - joice, And the is - lands join their voice,
3 Bless - ing, hon - or, glo - ry, might, Are the con-q'ror's na - tive right;

Now is come the prom-ised hour, Je - sus reigns with sov -'reign power.
Yea, the whole cre - a - tion sings, "Je-sus is the King of kings."
Thrones and powers be - fore Him fall, Lamb of God and Lord of all.

All ye na - tions, join and sing, Christ of lords and kings is King.
See the ran - som'd mil-lions stand, Palms of con - quest in their hands,
Time has near - ly reached its sum; All things with the bride say, "Come,"

Let it sound from shore to shore Je - sus reigns for-ev - er - more.
This be - fore the throne their strain, Hell is van-quished, death is slain.
Je - sus, whom all worlds a - dore, Come, and reign for-ev-er - more. A - men.

JESUS CHRIST: REIGN AND KINGDOM

200 SEEK YE FIRST THE KINGDOM

KINGDOM OF GOD 6.5.6.5.D.

Norman Elliott, b. 1893

English Melody from
Y Llawlyfr Moliant, 1890

1 "Seek ye first the king - dom, 'Tis your Fa - ther's will";
2 As for hid - den trea - sure, Or for match - less pearl,
3 As the si - lent leav - en Works its se - cret way,
4 As the ten - der seed - ling Grows up tall and strong,
5 Hum - blest shall be great - est, Poor in spir - it reign;

So the voice of Je - sus Bids us fol - low still.
When at last dis - cov - ered, Men will sell their all;
Or as grows the seed grain Through the night and day;
And the birds of heav - en To its branch - es throng;
Home shall come the child - like Born through Thee a - gain;

Sav - ior, we would hear Thee, Fol - low, find, and see;
So, when breaks the vi - sion Of that king - dom fair,
Lord, so be the in - crease, Peace - a - ble but sure,
So shall all God's chil - dren From the east and west
Ea - ger hearts ar - rive there On the pil - grim's road.

And, in life's ad - ven - ture, Thy dis - ci - ples be.
Ours shall be its rich - es And its beau - ty rare.
Of Thy Word with - in us And Thy king - dom's power.
Gath - er to His king - dom, In its shad - ow rest.
Hail! The king - dom glo - rious Of the liv - ing God!

JESUS CHRIST: REIGN AND KINGDOM

HARK! TEN THOUSAND HARPS 201

HARWELL 8.7.8.7.7.7. with Refrain

Thomas Kelly, 1806

Lowell Mason, 1840

1 Hark! ten thou-sand harps and voic - es Sound the note   of praise a - bove;
2 King of glo - ry! reign for - ev - er, Thine an ev - er - last-ing crown;
3 Sav - ior! has - ten Thine ap - pear-ing; Bring, O bring the glo-rious day,

Je - sus reigns, and heav'n re-joic - es; Je - sus reigns, the God of love.
Noth-ing, from Thy love, shall sev - er Those whom Thou hast made Thine own;
When, the awe - ful sum-mons hear-ing, Heav'n and earth shall pass a - way;

See, He sits on yon-der throne;   Je - sus rules the world a - lone.
Hap - py ob-jects of Thy grace   Des-tined to be-hold Thy face.
Then, with gold-en harps we'll sing,   "Glo-ry, glo-ry to our King!"

See, He sits   on yon-der throne; Je - sus rules   the world a - lone.
Hap - py ob - jects of Thy grace Des-tined to   be-hold Thy face.
Then, with gold - en harps we'll sing, "Glo-ry, glo - ry to our King!"

Al - le - lu - ia, Al - le - lu - ia, Al - le - lu - ia! A - men.

JESUS CHRIST: REIGN AND KINGDOM

202 O WHEREFORE DO THE NATIONS RAGE

UXBRIDGE L.M.

Based on Psalm 2
Psalter, 1912

Lowell Mason, 1830

1 O where-fore do the na - tions rage, And kings and
2 Their strength is weak - ness in the sight Of Him who
3 By God's de - cree His Son re - ceives The na - tions

rul - ers strive in vain, A - gainst the Lord of
sits en - throned a - bove; He speaks, and judg - ments
for His her - it - age; The con - qu'ring Christ su -

earth and heav'n To o - ver - throw Mes - si - ah's reign?
fall on them Who tempt His wrath and scorn His love.
preme shall reign As King of kings, from age to age.

203 JESUS SHALL REIGN

DUKE STREET L.M.

Based on Psalm 72
Isaac Watts, 1719

H. Boyd's *Psalm and Hymn Tunes*, 1793
Attributed to John Hatton, d. 1793

1 Je - sus shall reign wher-e'er the sun Does his suc - ces - sive jour-neys run;
2 For Him shall end - less prayer be made, And prais-es throng to crown His head;
3 Peo - ple and realms of ev - ery tongue Dwell on His love with sweet-est song;
4 Bless-ings a - bound wher-e'er He reigns; The pris-'ner leaps to lose his chains,
5 Let ev - ery crea - ture rise and bring Pe - cu - liar hon - ors to our King;

JESUS CHRIST: REIGN AND KINGDOM

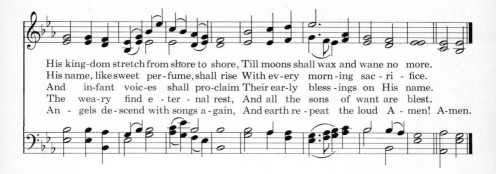

His king-dom stretch from shore to shore, Till moons shall wax and wane no more.
His name, like sweet per-fume, shall rise With ev-ery morn-ing sac-ri - fice.
And in-fant voic-es shall pro-claim Their ear-ly bless-ings on His name.
The wea-ry find e - ter - nal rest, And all the sons of want are blest.
An - gels de-scend with songs a-gain, And earth re-peat the loud A - men! A-men.

THE LORD IS KING 204

CREATION L.M.

Josiah Condert, 1824

Arranged from Franz Joseph Haydn, 1798

1 The Lord is King! lift up your voice, O earth; and
2 The Lord is King! who then shall dare Re - sist His
3 The Lord is King! Child of the dust, The Judge of
4 One Lord, one em - pire, all se - cures; He reigns, and

all ye heav'ns, re - joice: From world to world the
will, dis - trust His care, Or mur - mur at His
all the earth is just; Ho - ly and true are
life and death are yours: Through earth and heav'n one

joy shall ring, "The Lord om - nip - o - tent is King!"
wise de - crees, Or doubt His roy - al prom - is - es?
all His ways; Let ev - ery crea - ture speak His praise.
song shall ring, "The Lord om - nip - o - tent is King!"

JESUS CHRIST: REIGN AND KINGDOM

205 O SPIRIT OF LIFE

O HEILIGER GEIST 10.8.8.8.10.

Johann Niedling, 1651
O Heiliger Geist
Tr. John Caspar Mattes, 1913

Geistliche Kirchengesang, Köln, 1623

1 O Spir - it of Life, O Spir - it of God, In ev - ery
2 O Spir - it of Life, O Spir - it of God, Make us to
3 O Spir - it of Life, O Spir - it of God, In - crease our
4 O Spir - it of Life, O Spir - it of God, En - light - en

need Thou bring - est aid, Thou cam-est forth from God's great throne, From God, the
love Thy sa - cred Word; The ho - ly flame of love im - part, That char - i -
faith in our dear Lord; Un - less Thy grace the power should give, None can be -
us by Thy blest Word; Teach us to know the Fa - ther's love, And His dear

Fa - ther and the Son; O Spir - it of Life, O Spir - it of God.
ty may warm each heart; O Spir - it of Life, O Spir - it of God.
lieve in Christ and live; O Spir - it of Life, O Spir - it of God.
Son, who reigns a - bove: O Spir - it of Life, O Spir - it of God. A - men.

206 GRACIOUS SPIRIT! LOVE DIVINE

BUCKLAND 7.7.7.7.

"J. Stocker" in *Gospel Magazine*, 1777

Leighton G. Hayne, 1863

1 Gra - cious Spir - it! Love di - vine! Let Thy light with - in me shine;
2 Speak Thy par - d'ning grace to me; Set the bur - dened sin - ner free;
3 Life and peace to me im - part; Seal sal - va - tion on my heart;
4 Let me nev - er from Thee stray; Keep me in the nar - row way;

THE HOLY SPIRIT

All my guilt-y fears re-move; Fill me with Thy heav'n-ly love.
Lead me to the Lamb of God; Wash me in His pre-cious blood.
Dwell Thy-self with-in my breast, Ear-nest of im-mor-tal rest.
Fill my soul with joy di-vine; Keep me, Lord, for-ev-er Thine. A-men.

HOLY SPIRIT, TRUTH DIVINE 207

WEST END 7.7.7.7.

Samuel Longfellow, 1864

Alice Parker, 1966

1 Ho - ly Spir - it, truth di - vine, Dawn up - on this
2 Ho - ly Spir - it, love di - vine, Glow with - in this
3 Ho - ly Spir - it, power di - vine, Fill and nerve this
4 Ho - ly Spir - it, peace di - vine, Still this rest - less
5 Ho - ly Spir - it, right di - vine, King with - in my

soul of mine; Word of God, and in - ward light,
heart of mine; Kin - dle ev - ery high de - sire;
will of mine; By Thee may I strong - ly live;
heart of mine; Speak to calm this toss - ing sea,
con - science reign; Be my law, and I shall be

Wake my spir - it, clear my sight.
Per - ish self in Thy pure fire.
Brave - ly bear, and no - bly strive.
Stayed in Thy tran - quil - li - ty.
Firm - ly bound, for - ev - er free. A - men.

THE HOLY SPIRIT

208 O HOLY SPIRIT, ENTER IN

WIE SCHÖN LEUCHTET DER MORGENSTERN 8.8.7.8.8.7.4.12.8.

Michael Schirmer, 1640
O heilger Geist, kehr bei uns ein
Tr. Catherine Winkworth, 1863

Philipp Nicolai, 1599

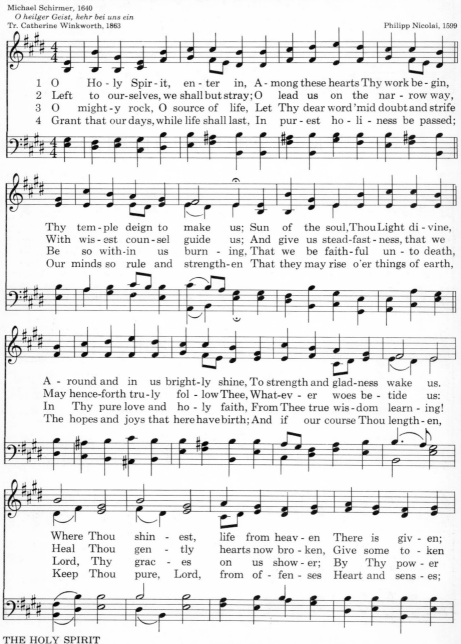

1 O   Ho - ly Spir - it, en - ter in, A - mong these hearts Thy work be - gin,
2 Left   to our-selves, we shall but stray; O   lead us on the nar - row way,
3 O   might-y rock, O source of life, Let Thy dear word 'mid doubt and strife
4 Grant that our days, while life shall last, In   pur - est ho - li - ness be passed;

Thy tem - ple deign to   make   us; Sun of the soul, Thou Light di - vine,
With wis - est coun - sel   guide   us; And give us stead-fast - ness, that we
Be   so with-in   us   burn - ing, That we be faith-ful un - to death,
Our minds so rule and strength-en That they may rise o'er things of earth,

A - round and in us bright-ly shine, To strength and glad-ness wake   us.
May hence-forth tru-ly fol - low Thee, What-ev - er   woes be - tide   us!
In   Thy pure love and ho - ly faith, From Thee true wis-dom learn - ing!
The hopes and joys that here have birth; And if   our course Thou length-en,

Where Thou   shin - est,   life from heav - en There is   giv - en;
Heal Thou   gen - tly   hearts now bro - ken, Give some to - ken
Lord, Thy   grac - es   on us show-er; By Thy pow - er
Keep Thou   pure, Lord, from of - fen - ses Heart and sens - es;

THE HOLY SPIRIT

we be - fore Thee For that pre-cious gift im - plore Thee.
Thou art near us, Whom we trust to light and cheer us.
Christ con - fess - ing, Let us win His grace and bless - ing.
bless - ed Spir - it, Bid us thus true life in - her - it. A - men.

MAY THE HOLY SPIRIT'S SWORD 209

JU MENG LING 7.9.7.10.4.10.

Tzu-ch'en Chao, b. 1887
Tr. Frank W. Price, b. 1895

Twelfth-century Chinese Melody

1 May the Ho - ly Spir - it's sword My soul with long-ing pierce, pierce my shield.
2 May the Ho - ly Spir - it pray With strong and word-less sighs, sighs for me.
3 May the Ho - ly Spir - it shine In ra - diant truth and make, make me free.

May He take my ev - ery-thing That I on earth may noth-ing se - cret hoard,
May He com-fort bring and lift The press-ing load and care of life a - way.
May He cast all doubt a - way, His joy and peace and rest be ful - ly mine.

I yield, I yield, To Christ, my Sav-ior, Je - sus Christ, my Lord.
To Thee, to Thee, I come, my Mas- ter. Lo, I come to - day.
On me, on me, Be shed Thy love, O Lord, Thy love di - vine.

THE HOLY SPIRIT

210 COME DOWN, O LOVE DIVINE

DOWN AMPNEY 6.6.11.6.6.11.

Bianco da Siena, d. 1434
Discendi, Amor santo
Tr. Richard Frederick Littledale, 1867

Ralph Vaughan Williams, 1906

1 Come down, O Love di - vine, Seek Thou this soul of mine,
2 O let it free - ly burn, Till earth - ly pas - sions turn
3 Let ho - ly char - i - ty Mine out - ward ves - ture be,
4 And so the yearn - ing strong, With which the soul will long,

And vis - it it with Thine own ar - dor glow - ing;
To dust and ash - es in its heat con - sum - ing;
And low - li - ness be - come my in - ner cloth - ing;
Shall far out - pass the power of hu - man tell - ing;

O Com - fort - er, draw near, With - in my heart ap - pear,
And let Thy glo - rious light Shine ev - er on my sight,
True low - li - ness of heart Which takes the hum - bler part,
For none can guess its grace, Till he be - come the place

And kin - dle it, Thy ho - ly flame be - stow - ing.
And clothe me round, the while my path il - lum - ing.
And o'er its own short - com - ings weeps with loath - ing.
Where - in the Ho - ly Spir - it makes His dwell - ing.

THE HOLY SPIRIT

COME, O CREATOR SPIRIT, COME 211

VENI CREATOR SPIRITUS L.M.

Ninth century
Veni Creator Spiritus
Tr. Robert Bridges, 1899
Sts. 3 and 5 omitted with permission

Fourth Century Plainsong

1 Come, O Cre - a - tor Spir - it, come, And make with - in our
2 O Com - fort - er, that name is Thine, Of God most high the
3 Our sens - es with Thy light in - flame, Our hearts to heav'n - ly
4 May we by Thee the Fa - ther learn, And know the Son, and

hearts Thy home; To us Thy grace ce - les - tial give,
gift di - vine; The well of life, the fire of love,
love re - claim; Our bod - ies' poor in - fir - mi - ty
Thee dis - cern, Who art of both; and so a - dore

Who of Thy breath - ing move and live.
Our souls' a - noint - ing from a - bove.
With strength per - pet - ual for - ti - fy.
In per - fect faith for - ev - er - more. A - men.

THE HOLY SPIRIT

212 COME, O COME, THOU QUICKENING SPIRIT

KOMM, O KOMM 8.7.8.7.7.7.

Heinrich Held, d. 1659
Komm, o komm, du Geist des Lebens
Tr. Edward Traill Horn III, b. 1909

Neu-vermehrtes Gesangbuch, Meiningen, 1693

1 Come, O come, Thou quick-ening Spir-it, God be - fore the dawn of time!
2 On - ly that which Thou de - sir - est Be our ob - ject; with Thy hand
3 Bless - ed Spir - it, who re - new - est All that dwell up - on the earth,
4 Help us keep the faith for - ev - er; Let not Sa - tan, death or shame

Fire our hearts with ho - ly ar - dor, Bless - ed Com - fort - er sub - lime!
Lead our ev - ery thought and ac - tion That they be but Thy com - mand.
When the e - vil one as - sails us Help us prove our heav'n-ly birth;
Draw us from Thee, or de - prive us Of the hon - or of Thy name.

Let Thy ra - diance fill our night, Turn-ing dark-ness in - to light.
All our sin - ful-ness e - rase With the in - crease of Thy grace.
Arm us with Thy might-y sword In the le - gions of the Lord.
When the foe would lure us hence, Be thou, God, our sure de - fense. A - men.

213 SPIRIT OF HOLINESS, DESCEND

NAOMI C.M.

Samuel Francis Smith, 1841

Johann G. Nägeli, 1832
Arranged by Lowell Mason, 1836

1 Spir - it of ho - li - ness, de - scend; Thy peo - ple wait for Thee;
2 Thy light that on our souls hath shone, Leads us in hope to Thee;
3 O bring our dear - est friends to God; Re - mem - ber those we love;
4 Spir - it of ho - li - ness, 'tis Thine To hear our fee - ble prayer;

THE HOLY SPIRIT

Thine ear in kind com - pas - sion lend; Let us Thy mer - cy see.
Let us not feel its rays a - lone, A - lone Thy peo - ple be.
Fit them on earth for Thine a - bode, Fit them for joys a - bove.
Come, for we wait Thy power di - vine, Let us Thy mer - cy share. A-men.

COME, HOLY SPIRIT, COME 214

MORNINGTON S.M.

Joseph Hart, 1759

Garret Wellesley, c. 1760

1 Come, Ho - ly Spir - it, come! Let Thy bright
2 Re - vive our droop - ing faith, Our doubts and
3 Con - vince us of our sin; Then lead to
4 If Thou, ce - les - tial dove, Thine in - flu -
5 Dwell, there - fore, in our hearts; Our minds from

beams a - rise; Dis - pel all dark - ness from our
fears re - move, And kin - dle in our breasts the
Je - sus' blood, And to our won - d'ring view re -
ence with - draw, What eas - y vic - tims soon we
bond - age free; Then shall we know, and praise, and

minds, And o - pen all our eyes.
flame Of nev - er - dy - ing love.
veal The se - cret love of God.
fall To con - science, wrath, and law!
love, The Fa - ther, Son, and Thee. A - men.

THE HOLY SPIRIT

215 COME, GRACIOUS SPIRIT

BACA L.M.

Simon Browne, 1720, and Others

William Batchelder Bradbury, c. 1858

1 Come, gra-cious Spir - it, heav'n-ly dove, With light and com - fort
2 The light of truth to us dis - play, And make us know and
3 Lead us to ho - li - ness, the road Which we must take to
4 Lead us to God, our fi - nal rest, To be with Him for -

from a - bove; Be Thou our guard-ian, Thou our guide, O'er ev - ery
choose Thy way; Plant ho - ly fear in ev - ery heart, That we from
dwell with God; Lead us to Christ, the liv - ing way, Nor let us
ev - er blest; Lead us to heav'n, its bliss to share, Full - ness of

thought and step pre - side, O'er ev - ery thought and step pre - side.
God may ne'er de - part, That we from God may ne'er de - part.
from His pas - tures stray, Nor let us from His pas - tures stray.
joy for - ev - er there, Full - ness of joy for - ev - er there.

216 BREATHE ON ME, BREATH OF GOD

TRENTHAM S.M.

Edwin Hatch†, 1878

Robert Jackson, 1888

1 Breathe on me, Breath of God, Fill me with life a - new, That I may
2 Breathe on me, Breath of God, Un - til my heart is pure; Un - til with
3 Breathe on me, Breath of God, Till I am whol - ly Thine; Un - til this
4 Breathe on me, Breath of God, So shall I nev - er die, But live with

THE HOLY SPIRIT

love what Thou dost love, And do what Thou wouldst do.
Thee I will one will, To do and to en - dure.
earth - ly part of me Glows with Thy fire di - vine.
Thee the per - fect life Of Thine e - ter - ni - ty. A - men.

SPIRIT OF GOD 217

MORECAMBE 10.10.10.10.

George Croly, 1854

Frederick Cook Atkinson, 1870

1 Spir - it of God! de - scend up - on my heart; Wean it from
2 I ask no dream, no proph - et ec - sta - sies; No sud - den
3 Hast Thou not bid us love Thee, God and King? All, all Thine
4 Teach me to feel that Thou art al - ways nigh; Teach me the
5 Teach me to love Thee as Thine an - gels love, One ho - ly

earth; through all its puls - es move; Stoop to my weak - ness,
rend - ing of the veil of clay; No an - gel vis - it -
own, soul, heart, and strength, and mind; I see Thy cross, there
strug - gles of the soul to bear; To check the ris - ing
pas - sion fill - ing all my frame; The bap - tism of the

might - y as Thou art, And make me love Thee as I ought to love.
ant, no op - 'ning skies; But take the dim - ness of my soul a - way.
teach my heart to cling: O let me seek Thee, and O let me find!
doubt, the reb - el sigh; Teach me the pa - tience of un - an - swered prayer.
heav'n - de - scend - ed dove, My heart an al - tar, and Thy love the flame. A - men.

THE HOLY SPIRIT

218 THY WORD, O LORD, LIKE GENTLE DEWS

RELEASE C.M.D.

Carl Bernhard Garve, 1825
Dein Wort, O Herr, ist milder Thau
Tr. Catherine Winkworth, 1855, and Others

Danish Melody
Version from *Service Book and Hymnal*, 1958

1 Thy Word, O Lord, like gen - tle dews, Falls soft on hearts that pine;
2 Thy Word is like a flam - ing sword, A wedge that cleav - eth stone;
3 Thy Word, a won - drous guid - ing star, On pil - grim hearts doth rise,

Lord, to Thy gar - den ne'er re - fuse This heav'n - ly balm of Thine.
Keen as a fire, so burns Thy Word, And pierc - eth flesh and bone.
Leads those to God who dwell a - far, And makes the sim - ple wise.

Wa - tered by Thee, let ev - ery tree Then blos - som to Thy praise,
Let it go forth o'er all the earth To cleanse our hearts with - in,
Let not its light e'er sink in night, But in each spir - it shine,

By grace of Thine bear fruit di - vine Through all the com - ing days.
To show Thy power in Sa - tan's hour, And break the might of sin.
That none may miss heav'n's fi - nal bliss, Led by Thy light di - vine. A - men.

THE HOLY SCRIPTURES

O WORD OF GOD INCARNATE 219

MUNICH 7.6.7.6.D.

Neu-vermehrtes Gesangbuch, Meiningen, 1693
Harmony by Felix Mendelssohn, 1847

William Walsham How, 1867

1 O Word of God in - car - nate, O wis - dom from on high,
2 The church from her dear Mas - ter, Re - ceived the gift di - vine,
3 It float-eth like a ban - ner Be - fore God's host un - furled;
4 O make Thy church, dear Sav - ior, A lamp of pur - est gold,

O truth un-changed, un - chang-ing, O light of our dark sky:
And still that light she lift - eth O'er all the earth to shine.
It shin-eth like a bea - con A - bove the dark - ling world.
To bear be - fore the na - tions Thy true light, as of old.

We praise Thee for the ra - diance That from the hal - lowed page,
It is the gold - en cas - ket, Where gems of truth are stored;
It is the chart and com - pass That o'er life's surg - ing sea,
O teach Thy wan-d'ring pil - grims By this their path to trace,

A lan - tern to our foot-steps, Shines on from age to age.
It is the heav'n-drawn pic - ture Of Christ, the liv - ing Word.
'Mid mists and rocks and quick-sands, Still guides, O Christ, to Thee.
Till, clouds and dark-ness end - ed, They see Thee face to face. A-men.

THE HOLY SCRIPTURES

220 THE HEAVENS DECLARE THY GLORY

UXBRIDGE L.M.

Based on Psalm 19
Isaac Watts†, 1719

Lowell Mason, 1830

1 The heav'ns de-clare Thy glo - ry, Lord, In ev - ery star Thy
2 Sun, moon and stars con - vey Thy praise Round the whole earth, and
3 Nor shall Thy spread-ing gos - pel rest Till through the world Thy
4 Great Sun of right-eous - ness, a - rise, Bless the dark world with
5 Thy no - blest won-ders here we view In souls re - new'd and

wis - dom shines: But when our eyes be - hold Thy
nev - er stand: So when Thy truth be - gan its
truth has run; Till Christ has all the na - tions
heav'n - ly light; Thy gos - pel makes the sim - ple
sins for - given: Lord, cleanse my sins, my soul re -

Word, We read Thy name in fair - er lines.
race, It touched and glanced on ev - ery land.
blest That see the light, or feel the sun.
wise; Thy laws are pure, Thy judg - ments right.
new, And make Thy Word my guide to heav'n. A - men.

221 LORD, THY WORD ABIDETH

RAVENSHAW 6.6.6.6.

M. Weisse's *Gesengbuchlein*, 1531
Adapted by William Henry Monk, 1861

Henry W. Baker†, 1861

1 Lord, Thy Word a - bid - eth, And our foot-steps guid - eth;
2 When our foes are near us, Then Thy Word doth cheer us,
3 When the storms are o'er us, And dark clouds be - fore us,
4 Word of mer - cy, giv - ing Help un - to the liv - ing,
5 O that we dis - cern - ing Its most ho - ly learn - ing,

THE HOLY SCRIPTURES

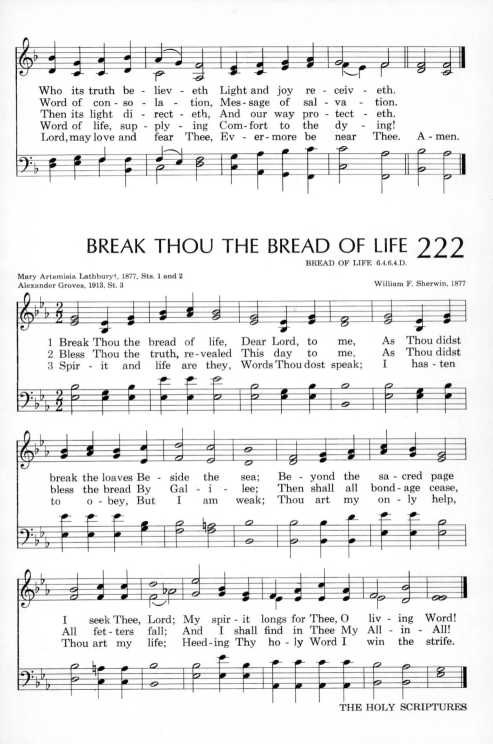

Who its truth be - liev - eth Light and joy re - ceiv - eth.
Word of con - so - la - tion, Mes-sage of sal - va - tion.
Then its light di - rect - eth, And our way pro - tect - eth.
Word of life, sup - ply - ing Com-fort to the dy - ing!
Lord, may love and fear Thee, Ev - er-more be near Thee. A - men.

BREAK THOU THE BREAD OF LIFE 222

BREAD OF LIFE 6.4.6.4.D.

Mary Artemisia Lathbury†, 1877, Sts. 1 and 2
Alexander Groves, 1913, St. 3

William F. Sherwin, 1877

1 Break Thou the bread of life, Dear Lord, to me, As Thou didst
2 Bless Thou the truth, re-vealed This day to me, As Thou didst
3 Spir - it and life are they, Words Thou dost speak; I has - ten

break the loaves Be - side the sea; Be - yond the sa - cred page
bless the bread By Gal - i - lee; Then shall all bond - age cease,
to o - bey, But I am weak; Thou art my on - ly help,

I seek Thee, Lord; My spir - it longs for Thee, O liv - ing Word!
All fet - ters fall; And I shall find in Thee My All - in - All!
Thou art my life; Heed-ing Thy ho - ly Word I win the strife.

THE HOLY SCRIPTURES

223 LAMP OF OUR FEET
NUN DANKET ALL' C.M.

Bernard Barton, 1836

Johann Crüger, 1653

1 Lamp of our feet, where - by we trace Our path when wont to stray;
2 Bread of our souls, where - on we feed, True man - na from on high;
3 Word of the ev - er - liv - ing God, Will of His glo - rious Son;
4 Yet to un - fold thy hid - den worth, Thy mys - ter - ies to re - veal,

Stream from the fount of heav'n - ly grace, Brook by the trav - 'ler's way;
Our guide and chart, where - in we read Of realms be - yond the sky;
With - out thee how could earth be trod, Or heav'n it - self be won?
That Spir - it which first gave thee forth Thy vol - ume must un - seal!

224 SPREAD, STILL SPREAD, THOU MIGHTY WORD
GOTT SEI DANK 7.7.7.7.

Jonathan Friedrich Bahnmaier, 1827
Walte, walte, nah und fern
Paraphrase by Percy Dearmer, 1931

J. A. Freylinghausen's *Neues Geistreiches Gesangbuch*, 1704

1 Spread, still spread, thou might - y Word, Show the king - dom of the Lord,
2 Tell them how the Fa - ther's will Made the world, and makes it still,
3 Might - y Word of man - y hues, Heav'n - ward point - ing, tell the news,
4 Word of life, so clean and strong, Word for which the na - tions long,

Spread to ev - ery soul on earth, Tell them their im - mor - tal worth.
How the Christ pro-claimed His love, Taught the wis - dom from a - bove.
Word, by Thy di - vine im - pact, Teach men how to will and act.
Spread, till from its tan - gled night All the earth stirs up to light.. A - men.

THE HOLY SCRIPTURES

COME TO THE SAVIOR NOW 225

INVITATION (MAKER) 6.6.6.6.D.

John M. Wigner, 1871

Frederick Charles Maker, 1881

1 Come to the Sav - ior now, He gen - tly call - eth thee;
2 Come to the Sav - ior now, Ye who have wan - dered far,
3 Come to the Sav - ior, all, What - e'er your bur - dens be;

In true re - pent - ance bow, Be - fore Him bend the knee:
Re - new your sol - emn vow, For His by right you are;
Hear now His lov - ing call, "Cast all your care on Me."

He wait - eth to be-stow Sal - va - tion, peace, and love,
Come, like poor wan-d'ring sheep Re - turn - ing to His fold;
Come, and for ev - ery grief In Je - sus you will find

True joy on earth be - low, A home in heav'n a - bove.
His arm will safe - ly keep, His love will ne'er grow cold.
A sure and safe re - lief, A lov - ing Friend, and kind.

LIFE IN CHRIST: CALL OF CHRIST

226 COME UNTO ME, YE WEARY

MEIRIONYDD 7.6.7.6.D.

William Chatterton Dix, 1867

William Lloyd, 1840

1 "Come un-to Me, ye wea-ry, And I will give you rest,"
2 "Come un-to Me, ye faint-ing, And I will give you life,"
3 "And who-so-ev-er com-eth, I will not cast him out,"

O bless-ed voice of Je-sus, Which comes to hearts op-pressed!
O peace-ful voice of Je-sus, Which comes to end our strife!
O pa-tient love of Je-sus, Which drives a-way our doubt!

It tells of ben-e-dic-tion, Of par-don, grace, and peace,
The foe is stern and ea-ger, The fight is fierce and long;
Which calls us, ver-y sin-ners, Un-wor-thy though we be

Of joy that hath no end-ing, Of love which can-not cease.
But Thou hast made us might-y, And strong-er than the strong.
Of love so free and bound-less, To come, dear Lord, to Thee!

LIFE IN CHRIST: CALL OF CHRIST

O JESUS, THOU ART STANDING 227

ST. HILDA 7.6.7.6.D.

William Walsham How, 1867

Justin Heinrich Knecht, 1793
and Edward Husband, 1871

1 O Je - sus, Thou art stand - ing Out - side the fast-closed door,
2 O Je - sus, Thou art knock - ing; And lo, that hand is scarred,
3 O Je - sus, Thou art plead - ing In ac - cents meek and low,

In low - ly pa - tience wait - ing To pass the thresh - old o'er:
And thorns Thy brow en - cir - cle, And tears Thy face have marred:
"I died for you, My chil - dren, And will ye treat Me so?"

Shame on us, Chris - tian broth - ers, His name and sign who bear,
O love that pass - eth knowl - edge, So pa - tient - ly to wait!
O Lord, with shame and sor - row We o - pen now the door;

O shame, thrice shame up - on us, To keep Him stand - ing there!
O sin that hath no e - qual, So fast to bar the gate!
Dear Sav - ior, en - ter, en - ter, And leave us nev - er - more! A-men.

LIFE IN CHRIST: CALL OF CHRIST

228 I SOUGHT THE LORD

FAITH 10.10.10.6.

The Pilgrim Hymnal, 1904

J. Harold Moyer, 1965

1 I sought the Lord, and af-ter-ward I knew He moved my
2 Thou didst reach forth Thy hand and mine en-fold, I walked and
3 I find, I walk, I love, but, O the whole Of love is

soul to seek Him, seek-ing me; It was not I that
sank not on the storm-vexed sea; 'Twas not so much that
but my an-swer, Lord, to Thee! For Thou wert long be-

found, O Sav-ior true, No, I was found of Thee.
I on Thee took hold As Thou, dear Lord, on me.
fore-hand with my soul; Al-ways Thou lov-edst me. A-men.

229 JESUS CALLS US

GALILEE 8.7.8.7.

Cecil Frances Alexander†, 1852

William Herbert Jude, 1888

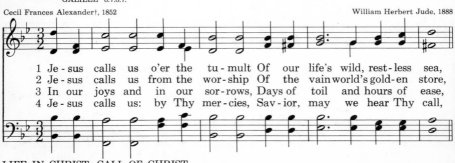

1 Je-sus calls us o'er the tu-mult Of our life's wild, rest-less sea,
2 Je-sus calls us from the wor-ship Of the vain world's gold-en store,
3 In our joys and in our sor-rows, Days of toil and hours of ease,
4 Je-sus calls us: by Thy mer-cies, Sav-ior, may we hear Thy call,

LIFE IN CHRIST: CALL OF CHRIST

Day by day His sweet voice sound-eth, Say-ing, "Chris-tian, fol-low Me."
From each i - dol that would keep us, Say-ing, "Chris-tian, love Me more."
Still He calls, in cares and pleas-ures, "Chris-tian, love Me more than these."
Give our hearts to Thine o - be-dience, Serve and love Thee best of all.

ART THOU WEARY, ART THOU LANGUID 230

STEPHANOS 8.5.8.3.

John Mason Neale,† 1862

Henry Williams Baker, 1868

1 Art thou wea - ry, art thou lan - guid,
2 Hath He marks to lead me to Him,
3 Is there di - a - dem, as Mon - arch,
4 If I find Him, if I fol - low,

Art thou sore dis - tressed? "Come to Me," saith
If He be my Guide? "In His feet and
That His brow a - dorns? "Yea, a crown, in
What His por - tion here? "Many a sor - row,

One, "and com - ing, Be at rest."
hands are wound - prints, And His side."
ver - y sure - ty, But of thorns."
many a la - bor, Many a tear."

5 If I still hold closely to Him,
   What hath He at last?
   "Sorrow vanquished, labor ended,
   Jordan passed."

6 If I ask Him to receive me,
   Will He say me nay?
   "Not till earth and not till heaven
   Pass away."

LIFE IN CHRIST: CALL OF CHRIST

231 I HEARD THE VOICE OF JESUS

KINGSFOLD C.M.D.

Horatius Bonar, 1846

Melody by Lucy Broadwood
Arranged and harmonized by
Ralph Vaughan Williams, 1906

1 I heard the voice of Je - sus say, "Come un - to Me and rest;
2 I heard the voice of Je - sus say, "Be - hold, I free - ly give
3 I heard the voice of Je - sus say, "I am this dark world's light;

Lay down, thou wea - ry one, lay down Thy head up - on My breast."
The liv - ing wa - ter; thirst - y one, Stoop down and drink and live."
Look un - to Me, thy morn shall rise, And all thy day be bright."

I came to Je - sus as I was, Wea-ry and worn and sad;
I came to Je - sus, and I drank Of that life-giv - ing stream;
I looked to Je - sus, and I found In Him my star, my sun;

I found in Him a rest - ing place, And He has made me glad.
My thirst was quench'd, my soul re - vived, And now I live in Him.
And in that light of life I'll walk, Till trav-'ling days are done. A-men.

LIFE IN CHRIST: CALL OF CHRIST

I HEARD THE VOICE OF JESUS 232

BONAR C.M.D.

Horatius Bonar, 1846

John David Brunk, 1911

1 I heard the voice of Je - sus say, "Come un - to Me and rest;
2 I heard the voice of Je - sus say, "Be - hold, I free - ly give
3 I heard the voice of Je - sus say, "I am this dark world's light;

Lay down, thou wea - ry one, lay down Thy head up - on My breast."
The liv - ing wa - ter; thirst - y one, Stoop down and drink and live."
Look un - to Me, thy morn shall rise, And all thy day be bright."

I came to Je - sus as I was, Wea - ry and worn and sad;
I came to Je - sus, and I drank Of that life - giv - ing stream;
I looked to Je - sus, and I found In Him my star, my sun;

I found in Him a rest - ing place, And He has made me glad.
My thirst was quench'd, my soul re - vived, And now I live in Him.
And in that light of life I'll walk, Till trav - 'ling days are done.

LIFE IN CHRIST: CALL OF CHRIST

233 DEPTH OF MERCY

BUCKLAND 7.7.7.7.

Charles Wesley, 1740

Leighton George Hayne, 1863

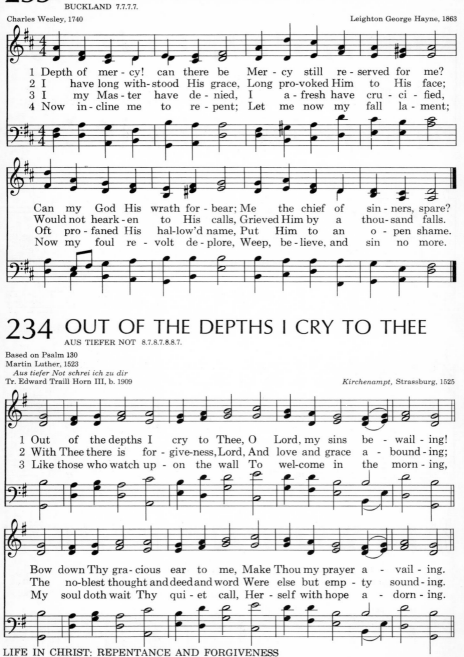

1 Depth of mer - cy! can there be Mer - cy still re - served for me?
2 I have long with - stood His grace, Long pro - voked Him to His face;
3 I my Mas - ter have de - nied, I a - fresh have cru - ci - fied,
4 Now in - cline me to re - pent; Let me now my fall la - ment;

Can my God His wrath for - bear; Me the chief of sin - ners, spare?
Would not heark - en to His calls, Grieved Him by a thou - sand falls.
Oft pro - faned His hal - low'd name, Put Him to an o - pen shame.
Now my foul re - volt de - plore, Weep, be - lieve, and sin no more.

234 OUT OF THE DEPTHS I CRY TO THEE

AUS TIEFER NOT 8.7.8.7.8.8.7.

Based on Psalm 130
Martin Luther, 1523
Aus tiefer Not schrei ich zu dir
Tr. Edward Traill Horn III, b. 1909

Kirchenampt, Strassburg, 1525

1 Out of the depths I cry to Thee, O Lord, my sins be - wail - ing!
2 With Thee there is for - give - ness, Lord, And love and grace a - bound - ing;
3 Like those who watch up - on the wall To wel - come in the morn - ing,

Bow down Thy gra - cious ear to me, Make Thou my prayer a - vail - ing.
The no - blest thought and deed and word Were else but emp - ty sound - ing.
My soul doth wait Thy qui - et call, Her - self with hope a - dorn - ing.

LIFE IN CHRIST: REPENTANCE AND FORGIVENESS

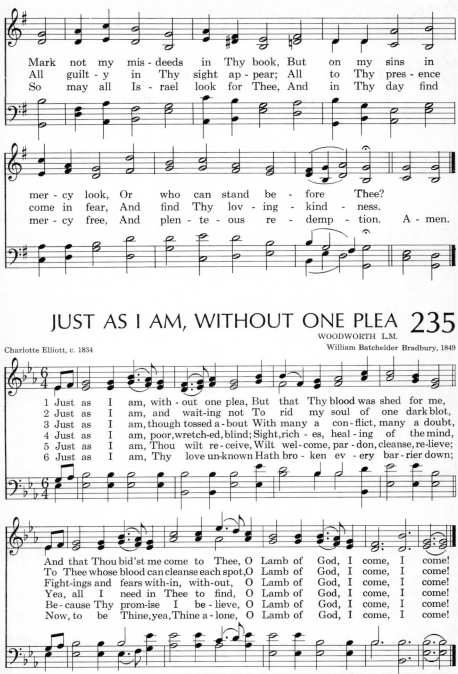

Mark not my mis-deeds in Thy book, But on my sins in
All guilt-y in Thy sight ap-pear; All to Thy pres-ence
So may all Is-rael look for Thee, And in Thy day find

mer-cy look, Or who can stand be-fore Thee?
come in fear, And find Thy lov-ing-kind-ness.
mer-cy free, And plen-te-ous re-demp-tion. A-men.

JUST AS I AM, WITHOUT ONE PLEA 235

WOODWORTH L.M.

Charlotte Elliott, c. 1834

William Batchelder Bradbury, 1849

1 Just as I am, with-out one plea, But that Thy blood was shed for me,
2 Just as I am, and wait-ing not To rid my soul of one dark blot,
3 Just as I am, though tossed a-bout With many a con-flict, many a doubt,
4 Just as I am, poor, wretch-ed, blind; Sight, rich-es, heal-ing of the mind,
5 Just as I am, Thou wilt re-ceive, Wilt wel-come, par-don, cleanse, re-lieve;
6 Just as I am, Thy love un-known Hath bro-ken ev-er-y bar-rier down;

And that Thou bid'st me come to Thee, O Lamb of God, I come, I come!
To Thee whose blood can cleanse each spot, O Lamb of God, I come, I come!
Fight-ings and fears with-in, with-out, O Lamb of God, I come, I come!
Yea, all I need in Thee to find, O Lamb of God, I come, I come!
Be-cause Thy prom-ise I be-lieve, O Lamb of God, I come, I come!
Now, to be Thine, yea, Thine a-lone, O Lamb of God, I come, I come!

LIFE IN CHRIST: REPENTANCE AND FORGIVENESS

236 JESUS, LOVER OF MY SOUL

MARTYN 7.7.7.7.D.

Charles Wesley, 1740

Simeon Butler Marsh, 1834

1 Je - sus, lov - er of my soul, Let me to Thy bos - om fly,
2 Oth - er ref - uge have I none; Hangs my help - less soul on Thee;
3 Thou, O Christ, art all I want, More than all in Thee I find;
4 Plen-teous grace with Thee is found, Grace to cov - er all my sin;

While the near - er wa - ters roll, While the tem - pest still is high;
Leave, ah, leave me not a - lone, Still sup-port and com - fort me.
Raise the fall - en, cheer the faint, Heal the sick, and lead the blind.
Let the heal - ing streams a-bound, Make and keep me pure with - in.

Hide me, O my Sav - ior, hide, Till the storm of life is past;
All my trust on Thee is stayed, All my help from Thee I bring;
Just and ho - ly is Thy name, I am all un - right - eous - ness;
Thou of life the foun - tain art, Free - ly let me take of Thee;

Safe in - to the ha - ven guide, O re - ceive my soul at last.
Cov - er my de - fence-less head With the shad-ow of Thy wing.
False and full of sin I am, Thou art full of truth and grace.
Spring Thou up with-in my heart, Rise to all e - ter - ni - ty. A-men.

LIFE IN CHRIST: REPENTANCE AND FORGIVENESS

JESUS, LOVER OF MY SOUL 237

ABERYSTWYTH 7.7.7.7.D.

Charles Wesley, 1740

Joseph Parry, 1879

1 Je - sus, lov - er of my soul, Let me to Thy bos - om fly,
2 Oth - er ref - uge have I none; Hangs my help - less soul on Thee;
3 Thou, O Christ, art all I want, More than all in Thee I find:
4 Plen - teous grace with Thee is found, Grace to cov - er all my sin;

While the near - er wa - ters roll, While the tem - pest still is high;
Leave, ah, leave me not a - lone, Still sup - port and com - fort me.
Raise the fall - en, cheer the faint, Heal the sick, and lead the blind,
Let the heal - ing streams a - bound, Make and keep me pure with - in.

Hide me, O my Sav - ior, hide, Till the storm of life is past;
All my trust on Thee is stayed, All my help from Thee I bring;
Just and ho - ly is Thy name, I am all un - right - eous-ness;
Thou of life the foun - tain art, Free - ly let me take of Thee;

Safe in - to the ha - ven guide, O re - ceive my soul at last.
Cov - er my de - fence-less head With the shad - ow of Thy wing.
False and full of sin I am, Thou art full of truth and grace.
Spring Thou up with - in my heart, Rise to all e - ter - ni - ty. A - men.

LIFE IN CHRIST: REPENTANCE AND FORGIVENESS

238 GOD, BE MERCIFUL TO ME

REDHEAD NO. 76 (AJALON) 7.7.7.7.7.7.

Based on Psalm 51
Psalter, 1912, Sts. 1-4
The Hymnbook, 1955, St. 5

Richard Redhead, 1853

1 God, be mer - ci - ful to me, On Thy grace I rest my plea;
2 My trans-gres-sions I con-fess, Grief and guilt my soul op-press;
3 I am e - vil, born in sin; Thou de - sir - est truth with - in.
4 Bro - ken, hum-bled to the dust By Thy wrath and judg-ment just,
5 Gra - cious God, my heart re-new, Make my spir - it right and true;

Plen-teous in com - pas - sion Thou, Blot out my trans - gres - sions now;
I have sinned a - gainst Thy grace And pro-voked Thee to Thy face;
Thou a - lone my Sav - ior art, Teach Thy wis - dom to my heart;
Let my con-trite heart re - joice And in glad-ness hear Thy voice;
Cast me not a - way from Thee, Let Thy Spir - it dwell in me;

Wash me, make me pure with-in, Cleanse, O cleanse me from my sin.
I con-fess Thy judg-ment just, Speech-less, I Thy mer - cy trust.
Make me pure, Thy grace be-stow, Wash me whit - er than the snow.
From my sins O hide Thy face, Blot them out in bound-less grace.
Thy sal - va-tion's joy im-part, Stead - fast make my will - ing heart. A-men.

239 APPROACH, MY SOUL, THE MERCY SEAT

BYEFIELD C.M.

John Newton, 1779

Thomas Hastings, c. 1840

1 Ap - proach, my soul, the mer - cy seat, Where Je - sus an - swers prayer;
2 Thy prom - ise is my on - ly plea, With this I ven - ture nigh;
3 Bowed down be-neath a load of sin, By Sa - tan sore - ly pressed,
4 O won-drous love! to bleed and die, To bear the cross and shame,

LIFE IN CHRIST: REPENTANCE AND FORGIVENESS

There hum-bly fall be-fore His feet, For none can per - ish there.
Thou call - est bur-dened souls to Thee, And such, O Lord, am I.
By war with-out, and fears with-in, I come to Thee for rest.
That guilt - y sin-ners, such as I, Might plead Thy gra - cious name! A-men.

LORD, THY MERCY NOW ENTREATING 240

RINGE RECHT 8.7.8.7.

Mary Ann Sidebotham, 1881

J. Thommen's *Erbaulicher Musicalischer Christen-Schatz*, 1745

1 Lord, Thy mer - cy now en - treat - ing, Low be -
2 Sin - ful thoughts and words un - lov - ing Rise a -
3 Hearts that far from Thee were stray - ing, While in
4 Pre - cious mo - ments i - dly wast - ed, Pre - cious
5 Lord, Thy mer - cy still en - treat - ing, We with

fore Thy throne we fall; Our mis - deeds to Thee con -
gainst us one by one; Acts un - wor - thy, deeds un -
prayer we bowed the knee; Lips that, while Thy prais - es
hours in fol - ly spent; Chris - tian vow and fight un -
shame our sins would own; From hence - forth, the time re -

fess - ing, On Thy name we hum - bly call.
think - ing, Good that we have left un - done;
sound - ing, Lift - ed not the soul to Thee;
heed - ed; Scarce a thought to wis - dom lent.
deem - ing, May we live to Thee a - lone. A - men.

LIFE IN CHRIST: REPENTANCE AND FORGIVENESS

241 LORD, FROM THE DEPTHS TO THEE

CHESHIRE C.M.

Based on Psalm 130
Scottish Psalter, 1650

Thomas Est's *Psalms*, 1592

1 Lord, from the depths to Thee I cried: My
2 Lord, who shall stand, if Thou, O Lord, Shouldst
3 I wait for God, my soul doth wait; My
4 I say, more than they that do watch The
4 Re - demp - tion al - so plen - te - ous Is

voice, Lord, do Thou hear: Un - to my sup - pli -
mark in - iq - ui - ty? But yet with Thee for -
hope is in His Word. More than they that for
morn - ing light to see, Let Is - ra - el hope
ev - er found with Him: And from all his in -

ca - tion's voice Give an at - ten - tive ear.
give - ness is, That feared Thou may - est be.
morn - ing watch, My soul waits for the Lord;
in the Lord, For with Him mer - cies be.
iq - ui - ties He Is - rael shall re - deem. A - men.

242 AMAZING GRACE! HOW SWEET

SOLON (AMAZING GRACE) C.M.

Folk Hymn

John Newton, 1779

Joseph Funk's *Genuine Church Music*, 1832 (*Harmonia Sacra*)

1 A - maz - ing grace! how sweet the sound That saved a wretch like me!
2 'Twas grace that taught my heart to fear, And grace my fears re - lieved;
3 Through man-y dan-gers, toils and snares, I have al - read - y come;
4 The Lord has prom-ised good to me, His Word my hope se - cures;

LIFE IN CHRIST: REPENTANCE AND FORGIVENESS

I once was lost, but now am found, Was blind, but now I see.
How pre - cious did that grace ap - pear, The hour I first be - lieved!
'Tis grace has brought me safe thus far, And grace will lead me home.
He will my shield and por - tion be, As long as life en - dures.

FAR, FAR AWAY 243

RESTORATION (I WILL ARISE) Irregular

Folk Hymn

P. P. Bliss' *Gospel Songs*, 1874

W. Walker's *Southern Harmony*, 1835

1 Far, far a - way from my lov - ing Fa - ther, I
2 Fain had I fed on the husks a - round me, Till
3 "I will a - rise, though faint and wear - y, Home
4 "Fa - ther," I'll say, "I have sinned be - fore Thee, No
5 Then I a - rose and came to my Fa - ther, Mer -

REFRAIN: I will a - rise and go to Je - sus, He

had been wan - d'ring, way - ward, wild, Fear - ing on - ly
to my - self I came, and said, "Plen - ty have my
to my Fa - ther I will go; Woe is me that
more may I be called Thy son: Make me on - ly
cy a - maz - ing! Love un - known! He be - held me,

will em - brace me in His arms; In the arms of

lest His an - ger O - ver - take His sin - ful child.
Fa - ther's ser - vants, Per - ish I for want of bread."
e'er I wan - dered, Ah, that I such need should know."
as Thy ser - vant, Pit - y me, a wretch un - done!"
ran, em - braced me, Par - doned, wel - comed, called me "son!"

my dear Sav - ior, O there are ten thou - sand charms.

LIFE IN CHRIST: REPENTANCE AND FORGIVENESS

244 ARISE, MY SOUL, ARISE

LENOX 6.6.6.6.8.8.

Charles Wesley, 1742

Lewis Edson, 1782

1 A - rise, my soul, a - rise, Shake off thy guilt - y fears,
2 He ev - er lives a - bove For me to in - ter - cede,
3 Five bleed - ing wounds He bears, Re - ceived on Cal - va - ry;
4 My God is rec - on - ciled, His pard -'ning voice I hear,

The bleed - ing sac - ri - fice In my be - half ap - pears;
His all - re - deem - ing love, His pre - cious blood to plead;
They pour ef - fec - tual prayers, They strong - ly speak for me;
He owns me for His child, I can no long - er fear;

Be - fore the throne my sure - ty stands, Be - fore the throne
His blood a - toned for all our race, His blood a - toned
For - give him, O for - give, they cry, For - give him, O
With con - fi - dence I now draw nigh, With con - fi - dence

my sure - ty stands, My name is writ - ten on His hands.
for all our race, And sprin - kles now the throne of grace.
for - give, they cry, Nor let that ran - somed sin - ner die!
I now draw nigh, And Fa - ther, Ab - ba Fa - ther, cry!

LIFE IN CHRIST: REPENTANCE AND FORGIVENESS

O BLESS THE LORD, MY SOUL 245

ST. THOMAS S.M.

Based on Psalm 103
Isaac Watts, 1719

Aaron Williams, 1762

1 O bless the Lord, my soul! Let all with-in me join,
2 O bless the Lord, my soul! Nor let His mer-cies lie
3 'Tis He for-gives thy sins; 'Tis He re-lieves thy pain;
4 He crowns thy life with love, When ran-somed from the grave;
5 He fills the poor with good; He gives the suf-f'rers rest;

And aid my tongue to bless His name Whose fa-vors are di-vine.
For-got-ten in un-thank-ful-ness, And with-out prais-es die.
'Tis He that heals thy sick-ness-es, And makes thee young a-gain.
He, that re-deemed my soul from hell Hath sov-ereign power to save.
The Lord hath judg-ments for the proud, And just-ice for th' op-pressed. A-men.

LORD JESUS, THINK ON ME 246

SOUTHWELL S.M.

Synesius of Cyrene, c. 410
Μνωέο Χριστέ
Tr. Allen W. Chatfield†, 1876

W. Damon's *Psalms*, 1579

1 Lord Je-sus, think on me, And purge a-way my sin;
2 Lord Je-sus, think on me, With care and woe op-pressed;
3 Lord Je-sus, think on me, Nor let me go a-stray;
4 Lord Je-sus, think on me, When flows the tem-pest high:
5 Lord Je-sus, think on me, That, when the flood is past,

From earth-born pas-sions set me free, And make me pure with-in.
Let me Thy lov-ing serv-ant be, And taste Thy prom-ised rest.
Through dark-ness and per-plex-i-ty Point Thou the heav'n-ly way.
When on doth rush the en-e-my, O Sav-ior, be Thou nigh.
I may th' e-ter-nal bright-ness see, And share Thy joy at last. A-men.

LIFE IN CHRIST: REPENTANCE AND FORGIVENESS

247 LORD CHRIST, WHEN FIRST THOU CAM'ST

MIT FREUDEN ZART 8.7.8.7.8.8.7.

Walter Russell Bowie, 1928

Adapted from *Geneva 138, Pseaulmes* . . . , Lyon, 1547
Bohemian Brethren's *Kirchengeseng* . . . , 1566

1 Lord Christ, when first Thou cam'st to men, Up - on a cross they bound Thee,
2 O awe-ful love, which found no room In life where sin de - nied Thee,
3 New ad-vent of the love of Christ, Shall we a-gain re - fuse Thee,
4 O wound-ed hands of Je-sus, build In us Thy new cre - a - tion;

And mocked Thy sav-ing king-ship then By thorns with which they crowned Thee;
And, doomed to death, must bring to doom The power which cru - ci - fied Thee;
Till in the night of hate and war We per-ish as we lose Thee?
Our pride is dust; our vaunt is stilled; We wait Thy rev - e - la - tion.

And still our wrongs may weave Thee now New thorns to pierce that
Till not a stone was left on stone, And all a na - tion's
From old un-faith our souls re-lease To seek the king - dom
O love that tri - umphs o - ver loss, We bring our hearts be -

stead - y brow, And robe of sor - row round Thee.
pride o'er-thrown, Went down to dust be - side Thee!
of Thy peace, By which a - lone we choose Thee.
fore Thy cross, To fin - ish Thy sal - va - tion. A - men.

LIFE IN CHRIST: REPENTANCE AND FORGIVENESS

I LAY MY SINS ON JESUS 248

ST. HILDA 7.6.7.6.D.

Justin Heinrich Knecht, 1793
and Edward Husband, 1871

Horatius Bonar, 1843

1 I lay my sins on Je-sus, The spot-less Lamb of God;
2 I lay my wants on Je-sus, All full-ness dwells in Him;
3 I rest my soul on Je-sus, This wea-ry soul of mine;
4 I long to be, like Je-sus, Meek, lov-ing, low-ly, mild;

He bears them all, and frees us From the ac-curs-ed load.
He heals all my dis-eas-es, He doth my soul re-deem.
His right hand me em-brac-es, I on His breast re-cline.
I long to be, like Je-sus, The Fa-ther's ho-ly child.

I bring my guilt to Je-sus, To wash my crim-son stains,
I lay my griefs on Je-sus, My bur-dens and my cares;
I love the name of Je-sus: Im-man-uel, Christ, the Lord;
I long to be with Je-sus, A-mid the heav'n-ly throng,

White in His blood most pre-cious, Till not a spot re-mains.
He from them all re-leas-es, He all my sor-rows shares.
Like fra-grance on the breez-es His name a-broad is poured.
To sing with saints His prais-es, To learn the an-gels' song.

LIFE IN CHRIST: REPENTANCE AND FORGIVENESS

249 FAITH IS A LIVING POWER

SESSIONS L.M.

Petrus Herbert, 1566
Der Glaub' ist ein' lebendig' Kraft
Tr. Composite

Luther Orlando Emerson, 1847

1 Faith is a liv - ing power from heav'n Which grasps the
2 Faith finds in Christ what - e'er we need To save and
3 Faith to the con - science whis - pers peace; And bids the
4 Such faith in us, O God, im - plant, And to our

prom - ise God has giv'n; Se - cure - ly fixed on
strength - en, guide and feed; Strong in His grace it
mourn - er's sigh - ing cease; By faith the chil - dren's
prayers Thy fa - vor grant, In Je - sus Christ, Thy

Christ a - lone, A trust that can - not be o'er - thrown.
joys to share His cross, in hope His crown to wear.
right we claim, And call up - on our Fa - ther's name.
sav - ing Son, Who is our fount of health a - lone. A - men.

250 WE WALK BY FAITH

LOBT GOTT C.M.

Henry Alford†, 1844

Nicolaus Herman, 1554

1 We walk by faith, and not by sight; No gra - cious words we hear From Him who
2 We may not touch His hands and side, Nor fol - low where He trod; But in His
3 Help then, O Lord, our un - be - lief; And may our faith a - bound, To call on
4 That, when our life of faith is done, In realms of clear - er light We may be -

LIFE IN CHRIST: FAITH AND ASSURANCE

spake as man ne'er spake; But we be-lieve Him near, But we be-lieve Him near.
prom - ise we re - joice, And cry, "My Lord and God!" And cry, "My Lord and God!"
Thee when Thou art near, And seek where Thou art found; And seek where Thou art found:
hold Thee as Thou art, With full and end-less sight, With full and end-less sight.

MY FAITH LOOKS UP TO THEE 251

OLIVET 6.6.4.6.6.6.4.

Ray Palmer, 1830

Lowell Mason, 1832

1 My faith looks up to Thee, Thou Lamb of Cal - va - ry,
2 May Thy rich grace im - part Strength to my faint - ing heart,
3 While life's dark maze I tread, And griefs a - round me spread,
4 When ends life's tran - sient dream, When death's cold, sul - len stream

Sav - ior di - vine: Now hear me while I pray, Take all my
My zeal in - spire; As Thou hast died for me, O may my
Be Thou my guide; Bid dark-ness turn to day, Wipe sor - row's
Shall o'er me roll, Blest Sav - ior, then, in love, Fear and dis -

guilt a - way, O let me from this day Be whol - ly Thine.
love to Thee, Pure, warm, and change-less be, A liv - ing fire.
tears a - way, Nor let me ev - er stray From Thee a - side.
trust re - move; O bear me safe a - bove, A ran - somed soul. A - men.

LIFE IN CHRIST: FAITH AND ASSURANCE

252 IN HEAVENLY LOVE ABIDING

NYLAND 7.6.7.6.D.

Anna Laetita Waring, 1850

Finnish Folk Melody
Harmonized by David Evans, 1927

1 In heav'n-ly love a - bid - ing, No change my heart shall fear,
2 Wher - ev - er He may guide me, No want shall turn me back;
3 Green pas - tures are be - fore me, Which yet I have not seen;

And safe is such con - fid - ing, For noth - ing chan - ges here.
My Shep-herd is be - side me, And noth - ing can I lack.
Bright skies will soon be o'er me, Where the dark clouds have been.

The storm may roar with - out me, My heart may low be laid;
His wis - dom ev - er wak - eth, His sight is nev - er dim;
My hope I can - not meas - ure, The path to life is free;

But God is round a - bout me, And can I be dis-mayed?
He knows the way He tak - eth, And I will walk with Him.
My Sav - ior has my treas - ure, And He will walk with me.

LIFE IN CHRIST: FAITH AND ASSURANCE

SOMETIMES A LIGHT SURPRISES 253

RHYDDID 7.6.7.6.D.

William Cowper†, 1779

J. Parry's *Peroriaeth Hyfryd*, 1837

1. Some-times a light sur - pris - es The Chris - tian while he sings;
2. In ho - ly con - tem - pla - tion We sweet - ly then pur - sue
3. It can bring with it noth-ing But He will bear us through;
4. Though vine nor fig tree nei - ther Their wont - ed fruit should bear,

It is the Lord who ris - es With heal - ing in His wings;
The theme of God's sal - va - tion, And find it ev - er new;
Who gives the lil - ies cloth-ing Will clothe His peo - ple, too;
Though all the fields should with-er, Nor flocks nor herds be there;

When com-forts are de - clin - ing, He grants the soul a - gain A
Set free from pres - ent sor - row, We cheer-ful - ly can say, Let
Be - neath the spread-ing heav-ens No crea - ture but is fed, And
Yet God, the same a - bid - ing, His praise shall tune my voice; For

sea - son of clear shin - ing, To cheer it af - ter rain.
the un-known to - mor - row Bring with it what it may.
He who feeds the ra - vens Will give His chil - dren bread.
while in Him con - fid - ing I can - not but re - joice.

LIFE IN CHRIST: FAITH AND ASSURANCE

254 ROCK OF AGES! CLEFT FOR ME

TOPLADY 7.7.7.7.7.7.

Augustus Montague Toplady, 1776
Altered by Thomas Cotterill, 1815

Thomas Hastings, 1830

1 Rock of A - ges! cleft for me, Let me hide my - self in Thee;
2 Should my tears for - ev - er flow, Should my zeal no lan - guor know,
3 While I draw this fleet-ing breath, When mine eye - lids close in death,

Let the wa - ter and the blood From Thy wound - ed side which flowed,
This for sin could not a - tone: Thou must save, and Thou a - lone;
When I rise to worlds un - known, And be - hold Thee on Thy throne,

Be of sin the dou - ble cure, Save from wrath, and make me pure.
In my hand no price I bring, Sim - ply to Thy cross I cling.
Rock of a - ges! cleft for me! Let me hide my - self in Thee. A - men.

255 HAVE FAITH IN GOD, MY HEART

SOUTHWELL S.M.

Bryn A. Rees, b. 1911

W. Damon's *Psalms*, 1579

1 Have faith in God, my heart; Trust and be un - a - fraid;
2 Have faith in God, my mind, Though oft thy light burns low;
3 Have faith in God, my soul; His cross for - ev - er stands,
4 Lord Je - sus, make me whole; Grant me no rest - ing place,

LIFE IN CHRIST: FAITH AND ASSURANCE

God will ful - fill in ev - ery part Each prom-ise He has made.
God's mer - cy holds a wis - er plan Than thou canst ful - ly know.
And nei - ther life nor death can pluck His chil-dren from His hands.
Un - til I rest, heart, mind, and soul, The cap-tive of Thy grace. A-men.

FATHER, I STRETCH MY HANDS TO THEE 256

CONSOLATION (MORNING SONG) C.M.

Folk Hymn
J. Wyeth's *Repository of Sacred Music,*
Part Second, 1813

Charles Wesley, 1741

1 Fa - ther, I stretch my hands to Thee, No
2 What did Thy on - ly Son en - dure, Be -
3 O Je - sus, could I this be - lieve, I
4 Au - thor of faith, to Thee I lift My

oth - er help I know; If Thou with - draw Thy -
fore I drew my breath! What pain, what la - bor
now should feel Thy power; Now my poor soul Thou
wea - ry, long - ing eyes; O let me now re -

self from me, Ah, whith - er shall I go?
to se - cure My soul from end - less death!
wouldst re - trieve, Nor let me wait one hour.
ceive that gift, My soul with - out it dies. A - men.

LIFE IN CHRIST: FAITH AND ASSURANCE

257 UNTO THE HILLS AROUND

SANDON 10.4.10.4.10.10.

Based on Psalm 121
John Campbell, 1866

Charles Purday, 1860

1 Un - to the hills a-round do I lift up My long - ing eyes:
2 He will not suf - fer that thy foot be moved: Safe shalt thou be.
3 Je - ho - vah is Him-self thy keep-er true, Thy change-less shade;
4 From ev - ery e - vil shall He keep thy soul, From ev - ery sin:

O whence for me shall my sal - va - tion come, From whence a - rise?
No care-less slum - ber shall His eye-lids close, Who keep-eth thee.
Je - ho - vah thy de - fense on thy right hand Him - self hath made.
Je - ho - vah shall pre-serve thy go - ing out, Thy com - ing in.

From God the Lord doth come my cer - tain aid,
Be - hold, He sleep - eth not, He slum - b'reth ne'er,
And thee no sun by day shall ev - er smite;
A - bove thee watch - ing, He whom we a - dore

From God the Lord who heav'n and earth hath made.
Who keep - eth Is - rael in His ho - ly care.
No moon shall harm thee in the si - lent night.
Shall keep thee hence - forth, yea, for - ev - er - more. A - men.

LIFE IN CHRIST: FAITH AND ASSURANCE

I TO THE HILLS WILL LIFT MINE EYES 258
DUNDEE C.M.

Based on Psalm 121
Scottish Psalter, 1650

Scottish Psalter, 1615

1 I to the hills will lift mine eyes, from whence doth come mine aid.
2 Thy foot He'll not let slide, nor will He slum - ber that thee keeps.
3 The Lord thee keeps, the Lord thy shade on thy right hand doth stay:
4 The Lord shall keep thy soul; He shall pre - serve thee from all ill.

My safe - ty com - eth from the Lord, who heav'n and earth hath made.
Be - hold, He that keeps Is - ra - el, He slum - bers not, nor sleeps.
The moon by night thee shall not smite, nor yet the sun by day.
Hence-forth thy go - ing out and in God keep for - ev - er will. A - men.

O FOR A FAITH THAT WILL NOT SHRINK 259
EVAN C.M.

William H. Havergal, d. 1870
Arranged by Lowell Mason, 1850

William Hiley Bathurst, 1831

1 O for a faith that will not shrink Though pressed by man - y a foe,
2 That will not mur - mur nor com-plain Be - neath the chas-tening rod,
3 A faith that shines more bright and clear When tem-pests rage with - out,
4 A faith that keeps the nar - row way Till life's last spark is fled,
5 Lord, give me such a faith as this, And then, what-e'er may come,

That will not trem - ble on the brink Of pov - er - ty or woe.
But in the hour of grief or pain Can lean up - on its God.
That, when in dan - ger, knows no fear, In dark-ness feels no doubt.
And with a pure and heav'n-ly ray Lights up the dy - ing bed.
I'll taste e'en here the hal-lowed bliss Of an e - ter - nal home. A - men.

LIFE IN CHRIST: FAITH AND ASSURANCE

260 HOW FIRM A FOUNDATION

BELLEVUE (FOUNDATION) 11.11.11.11.

Folk Hymn
Joseph Funk's *Genuine Church Music*, 1832 (*Harmonia Sacra*)

"K"† in John Rippon's *Selection of Hymns*, 1787

1 How firm a foun-da-tion, ye saints of the Lord,
2 "Fear not, I am with thee, O be not dis-mayed;
3 "When through the deep wa-ters I call thee to go,
4 "When through fi-ery tri-als thy path-way shall lie,
5 "The soul that on Je-sus hath leaned for re-pose,

Is laid for your faith in His ex-cel-lent Word!
For I am thy God, and will still give thee aid;
The riv-ers of sor-row shall not o-ver-flow;
My grace, all-suf-fi-cient, shall be thy sup-ply;
I will not, I will not de-sert to his foes;

What more can He say than to you He hath said,
I'll strength-en thee, help thee, and cause thee to stand,
For I will be with thee, thy trou-bles to bless,
The flame shall not hurt thee; I on-ly de-sign
That soul, though all hell should en-deav-or to shake,

To you who for ref-uge to Je-sus have fled?
Up-held by My righ-teous, om-nip-o-tent hand.
And sanc-ti-fy to thee thy deep-est dis-tress.
Thy dross to con-sume, and thy gold to re-fine.
I'll nev-er, no nev-er, no nev-er for-sake!"

LIFE IN CHRIST: FAITH AND ASSURANCE

HOW FIRM A FOUNDATION 261

ADESTE FIDELES 11.11.11.11.

"K"† in John Rippon's *Selection of Hymns*, 1787

John Francis Wade? c. 1740-43

1 How firm a foun-da-tion, ye saints of the Lord, Is
2 "Fear not, I am with thee, O be not dis-mayed; For
3 "When through the deep wa-ters I call thee to go, The
4 "The soul that on Je-sus hath leaned for re-pose, I

laid for your faith in His ex-cel-lent Word! What more can He
I am thy God, and will still give thee aid; I'll strength-en thee,
riv-ers of sor-row shall not o-ver-flow; For I will be
will not, I will not de-sert to his foes; That soul, though all

say than to you He hath said, Who un-to the Sav-ior for
help thee,and cause thee to stand, Up-held by My righ-teous,om-
with thee,thy trou-bles to bless, And sanc-ti-fy to thee thy
hell should en-deav-or to shake, I'll nev-er, no nev-er, no

ref-uge have fled? Who un-to the Sav-ior for ref-uge have fled?
nip-o-tent hand,Up-held by My righ-teous,om-nip-o-tent hand.
deep-est dis-tress, And sanc-ti-fy to thee thy deep-est dis-tress.
nev-er for-sake, I'll nev-er, no nev-er, no nev-er for-sake!"

LIFE IN CHRIST: FAITH AND ASSURANCE

262 FAITH OF OUR FATHERS

ST. CATHERINE L.M. with Refrain

Frederick W. Faber, 1849

Henri Frederick Hemy, 1864
Adapted by James G. Walton, 1874

1 Faith of our fa - thers, liv - ing still In spite of dun-geon, fire, and sword;
2 Our fa - thers, chained in pris-ons dark, Were still in heart and con-science free:
3 Faith of our fa - thers, we will love Both friend and foe in all our strife;

O how our hearts beat high with joy When-e'er we hear that glo-rious word.
How sweet would be their chil-dren's fate, If they, like them, could die for thee.
And preach thee, too, as love knows how, By kind-ly words and vir-tuous life:

Faith of our fa - thers, ho - ly faith. We will be true to thee till death!
Faith of our fa - thers, ho - ly faith. We will be true to thee till death!
Faith of our fa - thers, ho - ly faith. We will be true to thee till death!

263 O HOLY SAVIOR, FRIEND UNSEEN

INTEGER VITAE 8.8.8.6.

Charlotte Elliott, 1836

Friedrich F. Flemming, 1811

1 O ho - ly Sav - ior, friend un - seen, The faint, the weak on Thee may
2 Blest with com-mu - nion so di - vine, Take what Thou wilt, shall I re -
3 Though faith and hope a - while be tried, I ask not, need not aught be -
4 Blest is my lot, what - e'er be - fall; What can dis - turb me, who ap -

LIFE IN CHRIST: FAITH AND ASSURANCE

lean, Help me, through-out life's var - y-ing scene, By faith to cling to Thee.
pine, When as the branch-es to the vine, My soul would cling to Thee?
side; How safe, how calm, how sat - is - fied, The souls that cling to Thee?
pall, While as my strength, my rock, my all, Sav-ior, I cling to Thee?

WHEN IN THE HOUR OF UTMOST NEED 264

WENN WIR IN HÖCHSTEN NÖTEN SEIN L.M.

Paul Eber, 1566
Wenn wir in höchsten Nöten sein
Tr. Catherine Winkworth, 1858

Adapted from *Les commandemens de Dieu*
La forme des prieres . . . , Strasbourg, 1545
In German, Wittenberg, 1567

1 When in the hour of ut - most need We know not
2 Then this our com - fort is a - lone, That we may
3 That so with all our hearts we may Once more our

where to look for aid, When days and nights of anx - ious
meet be - fore Thy throne, And cry, O faith - ful God, to
glad thanks - giv - ings pay, And walk o - be - dient to Thy

thought Nor help nor coun - sel yet have brought,
Thee For res - cue from our mis - er - y:
Word, And now and ev - er praise the Lord. A - men.

LIFE IN CHRIST: FAITH AND ASSURANCE

265 MY JESUS, I LOVE THEE

GORDON 11.11.11.11.

William Ralph Featherston, c. 1862

Adoniram J. Gordon, 1876

1 My Je - sus, I love Thee, I know Thou art mine,
2 I love Thee, be - cause Thou hast first lov - ed me,
3 I will love Thee in life, I will love Thee in death,
4 In man - sions of glo - ry and end - less de - light,

For Thee all the fol - lies of sin I re - sign;
And pur - chased my par - don on Cal - va - ry's tree;
And praise Thee as long as Thou lend - est me breath;
I'll ev - er a - dore Thee in heav - en so bright;

My gra - cious Re - deem - er, my Sav - ior art Thou;
I love Thee for wear - ing the thorns on Thy brow;
And say when the death - dew lies cold on my brow,
I'll sing with the glit - ter - ing crown on my brow,

If ev - er I loved Thee, my Je - sus, 'tis now.

LIFE IN CHRIST: LOVE AND GRATITUDE

JESUS, THY BOUNDLESS LOVE TO ME 266

STELLA 8.8.8.8.8.8.

Paul Gerhardt, 1653
O Jesu Christ, mein schönstes Licht
Tr. John Wesley, 1739

Easy Tunes for Catholic Schools, 1852

1 Je - sus, Thy bound-less love to me No thought can
2 O Love, how cheer-ing is Thy ray! All pain be -
3 O draw me, Sav - ior, af - ter Thee; So shall I
4 In suf - fering be Thy love my peace, In weak - ness

reach, no tongue de-clare; O knit my thank-ful heart to Thee,
fore Thy pres - ence flies; Care, an - guish, sor - row melt a - way
run and nev - er tire: With gra - cious words still com - fort me;
be Thy love my power; And when the storms of life shall cease,

And reign with - out a ri - val there. Thine whol - ly,
Wher - e'er Thy heal - ing beams a - rise: O Je - sus,
Be Thou my hope, my sole de - sire. Free me from
Je - sus, in that im - por - tant hour, In death as

Thine a - lone I am: Be Thou a - lone my con - stant flame.
noth - ing may I see, Noth-ing hear, feel, or think but Thee!
ev - ery weight: nor fear Nor sin can come, if Thou art here.
life be Thou my guide, And save me, who for me hast died! A-men.

LIFE IN CHRIST: LOVE AND GRATITUDE

267 MY GOD, I THANK THEE

WENTWORTH 8.4.8.4.8.4.

Adelaide Anne Procter, 1858

Frederick Charles Maker, 1876

1 My God, I thank Thee, who hast made The earth so bright,
So full of splen-dor and of joy, Beau - ty and light,
So man - y glo-rious things are here, No - ble and right.

2 I thank Thee, too, that Thou hast made Joy to a - bound,
So man - y gen - tle thoughts and deeds Cir - cling us round;
That in the dark-est spot of earth Some love is found.

3 I thank Thee more that all our joy Is touched with pain;
That shad-ows fall on bright-est hours, That thorns re - main,
So that earth's bliss may be our guide, And not our chain.

4 I thank Thee, Lord, that Thou hast kept The best in store;
We have e - nough, yet not too much To long for more,
A yearn-ing for a deep - er peace Not known be - fore. A - men.

268 THE SAVIOR DIED, BUT ROSE AGAIN

WINCHESTER OLD C.M.

Based on Romans 8:34-39
Scottish Paraphrases, 1781

T. Est's *Whole Booke of Psalmes,* 1592

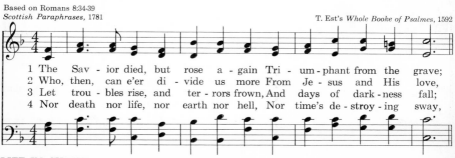

1 The Sav - ior died, but rose a - gain Tri - um-phant from the grave;

2 Who, then, can e'er di - vide us more From Je - sus and His love,

3 Let trou - bles rise, and ter - rors frown, And days of dark - ness fall;

4 Nor death nor life, nor earth nor hell, Nor time's de - stroy - ing sway,

LIFE IN CHRIST: LOVE AND GRATITUDE

And pleads our cause at God's right hand, Om - nip - o - tent to save.
Or break the sa - cred chain that binds The earth to heav'n a - bove?
Through Him all dan - gers we'll de - fy, And more than con - quer all.
Can e'er ef - face us from His heart, Or make His love de - cay. A - men.

O LOVE THAT WILT NOT LET ME GO 269

ST. MARGARET 8.8.8.8.6.

George Matheson, 1882   Albert Lister Peace, 1884

1 O Love that wilt not let me go, I rest my wea - ry soul in
2 O Light that fol - low'st all my way, I yield my flick'ring torch to
3 O Joy that seek - est me through pain, I can - not close my heart to
4 O Cross that lift - est up my head, I dare not ask to fly from

Thee; I give Thee back the life I owe, That in Thine
Thee; My heart re - stores its bor - rowed ray, That in Thy
Thee; I trace the rain - bow through the rain, And feel the
Thee; I lay in dust life's glo - ry dead, And from the

o - cean depths its flow May rich - er, full - er be.
sun - shine's blaze its day May bright - er, fair - er be.
prom - ise is not vain That morn shall tear - less be.
ground there blos - soms red Life that shall end - less be. A - men.

LIFE IN CHRIST: LOVE AND GRATITUDE

270 GRACIOUS SPIRIT, HOLY GHOST

CAPETOWN 7.7.7.5.

Christopher Wordsworth, 1862

Friedrich Filitz, 1847

1 Gra - cious Spir - it, Ho - ly Ghost, Taught by Thee, we cov - et most
2 Faith, that moun-tains could re-move, Tongues of earth or heav'n a - bove,
3 Love is kind, and suf - fers long, Love is meek, and thinks no wrong,
4 Proph-e - cy will fade a - way, Melt - ing in the light of day;
5 Faith and hope and love we see, Join - ing hand in hand, a - gree;

Of Thy gifts at Pen - te - cost, Ho - ly, heav'n-ly love.
Knowl-edge, all things, emp - ty prove, With-out heav'n-ly love.
Love than death it - self more strong; There-fore give us love.
Love will ev - er with us stay; There-fore give us love.
But the great-est of the three, And the best, is love. A - men.

LIFE IN CHRIST: LOVE AND GRATITUDE

271 PEACE, PERFECT PEACE

PAX TECUM 10.10.

Edward Henry Bickersteth, 1875

George Thomas Caldbeck, 1877

1 Peace, per - fect peace, in this dark world of sin?
2 Peace, per - fect peace, by throng - ing du - ties pressed?
3 Peace, per - fect peace, with loved ones far a - way?
4 Peace, per - fect peace, our fu - ture all un - known?
5 Peace, per - fect peace, death shad - 'wing us and ours?

The blood of Je - sus whis - pers peace with - in.
To do the will of Je - sus, this is rest.
In Je - sus' keep - ing we are safe and they.
Je - sus we know, and He is on the throne.
Je - sus has van-quished death and all its powers.

LIFE IN CHRIST: JOY AND PEACE

O HOW HAPPY ARE THEY 272

NEW CONCORD 6.6.9.6.6.9.

Folk Hymn
Joseph Funk's *Genuine Church Music*, 1832 (*Harmonia Sacra*)

Charles Wesley†, 1749

1 O how hap - py are they Who the Sav - ior o - bey,
2 O that com - fort was mine, When the fa - vor di - vine
3 'Twas a heav - en be - low My Re - deem - er to know,
4 Je - sus all the day long Was my joy and my song;

And have laid up their treas - ures a - bove,
I first found in the blood of the Lamb;
And the an - gels could do noth - ing more,
O that all His sal - va - tion may see!

O what tongue can ex - press The sweet com - fort and peace
When my heart it be - lieved, What a joy it re - ceived,
Than to fall at His feet, And the sto - ry re - peat,
"He hath loved me," I cried, "He hath suf - fered and died,

Of a soul in its ear - li - est love.
What a heav - en in Je - sus His name!
And the lov - er of sin - ners a - dore.
To re - deem such a reb - el as me!"

LIFE IN CHRIST: JOY AND PEACE

273 O THOU, IN WHOSE PRESENCE

ZION'S PILGRIM   11.8.11.8.D.

Joseph Swain, 1791

Folk Hymn
J. Leavitt's *Christian Lyre*, 1831

1 O Thou, in whose pres-ence my soul takes de - light, On whom in af -
2 O why should I wan-der an al - ien from Thee, Or cry in the

flic - tion I call, My com-fort by day, and my song in the night,
des - ert for bread? Thy foes will re - joice when my sor - rows they see,

My hope, my sal - va - tion, my all. Where dost Thou, dear Shep - herd, re -
And smile at the tears I have shed. He looks, and ten thou-sands of

sort with Thy sheep? To feed in the pas-tures of love? Say, why in the
an - gels re - joice, And myr - i - ads wait for His word; He speaks, and e -

LIFE IN CHRIST: JOY AND PEACE

val - ley of death should I weep, Or lone in the wil - der - ness rove?
ter - ni - ty, filled with His voice, Re - ech - oes the praise of the Lord.

DEAR LORD AND FATHER OF MANKIND 274

REST (WHITTIER) 8.6.8.8.6.

John Greenleaf Whittier, 1872

Frederick Charles Maker, 1887

1 Dear Lord and Fa - ther of man - kind, For - give our fool - ish ways;
2 In sim - ple trust like theirs who heard, Be - side the Syr - ian sea,
3 O Sab - bath rest by Gal - i - lee, O calm of hills a - bove,
4 Drop Thy still dews of qui - et - ness, Till all our striv - ings cease;
5 Breathe through the heats of our de - sire Thy cool - ness and Thy balm;

Re - clothe us in our right - ful mind, In pur - er lives Thy
The gra - cious call - ing of the Lord, Let us, like them, with -
Where Je - sus knelt to share with Thee The si - lence of e -
Take from our souls the strain and stress, And let our or - dered
Let sense be dumb, let flesh re - tire; Speak through the earth - quake,

serv - ice find, In deep - er rev - erence, praise.
out a word Rise up and fol - low Thee.
ter - ni - ty, In - ter - pret - ed by love!
lives con - fess The beau - ty of Thy peace.
wind, and fire, O still, small voice of calm! A - men.

LIFE IN CHRIST: JOY AND PEACE

275 ETERNAL SOURCE OF JOYS DIVINE

EDEN (ST. NICHOLAS) C.M.

Anne Steele, 1760

William Henry Havergal, 1853

1 E - ter - nal Source of joys di - vine, To Thee my soul as - pires;
2 My hope, my trust, my life, my Lord, As - sure me of Thy love;
3 Then shall my thank-ful powers re - joice, And tri - umph in my God,

O could I say, "The Lord is mine," 'Tis all my soul de - sires.
O speak the kind, trans-port-ing word, And bid my fears re - move.
Till heav'n-ly rap-ture tune my voice, To spread Thy praise a - broad.

276 PRINCE OF PEACE, CONTROL MY WILL

ALETTA 7.7.7.7.

Mary Ann Serrett Barber, 1838

William Batchelder Bradbury, 1857

1 Prince of Peace, con - trol my will; Bid this strug-gling heart be still;
2 Thou hast bought me with Thy blood, O - pened wide the gate to God:
3 May Thy will, not mine, be done; May Thy will and mine be one;
4 Sav - ior, at Thy feet I fall, Thou my life, my God, my all!

Bid my fears and doubt-ings cease, Hush my spir - it in - to peace.
Peace I ask, but peace must be, Lord, in be - ing one with Thee.
Chase these doubt-ings from my heart, Now Thy per - fect peace im - part.
Let Thy hap - py serv-ant be One for - ev - er - more with Thee. A-men.

LIFE IN CHRIST: JOY AND PEACE

REJOICE, YE PURE IN HEART 277

MARION S.M. with Refrain

Edward Hayes Plumptre, 1865

Arthur Henry Messiter, 1883

1 Re - joice, ye pure in heart, Re - joice, give thanks and sing;
2 Bright youth and snow-crowned age, Strong men and maid - ens meek,
3 With all the an - gel choirs, With all the saints on earth,
4 Yes on, through life's long path, Still chant - ing as ye go,

Your fes - tal ban - ner wave on high, The cross of Christ your King.
Raise high your free ex - ult - ing song, God's won-drous prais - es speak.
Pour out the strains of joy and bliss, True rap - ture, no - blest mirth.
From youth to age, by night and day, In glad - ness and in woe.

Re - joice, re - joice, Re - joice, give thanks and sing. A - men.

Re - joice, re - joice,

5 At last the march shall end,
   The wearied ones shall rest,
   The pilgrims find their Father's house,
   Jerusalem the blest.

6 Praise Him who reigns on high,
   The Lord whom we adore,
   The Father, Son, and Holy Ghost,
   One God for evermore.

LIFE IN CHRIST: JOY AND PEACE

278 THAT MAN HATH PERFECT BLESSEDNESS

DUNFERMLINE C.M.

Based on Psalm 1
Nichol Grieve, 1940

Scottish Psalter, 1615

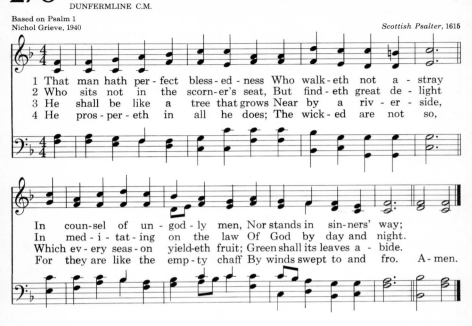

1 That man hath per - fect bless - ed - ness Who walk - eth not a - stray
2 Who sits not in the scorn-er's seat, But find - eth great de - light
3 He shall be like a tree that grows Near by a riv - er - side,
4 He pros - per - eth in all he does; The wick - ed are not so,

In coun-sel of un - god - ly men, Nor stands in sin-ners' way;
In med - i - tat-ing on the law Of God by day and night.
Which ev - ery seas-on yield-eth fruit; Green shall its leaves a - bide.
For they are like the emp-ty chaff By winds swept to and fro. A-men.

5 For evil-doers shall not stand
    When judgment draweth near;
  Nor in assemblies of the just
    Shall godless men appear.

6 The Lord takes knowledge of the way
    In which the righteous go:
  The course which men of sin pursue
    Ends in their overthrow.

LIFE IN CHRIST: JOY AND PEACE

279 BLEST ARE THE PURE IN HEART

FRANCONIA S.M.

J. B. König's *Harmonischer Liederschatz*, 1738
Adapted by William Henry Havergal, 1847

John Keble and Others, 1819 and 1836

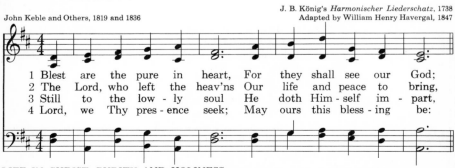

1 Blest are the pure in heart, For they shall see our God;
2 The Lord, who left the heav'ns Our life and peace to bring,
3 Still to the low - ly soul He doth Him - self im - part,
4 Lord, we Thy pres - ence seek; May ours this bless - ing be:

LIFE IN CHRIST: PURITY AND HOLINESS

The se-cret of the Lord is theirs, Their soul is Christ's a - bode.
To dwell in low - li - ness with men, Their pat-tern and their King;
And for His dwell-ing and His throne Choos-eth the pure in heart.
Give us a pure and low - ly heart, A tem - ple fit for Thee. A - men.

PURER IN HEART, O GOD 280

PURER IN HEART 6.4.6.4.6.6.4.4.

Fannie Estelle Davison, 1877

James Henry Fillmore, 1877

1 Pur - er in heart, O God, Help me to be; May I de -
2 Pur - er in heart, O God, Help me to be; Teach me to
3 Pur - er in heart, O God, Help me to be; That I Thy

vote my life Whol - ly to Thee. Watch Thou my way - ward feet,
do Thy will Most lov - ing - ly. Be Thou my friend and guide,
ho - ly face One day may see. Keep me from se - cret sin,

Guide me with coun-sel sweet; Pur - er in heart, Help me to be.
Let me with Thee a-bide; Pur - er in heart, Help me to be.
Reign Thou my soul with-in; Pur - er in heart, Help me to be. A-men.

LIFE IN CHRIST: PURITY AND HOLINESS

281 KEEP THYSELF PURE

PENTECOST L.M.

Adelaide M. Plumtre, 1908

William Boyd, 1864

1 Keep thy - self pure! Christ's sol - dier, hear, Through life's loud
2 Keep thy - self pure! Thrice bless - ed he Whose heart from
3 Keep thy - self pure! For He who died, Him - self for
4 O Ho - ly Spir - it, keep us pure, Grant us Thy

strife, the call rings clear. Thy cap - tain speaks: His
taint of sin is free; His feet shall stand where
thy sake sanc - ti - fied; Then hear Him speak - ing
strength when sins al - lure; Our bod - ies are Thy

word o - bey; So shall thy strength be as thy day.
saints have trod, He with rapt eyes shall see his God.
from the skies, And vic - tor o'er temp - ta - tion rise.
tem - ple, Lord; Be Thou in thought and act a - dored. A - men.

282 WALK IN THE LIGHT

DEDHAM C.M.

Bernard Barton, 1826

Lowell Mason's *Boston Handel and Haydn Society* . . . , 1822

1 Walk in the light! so shalt thou know That fel - low - ship of love
2 Walk in the light! and thou shalt find Thy heart made tru - ly His,
3 Walk in the light! and thou shalt own Thy dark - ness passed a - way,
4 Walk in the light! and thine shall be A path, though thorn - y, bright;

LIFE IN CHRIST: PURITY AND HOLINESS

His Spir-it on-ly can be-stow Who reigns in light a-bove.
Who dwells in cloud-less light en-shrined, In whom no dark-ness is.
Be-cause that light hath on thee shone In which is per-fect day.
For God, by grace, shall dwell in thee, And God Him-self is light.

O FOR A HEART TO PRAISE 283

KILMARNOCK C.M.

Charles Wesley†, 1742

Neil Dougall, 1831

1 O for a heart to praise my God, A
2 A heart re-signed, sub-mis-sive, meek, My
3 A heart in ev-ery thought re-newed, And
4 An hum-ble, low-ly, con-trite heart, Be-
5 Thy na-ture, gra-cious Lord, im-part, Come

heart from sin set free! A heart that's sprin-kled
dear Re-deem-er's throne; Where on-ly Christ is
full of love di-vine; Per-fect, and right, and
liev-ing, true, and clean, Which nei-ther life nor
quick-ly from a-bove, Write Thy new name up-

with the blood So free-ly shed for me.
heard to speak, Where Je-sus reigns a-lone.
pure, and good, A cop-y, Lord, of Thine.
death can part From Him that dwells with-in.
on my heart, Thy new, best name of Love. A-men.

LIFE IN CHRIST: PURITY AND HOLINESS

284 AS THE HART WITH EAGER YEARNING

GENEVA 42   8.7.8.7.7.7.8.8.

Based on Psalm 42
Christine Turner Curtis†, 1939

Pseaumes octante trois . . ., Geneva, 1551
Harmony adapted from Claude Goudimel, 1565

1 As the hart with ea-ger yearn-ing Seeks the cool-ing
2 Day and night in griev-ous an-guish Bit-ter tears have

wa-ter-course, So my soul with ar-dor burn-ing
been my meat, While my long-ing soul doth lan-guish

Longs for God, its heav'n-ly source. When shall I be-hold His
To par-take His man-na sweet. O, my soul, be not dis-

face? When shall I re-ceive His grace? When shall I, His prais-es
mayed: Trust in God, who is our aid; Hope and joy His love pro-

LIFE IN CHRIST: HOPE AND ASPIRATION

voic - ing, Come be - fore Him with re - joic - ing?
vides thee; 'Tis His hand a - lone that guides thee. A - men.

AS PANTS THE HART 285
MARTYRDOM C.M.

Based on Psalm 42
Tate and Brady's *New Version*
of the Psalms, 1696 and 1698

Hugh Wilson, late 18th century
Adapted by Robert Archibald Smith, 1825

1 As pants the hart for cool - ing streams When
2 For Thee, my God, the liv - ing God, My
3 Why rest - less, why cast down, my soul? Trust
4 God of my strength, how long shall I Like
5 Why rest - less, why cast down, my soul? Hope

heat - ed in the chase, So longs my soul, O
thirst - y soul doth pine; O when shall I be -
God, who will em - ploy His aid for thee, and
one for - got - ten mourn, For - lorn, for - sak - en,
still, and thou shalt sing The praise of Him who

God, for Thee, And Thy re - fresh - ing grace.
hold Thy face, Thou Maj - es - ty di - vine?
change these sighs To thank - ful hymns of joy.
and ex - posed To my op - pres - sor's scorn?
is thy God, Thy health's e - ter - nal spring. A - men.

LIFE IN CHRIST: HOPE AND ASPIRATION

286 CHRIST, OF ALL MY HOPES

SONG XIII 7.7.7.7.

Ralph Wardlaw, 1817

Orlando Gibbons, 1623

1 Christ, of all my hopes the ground, Christ, the
2 Let Thy love my heart in - flame; Keep Thy
3 When new tri - umphs of Thy name Swell the
4 Foun - tain of o'er - flow - ing grace, Free - ly

spring of all my joy, Still in Thee may I be
fear be - fore my sight; Be Thy praise my high - est
rap - tured songs a - bove, May I feel the kin - dred
from Thy full - ness give; Till I close my earth - ly

found, Still for Thee my powers em - ploy!
aim; Be Thy smile my chief de - light!
flame, Full of zeal, and full of love!
race, May I prove it "Christ to live!" A - men.

287 O LOVE THAT CASTS OUT FEAR

ST. DENYS 6.6.6.6.

Horatius Bonar, 1861

Frank S. Spinney, 1876

1 O love that casts out fear, O love that casts out sin,
2 True sun - light of the soul, Sur - round me as I go;
3 Great love of God, come in, Well - spring of heav'n - ly peace;
4 Love of the liv - ing God, Of Fa - ther, and of Son,

LIFE IN CHRIST: HOPE AND ASPIRATION

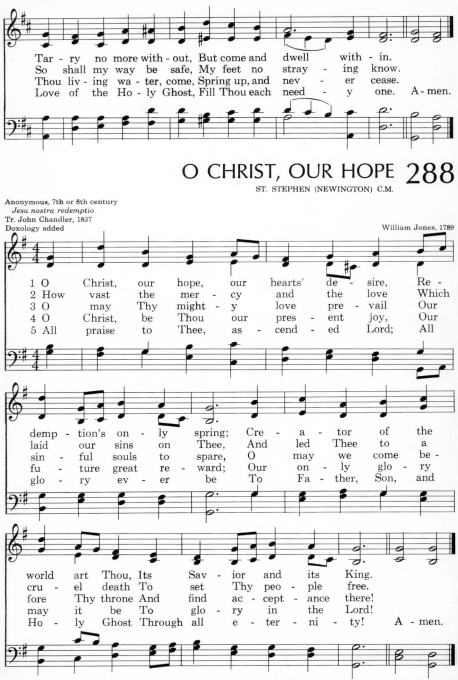

(Previous hymn, final verses)

Tar - ry no more with - out, But come and dwell with - in.
So shall my way be safe, My feet no stray - ing know.
Thou liv - ing wa - ter, come, Spring up, and nev - er cease.
Love of the Ho - ly Ghost, Fill Thou each need - y one. A - men.

O CHRIST, OUR HOPE 288

ST. STEPHEN (NEWINGTON) C.M.

Anonymous, 7th or 8th century
Jesu nostra redemptio
Tr. John Chandler, 1837
Doxology added

William Jones, 1789

1 O Christ, our hope, our hearts' de - sire, Re -
2 How vast the mer - cy and the love Which
3 O may Thy might - y love pre - vail Our
4 O Christ, be Thou our pres - ent joy, Our
5 All praise to Thee, as - cend - ed Lord; All

demp - tion's on - ly spring; Cre - a - tor of the
laid our sins on Thee, And led Thee to a
sin - ful souls to spare, O may we come be -
fu - ture great re - ward; Our on - ly glo - ry
glo - ry ev - er be To Fa - ther, Son, and

world art Thou, Its Sav - ior and its King.
cru - el death To set Thy peo - ple free.
fore Thy throne And find ac - cept - ance there!
may it be To glo - ry in the Lord!
Ho - ly Ghost Through all e - ter - ni - ty! A - men.

LIFE IN CHRIST: HOPE AND ASPIRATION

289 NEARER, MY GOD, TO THEE

BETHANY 6.4.6.4.6.6.6.4.

Sarah Adams†, 1841

Lowell Mason, 1856

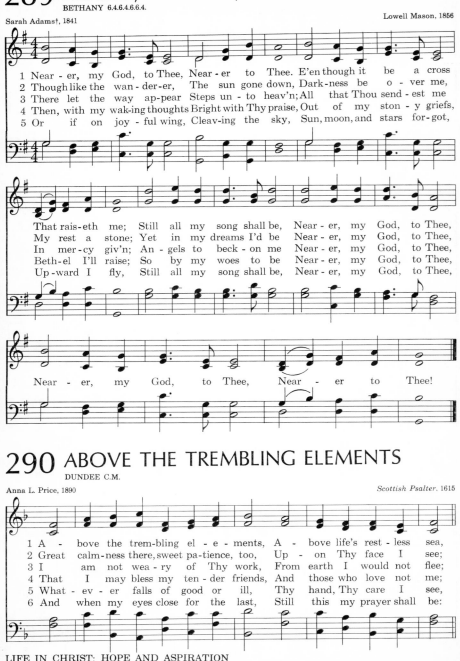

1 Near - er, my God, to Thee, Near - er to Thee. E'en though it be a cross
2 Though like the wan - der - er, The sun gone down, Dark-ness be o - ver me,
3 There let the way ap-pear Steps un - to heav'n; All that Thou send - est me
4 Then, with my wak-ing thoughts Bright with Thy praise, Out of my ston - y griefs,
5 Or if on joy - ful wing, Cleav-ing the sky, Sun, moon, and stars for-got,

That rais-eth me; Still all my song shall be, Near - er, my God, to Thee,
My rest a stone; Yet in my dreams I'd be Near - er, my God, to Thee,
In mer-cy giv'n; An - gels to beck - on me Near - er, my God, to Thee,
Beth-el I'll raise; So by my woes to be Near - er, my God, to Thee,
Up-ward I fly, Still all my song shall be, Near - er, my God, to Thee,

Near - er, my God, to Thee, Near - er to Thee!

290 ABOVE THE TREMBLING ELEMENTS

DUNDEE C.M.

Anna L. Price, 1890

Scottish Psalter, 1615

1 A - bove the trem-bling el - e - ments, A - bove life's rest - less sea,
2 Great calm-ness there, sweet pa-tience, too, Up - on Thy face I see;
3 I am not wea - ry of Thy work, From earth I would not flee;
4 That I may bless my ten - der friends, And those who love not me;
5 What - ev - er falls of good or ill, Thy hand, Thy care I see,
6 And when my eyes close for the last, Still this my prayer shall be:

LIFE IN CHRIST: HOPE AND ASPIRATION

Dear Sav - ior, lift my spir - it up, O lift me up to Thee!
I would be calm and pa - tient, Lord, O lift me up to Thee!
But while I walk and while I serve, O lift me up to Thee!
O lift me high a - bove my - self, Dear Je - sus, up to Thee!
And while these var - ied deal-ings pass, O lift me up to Thee!
Dear Sav - ior, lift my spir - it up, And lift me up to Thee! A-men.

ALL MY HOPE ON GOD IS FOUNDED 291

MEINE HOFFNUNG 8.7.8.7.3.3.7.

Joachim Neander, 1680
Meine Hoffnung stehet feste
Paraphrase by Robert Bridges, 1899

Joachim Neander, 1680

1 All my hope on God is found-ed; He doth still my trust re - new.
2 Pride of man and earth - ly glo - ry, Sword and crown be - tray his trust;
3 God's great good-ness aye en - dur-eth, Deep His wis-dom pass - ing thought:
4 Dai - ly doth th' al-might-y Giv - er Boun-teous gifts on us be - stow.
5 Still from man to God e - ter - nal Sac - ri - fice of praise be done,

Me through change and chance He guid-eth, On - ly good and on - ly true.
What with care and toil he build-eth, Tower and tem - ple fall to dust.
Splen - dor, light and life at - tend Him, Beau-ty spring-eth out of nought.
His de - sire our soul de - light-eth, Plea-sure leads us where we go.
High a - bove all prais - es prais-ing For the gift of Christ His Son.

God un-known, He a - lone Calls my heart to be His own.
But God's power Hour by hour, Is my tem - ple and my tower.
Ev - er - more From His store New-born worlds rise and a - dore.
Love doth stand At His hand; Joy doth wait on His com-mand.
Christ doth call One and all: Ye who fol - low shall not fall. A - men.

LIFE IN CHRIST: HOPE AND ASPIRATION

292 THE SANDS OF TIME ARE SINKING

RUTHERFORD 7.6.7.6.7.6.7.5.

Annie Ross Cousin†, 1857

Edward Francis Rimbault, 1867

1 The sands of time are sink - ing, The dawn of heav - en breaks,
2 O Christ! He is the foun - tain, The deep sweet well of love!
3 I've wres - tled on towards heav - en, 'Gainst storm, and wind, and tide;
4 With mer - cy and with judg - ment My web of time He wove,
5 O! I am my Be - lov - ed's, And my Be-loved is mine!
6 The bride eyes not her gar - ment, But her dear bride-groom's face;

The sum - mer morn I've sighed for, The fair sweet morn a - wakes:
The streams on earth I've tast - ed, More deep I'll drink a - bove:
Now, like a wea - ry trav - eler, That lean - eth on his guide,
And aye the dews of sor - row Were lus - tred by His love;
He brings a poor vile sin - ner In - to His house of wine:
I will not gaze at glo - ry, But on my King of grace;

Dark, dark hath been the mid - night, But day - spring is at hand,
There, to an o - cean full - ness, His mer - cy doth ex - pand,
A - mid the shades of eve - ning, While sinks life's lin-gering sand,
I'll bless the hand that guid - ed, I'll bless the heart that planned,
I stand up - on His mer - it, I know no oth - er stand,
Not at the crown He giv - eth, But on His pierc - ed hand:

And glo - ry, glo - ry dwell - eth In Em - man - uel's land.
And glo - ry, glo - ry dwell - eth In Em - man - uel's land.
I hail the glo - ry dawn - ing In Em - man - uel's land.
When throned where glo - ry dwell - eth, In Em - man - uel's land.
Not e'en where glo - ry dwell - eth In Em - man - uel's land.
The Lamb is all the glo - ry Of Em - man - uel's land.

LIFE IN CHRIST: HOPE AND ASPIRATION

LORD, I WANT TO BE A CHRISTIAN 293

LORD, I WANT TO BE A CHRISTIAN Irregular

Negro Spiritual

Traditional Melody

1 Lord, I want to be a Chris-tian In my heart, in my heart;
2 Lord, I want to be more lov - ing In my heart, in my heart;
3 Lord, I want to be more ho - ly In my heart, in my heart;
4 Lord, I want to be like Je - sus In my heart, in my heart;

Lord, I want to be a Chris - tian In my heart.
Lord, I want to be more lov - ing In my heart.
Lord, I want to be more ho - ly In my heart.
Lord, I want to be like Je - sus In my heart.

In my heart, In my heart,
In my heart, In my heart,

Lord, I want to be a Chris - tian In my heart.
Lord, I want to be more lov - ing In my heart.
Lord, I want to be more ho - ly In my heart.
Lord, I want to be like Je - sus In my heart.

LIFE IN CHRIST: HOPE AND ASPIRATION

294 ON JORDAN'S STORMY BANKS I STAND

BOUND FOR THE PROMISED LAND C.M. with Refrain

Folk Hymn

Samuel Stennett, 1787

W. Walker's *Southern Harmony*, 1835

1 On   Jor-dan's storm-y banks I stand, And cast a wish-ful   eye,
2 There gen-erous fruits that nev-er fail, On trees im-mor-tal grow;
3 All   o'er those wide ex-tend-ed plains Shines one e-ter-nal day;
4 When shall I   reach that hap-py place, And be for-ev-er blest?
5 Filled with de-light, my rap-tured soul Can here no long-er stay:

To   Ca-naan's fair and hap-py land, Where my   pos-ses-sions lie.
There rocks and hills and brooks and vales, With milk and hon-ey flow.
There God the sun for-ev-er reigns, And scat-ters night a-way.
When shall I   see my Fa-ther's face, And in   His bos-om rest?
Though Jor-dan's waves a-round me roll, Fear-less I'd launch a-way.

REFRAIN

I'm bound for the prom-ised land,   I'm bound for the prom-ised land;

O   who will come and go with me, I'm bound for the prom-ised land.

LIFE IN CHRIST: HOPE AND ASPIRATION

HOPE OF THE WORLD 295

GENEVA 12 (DONNE SECOURS, SEIGNEUR) 11.10.11.10.

Pseaumes octante trois . . . . , Geneva, 1551
Harmony adapted from Claude Goudimel, 1565

Georgia Harkness, 1953

1 Hope of the world, Thou Christ of great com - pas - sion,
2 Hope of the world, God's gift from high - est heav - en,
3 Hope of the world, a - foot on dust - y high - ways,
4 Hope of the world, who by Thy cross didst save us,
5 Hope of the world, O Christ, o'er death vic - to - rious,

Speak to our fear - ful hearts by con - flict
Bring - ing to hun - gry souls the bread of
Show - ing to wan - dering souls the path of
From death and dark de - spair, from sin and
Who by this sign didst con - quer grief and

rent; Save us, Thy peo - ple, from con - sum - ing pas - sion,
life, Still let Thy Spir - it un - to us be giv - en
light; Walk Thou be - side us lest the tempt-ing by - ways
guilt; We ren - der back the love Thy mer - cy gave us;
pain, We would be faith - ful to Thy gos - pel glo - rious:

Who by our own false hopes and aims are spent.
To heal earth's wounds and end her bit - ter strife.
Lure us a - way from Thee to end - less night.
Take Thou our lives and use them as Thou wilt.
Thou art our Lord! Thou dost for - ev - er reign! A - men.

LIFE IN CHRIST: HOPE AND ASPIRATION

296 SWEET HOUR OF PRAYER

SWEET HOUR L.M.D.

Anonymous, c. 1840   William Batchelder Bradbury, c. 1861

1 Sweet hour of prayer, sweet hour of prayer, That calls me from a world of care,
2 Sweet hour of prayer, sweet hour of prayer, The joys I feel, the bliss I share,
3 Sweet hour of prayer, sweet hour of prayer, Thy wings shall my pe - ti - tion bear

And bids me at my Fa-ther's throne Make all my wants and wish-es known;
Of those whose anx-ious spir - its burn With strong de-sires for thy re-turn!
To Him whose truth and faith-ful-ness En - gage the wait - ing soul to bless;

In sea-sons of dis - tress and grief, My soul has oft - en found re - lief;
With such I has - ten to the place Where God my Sav - ior shows His face,
And since He bids me seek His face, Be - lieve His Word and trust His grace,

And oft es-caped the tempt-er's snare, By thy re-turn, sweet hour of prayer!
And glad - ly take my sta - tion there, And wait for thee, sweet hour of prayer!
I'll cast on Him my ev - ery care, And wait for thee, sweet hour of prayer!

LIFE IN CHRIST: PRAYER

PRAYER IS THE SOUL'S SINCERE DESIRE 297

SHADDICK C.M.

James Montgomery, 1818

Bates Gilbert Burt, 1941

1 Prayer is the soul's sin - cere de - sire, Ut - ter'd or un - ex - press'd,
2 Prayer is the bur - den of a sigh, The fall - ing of a tear;
3 Prayer is the sim - plest form of speech That in - fant lips can try,
4 Prayer is the con - trite sin - ner's voice Re - turn - ing from his ways,
5 Prayer is the Chris-tian's vi - tal breath, The Chris-tian's na - tive air,

The mo - tion of a hid - den fire That trem - bles in the breast.
The up - ward glanc-ing of an eye When none but God is near.
Prayer the sub - lim - est strains that reach The Maj - es - ty on high!
While an - gels in their songs re - joice, And cry, "Be-hold, he prays!"
His watch-word at the gates of death; He en - ters heav'n with prayer.

O GOD OF MERCY! HEARKEN NOW 298

MENDON L.M.

Emily V. Clark, 1892

"German Air" in S. Dyer's *Selection of Sacred Music*, 1825

1 O God of mer - cy! heark-en now; Be - fore Thy throne we hum - bly bow;
2 We seek Thee where Thou dwell'st on high, Be-yond the glit - t'ring, star - ry sky:
3 Be ours the hearts and hands to bless The sor-r'wing sons of wretch-ed - ness;
4 Where pov-er - ty in pain must lie, Where lit-tle suf - f'ring chil - dren cry,
5 Be Thou, O God e - ter - nal, blest, Thy ho - ly name on earth con-fessed!

With heart and voice to Thee we cry, For all on earth who suf - f'ring lie.
We find Thee where Thou dwell'st be-low Be-side the beds of want and woe.
Send Thou the help we can-not give; Bid dy-ing souls a - rise and live.
Bid us haste forth as called by Thee, And in Thy poor, Thy-self to see.
Ech - o Thy praise from ev - ery shore For - ev - er and for - ev - er - more.

LIFE IN CHRIST: PRAYER

299 LORD, WHAT A CHANGE WITHIN US

FFIGYSBREN 10.10.10.10.

Richard C. Trench, c. 1856
Arranged by William Pierson Merrill, 1907

Welsh Hymn Melody

1 Lord, what a change with - in us one short hour
2 We kneel, and all a - round us seems to lower;
3 Why should we ev - er weak or heart - less be,

Spent in Thy pres - ence will pre - vail to make;
We rise, and all, the dis - tant and the near,
Why are we ev - er o - ver - borne with care,

What heav - y bur - dens from our bos - oms take,
Stands forth in sun - ny out - line, brave and clear;
Anx - ious or trou - bled, when with us is prayer,

What parch - ed fields re - fresh as with a shower!
We kneel, how weak; we rise, how full of power.
And joy, and strength, and cour - age are with Thee?

LIFE IN CHRIST: PRAYER

BE THOU MY VISION 300

SLANE 10.10.9.10.

Ancient Irish
Rob tu mo bhoile, a Comdi cride
Tr. Mary Byrne, 1905
Versified by Eleanor Hull, 1912

Irish Traditional Melody
Harmony by Martin Shaw, 1925
Arrangement slightly altered

1 Be Thou my vi - sion, O Lord of my heart;
2 Be Thou my wis - dom, be Thou my true word;
3 Be Thou my buck - ler, my sword for the fight;
4 Rich - es I heed not, nor man's emp - ty praise;
5 High King of heav - en, when vic - t'ry is won

Naught be all else to me save that Thou art,
I ev - er with Thee, and Thou with me, Lord;
Be Thou my dig - ni - ty, Thou my de - light,
Thou my in - her - it - ance, now and al - ways:
May I reach heav - en's joys, O bright heav'n's sun!

Thou my best thought, by day or by night,
Thou my great Fa - ther, I Thy true son;
Thou my soul's shel - ter, Thou my high tower;
Thou and Thou on - ly, first in my heart,
Heart of my heart, what - ev - er be - fall,

Wak - ing or sleep - ing, Thy pres - ence my light.
Thou in me dwell - ing, and I with Thee one.
Raise Thou me heav'n-ward, O power of my power.
High King of heav - en, my trea - sure Thou art.
Still be my vi - sion, O rul - er of all. A - men.

LIFE IN CHRIST: PRAYER

301 TEACH ME, MY GOD AND KING

ST. MICHAEL (OLD 134th) S.M.

George Herbert, 1633

From *Octante trois pseaumes. . .* , Geneva, 1554
Adapted by William Crotch, 1836

1 Teach me, my God and King, In all things Thee to see,
2 A man that looks on glass On it may stay his eye;
3 All may of Thee par - take: Noth - ing can be so mean,
4 A serv - ant with this clause Makes drudg - er - y di - vine:
5 This is the fa - mous stone That turn - eth all to gold:

And what I do in an - y - thing To do it as for Thee.
Or if he pleas-eth through it pass, And then the heav'n es - py.
Which with this tinc-ture,"For Thy sake," Will not grow bright and clean.
Who sweeps a room, as for Thy laws, Makes that and the ac - tion fine.
For that which God doth touch and own Can - not for less be told.

302 I WAITED FOR THE LORD MY GOD

ABBEY C.M.

Based on Psalm 40: 1-5
Scottish Psalter, 1650

Scottish Psalter, 1615

1 I wait - ed for the Lord my God, And pa - tient - ly did bear;
2 He took me from a fear - ful pit, And from the mir - y clay,
3 He put a new song in my mouth,Our God to mag - ni - fy:
4 O bless - ed is the man whose trust Up - on the Lord re - lies;
5 O Lord my God, full man - y are The won - ders Thou hast done;

At length to me He did in - cline My voice and cry to hear.
And on a rock He set my feet, Es - tab - lish - ing my way.
Man - y shall see it, and shall fear, And on the Lord re - ly.
Re - spect-ing not the proud,nor such As turn a - side to lies.
Thy gra - cious thoughts to us -ward far A - bove all thoughts are gone. A-men.

LIFE IN CHRIST: PRAYER

WE WOULD SEE JESUS 303

HENLEY 11.10.11.10.

Anna Bartlett Warner, 1852

Lowell Mason, 1854

1 We would see Je - sus; for the shad - ows length - en
2 We would see Je - sus, the great rock foun - da - tion,
3 We would see Je - sus! Oth - er lights are pal - ing
4 We would see Je - sus! This is all we're need - ing,

A - cross this lit - tle land - scape of our life;
Where - on our feet were set by sov - 'reign grace:
Which for long years we have re - joiced to see:
Strength, joy, and will - ing - ness come with the sight,

We would see Je - sus, our weak faith to strength - en
Not life nor death, with all their ag - i - ta - tion,
The bless - ings of our pil - grim - age are fail - ing;
We would see Je - sus, dy - ing, ris - en, plead - ing;

For the last wea - ri - ness, the fi - nal strife.
Can thence re - move us if we see His face.
We would not mourn them, for we go to Thee!
Then wel - come day and fare - well mor - tal night! A - men.

LIFE IN CHRIST: COMMUNION WITH CHRIST

304 THOU TRUE VINE, THAT HEALS

PLEADING SAVIOR 8.7.8.7.D.

Folk Hymn
J. Leavitt's *Christian Lyre*, 1831
Harmony by R. Vaughan Williams, 1906

"T.S.N." in *Songs of Praise*, 1925

1 Thou true vine, that heals the na-tions, Tree of life, Thy branch-es we.
2 Noth-ing can we do with-out Thee; On Thy life de-pends each one;

They who leave Thee fade and with-er, None bear fruit ex - cept in Thee.
If we keep Thy words and love Thee, All we ask for shall be done.

Cleanse us, make us sane and sim-ple, Till we merge our lives in Thine,
May we, lov-ing one an-oth-er, Ra-diant in Thy light a - bide;

Gain our-selves in Thee, the vint-age, Give our-selves through Thee, the vine.
So through us, made fruit-ful by Thee, Shall our God be glo - ri - fied.

LIFE IN CHRIST: COMMUNION WITH CHRIST

O FOR A CLOSER WALK WITH GOD 305

ELIZABETHTOWN C.M.

William Cowper, 1772

George Kingsley, 1838

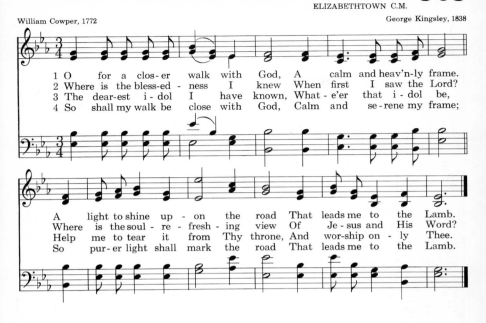

1 O for a clos-er walk with God, A calm and heav'n-ly frame.
2 Where is the bless-ed - ness I knew When first I saw the Lord?
3 The dear-est i - dol I have known, What - e'er that i - dol be,
4 So shall my walk be close with God, Calm and se-rene my frame;

A light to shine up - on the road That leads me to the Lamb.
Where is the soul - re - fresh - ing view Of Je - sus and His Word?
Help me to tear it from Thy throne, And wor-ship on - ly Thee.
So pur-er light shall mark the road That leads me to the Lamb.

O LOVE DIVINE 306

HESPERUS L.M.

Oliver Wendell Holmes, 1849

Henry Baker, 1854

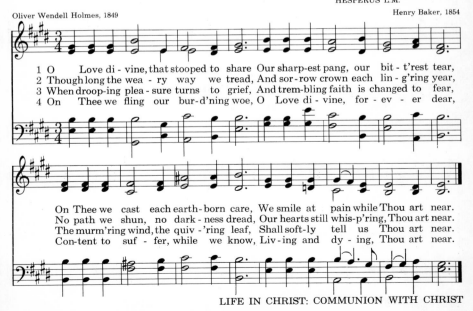

1 O Love di - vine, that stooped to share Our sharp-est pang, our bit - t'rest tear,
2 Though long the wea - ry way we tread, And sor-row crown each lin - g'ring year,
3 When droop-ing plea - sure turns to grief, And trem-bling faith is changed to fear,
4 On Thee we fling our bur-d'ning woe, O Love di - vine, for - ev - er dear,

On Thee we cast each earth-born care, We smile at pain while Thou art near.
No path we shun, no dark - ness dread, Our hearts still whis-p'ring, Thou art near.
The murm'ring wind, the quiv -'ring leaf, Shall soft-ly tell us Thou art near.
Con-tent to suf - fer, while we know, Liv - ing and dy - ing, Thou art near.

LIFE IN CHRIST: COMMUNION WITH CHRIST

307 DRAW THOU MY SOUL, O CHRIST

ST. EDMUND 6.4.6.4.6.6.6.4.

Lucy Larcom, 1892

Arthur Seymour Sullivan, 1872

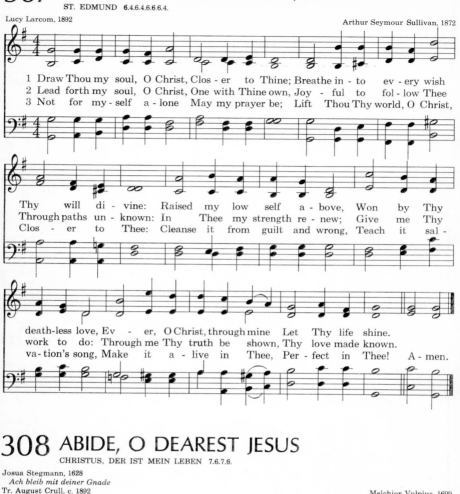

1 Draw Thou my soul, O Christ, Clos - er to Thine; Breathe in - to ev - ery wish
2 Lead forth my soul, O Christ, One with Thine own, Joy - ful to fol - low Thee
3 Not for my - self a - lone May my prayer be; Lift Thou Thy world, O Christ,

Thy will di - vine: Raised my low self a - bove, Won by Thy
Through paths un - known: In Thee my strength re - new; Give me Thy
Clos - er to Thee: Cleanse it from guilt and wrong, Teach it sal -

death-less love, Ev - er, O Christ, through mine Let Thy life shine.
work to do: Through me Thy truth be shown, Thy love made known.
va - tion's song, Make it a - live in Thee, Per - fect in Thee! A - men.

308 ABIDE, O DEAREST JESUS

CHRISTUS, DER IST MEIN LEBEN 7.6.7.6.

Josua Stegmann, 1628
Ach bleib mit deiner Gnade
Tr. August Crull, c. 1892

Melchior Vulpius, 1609

1 A - bide, O dear - est Je - sus, A - mong us with Thy grace,
2 A - bide, O dear Re - deem - er, A - mong us with Thy Word,
3 A - bide with heav'n-ly bright - ness A - mong us, pre - cious light;
4 A - bide with rich - est bless - ings A - mong us, boun-teous Lord;
5 A - bide, O faith - ful Sav - ior, A - mong us with Thy love,

LIFE IN CHRIST: COMMUNION WITH CHRIST

That Sa - tan may not harm us, Nor we to sin give place.
And thus now and here - af - ter True peace and joy af - ford.
Thy truth di - rect, and keep us From er - ror's gloom-y night.
Let us in grace and wis - dom Grow dai - ly through Thy Word.
Grant stead-fast-ness, and help us To reach our home a - bove. A - men.

DEAR LORD, WHO SOUGHT AT DAWN 309

ANGELUS L.M.

Scheffler's *Heilige Seelenlust*, 1657
and *Cantica Spiritualia*, 1847

Harry Webb Farrington‡, 1928

1 Dear Lord, who sought at dawn of day The sol - i -
2 O Mas - ter, who with kind - ly face At noon - day
3 Thou wea - ried Christ, at e - ven - tide Com - mun - ing
4 Strong Pi - lot, who at mid - night hour Could calm the

tar - y woods to pray, In qui - et - ness we come to ask
trod the mar - ket place, We crave a broth - er's smile and song
on the moun - tain - side, In mys - tic still - ness now we seek
sea with gen - tle power, Grant us the skill to aid the bark

Thy guid - ance for the dai - ly task.
While min - gling in the lone - ly throng.
Thy pres - ence for the com - ing week.
Of those who drift in storm and dark. A - men.

LIFE IN CHRIST: COMMUNION WITH CHRIST

310 COME, THOU FOUNT

NETTLETON 8.7.8.7.D.

Folk Hymn
John Wyeth's *Repository of Sacred Music, Part Second*, 1813

Robert Robinson†, 1758

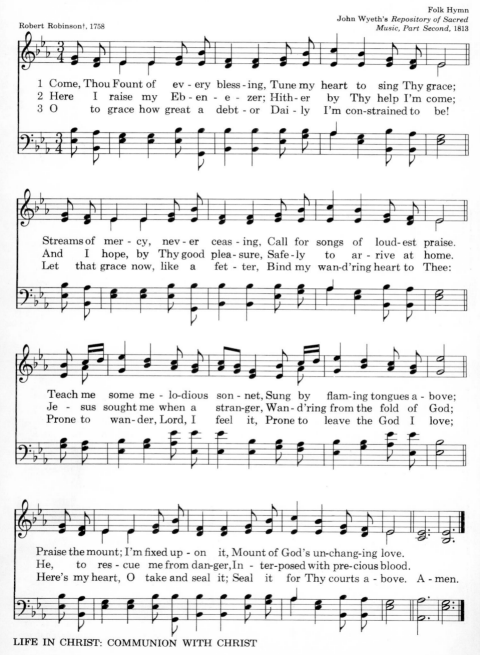

1 Come, Thou Fount of ev-ery bless-ing, Tune my heart to sing Thy grace;
2 Here I raise my Eb-en-e-zer; Hith-er by Thy help I'm come;
3 O to grace how great a debt-or Dai-ly I'm con-strained to be!

Streams of mer-cy, nev-er ceas-ing, Call for songs of loud-est praise.
And I hope, by Thy good plea-sure, Safe-ly to ar-rive at home.
Let that grace now, like a fet-ter, Bind my wan-d'ring heart to Thee:

Teach me some me-lo-dious son-net, Sung by flam-ing tongues a-bove;
Je-sus sought me when a stran-ger, Wan-d'ring from the fold of God;
Prone to wan-der, Lord, I feel it, Prone to leave the God I love;

Praise the mount; I'm fixed up-on it, Mount of God's un-chang-ing love.
He, to res-cue me from dan-ger, In-ter-posed with pre-cious blood.
Here's my heart, O take and seal it; Seal it for Thy courts a-bove. A-men.

LIFE IN CHRIST: COMMUNION WITH CHRIST

GUIDE ME, O THOU GREAT JEHOVAH 311

CWM RHONDDA 8.7.8.7.8.7.

William Williams, 1745
Arglwydd arwain trwy'r anialwch
Tr. Peter Williams and Others, 1771-2

John Hughes, 1907

1 Guide me, O Thou great Je - ho - vah, Pil - grim through this
2 O - pen now the crys - tal foun - tain, Whence the heal - ing
3 When I tread the verge of Jor - dan, Bid my anx - ious

bar - ren land; I am weak, but Thou art might - y; Hold me with Thy
streams do flow; Let the fi - ery cloud - y pil - lar Lead me all my
fears sub - side; Death of death, and hell's de - struc-tion, Land me safe on

power - ful hand; Bread of heav - en, bread of heav - en,
jour - ney through; Strong de - liv - erer, strong de - liv - erer,
Ca - naan's side; Songs of prais - es, songs of prais - es,

Feed me now and ev - er - more, Feed me now and ev - er - more.
Be Thou still my strength and shield, Be Thou still my strength and shield.
I will ev - er give to Thee, I will ev - er give to Thee. A - men.

LIFE IN CHRIST: PILGRIMAGE AND GUIDANCE

312 COME, COME, YE SAINTS

ALL IS WELL   10.6.10.6.8 8.8.6.

William Clayton, 1846
Altered by Joseph F. Green, 1960

Folk Hymn
Adapted from J. T. White's
Sacred Harp, 1844

1 Come, come, ye saints, no toil nor la - bor fear; But with joy
2 The world of care is with us ev - ery day; Let it not
3 We'll find the rest which God for us pre - pared, When at last

wend your way. Though hard to you the jour - ney may ap - pear,
this ob - scure: Here we can serve the Mas - ter on the way,
He will call; Where none will come to hurt or make a - fraid,

Grace shall be as your day. We have a liv - ing
And in Him be se - cure. Gird up your loins; fresh
He will reign o - ver all. We will make the air with

Lord to guide, And we can trust Him to pro - vide; Do
cour - age take; Our God will nev - er us for - sake; And
mu - sic ring, Shout praise to God our Lord and King: O

LIFE IN CHRIST: PILGRIMAGE AND GUIDANCE

this, and joy your hearts will swell: All is well! All is well!
so our song no fear can quell; All is well! All is well!
how we'll make the cho - rus swell: All is well! All is well!

ETERNAL ONE, THOU LIVING GOD 313

WINCHESTER NEW L.M.

From *Musicalisch Hand-buch*, published
by George Rebelein's Widow, 1690
Arranged by William Henry Havergal, 1847

Samuel Longfellow, 1875

1 E - ter - nal one, Thou liv - ing God, Whom
2 The same our trust, the same our need, In
3 We bless Thee for the grow - ing light, Th' ad -
4 With wid - er view, come loft - ier goal; With
5 A - new we pledge our - selves to Thee, To

chang - ing years un - chang'd re - veal, With Thee their way our
sor - row's stress, in du - ty's hour; We keep their faith, by
vanc - ing thought, the wid - 'ning view, The larg - er free - dom,
full - er light, more good to see; With free - dom, tru - er
fol - low where Thy truth shall lead; A - float up - on its

fa - thers trod; The hand they held, in ours we feel.
Thee de - creed, That faith the fount of all our power.
clear - er sight, Which from the old un - folds the new.
self - con - trol, With knowl - edge, deep - er rev - 'rence be.
bound - less sea, Who sails with God is safe in - deed!

LIFE IN CHRIST: PILGRIMAGE AND GUIDANCE

314 IF THOU BUT SUFFER GOD TO GUIDE

WER NUR DEN LIEBEN GOTT LÄSST WALTEN 9.8.9.8.8.8.

Georg Neumark, 1641
Wer nur den lieben Gott lässt walten
Tr. Catherine Winkworth†, 1863

Georg Neumark, 1641

1 If thou but suf - fer God to guide thee, And hope in
2 On - ly be still and wait His lei - sure In cheer - ful
3 He knows the time for joy, and tru - ly Will send it
4 Sing, pray, and keep His ways un - swerv - ing, So do thine

Him through all thy ways, He'll give thee strength what - e'er be -
hope, with heart con - tent To take what - e'er thy Fa - ther's
when He sees it meet, When He has tried and purged thee
own part faith - ful - ly, And trust His Word, though un - dis -

tide thee, And bear thee through the e - vil days. Who trusts in
plea - sure And all - de - serv - ing love hath sent, Nor doubt our
through-ly And finds thee free from all de - ceit, He comes to
cern - ing Thou yet shall find it true for thee; God nev - er

God's un - chang - ing love Builds on a rock that nought can move.
in - most wants are known To Him who chose us for His own.
thee all un - a - ware And makes thee own His lov - ing care.
yet for - sook at need The soul that trust - ed Him in - deed. A - men.

LIFE IN CHRIST: PILGRIMAGE AND GUIDANCE

1 Wer nur den lieben Gott lässt walten
   und hoffet auf ihn allezeit,
   den wird er wunderbar erhalten
   in aller Not und Traurigkeit.
   Wer Gott, dem Allerhöchsten, traut,
   der hat auf keinen Sand gebaut.

2 Man halte nur ein wenig stille
   und sei doch in sich selbst vergnügt,
   wie unsers Gottes Gnadenwille,
   wie sein Allwissenheit es fügt.
   Gott, der uns ihm hat auserwählt,
   der weiss am besten, was uns fehlt.

3 Er kennt die rechten Freudenstunden,
   er weiss wohl, was uns nützlich sei:
   Wenn er uns nur hat treu erfunden
   und merket keine Heuchelei,
   so kommt Gott, eh wir's uns versehn,
   und lässet uns viel Guts geschehn.

4 Sing, bet und geh auf Gottes Wegen,
   verricht das Deine nur getreu
   und trau des Himmels reichem Segen,
   so wird er bei dir werden neu;
   denn welcher seine Zuversicht
   auf Gott setzt, den verlässt er nicht.

TEACH ME THE MEASURE OF MY DAYS 315

ST. FLAVIAN C.M.

Based on Psalm 39
Isaac Watts, 1719

English Psalter, 1562
Arranged by Richard Redhead, 1853

1 Teach me the meas-ure of my days, Thou Mak-er of my frame;
2 A span is all that we can boast, An inch or two of time;
3 See the vain race of mor-tals move Like shad-ows o'er the plain,
4 What should I wish or wait for then From crea-tures, earth, and dust?
5 Now I for-bid my car-nal hope, My fond de-sires re-call;

I would sur-vey life's nar-row space, And learn how frail I am.
Man is but van-i-ty and dust In all his flower and prime.
They rage and strive, de-sire and love, But all the noise is vain.
They make our ex-pec-ta-tions vain, And dis-ap-point our trust.
I give my mor-tal in-terest up, And make my God my all. A-men.

316 LEAD, KINDLY LIGHT

SANDON 10.4.10.4.10.10.

John Henry Newman, 1833

Charles Henry Purday, 1860

1 Lead, kind-ly Light, a - mid th' en-cir-cling gloom, Lead Thou me on;
2 I was not ev - er thus, nor prayed that Thou Shouldst lead me on;
3 So long Thy power hath blest me, sure it still Will lead me on,

The night is dark, and I am far from home; Lead Thou me on.
I loved to choose and see my path, but now Lead Thou me on;
O'er moor and fen, o'er crag and tor - rent, till The night is gone,

Keep Thou my feet; I do not ask to see
I loved the gar - ish day, and, spite of fears,
And with the morn those an - gel fac - es smile,

The dis - tant scene, one step e - nough for me.
Pride ruled my will. Re - mem - ber not past years.
Which I have loved long since, and lost a - while. A - men.

LIFE IN CHRIST: PILGRIMAGE AND GUIDANCE

LEAD US, O FATHER 317

LONGWOOD 10.10.10.10.

William Henry Burleigh, 1859

Joseph Barnby, 1872

1 Lead us, O Fa - ther, in the paths of peace;
2 Lead us, O Fa - ther, in the paths of truth;
3 Lead us, O Fa - ther, in the paths of right:
4 Lead us, O Fa - ther, to Thy heav'n - ly rest,

With - out Thy guid - ing hand we go a - stray,
Un - helped by Thee, in er - ror's maze we grope,
Blind - ly we stum - ble when we walk a - lone,
How - ev - er rough and steep the path may be,

And doubts ap - pall, and sor - rows still in - crease;
While pas - sion stains and fol - ly dims our youth,
In - volv'd in shad - ows of a mor - al night;
Through joy or sor - row, as Thou deem - est best,

Lead us through Christ, the true and liv - ing way.
And age comes on un-cheered by faith and hope.
On - ly with Thee we jour - ney safe - ly on.
Un - til our lives are per - fect - ed in Thee. A - men.

LIFE IN CHRIST: PILGRIMAGE AND GUIDANCE

318 TAKE THOU MY HAND, O FATHER

SO NIMM DENN MEINE HÄNDE 7.4.7.4.D.

Julie Katharina Hausmann, 1862
So nimm denn meine Hände
Tr. Herman Brückner, d. 1942

Friedrich Silcher, 1842

1 Take Thou my hand, O Fa - ther, And lead Thou me, Un - til my
2 O cov - er with Thy mer - cy My poor, weak heart! Let ev - ery
3 Though naught of Thy great pow - er May move my soul, With Thee through

jour - ney end - eth, E - ter - nal - ly. A - lone I will not wan - der
thought re - bel - lious From me de - part. Per - mit Thy child to lin - ger
night and dark - ness I reach the goal. Take, then, my hands, O Fa - ther,

One sin - gle day; Be Thou my true com - pan - ion And with me stay.
Here at Thy feet, And blind - ly trust Thy good - ness With faith com - plete.
And lead Thou me Un - til my jour - ney end - eth E - ter - nal - ly. A - men.

1 So nimm denn meine Hände
    und führe mich
  bis an mein selig Ende
    und ewiglich!
  Ich kann allein nicht gehen,
    nicht einen Schritt;
  wo du wirst gehn und stehen,
    da nimm mich mit.

2 In deine Gnade hülle
    mein schwaches Herz,
  und mach es endlich stille
    in Freud und Schmerz.
  Lass ruhn zu deinen Füssen
    dein schwaches Kind;
  es will die Augen schliessen
    und folgen blind.

3 Wenn ich auch gar nichts fühle
    von deiner Macht,
  du bringst mich doch zum Ziele
    auch durch die Nacht.
  So nimm denn meine Hände
    und führe mich
  bis an mein selig Ende
    und ewiglich!

LIFE IN CHRIST: PILGRIMAGE AND GUIDANCE

JESUS, STILL LEAD ON 319

SEELENBRÄUTIGAM 5.5.8.8.5.5.

Nicolaus Ludwig von Zinzendorf, 1778
Jesu, geh' voran
Tr. Jane L. Borthwick, 1846

Adam Drese, 1698

1 Je - sus, still lead on, Till our rest be won, And, al -
2 If the way be drear, If the foe be near, Let not
3 When we seek re - lief From a long - felt grief, When op -
4 Je - sus, still lead on, Till our rest be won; Heav'n-ly

though the way be cheer - less, We will fol - low, calm and fear - less;
faith - less fears o'er - take us, Let not faith and hope for - sake us;
pressed by new temp-ta - tions, Lord, in - crease and per - fect pa - tience;
lead - er, still di - rect us, Still sup-port, con - sole, pro - tect us,

Guide us by Thy hand To our fa - ther - land.
For, through ma - ny a woe, To our home we go.
Show us that bright shore Where we weep no more.
Till we safe - ly stand In our fa - ther - land. A - men.

1 Jesu, geh voran
     auf der Lebensbahn,
   und wir wollen nicht verweilen,
   dir getreulich nachzueilen;
     führ uns an der Hand
     bis ins Vaterland.

2 Soll's uns hart ergehn,
     lass uns feste stehn
   und auch in den schwersten Tagen
   niemals über Lasten klagen;
     denn durch Trübsal hier
     geht der Weg zu dir.

3 Rühret eigner Schmerz
     irgend unser Herz,
   kümmert uns ein fremdes Leiden,
   o so gib Geduld zu beiden;
     richte unsern Sinn
     auf das Ende hin!

4 Ordne unsern Gang,
     Jesu, lebenslang.
   Führst du uns durch rauhe Wege,
   gib uns auch die nötge Pflege;
     tu uns nach dem Lauf
     deine Türe auf.

LIFE IN CHRIST: PILGRIMAGE AND GUIDANCE

320 SHEPHERD OF SOULS, REFRESH

WINDSOR C.M.

Collection of Hymns . . . of the United Brethren, 1832

W. Damon's *Booke of Musicke*, 1591

1 Shep - herd of souls, re - fresh and bless Thy cho - sen pil - grim flock
2 Hun - gry and thir - sty, faint and weak, As Thou when here be - low,
3 We would not live by bread a - lone, But by Thy word of grace,

With man - na in the wil - der - ness, With wa - ter from the rock.
Our souls the joys ce - les - tial seek, That from Thy sor - rows flow.
In strength of which we trav - el on To our a - bid - ing place. A - men.

321 MY SOUL, BE ON THY GUARD

LABAN S.M.

George Heath, 1781

Lowell Mason, 1830

1 My soul, be on thy guard; Ten thou - sand foes a - rise;
2 O watch, and fight, and pray; The bat - tle ne'er give o'er;
3 Ne'er think the vic - t'ry won, Nor lay thine ar - mor down;
4 Fight on, my soul, till death Shall bring thee to thy God;

The hosts of sin are press - ing hard To draw thee from the skies.
Re - new it bold - ly ev - ery day, And help di - vine im - plore.
Thy ar - duous work will not be done, Till thou ob - tain thy crown.
He'll take thee, at thy part - ing breath, To His di - vine a - bode. A - men.

LIFE IN CHRIST: CONFLICT AND VICTORY

COME, O THOU TRAVELER UNKNOWN 322

VERNON 8.8.8.8.8.8.

Folk Hymn
J. Ingall's *Christian Harmony*, 1805
Version from Joseph Funk's *Genuine Church Music*, 1832

Charles Wesley†, 1742

1 Come, O Thou Trav - el - er un - known, Whom still I hold,
2 Wilt Thou not yet to me re - veal Thy new, un - ut -
3 'Tis Love! tis' Love! Thou diedst for me, I hear Thy whis -
4 My prayer hath power with God; the grace Un - speak - a - ble

but can - not see, My com - pan - y be - fore is gone,
ter - a - ble name? Tell me, I still be - seech Thee, tell,
per in my heart. The morn - ing breaks, the shad - ows flee:
I now re - ceive, Through faith I see Thee face to face,

And I am left a - lone with Thee, With Thee all night
To know it now re - solved I am; Wres - tling I will
Pure u - ni - ver - sal love Thou art, To me, to all
I see Thee face to face and live: In vain I have

I mean to stay, And wres - tle till the break of day.
not let Thee go, Till I Thy name, Thy na - ture know.
Thy mer - cies move, Thy na - ture, and Thy name is Love.
not wept and strove, Thy na - ture, and Thy name is Love.

LIFE IN CHRIST: CONFLICT AND VICTORY

323 HE WHO WOULD VALIANT BE

ST. DUNSTANS 6.5.6.5.6.6.6.6.5.

Based on John Bunyan's
Who Would True Valor See, 1684
Percy Dearmer, 1906

Winfred Douglas, 1918

1 He who would val - iant be 'Gainst all dis - as - ter,
2 Who so be - set him round With dis - mal sto - ries,
3 Since, Lord, Thou dost de - fend Us with Thy Spir - it,

Let him in con - stan - cy Fol - low the Mas - ter.
Do but them - selves con-found, His strength the more is.
We know we at the end Shall life in - her - it.

There's no dis - cour - age-ment Shall make him once re - lent
No foes shall stay his might, Though he with gi - ants fight;
Then fan - cies flee a - way! I'll fear not what men say,

His first a - vowed in - tent To be a pil - grim.
He will make good his right To be a pil - grim.
I'll la - bor night and day To be a pil - grim.

LIFE IN CHRIST: CONFLICT AND VICTORY

IN THE HOUR OF TRIAL 324

PENITENCE 6.5.6.5.D.

James Montgomery, 1834

Spencer Lane, 1875

1 In the hour of tri - al, Je - sus, pray for me;
2 With its witch-ing plea - sures Would this vain world charm,
3 If with sore af - flic - tion Thou in love chas - tise,
4 When in dust and ash - es To the grave I sink,

Lest by base de - ni - al I de - part from Thee;
Or its sor - did trea - sures Spread to work me harm,
Pour Thy ben - e - dic - tion On the sac - ri - fice;
While heav'n's glo - ry flash - es O'er the shelv - ing brink,

When Thou seest me wav - er, With a look re - call,
Bring to my re - mem-brance Sad Geth-sem - a - ne,
Then, up - on Thine al - tar Free - ly of - fered up,
On Thy truth re - ly - ing Through that mor-tal strife,

Nor for fear or fa - vor Suf - fer me to fall.
Or in dark - er sem-blance, Cross-crowned Cal-va - ry.
Though the flesh may fal - ter, Faith shall drink the cup.
Lord, re - ceive me, dy - ing, To e - ter - nal life. A - men.

LIFE IN CHRIST: CONFLICT AND VICTORY

325 A MIGHTY FORTRESS IS OUR GOD

EIN' FESTE BURG 8.7.8.7.6.6.6.6.7.

Based on Psalm 46
Martin Luther, 1527 or 1528
Ein feste Burg ist unser Gott
Tr. Frederich H. Hedge, 1852

Martin Luther, 1529

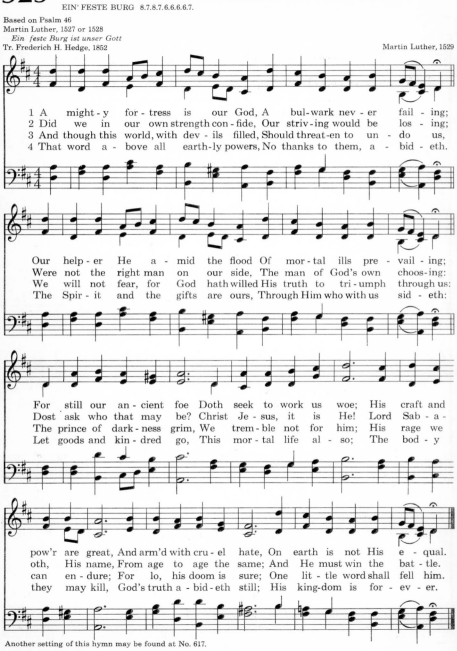

1 A might-y for-tress is our God, A bul-wark nev-er fail-ing;
2 Did we in our own strength con-fide, Our striv-ing would be los-ing;
3 And though this world, with dev-ils filled, Should threat-en to un-do us,
4 That word a-bove all earth-ly powers, No thanks to them, a-bid-eth.

Our help-er He a-mid the flood Of mor-tal ills pre-vail-ing;
Were not the right man on our side, The man of God's own choos-ing:
We will not fear, for God hath willed His truth to tri-umph through us:
The Spir-it and the gifts are ours, Through Him who with us sid-eth:

For still our an-cient foe Doth seek to work us woe; His craft and
Dost ask who that may be? Christ Je-sus, it is He! Lord Sab-a-
The prince of dark-ness grim, We trem-ble not for him; His rage we
Let goods and kin-dred go, This mor-tal life al-so; The bod-y

pow'r are great, And arm'd with cru-el hate, On earth is not His e-qual.
oth, His name, From age to age the same; And He must win the bat-tle.
can en-dure; For lo, his doom is sure; One lit-tle word shall fell him.
they may kill, God's truth a-bid-eth still; His king-dom is for-ev-er.

Another setting of this hymn may be found at No. 617.

LIFE IN CHRIST: CONFLICT AND VICTORY

GOD IS THE REFUGE OF HIS SAINTS 326

WARRINGTON L.M.

Based on Psalm 46
Isaac Watts, 1719

Ralph Harrison, 1784

1 God is the ref - uge of His saints, When storms of sharp dis -
2 Let moun-tains from their seats be hurled Down to the deep, and
3 Loud may the trou - bled o - cean roar; In sa - cred peace our
4 There is a stream, whose gen - tle flow Sup - plies the cit - y

tress in - vade; Ere we can of - fer our com - plaints,
bur - ied there, Con - vul - sions shake the sol - id world,
souls a - bide; While ev - ery na - tion, ev - ery shore,
of our God, Life, love, and joy still glid - ing through,

Be - hold Him pres - ent with His aid!
Our faith shall nev - er yield to fear.
Trem - bles, and dreads the swell - ing tide.
And wa - t'ring our di - vine a - bode. A - men.

5 That sacred stream, Thy holy Word,
    That all our raging fear controls;
  Sweet peace Thy promises afford,
    And give new strength to fainting souls.

6 Zion enjoys her Monarch's love,
    Secure against a threatening hour;
  Nor can her firm foundations move,
    Built on His truth and armed with power.

LIFE IN CHRIST: CONFLICT AND VICTORY

327 SO LET OUR LIPS AND LIVES EXPRESS

UXBRIDGE L.M.

Isaac Watts, c. 1707

Lowell Mason, 1830

1 So let our lips and lives express The ho - ly
2 Thus shall we best pro - claim a - broad The hon - or
3 Our flesh and sense must be de - nied; Pas - sion and
4 Re - lig - ion bears our spir - its up, While we ex -

gos - pel we pro - fess; So let our works and
of our Sav - ior God; When the sal - va - tion
en - vy, lust and pride; While jus - tice, tem - p'rance,
pect that bless - ed hope, The bright ap - pear - ance

vir - tues shine, To prove the doc - trine all di - vine.
reigns with - in, And grace sub - dues the power of sin.
truth and love Our in - ward pi - e - ty ap - prove.
of the Lord, And faith stands lean - ing on His Word.

328 STRIVE ARIGHT WHEN GOD DOTH CALL

RINGE RECHT 8.7.8.7.

Johann Joseph Winckler, 1714
Ringe recht wenn Gottes Gnade
Catherine Winkworth, 1855

J. Thommen's *Erbaulicher*
Musicalischer Christen-Schatz, 1745

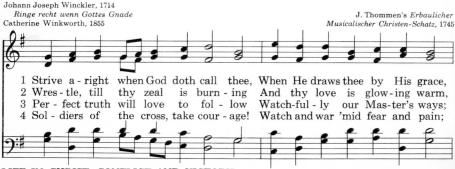

1 Strive a - right when God doth call thee, When He draws thee by His grace,
2 Wres - tle, till thy zeal is burn - ing And thy love is glow-ing warm,
3 Per - fect truth will love to fol - low Watch-ful - ly our Mas-ter's ways;
4 Sol - diers of the cross, take cour - age! Watch and war 'mid fear and pain;

LIFE IN CHRIST: CONFLICT AND VICTORY

Cast off all that would en-thrall thee, And de - ter thee from the race.
All that earth can give thee spurn - ing, Half love will not bide the storm.
Seeks not com - fort poor and hol - low, Looks not for re - ward or praise.
Dai - ly con-quering sin and sor - row, Till our King o'er earth shall reign.

I AM THE LORD, O HEAR 329

MACH'S MIT MIR 8.7.8.7.8.8.

Johann Scheffler, 1668
Mir nach, spricht Christus, unser Held
Tr. Joanna Sudermann Andres, 1940

Johann Hermann Schein, 1628

1 I am the Lord, O hear My voice, A - rise, ye Chris-tians, fol - low!
2 I am the light, I light the way Un - to a life vic - to - rious.
3 Fear not, I am your con-stant stay Though strong the foe as - sail - eth;
4 Dear Lord, we rise to fol - low Thee, In Thee is grace suf - fi - cient;

De - ny your-self, for - sake the world, My name a - lone to hal - low.
He that will come and fol - low Me Shall find his path - way glo - rious.
I am your vic - tor in the fight, No foe o'er Me pre - vail - eth.
In Thee is strength, is vic - to - ry, In Thee is love om - nis - cient.

Take up your cross, your bur-dens bear And fol - low Me, My life to share.
I am the way, the heav'n-ly light By which the soul may walk a - right.
Woe un - to him that stand-eth still And fol-lows not to do My will.
Help us to tri-umph in the strife And grant to us the crown of life. A-men.

LIFE IN CHRIST: CONFLICT AND VICTORY

330 SOLDIERS OF CHRIST, ARISE

SILVER STREET S.M.

Charles Wesley, 1749

Isaac Smith, 1770

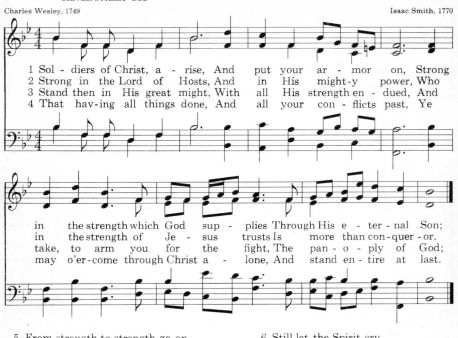

1 Sol - diers of Christ, a - rise, And put your ar - mor on, Strong
2 Strong in the Lord of Hosts, And in His might - y power, Who
3 Stand then in His great might, With all His strength en - dued, And
4 That hav - ing all things done, And all your con - flicts past, Ye

in the strength which God sup - plies Through His e - ter - nal Son;
in the strength of Je - sus trusts Is more than con - quer - or.
take, to arm you for the fight, The pan - o - ply of God;
may o'er - come through Christ a - lone, And stand en - tire at last.

5 From strength to strength go on,
Wrestle, and fight, and pray,
Tread all the powers of darkness down,
And win the well-fought day;

6 Still let the Spirit cry
In all His soldiers, "Come";
Till Christ the Lord descends from high
And takes the conqu'rors home.

331 FROM EVERY STORMY WIND

RETREAT L.M.

Hugh Stowell†, 1828

Thomas Hastings, 1842

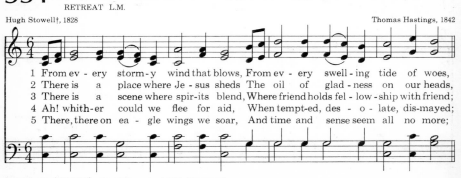

1 From ev - ery storm - y wind that blows, From ev - ery swell - ing tide of woes,
2 There is a place where Je - sus sheds The oil of glad - ness on our heads,
3 There is a scene where spir - its blend, Where friend holds fel - low - ship with friend;
4 Ah! whith - er could we flee for aid, When tempt - ed, des - o - late, dis - mayed;
5 There, there on ea - gle wings we soar, And time and sense seem all no more;

LIFE IN CHRIST: CONFLICT AND VICTORY

There is a calm, a sure re-treat; 'Tis found be-neath the mer-cy seat.
A place than all be-sides more sweet; It is the blood-stained mer-cy seat.
Though sun-dered far, by faith they meet A-round one com-mon mer-cy seat.
Or how the hosts of hell de-feat, Had suf-f'ring saints no mer-cy seat?
And heav'n comes down our souls to greet, And glo-ry crowns the mer-cy seat.

AWAKE, MY SOUL, STRETCH EVERY NERVE 332

CHRISTMAS C.M.

Philip Doddridge, 1755

Arranged from George Frideric Handel, 1728

1 A - wake, my soul, stretch ev - ery nerve, And press with vig - or
2 A cloud of wit - ness - es a - round Hold thee in full sur-
3 'Tis God's all - an - i - mat - ing voice, That calls thee from on
4 Blest Sav - ior, in - tro - duced by Thee Have I my race be-

on; A heav'n - ly race de - mands thy zeal, And
vey: For - get the steps al - read - y trod, And
high; 'Tis His own hand pre - sents the prize To
gun; And crowned with vic - t'ry at Thy feet I'll

an im - mor - tal crown, And an im - mor - tal crown.
on - ward urge thy way, And on - ward urge thy way.
thine as - pir - ing eye, To thine as - pir - ing eye.
lay my hon - ors down, I'll lay my hon - ors down.

LIFE IN CHRIST: CONFLICT AND VICTORY

333 COME, YE DISCONSOLATE

CONSOLATOR 11.10.11.10.

Thomas Moore and Thomas Hastings, 1824 and 1831

Samuel Webbe, 1792

1 Come, ye dis - con - so - late, wher - e'er ye lan - guish;
2 Joy of the des - o - late, light of the stray - ing,
3 Here see the bread of life, see wa - ters flow - ing

Come to the mer - cy - seat, fer - vent - ly kneel;
Hope of the pen - i - tent, fade - less and pure,
Forth from the throne of God, pure from a - bove;

Here bring your wound - ed hearts, here tell your an - guish;
Here speaks the Com - fort - er, ten - der - ly say - ing,
Come to the feast of love, come, ev - er know - ing,

Earth has no sor - row that heav'n can - not heal.
"Earth has no sor - row that heav'n can - not cure."
Earth has no sor - row but heav'n can re - move.

LIFE IN CHRIST: COURAGE AND COMFORT

I LOOK TO THEE IN EVERY NEED 334

O JESU, WARUM LEGST DU MIR   8.6.8.6.8.8.

Samuel Longfellow†, 1864

Gesangbuch, Hirschberg, 1741

1 I look to Thee in ev - ery need,
2 Dis - cour - aged in the work of life,
3 Thy calm - ness bends se - rene a - bove,
4 En - fold - ed deep in Thy dear love,

And nev - er look in vain; I feel Thy strong and ten - der love,
Dis - heart-ened by its load, Shamed by its fail - ures or its fears,
My rest - less - ness to still; A - round me flows Thy quick - ening life,
Held in Thy law, I stand; Thy hand in all things I be - hold,

And all is well a - gain: The thought of Thee is might - ier far
I sink be - side the road; But let me on - ly think of Thee
To nerve my fal - tering will: Thy pres - ence fills my sol - i - tude;
And all things in Thy hand; Thou lead - est me by un - sought ways,

Than sin and pain and sor - row are.
And then new heart springs up in me.
Thy prov - i - dence turns all to good.
And turn'st my mourn - ing in - to praise. A - men.

LIFE IN CHRIST: COURAGE AND COMFORT

335 CHILDREN OF THE HEAVENLY FATHER

SANDELL L.M.

Caroline V. Sandell Berg, 1858
Trygare kan ingen vara
Tr. Ernst William Olson, d. 1958

Swedish Melody

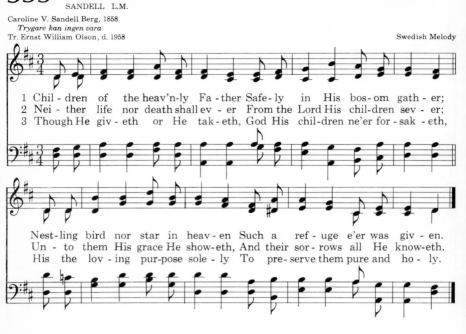

1 Chil - dren of the heav'n-ly Fa -ther Safe- ly in His bos-om gath - er;
2 Nei - ther life nor death shall ev - er From the Lord His chil-dren sev - er;
3 Though He giv - eth or He tak-eth, God His chil-dren ne'er for-sak - eth,

Nest-ling bird nor star in heav-en Such a ref - uge e'er was giv - en.
Un - to them His grace He show-eth, And their sor - rows all He know-eth.
His the lov - ing pur-pose sole - ly To pre-serve them pure and ho - ly.

336 FATHER, WHATE'ER OF EARTHLY BLISS

NAOMI C.M.

Anne Steele†, 1760

Johann Georg Nägeli, 1832
Arranged by Lowell Mason, 1836

1 Fa - ther, what-e'er of earth-ly bliss Thy sov-'reign will de - nies,
2 Give me a calm, a thank-ful heart, From ev - ery mur-mur free;
3 Let the sweet hope that Thou art mine My path of life at - tend;

Ac - cept-ed at Thy throne of grace, Let this pe - ti - tion rise:
The bless-ings of Thy grace im-part, And let me live to Thee.
Thy pres-ence through my jour-ney shine, And bless its hap - py end. A-men.

LIFE IN CHRIST: COURAGE AND COMFORT

WHAT A FRIEND WE HAVE IN JESUS 337

ERIE 8 7.8.7.D.

Joseph Medlicott Scriven†, 1855

Charles Crozat Converse, 1868

1 What a friend we have in Je - sus, All our sins and griefs to bear;
2 Have we tri - als and temp-ta-tions? Is there trou-ble an - y - where?
3 Are we weak and heav-y la - den, Cum-bered with a load of care?

What a priv - i - lege to car - ry Ev - ery-thing to God in prayer!
We should nev - er be dis - cour-aged: Take it to the Lord in prayer!
Pre - cious Sav - ior, still our re - fuge, Take it to the Lord in prayer!

O what peace we of - ten for - feit, O what need-less pain we bear,
Can we find a friend so faith - ful, Who will all our sor-rows share?
Do thy friends de-spise, for - sake thee? Take it to the Lord in prayer!

All be-cause we do not car - ry Ev - ery-thing to God in prayer.
Je - sus knows our ev - ery weak-ness; Take it to the Lord in prayer!
In His arms He'll take and shield thee, Thou wilt find a sol - ace there.

LIFE IN CHRIST: COURAGE AND COMFORT

338 THY WAY AND ALL THY SORROWS

BEFIEHL DU DEINE WEGE   7.6.7.6.D.

Paul Gerhardt, 1656
Befiehl du deine Wege
Tr. Arthur Tozer Russell, 1851

Johann Michael Haydn, d. 1806

1 Thy way and all thy sor - rows, Give thou in - to His hand,
2 On Him be thy re - li - ance, As thou wouldst pros-per well;
3 Leave all to His di - rec - tion; In wis - dom He doth reign;
4 Give, Lord, the con - sum - ma - tion To all our hearts' dis - tress;

His gra - cious care un - fail - ing, Who doth the heav'ns com - mand.
To make thy work en - dur - ing Thy mind on His must dwell.
Thy won - der far ex - ceed - ing, He will His course main - tain;
Our hands, our feet, O strength-en; In death our spir - its bless.

Their course and path He giv - eth To clouds and air and wind;
God yield-eth nought to sor - row And self - tor - ment - ing care;
So He as Him be - seem - eth, With won - der-work - ing skill,
Thy truth and Thy pro - tec - tion For ev - er - more we pray:

A way thy feet may fol - low, He too for thee will find.
Nought, nought with Him a - vail - eth; No power save that of prayer.
Shall put a - way the sor - rows That now thy spir - it fill.
With these in heav'n - ly glo - ry Shall end our cer - tain way.

LIFE IN CHRIST: COURAGE AND COMFORT

JESUS MERCIFUL 339

HUBBARD 5.5.5.5.

Tzu-ch'en Chao, 1931
Tr. Frank W. Price, 1952

Chinese Traditional Melody
Arranged by Bliss Wiant, 1936

1 Je - sus mer - ci - ful, Je - sus pit - y - ing,
2 Je - sus val - or - ous, Je - sus wise and good,
3 Je - sus, broth - er man, Je - sus, friend who knows,
4 Je - sus, ho - ly Lord, Je - sus, Mas - ter true,

Melt my ston - y heart, Com - fort to me bring.
Save me by Thy blood, Feed me with Thy food.
Shar - ing all my load, Bear - ing all my woes.
Re - in - spire me now, Thy great work to do. A - men.

GIVE TO THE WINDS THY FEARS 340

ST. BRIDE S.M.

Paul Gerhardt, 1656
Befiehl du deine Wege
Tr. John Wesley, 1739

Samuel Howard, 1762

1 Give to the winds thy fears; Hope and be un - dis - mayed; God
2 Through waves, and clouds, and storms, He gen - tly clears thy way; Wait
3 Leave to His sov-ereign sway To choose and to com - mand; So
4 Far, far a - bove thy thought His coun - sel shall ap - pear, When

hears thy sighs and counts thy tears; God shall lift up thy head.
thou His time; so shall this night Soon end in joy - ous day.
shalt thou, won-dering, own His way How wise, how strong His hand!
ful - ly He the work hath wrought That caused thy need-less fear. A - men.

LIFE IN CHRIST: COURAGE AND COMFORT

341 THY WAY, NOT MINE, O LORD

QUAM DILECTA 6.6.6.6.

Horatius Bonar, 1857

Henry Lascelles Jenner, 1861

1 Thy way, not mine, O Lord, How - ev - er dark it be!
2 Smooth let it be or rough, It will be still the best,
3 The king - dom that I seek Is Thine; so let the way
4 Not mine, not mine the choice, In things or great or small;

Lead me by Thine own hand, Choose out the path for me.
Wind - ing or straight, it leads Right on - ward to Thy rest.
That leads to it be Thine, Else I must sure - ly stray.
Be Thou my guide, my strength, My wis - dom, and my all. A - men.

342 GOD IS MY STRONG SALVATION

CHRISTUS, DER IST MEIN LEBEN 7.6.7.6.

James Montgomery, 1822

Melchior Vulpius, 1609

1 God is my strong sal - va - tion; What foe have I to fear?
2 Though hosts en - camp a - round me, Firm to the fight I stand;
3 Place on the Lord re - li - ance, My soul, with cour - age wait;
4 His might thine heart shall strength - en, His love thy joy in - crease;

In dark - ness and temp - ta - tion My light, my help, is near.
What ter - ror can con - found me, With God at my right hand?
His truth be thine af - fi - ance, When faint and des - o - late.
Mer - cy thy days shall length - en; The Lord will give thee peace. A - men.

LIFE IN CHRIST: COURAGE AND COMFORT

O JESUS, I HAVE PROMISED 343

ANGEL'S STORY 7.6.7.6.D.

John Ernest Bode, 1869

Arthur H. Mann, 1881

1 O Je - sus, I have prom - ised To serve Thee to the end;
2 O let me feel Thee near me, The world is ev - er near;
3 O let me hear Thee speak - ing In ac - cents clear and still;
4 O Je - sus, Thou hast prom - ised To all who fol - low Thee

Be Thou for - ev - er near me, My Mas - ter and my friend;
I see the sights that daz - zle, The tempt - ing sounds I hear:
A - bove the storms of pas - sion, The mur - murs of self - will:
That where Thou art in glo - ry There shall Thy serv - ant be;

I shall not fear the bat - tle If Thou art by my side,
My foes are ev - er near me, A - round me and with - in;
O speak to re - as - sure me, To has - ten or con - trol;
And, Je - sus, I have prom - ised To serve Thee to the end;

Nor wan - der from the path - way If Thou wilt be my guide.
But, Je - sus, draw Thou near - er, And shield my soul from sin.
O speak, and make me lis - ten, Thou guard - ian of my soul.
O give me grace to fol - low, My Mas - ter and my friend. A - men.

LIFE IN CHRIST: OBEDIENCE AND CONSECRATION

344 HE WHO WOULD FOLLOW CHRIST

WARUM BETRÜBST DU DICH, MEIN HERZ 8.8.6.8.6.

Jörg Wagner, 1527, in the *Ausbund*, 1564
Wer Christo jetzt will folgen nach
Tr. David Augsburger, 1962

Bartholomeus Monoetius, 1565

1 He who would fol - low Christ in life Must scorn the world's
2 Christ's serv - ants fol - low Him to death, And give their bod -
3 Re - nounc - ing all, they choose the cross, And claim - ing it,

in - sult and strife, And bear his cross each day. For this
y life and breath On cross and rack and pyre. As gold
count all as loss, E'en home and child and wife. For - sak -

a - lone leads to the throne; Christ is the on - ly way.
is tried and pur - i - fied They stand the test of fire.
ing gain, for - get - ting pain, They en - ter in - to life.

345 MUST JESUS BEAR THE CROSS ALONE

MAITLAND C.M.

Thomas Shepherd, 1693, and Others

George Nelson Allen, 1844

1 Must Je - sus bear the cross a - lone, And all the world go free?
2 Dis - owned on earth, 'mid griefs and cares He led His toil - some way;
3 The con - se - crat - ed cross I'll bear, Till from the cross set free,

LIFE IN CHRIST: OBEDIENCE AND CONSECRATION

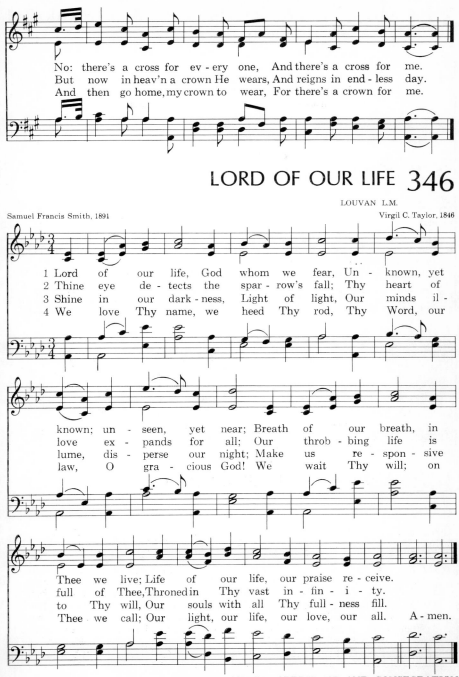

No: there's a cross for ev-er-y one, And there's a cross for me.
But now in heav'n a crown He wears, And reigns in end-less day.
And then go home, my crown to wear, For there's a crown for me.

LORD OF OUR LIFE 346

LOUVAN L.M.

Samuel Francis Smith, 1891

Virgil C. Taylor, 1846

1 Lord of our life, God whom we fear, Un - known, yet
2 Thine eye de - tects the spar - row's fall; Thy heart of
3 Shine in our dark - ness, Light of light, Our minds il -
4 We love Thy name, we heed Thy rod, Thy Word, our

known; un - seen, yet near; Breath of our breath, in
love ex - pands for all; Our throb - bing life is
lume, dis - perse our night; Make us re - spon - sive
law, O gra - cious God! We wait Thy will; on

Thee we live; Life of our life, our praise re - ceive.
full of Thee, Throned in Thy vast in - fin - i - ty.
to Thy will, Our souls with all Thy full - ness fill.
Thee we call; Our light, our life, our love, our all. A - men.

LIFE IN CHRIST: OBEDIENCE AND CONSECRATION

347 MASTER, SPEAK! THY SERVANT HEARETH

AMEN, JESUS HAN SKAL RAADE 8.7.8.7.7.7.

Frances Ridley Havergal, 1867

Anton P. Berggreen, 1849

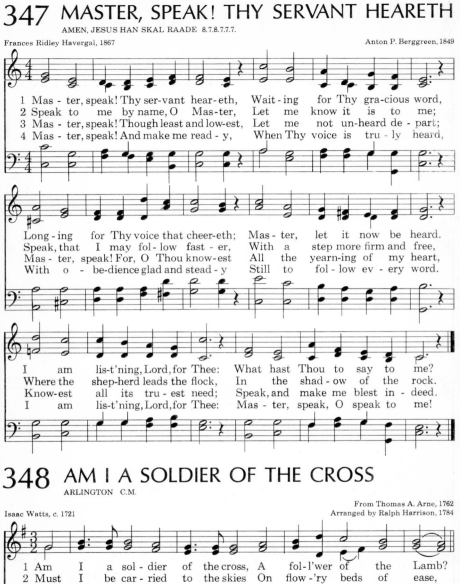

1 Mas - ter, speak! Thy ser-vant hear-eth, Wait - ing for Thy gra-cious word,
2 Speak to me by name, O Mas-ter, Let me know it is to me;
3 Mas - ter, speak! Though least and low-est, Let me not un-heard de - part;
4 Mas - ter, speak! And make me read - y, When Thy voice is tru - ly heard,

Long - ing for Thy voice that cheer-eth; Mas - ter, let it now be heard.
Speak, that I may fol - low fast - er, With a step more firm and free,
Mas - ter, speak! For, O Thou know-est All the yearn-ing of my heart,
With o - be-dience glad and stead - y Still to fol - low ev - ery word.

I am list'-ning, Lord, for Thee: What hast Thou to say to me?
Where the shep-herd leads the flock, In the shad - ow of the rock.
Know-est all its tru - est need; Speak, and make me blest in - deed.
I am list'-ning, Lord, for Thee: Mas - ter, speak, O speak to me!

348 AM I A SOLDIER OF THE CROSS

ARLINGTON C.M.

Isaac Watts, c. 1721

From Thomas A. Arne, 1762
Arranged by Ralph Harrison, 1784

1 Am I a sol - dier of the cross, A fol-l'wer of the Lamb?
2 Must I be car - ried to the skies On flow-'ry beds of ease,
3 Are there no foes for me to face? Must I not stem the flood?
4 Sure I must fight, if I would reign; In - crease my cour - age, Lord;
5 Thy saints in all this glo - rious war Shall con-quer, though they die:
6 When that il - lus-trious day shall rise, And all Thy ar - mies shine

LIFE IN CHRIST: OBEDIENCE AND CONSECRATION

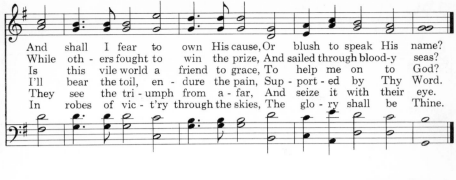

And shall I fear to own His cause, Or blush to speak His name?
While oth - ers fought to win the prize, And sailed through blood-y seas?
Is this vile world a friend to grace, To help me on to God?
I'll bear the toil, en - dure the pain, Sup - port - ed by Thy Word.
They see the tri - umph from a - far, And seize it with their eye.
In robes of vic - t'ry through the skies, The glo - ry shall be Thine.

HOW SHALL I FOLLOW HIM 349

GERMANY L.M.

Josiah Conder†, 1836

W. Gardiner's *Sacred Melodies*, 1815

1 How shall I fol - low Him I serve? How shall I
2 Lord, should my path through suf - f'ring lie, For - bid it
3 O let me think how Thou didst leave Un - tast - ed
4 To faint, to grieve, to die for me! Thou cam - est
5 Yes! I would count them all but loss To gain the

learn of Him I love? Nor from those bless - ed
I should e'er re - pine; Still let me turn to
ev - ery pure de - light, To fast, to faint, to
not Thy - self to please: And, dear as earth - ly
no - tice of Thine eye: Flesh shrinks and trem - bles

foot - steps swerve, Which lead me to His seat a - bove?
Cal - va - ry, Nor heed my griefs, re - mem - b'ring Thine.
watch, to grieve, The toil - some day, the home - less night:
com - forts be, Shall I not love Thee more than these?
at the cross, But Thou canst give the vic - to - ry.

LIFE IN CHRIST: OBEDIENCE AND CONSECRATION

350 A CHARGE TO KEEP I HAVE

BOYLSTON S.M.

Charles Wesley†, 1762

Lowell Mason, 1832

1 A charge to keep I have, A God to glo - ri - fy;
2 To serve the pres - ent age, My call - ing to ful - fill,
3 Arm me with zeal - ous care, As in Thy sight to live;
4 Help me to watch and pray, And on Thy-self re - ly;

A nev - er - dy - ing soul to save, And fit it for the sky;
O may it all my powers en-gage To do my Mas - ter's will!
And O! Thy ser - vant, Lord, pre-pare A strict ac-count to give.
As - sured, if I my trust be-tray, I shall for-ev - er die. A - men.

351 A CHARGE TO KEEP I HAVE

FERGUSON S.M.

Charles Wesley†, 1762

George Kingsley, 1842

1 A charge to keep I have, A God to glo - ri - fy;
2 To serve the pres - ent age, My call - ing to ful - fill,
3 Arm me with zeal - ous care, As in Thy sight to live;
4 Help me to watch and pray, And on Thy - self re - ly;

A nev - er - dy - ing soul to save, And fit it for the sky.
O, may it all my powers en-gage To do my Mas - ter's will!
And O, Thy serv ant, Lord, pre-pare A strict ac-count to give.
As - sured, if I my trust be-tray, I shall for - ev - er die. A - men.

LIFE IN CHRIST: OBEDIENCE AND CONSECRATION

O GOD, THOU FAITHFUL GOD 352

O GOTT, DU FROMMER GOTT 6.7.6.7.6.6.6.6.

Johann Heermann, 1630
O Gott, du frommer Gott
Tr. Catherine Winkworth‡, 1858

A. Fritzsch's *Himmels-Lust*, 1679
Harmony by Johann Sebastian Bach, c. 1740

1 O God, Thou faith-ful God, Thou foun-tain ev - er flow - ing,
2 And grant me, Lord, to do, With read - y heart and will - ing,
3 If dan - gers gath - er round, Still keep me calm and fear - less;

With - out whom noth - ing is, All per - fect gifts be - stow - ing,
What - e'er Thou shalt com - mand, My call - ing here ful - fill - ing;
Help me to bear the cross When life is dark and cheer - less,

Grant me a health - y frame, And give me, Lord, with - in,
And do it when I ought, With zeal and joy - ful - ness;
To o - ver - come my foe With words and ac - tions kind;

A con-science free from blame, A soul un - hurt by sin.
And bless the work I've wrought, For Thou must give suc - cess.
When coun - sel I would know, Good coun - sel let me find. A-men.

LIFE IN CHRIST: OBEDIENCE AND CONSECRATION

353 I BIND MY HEART THIS TIDE

UNION 6.7.7.7.

Lauchlan MacLean Watt, 1907

J. Randall Zercher, 1965

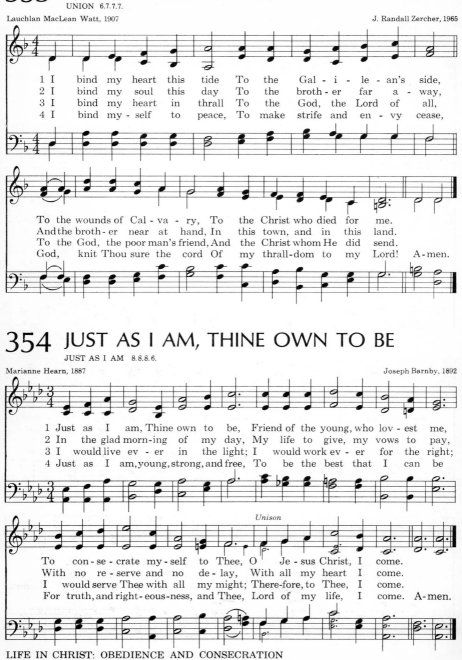

1 I bind my heart this tide To the Gal - i - le - an's side,
2 I bind my soul this day To the broth - er far a - way,
3 I bind my heart in thrall To the God, the Lord of all,
4 I bind my - self to peace, To make strife and en - vy cease,

To the wounds of Cal - va - ry, To the Christ who died for me.
And the broth - er near at hand, In this town, and in this land.
To the God, the poor man's friend, And the Christ whom He did send.
God, knit Thou sure the cord Of my thrall-dom to my Lord! A - men.

354 JUST AS I AM, THINE OWN TO BE

JUST AS I AM 8.8.8.6.

Marianne Hearn, 1887

Joseph Barnby, 1892

1 Just as I am, Thine own to be, Friend of the young, who lov - est me,
2 In the glad morn-ing of my day, My life to give, my vows to pay,
3 I would live ev - er in the light; I would work ev - er for the right;
4 Just as I am, young, strong, and free, To be the best that I can be

Unison

To con - se - crate my - self to Thee, O Je - sus Christ, I come.
With no re - serve and no de - lay, With all my heart I come.
I would serve Thee with all my might; There-fore, to Thee, I come.
For truth, and right-eous-ness, and Thee, Lord of my life, I come. A - men.

LIFE IN CHRIST: OBEDIENCE AND CONSECRATION

SAVIOR, THY DYING LOVE 355

SOMETHING FOR THEE 6.4.6.4.6.6.6.4.

Sylvanus D. Phelps, 1862

Robert Lowry, 1871

1 Sav - ior, Thy dy - ing love Thou gav - est me,
2 At the blest mer - cy-seat, Plead - ing for me;
3 Give me a faith - ful heart, Like - ness to Thee,
4 All that I am and have, Thy gifts so free,

Nor should I aught with-hold, Dear Lord, from Thee;
My fee - ble faith looks up, Je - sus, to Thee.
That each de - part - ing day Hence-forth may see
In joy, in grief, through life, Dear Lord, for Thee!

In love my soul would bow, My heart ful - fill its vow,
Help me the cross to bear, Thy won - drous love de - clare,
Some work of love be - gun, Some deed of kind - ness done,
And when Thy face I see, My ran - somed soul shall be,

Some off - 'ring bring Thee now, Some - thing for Thee.
Some song to raise, or prayer, Some - thing for Thee.
Some wan - d'rer sought and won, Some - thing for Thee.
Through all e - ter - ni - ty, Some - thing for Thee. A - men.

LIFE IN CHRIST: OBEDIENCE AND CONSECRATION

356 TEACH ME, O LORD

BISHOP L.M.

Based on Psalm 119: 33-40
Psalter, 1912

Joseph P. Holbrook, c. 1878

1 Teach me, O Lord, Thy way of truth, And from it
2 In Thy com - mand -ments make me walk, For in Thy
3 Turn Thou my eyes from van - i - ty, And cause me
4 Turn Thou a - way re - proach and fear, Thy right - eous

I will not de - part; That I may stead - fast -
law my joy shall be; Give me a heart that
in Thy ways to tread; O let Thy serv - ant
judg - ments I con - fess; To know Thy pre - cepts

ly o - bey, Give me an un - der - stand - ing heart.
loves Thy will, From dis - con - tent and en - vy free.
prove Thy Word, And thus to god - ly fear be led.
I de - sire, Re - vive me in Thy right- eous - ness. A - men.

357 TAKE UP THY CROSS, THE SAVIOR SAID

KEDRON L.M.

Folk Hymn

A. Pilsbury's *United States Sacred Harmony*, 1799
Version from Joseph Funk's *Genuine Church Music*, 1832

Charles William Everest, 1833

1 Take up thy cross, the Sav - ior said, If thou wouldst My dis - ci - ple be;
2 Take up thy cross; let not its weight Fill thy weak soul with vain a - larm;
3 Take up thy cross, nor heed the shame; And let thy fool - ish pride be still;
4 Take up thy cross, then, in His strength, And calm - ly sin's temp-ta-tions brave;
5 Take up thy cross, and fol - low on, Nor think till death to lay it down;

LIFE IN CHRIST: OBEDIENCE AND CONSECRATION

Take up thy cross with will-ing heart, And hum-bly fol-low af-ter Me.
His strength shall bear thy spir-it up, And brace thy heart, and nerve thine arm.
The Lord re-fused not e'en to die Up-on a cross on Cal-v'ry's hill.
'Twill guide thee to a bet-ter home; And point to glo-ry o'er the grave.
For on-ly he who bears the cross May hope to wear the glo-rious crown.

TAKE MY LIFE AND LET IT BE CONSECRATED 358

HENDON 7.7.7.7.

Frances Ridley Havergal, 1874

Henri Alexander César Malan, 1827
Arranged by Lowell Mason, c. 1827

1 Take my life and let it be Con-se-crat-ed, Lord, to Thee; Take my mo-ments and my days; Let them flow in cease-less praise, Let them flow in cease-less praise.
2 Take my hands, and let them move At the im-pulse of Thy love. Take my feet, and let them be Swift and beau-ti-ful for Thee, Swift and beau-ti-ful for Thee.
3 Take my voice, and let me sing, Al-ways, on-ly, for my King. Take my lips, and let them be Filled with mes-sag-es from Thee, Filled with mes-sag-es from Thee.
4 Take my sil-ver and my gold; Not a mite would I with-hold. Take my in-tel-lect and use Ev-ery power as Thou shalt choose, Ev-ery power as Thou shalt choose.
5 Take my will and make it Thine, It shall be no long-er mine: Take my heart, it is Thine own, It shall be Thy roy-al throne, It shall be Thy roy-al throne.
6 Take my love; my Lord, I pour At Thy feet its trea-sure store; Take my-self, and I will be Ev-er, on-ly, all for Thee, Ev-er, on-ly, all for Thee. A-men.

359 SON OF GOD, ETERNAL SAVIOR

IN BABILONE 8.7.8.7.D.

Somerset Corry Lowry, 1893

Dutch Traditional Melody
Oude en Nieuwe Hollantse Boerenlilies, c. 1710

1 Son of God, e - ter - nal Sav-ior, Source of life and truth and grace,
2 As Thou, Lord, hast lived for oth-ers, So may we for oth - ers live,

Son of man, whose birth a-mongst us Hal - lows all our hu - man race,
Free - ly have Thy gifts been grant-ed, Free - ly may Thy serv - ants give.

Thou, our head, who, throned in glo - ry, For Thine own dost
Thine the gold and Thine the sil - ver, Thine the wealth of

ev - er plead, Fill us with Thy love and pit - y,
land and sea, We but stew - ards of Thy boun - ty,

LIFE IN CHRIST: STEWARDSHIP

Heal our wrongs, and help our need. A - men.
Held in sol - emn trust for Thee.

GOD OF THE FERTILE FIELDS 360

ITALIAN HYMN 6.6.4.6.6.6.4.

Georgia Harkness, 1953

Felice de Giardini, 1769

1 God of the fer - tile fields, Lord of the earth that yields
2 We would Thy stew - ards be, Hold-ing in trust from Thee
3 As grows the hid - den seed To fruit that serves men's need,
4 God of the coun - try - side, Dear to our Lord who died

Our dai - ly bread; Forth from Thy boun-teous hand Come gifts Thy
All Thou dost give; Help us in love to share, Teach us like
Thy king-dom grows. So let our toil be used, No gift of
To make men one; We pledge our lives to Thee, To serve Thee

love has planned, That men through all the land Be clothed and fed.
Thee to care, That earth may all be fair, And men may live.
Thine a-bused, No hum-blest task re-fused, Thy love be - stows.
faith - ful - ly Till in e - ter - ni - ty Our day is done. A - men.

LIFE IN CHRIST: STEWARDSHIP

361 LORD, THOU DOST LOVE THE CHEERFUL GIVER

PLEADING SAVIOR 8.7.8.7.D.

Robert Murray†, d. 1910

J. Leavitt's *Christian Lyre*, 1831
Harmony by Ralph Vaughan Williams, 1906

1 Lord, Thou dost love the cheer-ful giv-er, Who with o-pen heart and hand
2 We are Thine, Thy mer-cy sought us, Found us in death's dread-ful way,
3 Blest by Thee with gifts and grac-es, May we heed Thy church's call;
4 Sav-ior, Thou hast free-ly giv-en All the bless-ings we en-joy,

Bless-es free-ly, as a riv-er That re-fresh-es all the land;
To the fold in safe-ty brought us, Nev-er-more from Thee to stray.
Glad-ly in all times and plac-es Give to Thee who giv-est all.
Earth-ly store and bread of heav-en, Love and peace with-out al-loy;

Grant us, then, the grace of giv-ing With a spir-it large and free,
Thine own life Thou free-ly gav-est As an of-fering on the cross
Thou hast bought us, and no long-er Can we claim to be our own;
Hum-bly now we bow be-fore Thee, And our all to Thee re-sign;

That our life and all our liv-ing We may con-se-crate to Thee.
For each sin-ner whom Thou sav-est From e-ter-nal shame and loss.
Ev-er free and ev-er strong-er, We shall serve Thee, Lord, a-lone.
For the king-dom, power, and glo-ry Are, O Lord, for-ev-er Thine. A-men.

LIFE IN CHRIST: STEWARDSHIP

HEART AND MIND, POSSESSIONS, LORD 362

TANA MANA DHANA Irregular

Krishnarao Rathnaji Sangle, d. 1908
Tr. Alden H. Clark, b. 1878, and Others

Ancient Indian Melody
Adapted by Marion Jean Chute, b. 1901

1 Heart and mind, pos - ses - sions, Lord, I of - fer un - to Thee;
2 Heart and mind, pos - ses - sions, Lord, I of - fer un - to Thee;

All these were Thine, Lord; Thou didst give them all to me.
Thou art the way, the truth; Thou art the life.

Won-drous are Thy do - ings un - to me. Plans and my thoughts and
Sin - ful, I com - mit my - self to Thee. Je - sus Christ is fill - ing

ev - ery-thing I ev - er do are de - pend - ent on Thy
all the heart of me. He can give me vic - t'ry o'er

will and love a - lone. I com - mit my spir - it un - to Thee.
all that threat-ens me. Je - sus Christ is fill - ing all my heart.

LIFE IN CHRIST: STEWARDSHIP

363 GOD, WHOSE GIVING

HYFRYDOL 8.7.8.7.D.

Robert Lansing Edwards, 1961

Rowland Hugh Pritchard, c. 1830
Harmony by Ralph Vaughan Williams, 1951

1 God, whose giv - ing knows no end - ing, All our life is from Thy store:
2 Skills and time are ours for press - ing Toward the goals of Christ, Thy Son:
3 Trea - sure, too. Thou hast en - trust - ed, Gain through powers Thy grace con - ferred;
4 Lend Thy joy to all our giv - ing, Let it light our pil - grim way;

Na - ture's won - der, Je - sus' wis - dom, Cost - ly cross, grave's shat - tered door.
Men at peace in health and free - dom, Rac - es joined, the church made one.
Ours to use for home and kin - dred, And to spread the gos - pel Word.
From the dark of anx - ious keep - ing, Loose us in - to gen - erous day.

Gift - ed by Thee, turn we to Thee, Of - fering up our - selves in praise;
Now di - rect our dai - ly la - bor, Lest we strive for self a - lone;
O - pen wide our hands in shar - ing, As we heed Christ's age - less call,
Then when years on earth are o - ver, Rich toward Thee and fel - low man,

Thank - ful song shall rise for - ev - er; Gra - cious don - or of our days.
Born with tal - ents make us ser - vants Fit to an - swer at Thy throne.
Heal - ing, teach - ing, and re - claim - ing, Serv - ing Thee who lov - est all.
Lord, ful - fill be - yond our dream - ing All our stew - ard life be - gan. A - men.

LIFE IN CHRIST: STEWARDSHIP

WE GIVE THEE BUT THINE OWN 364

SCHUMANN S.M.

William Walsham How, 1858

Mason and Webb's *Cantica Laudis*, 1850

1 We give Thee but Thine own, What - e'er the gift may be:
2 May we Thy boun - ties thus As stew - ards true re - ceive,
3 To com - fort and to bless, To find a balm for woe,
4 The cap - tive to re - lease, To God the lost to bring,
5 And we be - lieve Thy word, Though dim our faith may be,

All that we have is Thine a - lone, A trust, O Lord, from Thee.
And glad - ly, as Thou bless - est us, To Thee our first - fruits give.
To tend the lone and fa - ther-less, Is an - gels' work be - low.
To teach the way of life and peace; That is a Christ-like thing.
What - e'er for Thine we do, O Lord, We do it un - to Thee.

ALL THINGS ARE THINE 365

O JESU CHRISTE, WAHRES LICHT L.M.

John Greenleaf Whittier, 1873

Gesangbuch, Nürnberg, 1676

1 All things are Thine; no gift have we, Lord of all gifts, to of - fer Thee;
2 Thy will was in the build - ers' thought; Thy hand un - seen a - midst us wrought;
3 In weak - ness and in want we call On Thee for whom the heav'ns are small;
4 O Fa - ther, deign these walls to bless; Fill with Thy love their emp - ti - ness;

And hence with grate - ful hearts to - day, Thine own be - fore Thy feet we lay.
Through mor - tal mo - tive, scheme, and plan, Thy wise e - ter - nal pur - pose ran.
Thy glo - ry is Thy chil - dren's good, Thy joy Thy ten - der fa - ther-hood.
And let their door a gate - way be To lead us from our - selves to Thee. A - men.

LIFE IN CHRIST: STEWARDSHIP

366 I HEARD A SOUND OF VOICES

PATMOS 7.6.8.6.D

Godfrey Thring. 1886

Henry Johnson Storer, 1891

1 I heard a sound of voic - es A - round the great white throne,
2 From ev - ery clime and kin - dred, And na - tions from a - far,
3 O great and glo - rious vi - sion! The Lamb up - on His throne;
4 And there no sun was need - ed, Nor moon to shine by night,

With harp - ers harp-ing on their harps To Him that sat there - on:
As ser - ried ranks re - turn - ing home In tri - umph from a war,
O won - drous sight for man to see! The Sav - ior with His own:
God's glo - ry did en - light - en all, The Lamb Him-self the light;

"Sal - va - tion, glo - ry, hon - or!" I heard the song a - rise,
I heard the saints up - rais - ing, The myr - iad hosts a - mong,
To drink the liv - ing wa - ters And stand up - on the shore,
And there His serv - ants serve Him, And, life's long bat - tle o'er,

As through the courts of heav'n it rolled In won-drous har - mo - nies.
In praise of Him who died and lives, Their one glad tri - umph song.
Where nei - ther sor - row, sin, nor death Shall ev - er en - ter more.
En - throned with Him, their Sav - ior, King, They reign for - ev - er - more.

LIFE IN CHRIST: LIFE ETERNAL

NOW IS ETERNAL LIFE 367

EASTVIEW 6.6.6.6.8.8.

George Wallace Briggs, 1951

Vernon Lee, 1951

1 Now is e - ter - nal life, If risen with
2 Man long in bond - age lay, Brood - ing o'er
3 And God, the liv - ing God, Stooped down to
4 Un - fath - omed love di - vine, Reign Thou with -
5 Thee will I love and serve Now in time's

Christ we stand, In Him to life re - born,
life's brief span; Was it, O God, for nought,
man's es - tate; By death de - stroy - ing death
in my heart; From Thee nor depth nor height,
pass - ing day; Thy hand shall hold me fast

And hold - en in His hand; No more we fear death's
For nought, Thou mad - est man? Thou art our hope, our
Christ o - pened wide life's gate; He lives, who died; He
Nor life nor death can part; My life is hid in
When time is done a - way, In God's un - known e -

an - cient dread, In Christ a - ris - en from the dead.
vi - tal breath; Shall hope un - dy - ing end in death?
reigns on high; Who live in Him shall nev - er die.
God with Thee, Now and through all e - ter - ni - ty.
ter - nal spheres To serve Him through e - ter - nal years.

LIFE IN CHRIST: LIFE ETERNAL

368 SING WE THE SONG
NATIVITY C.M.

James Montgomery, 1824

Henry Lahee, 1855

1 Sing we the song of those who stand A - round th'e-
2 Toil, tri - al, suf - fering, still a - wait On earth the
3 "Wor - thy the Lamb for sin - ners slain," Cry the re-
4 "Wor - thy the Lamb!" on earth we sing, "Who died our
5 Then, Al - le - lu - ia! power and praise To God in

ter - nal throne, Of ev - ery kin - dred,
pil - grim throng, Yet learn we, in our
deem'd a - bove, "Bless - ing and hon - or
souls to save; Hence - forth, O death! where
Christ be given; May all who now this

clime, and land, A mul - ti - tude un - known.
low es - tate, The church - tri - um - phant's song.
to ob - tain, And ev - er - last - ing love."
is thy sting? Thy vic - to - ry, O grave?"
an - them raise Re - new the strain in heav'n!

369 ALMIGHTY MAKER OF MY FRAME
WINSCOTT L.M.

Anne Steele, 1760

Samuel Sebastian Wesley, 1872

1 Al - might-y Mak - er of my frame! Teach me the mea - sure of my days,
2 My days are short - er than a span, A lit - tle point my life ap - pears;
3 Vain his am - bi - tion, noise and show; Vain are the cares which rack his mind;
4 O be a no - bler por - tion mine! My God, I bow be - fore Thy throne;

LIFE IN CHRIST: LIFE ETERNAL

Teach me to know how frail I am, And spend the rem-nant to Thy praise.
How frail at best is dy-ing man! How vain are all his hopes and fears!
He heaps up trea-sures mixed with woe, And dies and leaves them all be-hind.
Earth's fleet-ing trea-sures I re-sign, And fix my hope on Thee a-lone.

JERUSALEM! MY HAPPY HOME 370
LAND OF REST C.M.

Joseph Bromehead, 1795

Folk Hymn
Adapted from J. James' *Original Sacred Harp*, 1911

1 Je - ru - sa - lem! my hap - py home, Name
2 When shall these eyes thy heav'n - built walls And
3 O when, thou cit - y of my God, Shall
4 A - pos - tles, mar - tyrs, proph - ets there, A -
5 Je - ru - sa - lem! my hap - py home, My

ev - er dear to me! When shall my la - bors
pearl - y gates be - hold; Thy bul - warks with sal -
I thy courts as - cend; Where con - gre - ga - tions
round my Sav - ior stand; And soon my friends in
soul still pants for thee; Then shall my la - bors

have an end In joy, and peace, and thee?
va - tion strong, And streets of shin - ing gold!
ne'er break up, And Sab - baths have no end?
Christ be - low, Will join the glo - rious band.
have an end, When I thy joys shall see.

LIFE IN CHRIST: LIFE ETERNAL

371 LORD, IT BELONGS NOT TO MY CARE

COLESHILL C.M.

Richard Baxter‡, 1681

W. Barton's *Psalms*, 1706

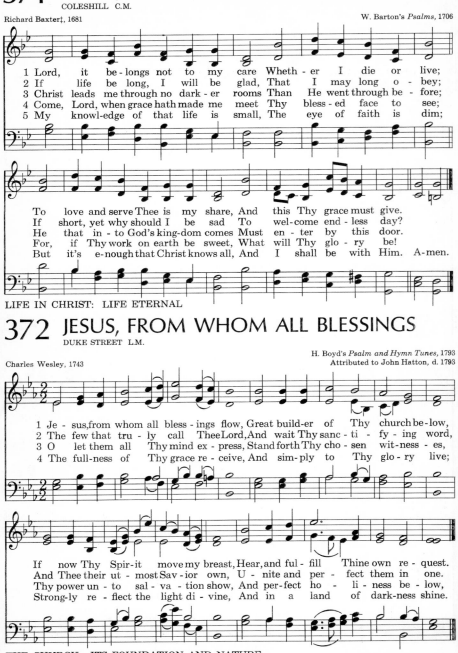

1 Lord, it be - longs not to my care Wheth - er I die or live;
2 If life be long, I will be glad, That I may long o - bey;
3 Christ leads me through no dark - er rooms Than He went through be - fore;
4 Come, Lord, when grace hath made me meet Thy bless - ed face to see;
5 My knowl-edge of that life is small, The eye of faith is dim;

To love and serve Thee is my share, And this Thy grace must give.
If short, yet why should I be sad To wel-come end - less day?
He that in - to God's king-dom comes Must en - ter by this door.
For, if Thy work on earth be sweet, What will Thy glo - ry be!
But it's e-nough that Christ knows all, And I shall be with Him. A-men.

LIFE IN CHRIST: LIFE ETERNAL

372 JESUS, FROM WHOM ALL BLESSINGS

DUKE STREET L.M.

H. Boyd's *Psalm and Hymn Tunes*, 1793

Charles Wesley, 1743

Attributed to John Hatton, d. 1793

1 Je - sus, from whom all bless - ings flow, Great build-er of Thy church be-low,
2 The few that tru - ly call Thee Lord, And wait Thy sanc - ti - fy - ing word,
3 O let them all Thy mind ex - press, Stand forth Thy cho - sen wit-ness - es,
4 The full-ness of Thy grace re - ceive, And sim-ply to Thy glo - ry live;

If now Thy Spir-it move my breast, Hear, and ful - fill Thine own re - quest.
And Thee their ut - most Sav - ior own, U - nite and per - fect them in one.
Thy power un - to sal - va - tion show, And per-fect ho - li - ness be - low,
Strong-ly re - flect the light di - vine, And in a land of dark-ness shine.

THE CHURCH: ITS FOUNDATION AND NATURE

CHRIST IS MADE THE SURE FOUNDATION 373

REGENT SQUARE 8.7.8.7.8.7.

Anonymous Latin
Angularis fundamentum lapis
Tr. J. M. Neale and Compilers
of *Hymns Ancient and Modern*, 1861

Henry Smart, 1867

1 Christ is made the sure foun-da-tion, Christ the head and cor-ner-stone, Cho-sen of the Lord and pre-cious, Bind-ing all the church in one, Ho-ly Zi-on's help for-ev-er, And her con-fi-dence a-lone.

2 To this tem-ple, where we call Thee, Come, O Lord of hosts, to-day: With Thy wont-ed lov-ing-kind-ness Hear Thy peo-ple as they pray, And Thy full-est ben-e-dic-tion Shed with-in its walls al-way.

3 Here vouch-safe to all Thy serv-ants What they ask of Thee to gain, What they gain from Thee for-ev-er With the bless-ed to re-tain, And here-af-ter in Thy glo-ry Ev-er-more with Thee to reign.

4 Praise and hon-or to the Fa-ther, Praise and hon-or to the Son, Praise and hon-or to the Spir-it, Ev-er three, and ev-er one, One in might and one in glo-ry, While e-ter-nal a-ges run. A-men.

THE CHURCH: ITS FOUNDATION AND NATURE

374 CHRIST IS OUR CORNERSTONE

DARWALL 148   6.6.6.6.8.8.

Anonymous Latin
Angularis fundamentum lapis
Tr. John Chandler†, 1837

John Darwall, 1770

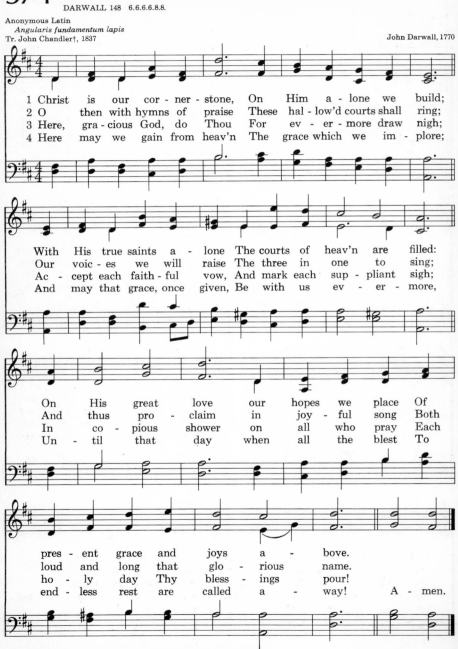

1 Christ is our cor - ner - stone, On Him a - lone we build;
2 O then with hymns of praise These hal - low'd courts shall ring;
3 Here, gra - cious God, do Thou For ev - er - more draw nigh;
4 Here may we gain from heav'n The grace which we im - plore;

With His true saints a - lone The courts of heav'n are filled:
Our voic - es we will raise The three in one to sing;
Ac - cept each faith - ful vow, And mark each sup - pliant sigh;
And may that grace, once given, Be with us ev - er - more,

On His great love our hopes we place Of
And thus pro - claim in joy - ful song Both
In co - pious shower on all who pray Each
Un - til that day when all the blest To

pres - ent grace and joys a - bove.
loud and long that glo - rious name.
ho - ly day Thy bless - ings pour!
end - less rest are called a - way! A - men.

THE CHURCH: ITS FOUNDATION AND NATURE

THE CHURCH'S ONE FOUNDATION 375

AURELIA 7.6.7.6.D.

Samuel John Stone, 1868   Samuel Sebastian Wesley, 1864

1 The church's one foun - da - tion Is Je - sus Christ her Lord;
2 E - lect from ev - ery na - tion Yet one o'er all the earth,
3 Though with a scorn - ful won - der Men see her sore op - pressed,
4 'Mid toil and trib - u - la - tion, And tu - mult of her war,
5 Yet she on earth hath un - ion With God the three in one,

She is His new cre - a - tion By wa - ter and the word:
Her char - ter of sal - va - tion One Lord, one faith, one birth;
By schisms rent a - sun - der, By her - e - sies dis - tressed,
She waits the con - sum - ma - tion Of peace for ev - er - more;
And mys - tic sweet com - mun - ion With those whose rest is won:

From heav'n He came and sought her To be His ho - ly bride;
One ho - ly name she bless - es, Par - takes one ho - ly food;
Yet saints their watch are keep - ing, Their cry goes up, "How long?"
Till with the vi - sion glo - rious Her long - ing eyes are blest,
O hap - py ones and ho - ly! Lord, give us grace that we,

With His own blood He bought her, And for her life He died.
And to one hope she press - es, With ev - ery grace en - dued.
And soon the night of weep - ing Shall be the morn of song.
And the great church vic - to - rious Shall be the church at rest.
Like them the meek and low - ly, On high may dwell with Thee. A - men.

THE CHURCH: ITS FOUNDATION AND NATURE

376 GLORIOUS THINGS OF THEE ARE SPOKEN

AUSTRIAN HYMN 8.7.8.7.D.

John Newton, 1779

Franz Joseph Haydn, 1797

1 Glo-rious things of thee are spo-ken, Zi-on, cit-y of our God;
2 See the streams of liv-ing wa-ters, Spring-ing from e-ter-nal love,
3 Round each hab-i-ta-tion hov-'ring, See the cloud and fire ap-pear
4 Sav-ior, if of Zi-on's cit-y I, through grace, a mem-ber am,

He whose word can-not be bro-ken Formed thee for His own a-bode:
Well sup-ply thy sons and daugh-ters, And all fear of want re-move:
For a glo-ry and a cov-'ring, Show-ing that the Lord is near:
Let the world de-ride or pit-y, I will glo-ry in Thy name:

On the rock of a-ges found-ed, What can shake thy sure re-pose?
Who can faint while such a riv-er Ev-er flows their thirst to assuage;
Thus de-riv-ing from their ban-ner Light by night and shade by day,
Fad-ing is the world-ling's plea-sure, All his boast-ed pomp and show;

With sal-va-tion's walls sur-round-ed, Thou mayst smile at all thy foes.
Grace which, like the Lord the giv-er, Nev-er fails from age to age?
Safe they feed up-on the man-na Which He gives them when they pray.
Sol-id joys and last-ing trea-sure None but Zi-on's chil-dren know.

THE CHURCH: ITS FOUNDATION AND NATURE

HERE, O LORD, THY SERVANTS GATHER 377

TOKYO 7.5.7.5.D.

Tokuo Yamaguchi, 1958
Sekai no tomo to te o tsunagi
Tr. Everett M. Stowe†, 1958

Japanese Melody
Isao Koizumi, 1958
Altered by permission

1 Here, O Lord, Thy serv-ants gath-er, Hand we link with hand;
2 Man-y are the tongues we speak, Scat-tered are the lands,
3 Na-ture's se-crets o-pen wide, Chang-es nev-er cease;
4 Grant, O God, an age re-newed, Filled with death-less love,

Look-ing toward our Sav-ior's cross, Joined in love we stand.
Yet our hearts are one in God And His love's de-mands.
Where, O where, can wea-ry men Find the source of peace?
Help us as we work and pray, Send us from a-bove

As we seek the realm of God, We u-nite to pray:
E'en in dark-ness hope ap-pears, Call-ing age and youth:
Un-to all those sore dis-tressed, Torn by end-less strife:
Truth and cour-age, faith and power Need-ed in our strife:

Je-sus, Sav-ior, guide our steps, For Thou art the way.
Je-sus, teach-er, dwell with us, For Thou art the truth.
Je-sus, heal-er, bring Thy balm, For Thou art the life.
Je-sus Christ, Thou art our way, Thou our truth, our life.

THE CHURCH: ITS FOUNDATION AND NATURE

378 O WHERE ARE KINGS AND EMPIRES

ST. ANNE C.M.

Arthur Cleveland Coxe‡, 1839

William Croft (?) 1708

1 O where are kings and em-pires now Of old that went and came?
2 We mark her good-ly bat-tle-ments, And her foun-da-tions strong;
3 For not like king-doms of the world, Thy ho-ly church, O God!
4 Un-shak-en as e-ter-nal hills, Im-mov-a-ble she stands,

But, Lord, Thy church is pray-ing yet, A thou-sand years the same.
We hear with-in the sol-emn voice Of her un-end-ing song.
Though earth-quake shocks are threat-'ning her, And tem-pests are a-broad.
A moun-tain that shall fill the earth, A house not made by hands.

379 JESUS, WITH THY CHURCH ABIDE

HERVEY'S LITANY 7.7.7.6.

Thomas Benson Pollock, 1871

Frederick A. J. Hervey, 1875
Harmony from *The Hymnal*, 1940

1 Je-sus, with Thy church a-bide, Be her Sav-ior, Lord, and Guide,
2 May she one in doc-trine be, One in truth and char-i-ty,
3 May she guide the poor and blind, Seek the lost un-til she find,
4 May the grace of Him who died, And the Fa-ther's love a-bide,

While on earth her faith is tried: We be-seech Thee, hear us.
Win-ning all to faith in Thee: We be-seech Thee, hear us.
And the bro-ken-heart-ed bind: We be-seech Thee, hear us.
And the Spir-it ev-er guide: We be-seech Thee, hear us. A-men.

THE CHURCH: ITS FOUNDATION AND NATURE

I LOVE THY KINGDOM, LORD 380

BEALOTH S.M.D.

Timothy Dwight, 1800

Lowell Mason, d. 1872

1 I love Thy king-dom, Lord, The house of Thine a - bode,
2 For her my tears shall fall, For her my prayers as - cend;
3 Je - sus, Thou friend di - vine, Our Sav - ior and our King,

The church our blest Re - deem - er saved With His own pre - cious blood.
To her my cares and toils be giv'n Till toils and cares shall end.
Thy hand from ev - ery snare and foe Shall great de - liv - 'rance bring.

I love Thy church, O God, Her walls be - fore Thee stand,
Be - yond my high - est joy I prize her heav'n - ly ways,
Sure as Thy truth shall last, To Zi - on shall be giv'n

Dear as the ap - ple of Thine eye, And grav - en on Thy hand.
Her sweet com-mun-ion, sol - emn vows, Her hymns of love and praise.
The bright-est glo - ries earth can yield, And bright-er bliss of heav'n.

THE CHURCH: ITS FOUNDATION AND NATURE

381 JESUS, WHERE'ER THY PEOPLE MEET

SHELTERING WING L.M.

William Cowper, 1779

Joseph Barnby, 1872

1 Je - sus, wher - e'er Thy peo - ple meet, There they be - hold Thy mer - cy seat; Wher - e'er they seek Thee, Thou art found, And ev - ery place is hal - lowed ground.

2 For Thou, with - in no walls con - fined, In - hab - it - est the hum - ble mind; Such ev - er bring Thee where they come, And, go - ing, take Thee to their home.

3 Dear Shep - herd of Thy cho - sen few, Thy for - mer mer - cies here re - new; Here, to our wait - ing hearts, pro - claim The sweet - ness of Thy sav - ing name.

4 Here may we prove the power of prayer To strength - en faith and sweet - en care; To teach our faint de - sires to rise, And bring all heav'n be - fore our eyes.

382 LO, WHAT A PLEASING SIGHT

GERAR S.M.

Based on Psalm 133
Isaac Watts, 1719, and Others

Lowell Mason, 1836

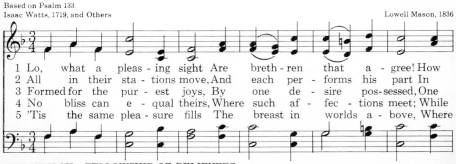

1 Lo, what a pleas - ing sight Are breth - ren that a - gree! How

2 All in their sta - tions move, And each per - forms his part In

3 Formed for the pur - est joys, By one de - sire pos - sessed, One

4 No bliss can e - qual theirs, Where such af - fec - tions meet; While

5 'Tis the same plea - sure fills The breast in worlds a - bove, Where

THE CHURCH: FELLOWSHIP OF BELIEVERS

blest are all whose hearts u - nite In bonds of pi - e - ty.
all the cares of life and love, With sym - pa - thiz - ing heart.
aim the zeal of all em - ploys, To make each oth - er blest.
praise de - vout, and min - gled prayers Make their com - mun-ion sweet.
joy, like morn-ing dew, dis - tils, And all the air is love.

ALL PRAISE TO OUR REDEEMING LORD 383

DEDHAM C.M.

Charles Wesley, 1747, Sts. 1 to 4
Supplement to Church and Sunday School Hymnal, 1911, St. 5

L. Mason's *Boston Handel and Haydn Society . . . , 1822*

1 All praise to our re - deem-ing Lord, Who joins us by His grace,
2 He bids us build each oth - er up; And, gath - ered in - to one,
3 The gift which He on one be - stows, We all de - light to prove;
4 We all par-take the joy of one; The com - mon peace we feel;

And bids us, each to each re - stored, To-geth - er seek His face.
To our high call-ing's glo - rious hope, We hand in hand go on.
The grace through ev-ery ves - sel flows, In pur - est streams of love.
A peace to world-ly minds un - known, A joy un - speak - a - ble.

5 The kiss of peace to each we give,
A pledge of Christian love;
In love, while here on earth we'll live,
In love we'll dwell above.

THE CHURCH: FELLOWSHIP OF BELIEVERS

384 OUR FATHER GOD, THY NAME

NUN FREUT EUCH 8.7.8.7.8.8.7.

Leenaerdt Clock, c. 1590
O Gott, Vater, wir loben dich
Tr. Ernest A. Payne, 1956 and 1962

J. Klug's *Geistliche Lieder*, 1535

1 Our Fa-ther God, Thy name we praise, To Thee our hymns ad-dress - ing,
2 Touch, Lord, the lips that speak for Thee; Set words of truth be - fore us,
3 Lord, make Thy pil-grim peo-ple wise, The gos-pel mes-sage know - ing,
4 As with our breth-ren here we meet, Thy grace a - lone can feed us,

And joy-ful - ly our voic-es raise Thy faith-ful-ness con - fess - ing:
That we may grow in con-stan - cy, The light of wis-dom o'er us.
That we may walk with light-ened eyes In grace and good-ness grow - ing.
As here we gath-er at Thy feet We pray that Thou wilt heed us.

As - sem - bled by Thy grace, O Lord, We seek fresh guid-ance
Give us this day our dai - ly bread; May hun - gry souls a-
The right-eous must Thy pre-cepts heed; Thy Word a - lone sup-
The power is Thine, O Lord di - vine, The king-dom and the

from Thy Word; Now grant a - new Thy bless - ing.
gain be fed; May heav'n - ly food re - store us.
plies their need, From heav'n their suc - cor flow - ing.
rule are Thine. May Je - sus Christ still lead us!

THE CHURCH: FELLOWSHIP OF BELIEVERS

1 O Gott Vater, wir loben dich
  und deine Güte preisen,
die du, o Herr, so gnädiglich
  an uns neu hast bewiesen;
und hast uns, Herr, zusammeng'führt,
uns zu ermahnen durch dein Wort.
  Gib uns Genad zu diesem!

2 Öffne den Mund, Herr, deiner Knecht,
  gib ihn'n Weisheit daneben,
dass sie dein Wort mög'n sprechen recht,
  was dient zum frommen Leben
und nützlich ist zu deinem Preis.
Gib uns Hunger nach solcher Speis,
  das is unser Begehren.

3 Gib unserm Herzen auch Verstand,
  Erleuchtung hier auf Erden,
dass dein Wort in uns werd bekannt,
  dass wir fromm mögen werden
und leben in Gerechtigkeit,
achten auf dein Wort allezeit.
  So bleib'n wir unbetrogen.

4 Dein, o Herr, ist das Reich allein
  und auch die Macht zusammen.
Wir loben dich in der Gemein
  und danken deinem Namen
und bitten dich aus Herzens Grund,
wollst bei uns sein zu dieser Stund,
  durch Jesum Christum, Amen.

BLEST BE THE TIE THAT BINDS 385

DENNIS S.M.

Arranged from J. G. Nägeli, 1832
by Lowell Mason, 1845

John Fawcett, c. 1772

1 Blest be the tie that binds Our hearts in Chris - tian love:
2 Be - fore our Fa - ther's throne We pour our ar - dent prayers;
3 We share our mu - tual woes, Our mu - tual bur - dens bear;
4 When we a - sun - der part It gives us in - ward pain;
5 This glo - rious hope re - vives Our cour - age by the way;
6 From sor - row, toil, and pain, And sin we shall be free;

The fel - low - ship of kin - dred minds Is like to that a - bove.
Our fears, our hopes, our aims are one, Our com - forts and our cares.
And oft - en for each oth - er flows The sym - pa - thiz - ing tear.
But we shall still be joined in heart, And hope to meet a - gain.
While each in ex - pec - ta - tion lives And longs to see the day.
And per - fect love and friend-ship reign Through all e - ter - ni - ty. A - men.

THE CHURCH: FELLOWSHIP OF BELIEVERS

386 HEART WITH LOVING HEART UNITED

O DU LEIBE MEINER LIEBE 8.7.8.7.D.

Nikolaus Ludwig von Zinzendorf, 1723
Herz und Herz vereint zusammen
Tr. Walter Klaassen, 1965

Manuscript Chorale Book,
Herrnhaag, 1735

1 Heart with lov - ing   heart u - nit - ed,   Met to know God's ho - ly will.
2 May we all so   love each oth - er   And all self - ish claims de - ny,
3 Since, O Lord, You   have de-mand-ed   That our lives Your love should show,

Let His love in   us   ig - nit - ed   More and more our   spir - its   fill.
That the broth-er   for   the broth-er   Will not hes - i - tate to   die.
So we wait to   be   com-mand-ed   Forth in - to Your world to   go.

He the head, we   are   His mem-bers; We re - flect the light He   is.
E - ven so   our Lord has loved us; For our lives He shed His blood.
Kin - dle in   us love's com-pas - sion So that ev - ery - one   may see

He the Mas-ter,   we the broth-ers, He   is ours and   we are His.
Still He grieves and still He suf - fers When we mar the broth-er - hood.
In   our fel - low - ship the prom-ise Of   the new hu - man - i - ty.   A-men.

THE CHURCH: FELLOWSHIP OF BELIEVERS

IN CHRIST THERE IS NO EAST OR WEST 387

ST. PETER C.M.

John Oxenham, 1908

Alexander Robert Reinagle, c. 1836

1 In Christ there is no East or West, In Him no South or North;
2 In Him shall true hearts ev-ery-where Their high com-mun-ion find;
3 Join hands, then, broth-ers of the faith, What-e'er your race may be.
4 In Christ now meet both East and West, In Him meet South and North;

But one great fel-low-ship of love Through-out the whole wide earth.
His serv-ice is the gold-en cord Close bind-ing all man-kind.
Who serves my Fa-ther as a son Is sure-ly kin to me.
All Christ-ly souls are one in Him Through-out the whole wide earth. A-men.

THE CHURCH: THE FELLOWSHIP OF BELIEVERS

POUR OUT THY SPIRIT FROM ON HIGH 388

MENDON L.M.

James Montgomery, 1833

"German Air" in Samuel Dyer's
Selection of Sacred Music, 1825

1 Pour out Thy Spir-it from on high; Lord, Thine as-sem-bled serv-ants bless;
2 With-in Thy tem-ple when we stand, To teach the truth, as taught by Thee,
3 Wis-dom and zeal and faith im-part, Firm-ness with meek-ness from a-bove,
4 To watch and pray, and nev-er faint; By day and night strict guard to keep;
5 Then, when our work is fin-ished here, In hum-ble hope our charge re-sign:

Grac-es and gifts to each sup-ply, And clothe Thy priests with right-eous-ness.
Sav-ior, like stars in Thy right hand The an-gels of the church-es be!
To bear Thy peo-ple on our heart, And love the souls whom Thou dost love;
To warn the sin-ner, cheer the saint, Nour-ish Thy lambs, and feed Thy sheep;
When the Chief Shepherd shall appear, O God, may they and we be Thine. A-men.

THE MINISTRY: PASTORS AND TEACHERS

389 LORD, SPEAK TO ME

CANONBURY L.M.

Frances Ridley Havergal, 1872

Arranged from Robert Schumann, 1839

1 Lord, speak to me, that I may speak In liv-ing ech-oes of Thy tone;
2 O lead me, Lord, that I may lead The wan-d'ring and the wav-'ring feet;
3 O strength-en me, that while I stand Firm on the Rock, and strong in Thee,
4 O teach me, Lord, that I may teach The pre-cious things Thou dost im-part;
5 O fill me with Thy full-ness, Lord, Un-til my ver-y heart o'er-flow

As Thou hast sought, so let me seek Thy err-ing chil-dren lost and lone.
O feed me, Lord, that I may feed Thy hun-g'ring ones with man-na sweet.
I may stretch out a lov-ing hand To wres-tlers with the trou-bled sea.
And wing my words, that they may reach The hid-den depths of many a heart.
In kin-dling thought and glow-ing word, Thy love to tell, Thy praise to show. A-men.

THE MINISTRY: PASTORS AND TEACHERS

390 TO THY TEMPLE I REPAIR

GUISBOROUGH 7.7.7.7.

James Montgomery, 1812

C. T. Bowen, b. 1833

1 To Thy tem-ple I re-pair; Lord, I love to wor-ship there,
2 While Thy glo-rious praise is sung, Touch my lips, un-loose my tongue,
3 While the prayers of saints as-cend, God of love, to mine at-tend;
4 While Thy min-is-ters pro-claim Peace and par-don in Thy name,
5 From Thy house when I re-turn, May my heart with-in me burn,

When with-in the veil I meet Christ be-fore the mer-cy seat.
That my joy-ful soul may bless Thee, the Lord my right-eous-ness.
Hear me, for Thy Spir-it pleads; Hear, for Je-sus in-ter-cedes.
Through their voice, by faith, may I Hear Thee speak-ing from the sky.
And at eve-ning let me say, "I have walked with God to-day." A-men.

THE CHURCH: THE LORD'S HOUSE

BLESSED JESUS, AT THY WORD 391

LIEBSTER JESU, WIR SIND HIER 7.8.7.8.8.8.

Tobias Clausnitzer, 1663
Liebster Jesu, wir sind hier
Tr. Catherine Winkworth†, 1858

Johann Rudolph Ahle, 1664

1 Bless - ed Je - sus, at Thy word We are gath - ered
2 All our knowl - edge, sense, and sight Lie in deep - est
3 Glo - rious Lord, Thy - self im - part! Light of light from

all to hear Thee; Let our hearts and souls be stirred
dark - ness shroud - ed, Till Thy Spir - it breaks our night
God pro - ceed - ing, O - pen Thou our ears and heart,

Now to seek and love and fear Thee; By Thy teach-ings true and
With the beams of truth un - cloud - ed; Thou a - lone to God canst
Help us by Thy Spir-it's plead - ing, Hear the cry Thy peo - ple

ho - ly Drawn from earth to love Thee sole - ly.
win us, Thou must work all good with - in us.
rais - es, Hear, and bless our prayers and prais - es! A - men.

392 LORD OF THE WORLDS ABOVE

DARWALL 148   6.6.6.6.8.8.

Based on Psalm 84
Isaac Watts, 1719

John Darwall, 1770

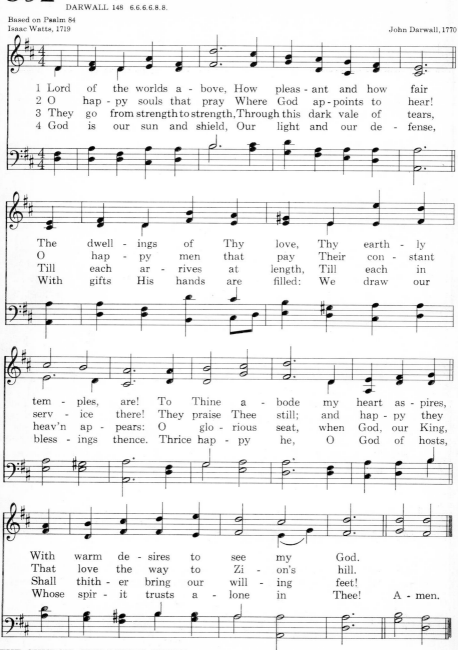

1 Lord of the worlds a - bove, How pleas - ant and how fair
2 O hap - py souls that pray Where God ap - points to hear!
3 They go from strength to strength, Through this dark vale of tears,
4 God is our sun and shield, Our light and our de - fense,

The dwell - ings of Thy love, Thy earth - ly
O hap - py men that pay Their con - stant
Till each ar - rives at length, Till each in
With gifts His hands are filled: We draw our

tem - ples, are! To Thine a - bode my heart as - pires,
serv - ice there! They praise Thee still; and hap - py they
heav'n ap - pears: O glo - rious seat, when God, our King,
bless - ings thence. Thrice hap - py he, O God of hosts,

With warm de - sires to see my God.
That love the way to Zi - on's hill.
Shall thith - er bring our will - ing feet!
Whose spir - it trusts a - lone in Thee! A - men.

THE CHURCH: THE LORD'S HOUSE

HOW LOVELY ARE THY DWELLINGS FAIR 393

WINCHESTER OLD C.M.

John Milton, 1648

T. Est's *Whole Booke of Psalmes*, 1592

1 How love - ly are Thy dwell-ings fair! O Lord of hosts, how dear
2 Hap - py, who in Thy house re - side, Where Thee they ev - er praise,
3 They pass through Ba - ca's thirst - y vale, That dry and bar - ren ground,
4 They jour - ney on from strength to strength With joy and glad - some cheer,
5 Lord God of hosts that reign'st on high, That man is tru - ly blest

The pleas - ant tab - er - na - cles are Where Thou dost dwell so near!
Hap - py, whose strength in Thee doth bide, And in their hearts Thy ways.
As through a fruit - ful wa - tery dale Where springs and show'rs a - bound.
Till all be - fore our God at length In Zi - on do ap - pear.
Who on - ly on Thee doth re - ly, And in Thee on - ly rest. A - men.

THE CHURCH: THE LORD'S HOUSE

COME, LET US JOIN OUR FRIENDS 394

DUNDEE C.M.

Charles Wesley‡, 1759

Scottish Psalter, 1615

1 Come, let us join our friends a - bove Who have ob - tained the prize,
2 Let saints on earth u - nite and sing, With those to glo - ry gone;
3 One fam - i - ly we dwell in Him, One church, a - bove, be - neath,
4 One ar - my of the liv - ing God, To His com - mand we bow;
5 E'en now by faith we join our hands With those that went be - fore,

And on the ea - gle wings of love To joy ce - les - tial rise.
For all the serv - ants of our King, In earth and heav'n, are one.
Though now di - vid - ed by the stream, The nar - row stream of death:
Part of His host have crossed the flood, And part are cross - ing now.
And greet the blood - re - deem - ed bands On the e - ter - nal shore.

THE CHURCH: COMMUNION OF SAINTS

395 FOR ALL THE SAINTS

SINE NOMINE 10.10.10. with Alleluias

William Walsham How, 1864

Ralph Vaughan Williams, 1906

In unison

1 For all the saints, who from their la - bors rest, Who
2 Thou wast their rock, their for - tress, and their might:
3 O may Thy sol - diers, faith - ful, true, and bold,
7 But lo! there breaks a yet more glo - rious day; The
8 From earth's wide bounds, from o - cean's far - thest coast, Through

Thee by faith be - fore the world con - fessed,
Thou, Lord, their cap - tain in the well-fought fight;
Fight as the saints who no - bly fought of old,
saints tri - um - phant rise in bright ar - ray;
gates of pearl streams in the count - less host,

Thy name, O Je - sus, be for ev - er blest.
Thou, in the dark - ness drear, the one true light.
And win, with them, the vic - tor's crown of gold.
The King of glo - ry pass - es on His way.
Sing - ing to Fa - ther, Son, and Ho - ly Ghost,

THE CHURCH: COMMUNION OF SAINTS

Al - le - lu - ia, al - le - lu - ia!

In harmony

A - men.

In harmony

4 O blest com-mun - ion, fel-low-ship di - vine! We fee-bly strug-gle,
5 And when the strife is fierce, the war-fare long, Steals on the ear the
6 The gold-en eve - ning bright-ens in the west; Soon, soon to faith-ful

(Small notes st. 6)

they in glo - ry shine; Yet all are one in Thee, for all are
dis - tant tri-umph song, And hearts are brave a - gain, and arms are
war-riors com-eth rest; Sweet is the calm of pa - ra - dise the

Thine.
strong. Al - le - lu - ia, al - le - lu - ia!
blest.

THE CHURCH: COMMUNION OF SAINTS

396 WE COME UNTO OUR FATHERS' GOD

NUN FREUT EUCH 8.7.8.7.8.8.7.

Thomas Hornblower Gill, 1868

J. Klug's *Geistliche Lieder*, 1535

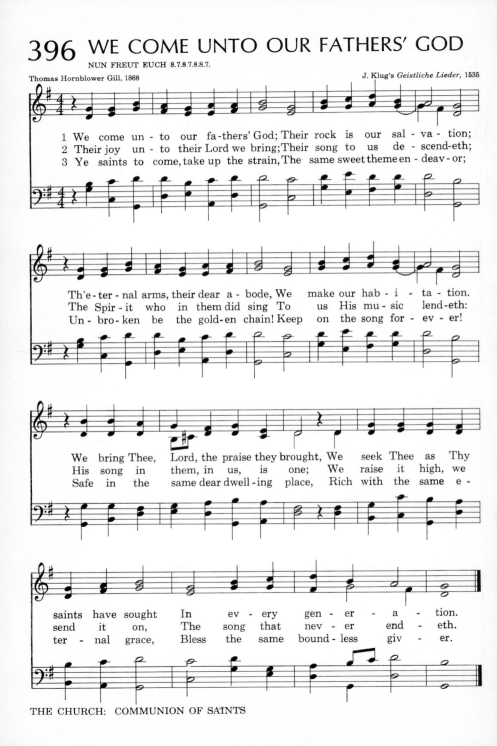

1 We come un-to our fa-thers' God; Their rock is our sal-va-tion;
2 Their joy un-to their Lord we bring; Their song to us de-scend-eth;
3 Ye saints to come, take up the strain, The same sweet theme en-deav-or;

Th'e-ter-nal arms, their dear a-bode, We make our hab-i-ta-tion.
The Spir-it who in them did sing To us His mu-sic lend-eth:
Un-bro-ken be the gold-en chain! Keep on the song for-ev-er!

We bring Thee, Lord, the praise they brought, We seek Thee as Thy
His song in them, in us, is one; We raise it high, we
Safe in the same dear dwell-ing place, Rich with the same e-

saints have sought In ev-ery gen-er-a-tion.
send it on, The song that nev-er end-eth.
ter-nal grace, Bless the same bound-less giv-er.

THE CHURCH: COMMUNION OF SAINTS

HE WANTS NOT FRIENDS 397

SONG XXXIV L.M.

Richard Baxter†, 1663

Orlando Gibbons, 1623

1 He wants not friends that hath Thy love, And may converse and walk with Thee, And with Thy saints here and a-
bove, With whom for ev - er I must be.

2 In the com - mun - ion of the saints Is wis - dom,
safe - ty and de - light; And, when my heart de - clines and
faints, It's rais - ed by their heat and light.

3 As for my friends, they are not lost; The sev - eral
ves - sels of Thy fleet, Though part - ed now, by tem - pests
tossed, Shall safe - ly in the ha - ven meet.

4 Still we are cen - tered all in Thee, Mem - bers, though
dis - tant, of one head; In the same fam - i - ly we
be, By the same faith and Spir - it led.

5 Before Thy throne we daily meet
  As joint-petitioners to Thee;
  In spirit we each other greet,
  And shall again each other see.

6 The heav'nly hosts, world without end,
  Shall be my company above;
  And Thou, my best and surest friend,
  Who shall divide me from Thy love?

THE CHURCH: COMMUNION OF SAINTS

398 O HAPPY DAY, THAT FIXED MY CHOICE

ROCKINGHAM NEW L.M.

Philip Doddridge, 1755

Lowell Mason, 1830

1 O hap - py day, that fixed my choice On Thee, my
2 O hap - py bond, that seals my vows, To Him who
3 'Tis done! the great trans - ac - tion's done; I am my
4 High heav'n, that heard the sol - emn vow, That vow re -

Sav - ior and my God! Well may this glow - ing
mer - its all my love! Let cheer - ful an - thems
Lord's, and He is mine; He drew me, and I
newed shall dai - ly hear, Till in life's lat - est

heart re - joice, And tell its rap - tures all a - broad.
fill His house, While to that sa - cred shrine I move.
fol - lowed on, Charmed to con - fess the voice di - vine.
hour I bow, And bless in death a bond so dear.

399 MY GOD, ACCEPT MY HEART

GLENLUCE C.M.

Matthew Bridges, 1848

Scottish Psalter, 1635

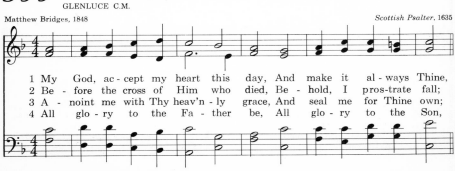

1 My God, ac - cept my heart this day, And make it al - ways Thine,
2 Be - fore the cross of Him who died, Be - hold, I pros - trate fall;
3 A - noint me with Thy heav'n - ly grace, And seal me for Thine own;
4 All glo - ry to the Fa - ther be, All glo - ry to the Son,

THE CHURCH: SACRAMENTS — BAPTISM

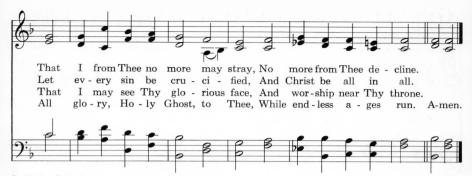

That   I from Thee no   more   may stray, No   more from Thee de - cline.
Let   ev - ery sin be   cru - ci - fied, And Christ be all in   all.
That   I may see Thy glo - rious face, And wor-ship near Thy throne.
All   glo - ry, Ho - ly Ghost, to   Thee, While end-less a - ges   run. A-men.

See Topical Index for other suitable hymns on "Baptism."

ACCORDING TO THY GRACIOUS WORD 400

ST. FLAVIAN C.M.

James Montgomery, 1825

English Psalter, 1562

1 Ac - cord - ing to Thy gra-cious Word, In meek hu - mil - i - ty,
2 Thy bod - y, bro - ken for my sake, My bread from heav'n shall be;
3 Geth - sem - a - ne can I for - get? Or there Thy con - flict see,
4 When to the cross I turn my eyes, And rest on Cal - va - ry,
5 Re - mem - ber Thee, and all Thy pains, And all Thy love to me:
6 And when these fail - ing lips grow dumb, And mind and mem - 'ry flee,

This will I do, my dy - ing Lord, I will re - mem - ber Thee.
Thy tes - ta - men - tal cup I take, And thus re - mem - ber Thee.
Thine ag - o - ny and blood - y sweat, And not re - mem - ber Thee?
O   Lamb of God, my sac - ri - fice, I must re - mem - ber Thee.
Yea, while a breath, a pulse re-mains Will I re - mem - ber Thee.
When Thou shalt in Thy king-dom come, Je - sus, re - mem - ber me. A - men.

THE CHURCH: SACRAMENTS — THE LORD'S SUPPER

401 BREAD OF HEAVEN! ON THEE WE FEED

O DU LIEBE MEINER LIEBE 7.7.7.7.7.7.

Josiah Conder‡, 1824

Manuscript Chorale Book, Herrnhaag, 1735

1 Bread of heav'n! on Thee we feed, For Thy flesh is meat in-deed.
2 Vine of heav'n! Thy blood sup-plies This blest cup of sac-ri-fice.

Ev - er may our souls be fed With this true and liv - ing bread;
'Tis Thy wounds our heal - ing give: To Thy cross we look, and live.

Day by day with strength sup-plied, Through the life of Him who died.
Thou our life! O let us be Root-ed, graft-ed, built on Thee. A-men.

402 BE KNOWN TO US IN BREAKING BREAD

DUNFERMLINE C.M.

James Montgomery, 1825

Scottish Psalter, 1615

1 Be known to us in break-ing bread, But do not then de - part;
2 There sup with us in love di - vine; Thy bod - y and Thy blood,

THE CHURCH: SACRAMENTS — THE LORD'S SUPPER

Sav - ior, a - bide with us, and spread Thy ta - ble in our heart.
That liv - ing bread, that heav'n-ly wine, Be our im - mor - tal food. A-men.

COME, RISEN LORD, AND DEIGN 403

BIRMINGHAM (CUNNINGHAM) 10.10.10.10.

George Wallace Briggs, 1926 and 1957

F. Cunningham's, *Selection of Psalm Tunes*, 1834

1 Come, ris - en Lord, and deign to be our guest; Nay, let us
2 We meet, as in that up - per room they met, Thou at the
3 One bod - y we, one bod - y who par - take, One church u -
4 One with each oth - er, Lord, for one in Thee, Who art one

be Thy guests; the feast is Thine; Thy - self at Thine own
ta - ble, bless - ing, yet dost stand: "This is My bod - y":
nit - ed in com - mun - ion blest; One name we bear, one
Sav - ior and one liv - ing head; Then o - pen Thou our

board make man-i - fest, In Thine own sac - ra - ment of bread and wine.
so Thou giv-est yet: Faith still re-ceives the cup as from Thy hand.
bread of life we break, With all Thy saints on earth and saints at rest.
eyes, that we may see; Be known to us in break - ing of the bread. A-men.

THE CHURCH: SACRAMENTS — THE LORD'S SUPPER

404 SING, MY TONGUE

PANGE LINGUA 8.7.8.7.8.7.

Thomas Aquinas, 1263
Pange lingua gloriosi
Tr. *New Congregational Hymn Book,* 1859

Sarum Plainsong

1 Sing, my tongue, the Sav-ior's glo - ry, Of His cross the mys-tery sing;
2 Born for us and for us giv - en, Son of man, like us be - low,
3 Word made flesh! His word life-giv - ing, Gives His flesh our meat to be,
4 Low in ad - o - ra-tion bend - ing, Now our hearts our God re - vere;
5 Praise for ev - er, thanks and bless - ing Thine, O gra-cious Fa - ther, be:

Lift on high the won-drous tro - phy, Tell the tri-umph of the King;
He as man with men a - bid - ing Dwells, the seed of life to sow,
Bids us drink His blood be - liev - ing, Through His death, we life shall see:
Faith her aid to sight is lend - ing, Though un-seen the Lord is near;
Praise be Thine, O Christ, who bring-est Life and im - mor-tal - i - ty;

He, the world's Re-deem-er, con-quers Death, thro' death now van-quish-ing.
He, our heav-y griefs par-tak-ing, Thus ful-fills His life of woe.
Bless-ed they who thus re-ceiv-ing Are from death and sin set free.
An - cient types and shad-ows end-ing, Christ our pas-chal Lamb is here.
Praise be Thine, Thou quick-ening Spir-it, Praise through all e - ter - ni - ty. A - men.

THE CHURCH: SACRAMENTS — THE LORD'S SUPPER

HERE, O MY LORD, I SEE THEE 405

LANGRAN 10.10.10.10.

Horatius Bonar, 1855

James Langran, 1861

1 Here, O my Lord, I see Thee face to face;
2 Here would I feed up - on the bread of God;
3 Too soon we rise; the sym - bols dis - ap - pear;
4 Feast af - ter feast thus comes and pass - es by;

Here would I touch and han - dle things un - seen;
Here drink with Thee the roy - al wine of heav'n;
The feast, though not the love, is passed and gone;
Yet, pass - ing, points to the glad feast a - bove,

Here grasp with firm - er hand th'e - ter - nal grace,
Here would I lay a - side each earth - ly load,
The bread and wine re - move, but Thou art here;
Giv - ing sweet fore - taste of the fes - tal joy,

And all my wea - ri - ness up - on Thee lean.
Here taste a - fresh the calm of sin for - given.
Near - er than ev - er; still my shield and sun.
The Lamb's great brid - al feast of bliss and love. A - men.

THE CHURCH: SACRAMENTS — THE LORD'S SUPPER

406 DECK THYSELF WITH JOY

SCHMÜCKE DICH, O LIEBE SEELE L.M.D.

Johann Franck, 1649
Schmücke dich, O liebe Seele
Tr. John Casper Mattes†, 1913

Johann Crüger, 1649

1 Deck thy-self with joy and glad-ness, Dwell no more, my soul, in sad-ness;
2 Has-ten, then, my soul, to meet Him, Ea-ger-ly and glad-ly greet Him.
3 Je-sus, source of life and plea-sure, Tru-est friend and dear-est trea-sure,

Let the day-light shine up-on thee, Put thy wed-ding gar-ment on thee,
As with-out He stand-eth knock-ing, Quick-ly, thy soul's gate un-lock-ing,
Joy, the sweet-est man e'er know-eth; Fount, whence all my be-ing flow-eth;

For the Lord of life un-end-ing Un-to
O-pen wide the fast-closed por-tal, Say-ing
Hum-bly now I bow be-fore Thee, And in

thee His call is send-ing, Come, for now the King most
to the Lord im-mor-tal, "Come, and leave Thy serv-ant
pen-i-tence a-dore Thee; Wor-thi-ly let me re-

THE CHURCH: SACRAMENTS — THE LORD'S SUPPER

ho - ly Stoops to thee in like-ness low - ly.
nev - er, Dwell with - in my heart for - ev - er."
ceive Thee, Per - fect peace and par-don give me. A - men.

BREAD OF THE WORLD IN MERCY 407

LES COMMANDEMENS DE DIEU 9.8.9.8.

La forme des prieres . . . , Strasbourg, 1545
Harmony adapted from Claude Goudimel, 1565

Reginald Heber, 1827

1 Bread of the world in mer - cy bro - ken,
2 Look on the heart by sor - row bro - ken,

Wine of the soul in mer - cy shed, By whom the
Look on the tears by sin - ners shed; And be Thy

words of life were spo - ken, And in whose death our sins are dead:
feast to us the to - ken That by Thy grace our souls are fed. A - men.

Another setting of this hymn may be found at No. 609

THE CHURCH: SACRAMENTS—THE LORD'S SUPPER

408 'TWAS ON THAT NIGHT

ROCKINGHAM OLD L.M.

Based on Matthew 26:26-29
Scottish Paraphrases, 1781

A. Williams' *Supplement to Psalmody*, c. 1780
Adapted by Edward Miller, 1790

1 'Twas on that night when doomed to know The ea - ger
2 And, af - ter thanks and glo - ry given To Him that
3 "My bro - ken bod - y thus I give For you, for
4 Then in His hands the cup He raised, And God a -

rage of ev - ery foe, That night in which He
rules in earth and heav'n, That sym - bol of His
all; take, eat, and live: And oft the sa - cred
new He thanked and praised, While kind - ness in His

was be-trayed The Sa - vior of the world took bread;
flesh He broke, And thus to all His fol - lowers spoke:
rite re - new That brings My won - drous love to view."
bos - om glowed, And from His lips sal - va - tion flowed. A - men.

5 "My blood I thus pour forth," He cries,
"To cleanse the soul in sin that lies;
In this the covenant is sealed,
And heav'n's eternal grace revealed.

6 "With love to man this cup is fraught,
Let all partake the sacred draught;
Through latest ages let it pour
In memory of My dying hour."

THE CHURCH: SACRAMENTS—THE LORD'S SUPPER

BY CHRIST REDEEMED 409

IN MEMORIAM 8.8.8.4.

George Rawson†, 1857

Frederick Charles Maker, 1876

1 By Christ re - deemed, in Christ re - stored, We keep the mem - o - ry a - dored, And show the death of our dear Lord Un - til He come.

2 His bod - y bro - ken in our stead Is shown in this me - mo - rial bread, And so our fee - ble love is fed Un - til He come.

3 The streams of His dread ag - on - y, His life - blood shed for us, we see; The wine shall tell the mys - ter - y Un - til He come.

4 And thus that dark be - tray - al night With the last ad - vent we u - nite By one blest chain of lov - ing rite Un - til He come. A - men.

5 Until the trump of God be heard,
Until the ancient graves be stirred,
And, with the great commanding word,
The Lord shall come,

6 O blessed hope! with this elate
Let not your hearts be desolate,
But, strong in faith, in patience wait
Until He come.

THE CHURCH: SACRAMENTS—THE LORD'S SUPPER

410 EXTOL THE LOVE OF CHRIST

ELLACOMBE C.M.D.

Samuel Frederick Coffman, 1925

Adapted from *Gesangbuch* . . . , Württemberg, 1784

1 Ex - tol the love of Christ, ye saints, And sing His won-drous
2 Ex - tol the love which sought to show The Fa - ther's bound-less
3 The Lord and Mas - ter hum - bly served To glo - ri - fy the
4 Let poor, vain man ex - am - ple take And from his pride re-

worth, Whose love, like God, e - ter - nal is In
grace; The Son, from Fa - ther's bos - om come, Be -
meek; His heav'n - ly glo - ry shared with those Who
pent; For Christ far great - er is than man, Or

heav - en and on earth. From God He brought His
held the Fa - ther's face: In serv - ile gar - ments
would His fa - vor seek. Lord, teach Thy saints in
serv - ant that is sent. Ex - am - ple, wor - thy,

bless - ing rare; To God He did as - cend; And
clothed up - on, With hum - ble serv - ice meet, The
Thee to know The full - ness of Thy love, The
Christ has giv'n, And hap - py shall they be Who

THE CHURCH: FOOTWASHING

con - stant in His heav'n-ly love He loved un - to the end.
Mas - ter loved as none could love And washed His serv - ants' feet.
fel - low-ship Thy serv - ice taught, Thy glo - ry, bright, a - bove.
wash each oth - er's feet, and love As deep and true as He.

LOVE CONSECRATES THE HUMBLEST ACT 411

LOVE'S CONSECRATION C.M.

S. B. McManus, 1902

Abram Bowman Kolb, 1902

1 Love con - se - crates the hum - blest act, And
2 When in the shad - ow of the cross, Christ
3 "As I have done this un - to you, My
4 Love serves, yet will - ing stoops to serve, What

sanc - ti - fies each deed; It sheds a ben - e -
bowed and washed the feet Of His dis - ci - ples,
breth - ren, here this night, Thus would I have you
Christ in love so true, Hath free - ly done for

dic - tion sweet, And hal - lows ev - ery need.
'twas a sign Of His great love com - plete.
do to each When I have passed from sight."
one and all, Shall we not glad - ly do?

THE CHURCH: FOOTWASHING

412 O PERFECT LOVE

SANDRINGHAM 11.10.11.10.

Dorothy F. Blomfield Gurney, 1883
Doxology by John Ellerton, 1875

Joseph Barnby, 1889

1 O per-fect Love, all hu-man thought trans-cend-ing,
2 O per-fect Life, be Thou their full as-sur-ance
3 Grant them the joy which bright-ens earth-ly sor-row;
4 Hear us, O Fa-ther, gra-cious and for-giv-ing,

Low-ly we kneel in prayer be-fore Thy throne,
Of ten-der char-i-ty and stead-fast faith,
Grant them the peace which calms all earth-ly strife,
Through Je-sus Christ Thy co-e-ter-nal Word,

That theirs may be the love which knows no end-ing,
Of pa-tient hope, and qui-et, brave en-dur-ance,
And to life's day the glo-rious, un-known mor-row
Who, with the Ho-ly Ghost, by all things liv-ing

Whom Thou for-ev-er-more dost join in one.
With child-like trust that fears nor pain nor death.
That dawns up-on e-ter-nal love and life.
Now and to end-less a-ges art a-dored. A-men.

THE CHURCH: MARRIAGE

SHEPHERD OF TENDER YOUTH 413

BRAUN 6.6.4.6.6.6.4.

Clement of Alexandria, d.c. 220
Στομίον πώλων άδαῶν
Tr. Henry Martyn Dexter, 1846

Johann G. Braun, 1675

1 Shep - herd of ten - der youth, Guid - ing, in
2 Thou art our ho - ly Lord, The all - sub -
3 Thou art our soul's high priest, Thou hast pre -
4 Ev - er be Thou our guide, Our Shep - herd
5 So now and till we die, Sound we Thy

love and truth, Through de - vious ways: Christ, our tri -
du - ing Word, Heal - er of strife: Thou didst Thy -
pared the feast Of ho - ly love: And in our
and our pride, Our staff and song: Je - sus, Thou
prais - es high, And joy - ful sing: In - fants, and

um - phant King, We come Thy name to sing;
self a - base, That from sin's deep dis - grace
mor - tal pain, None calls on Thee in vain;
Christ of God, By Thy per - en - nial Word,
the glad throng Who to Thy church be - long,

And here our chil - dren bring, To shout Thy praise.
Thou might - est save our race, And give us life.
Help Thou dost not dis - dain, Help from a - bove.
Lead us where Thou hast trod; Make our faith strong.
U - nite and swell the song To Christ our King. A - men.

THE CHURCH: CONSECRATION OF CHILDREN AND PARENTS

414 JESUS, FRIEND, SO KIND

SICILIAN MARINERS 8.7.8.7.8.7.

Philip E. Gregory, b. 1886

Tattersall's *Psalmody*, 1794

1 Je - sus, friend, so kind and gen - tle, Lit - tle ones we
2 Thou who didst re - ceive the chil - dren To Thy - self so

bring to Thee; Grant to them Thy dear - est bless - ing,
ten - der - ly, Give to all who teach and guide them,

Let Thine arms a - round them be; Now en - fold them
Wis - dom and hu - mil - i - ty, Vi - sion true to

in Thy good - ness, From all dan - ger keep them free.
keep them no - ble, Love to serve them faith - ful - ly. A - men.

THE CHURCH: CONSECRATION OF CHILDREN AND PARENTS

O JESUS CHRIST, OUR LORD MOST DEAR 415

VOM HIMMEL HOCH L.M.

Heinrich von Laufenburg, 1429
Ach lieber Herre Jesu Christ
Tr. Catherine Winkworth‡, 1869

V. Schumann's *Geistliche Lieder*, 1539

1 O Je - sus Christ, our Lord most dear, As
2 As in Thy heav'n - ly king - dom, Lord, Thy
3 And all his life, let an - gels keep Him

Thou wast once an in - fant here, So give this child of
mes - sen - gers o - bey Thy Word, Send forth the suc - cor
safe from harm, a - wake, a - sleep; May he not bear the

Thine, we pray, Thy grace and bless - ing day by day.
of Thy might To shield this child both day and night.
cross in vain, But with Thy saints a crown at - tain.

416 JERUSALEM, THE GOLDEN

EWING 7.6.7.6.D.

Bernard of Cluny, c. 1140
Urbs Syon aurea
Tr. John Mason Neale†, 1858, Sts. 1-3
Hymns Ancient and Modern, 1861, St. 4

Alexander Ewing, 1853

1 Je - ru - sa - lem the gold - en, With milk and hon - ey blest,
2 They stand, those halls of Zi - on, All ju - bi - lant with song,
3 There is the throne of Da - vid, And there, from care re - leased,
4 O sweet and bless - ed coun - try, The home of God's e - lect!

Be - neath thy con - tem - pla - tion Sink heart and voice op - pressed.
And bright with man - y an an - gel, And all the mar - tyr throng.
The shout of them that tri - umph, The song of them that feast;
O sweet and bless - ed coun - try, That ea - ger hearts ex - pect!

I know not, O I know not, What joys a - wait us there,
The Prince is ev - er in them; The day - light is se - rene;
And they, who with their lead - er, Have con - quered in the fight,
Je - sus, in mer - cy bring us To that dear land of rest,

What ra - dian - cy of glo - ry, What bliss be - yond com - pare!
The pas - tures of the bless - ed Are decked in glo - rious sheen.
For - ev - er and for - ev - er Are clad in robes of white.
Who art, with God the Fa - ther And Spir - it, ev - er blest!

THE CHURCH: BURIAL OF THE DEAD

THIS BODY IN THE GRAVE WE LAY 417

NUN LASST UNS DEN LEIB L.M.

Michael Weisse, 1531, Sts. 1-7
Anonymous St. 8
Nun lasst uns den Leib begraben
Tr. William M. Czamanske, 1938

G. Rhau's *Newe Deudsche*
Geistliche Gesenge, 1544

1 This bod - y in the grave we lay There to a -
2 And so to earth we now en - trust What came from
3 The soul for - ev - er lives with God, Who free - ly
4 All tri - als and all griefs are past, A bless - ed

wait that sol - emn day When God Him - self shall bid it
dust and turns to dust And from the dust shall rise that
hath His grace be - stowed And through His Son re - deemed it
end has come at last. Christ's yoke was borne with read - y

rise To mount tri - um - phant to the skies.
day In glo - rious tri - umph o'er de - cay.
here From ev - ery sin, from ev - ery fear.
will; Who die - eth thus is liv - ing still. A - men.

5 We have no cause to mourn or weep;
Securely shall this body sleep
Till Christ Himself shall death destroy
And raise the blessed dead to joy.

6 For they who with Him suffered here
Shall there be healed from woe and fear;
And when eternal bliss is won,
They'll shine in glory like the sun.

7 Then let us leave this place of rest
And homeward turn, for they are blest
Who heed God's warning and prepare
Lest death should find them unaware.

8 So help us, Jesus, ground of faith;
Thou hast redeemed us by Thy death
From endless death and set us free.
We laud and praise and worship Thee.

THE CHURCH: BURIAL OF THE DEAD

418 O LORD OF LIFE, WHERE'ER THEY BE

VICTORY 8.8.8. with Alleluia

Frederick Lucian Hosmer, 1888

Giovanni Pierluigi da Palestrina, 1591
Adapted by William Henry Monk, 1861

1 O Lord of life, wher-e'er they be, Safe in Thine own e-ter-ni-ty,
2 All souls are Thine, and, here or there, They rest with-in Thy shel-t'ring care;
3 Thy Word is true, Thy ways are just; A-bove the re-quiem, "Dust to dust,"
4 O hap-py they in God who rest, No more by fear and doubt op-pressed;

Our dead are liv-ing un-to Thee. Al-le-lu-ia!
One prov-i-dence a-like they share. Al-le-lu-ia!
Shall rise our psalm of grate-ful trust, Al-le-lu-ia!
Liv-ing or dy-ing, they are blest. Al-le-lu-ia! A-men.

THE CHURCH: BURIAL OF THE DEAD

419 LORD, BLESS AND PITY US

GOLDEN HILL S.M.

Folk Hymn

Based on Psalm 67
Psalter, 1912

A. Davisson's Kentucky Harmony, 1816
Version from Joseph Funk's Harmonia Sacra, 1851

1 Lord, bless and pit-y us, Shine on us with Thy face,
2 Thy praise, O gra-cious God, Let all the na-tions sing;
3 The na-tions Thou wilt judge And lead them in Thy ways;
4 The earth her fruit shall yield, For God, our God, will bless;

That all the earth Thy way may know And men may see Thy grace.
Let all men wor-ship Thee with joy And songs of glad-ness bring.
Let all men praise Thy name, O God, Let all the peo-ple praise.
We shall be blest, and all the world His glo-ry shall con-fess.

MISSION OF THE CHURCH: EVANGELISM AND MISSIONS

HERALDS OF CHRIST 420

NATIONAL HYMN 10.10.10.10.

Laura S. Copenhaver, 1894

George William Warren, c. 1892

1 Her - alds of Christ, who bear the King's com-mands,
2 Through des - ert ways, dark fen, and deep mor - ass,
3 Lord, give us faith and strength the road to build,

Im - mor - tal ti - dings in your mor - tal hands,
Through jun - gles, slug - gish seas, and moun - tain pass,
To see the prom - ise of the day ful - filled,

Pass on and car - ry swift the news ye bring;
Build ye the road, and fal - ter not nor stay;
When war shall be no more and strife shall cease

Make straight, make straight the high - way of the King.
Pre - pare a - cross the earth the King's high - way.
Up - on the high - way of the Prince of Peace. A - men.

MISSION OF THE CHURCH: EVANGELISM AND MISSIONS

421 O SPIRIT OF THE LIVING GOD

ALSTONE L.M.

James Montgomery, 1823

Christopher Edwin Willing, 1868

1 O Spir - it of the liv - ing God, In all Thy plen - i - tude of grace, Wher - e'er the foot of man hath trod, De - scend on our a - pos - tate race.

2 Give tongues of fire and hearts of love, To preach the rec - on - cil - ing word; Give power and unc - tion from a - bove, When-e'er the joy - ful sound is heard.

3 Be dark - ness, at Thy com - ing, light; Con - fu - sion or - der, in Thy path; Souls with - out strength in - spire with might; Bid mer - cy tri - umph o - ver wrath.

4 O Spir - it of the Lord, pre - pare All the round earth her God to meet; Breathe Thou a - broad like morn - ing air, Till hearts of stone be - gin to beat.

5 Bap - tize the na - tions; far and nigh The tri - umphs of the cross re - cord; The name of Je - sus glo - ri - fy, Till ev - ery kin - dred call Him Lord. A - men.

422 FATHER, WHOSE WILL IS LIFE

TALLIS' ORDINAL C.M.

Hardwick Drummond Rawnsley, 1922

Thomas Tallis, c. 1567

1 Fa - ther, whose will is life and good For all of mor - tal breath,

2 Em - power the hands and hearts and wills Of friends in lands a - far,

3 Wher - e'er they heal the maimed and blind, Let love of Christ at - tend:

4 For still His love works won-drous charms, And, as in days of old,

5 O Fa - ther, look from heav'n and bless, Wher-e'er Thy serv-ants be,

MISSION OF THE CHURCH: EVANGELISM AND MISSIONS

Bind strong the bond of broth-er-hood Of those who fight with death.
Who bat - tle with the bod - y's ills, And wage Thy ho - ly war.
Pro - claim the good Phy - si - cian's mind, And prove the Sav - ior friend.
He takes the wound-ed to His arms, And bears them to the fold.
Their works of pure un - self - ish - ness, Made con - se - crate to Thee! A - men.

HAIL TO THE BRIGHTNESS 423

WESLEY 11.10.11.10.

Thomas Hastings, 1830

Lowell Mason, 1830

1 Hail to the bright-ness of Zi - on's glad morn - ing, Joy to the
2 Hail to the bright-ness of Zi - on's glad morn - ing, Long by the
3 Lo, in the des - ert rich flow - ers are spring-ing, Streams ev - er
4 See, from all lands, from the isles of the o - cean, Praise to Je-

lands that in dark-ness have lain! Hushed be the ac-cents of sor - row and
proph-ets of Is - rael fore-told; Hail to the mil-lions from bond-age re-
co - pious are glid-ing a - long; Loud from the moun-tain-tops ech - oes are
ho - vah as - cend-ing on high; Fall'n are the en-gines of war and com-

mourn-ing, Zi - on in tri - umph be - gins her mild reign.
turn - ing, Gen - tiles and Jews the blest vi - sion be - hold.
ring - ing, Wastes rise in ver - dure and min - gle in song.
mo - tion, Shouts of sal - va - tion are rend-ing the sky. A - men.

MISSION OF THE CHURCH: EVANGELISM AND MISSIONS

424 CHRIST FOR THE WORLD WE SING

MALVERN (DORCHESTER) 6.6.4.6.6.6.4.

Samuel Wolcott, 1869

Gauntlett and Waite's *Hallelujah*, 1849

1 Christ for the world we sing; The world to
2 Christ for the world we sing; The world to
3 Christ for the world we sing; The world to
4 Christ for the world we sing; The world to

Christ we bring With lov - ing zeal; The poor and
Christ we bring With fer - vent prayer; The way - ward
Christ we bring With one ac - cord; With us the
Christ we bring With joy - ful song; The new - born

them that mourn, The faint and o - ver - borne,
and the lost, By rest - less pas - sions tossed,
work to share, With us re - proach to dare,
souls whose days, Re - claimed from er - ror's ways,

Sin - sick and sor - row - worn, Whom Christ doth heal.
Re - deemed at count - less cost From dark de - spair.
With us the cross to bear, For Christ our Lord.
In - spired with hope and praise, To Christ be - long.

MISSION OF THE CHURCH: EVANGELISM AND MISSIONS

CHRIST FOR THE WORLD WE SING 425

MILTON ABBAS 6.6.4.6.6.6.4.

Samuel Wolcott, 1869

Eric Harding Thiman, 1953

1 Christ for the world we sing; The world to
2 Christ for the world we sing; The world to
3 Christ for the world we sing; The world to
4 Christ for the world we sing; The world to

Christ we bring With lov - ing zeal; The poor and
Christ we bring With fer - vent prayer; The way - ward
Christ we bring With one ac - cord; With us the
Christ we bring With joy - ful song; The new - born

them that mourn, The faint and o - ver - borne,
and the lost, By rest - less pas - sions tossed,
work to share, With us re - proach to dare,
souls whose days, Re - claimed from er - ror's ways,

Sin - sick and sor - row - worn, Whom Christ doth heal.
Re - deemed at count - less cost From dark de - spair.
With us the cross to bear, For Christ our Lord.
In - spired with hope and praise, To Christ be - long.

MISSION OF THE CHURCH: EVANGELISM AND MISSIONS

426 THE WORK IS THINE, O CHRIST

DIE SACH' IST DEIN   8.6.8.6 8.8.8.8.4.6.

Samuel Preiswerk, 1829, Sts. 1, 2, and
Felician von Zaremba, d. 1874, St. 3
Die Sach' ist dein
Tr. Julius Henry Horstmann, 1908

Johann Michael Haydn, late 18th century

1 The   work is Thine, O   Christ our Lord, The   cause   for which we   stand;
2 Through suf-f'ring Thou, O   Christ, didst go Un - to   Thy throne a - bove,
3 Thou   hast, O Sav - ior, led   the way Through ag - o - ny   and death;

And   be - ing Thine, 'twill o - ver-come Its   foes   on   ev - ery   hand.
And   lead-est now the   self - same way Those true   in   faith and   love;
O   give, we pray, yet more and more Thy Spir - it's   liv - ing   breath!

Yet grains of wheat, be - fore they grow, Are bur - ied   in the earth be - low;
So   lead us, then, though suf-f'rings wait, To share Thy king-dom's heav'n-ly state,
Send mes - sen-gers o'er land and sea   To bring Thy chil-dren all   to Thee;

All   that   is   old doth per - ish there To form   a   life both new and fair:
Thy death has bro - ken Sa-tan's might, And leads the faith-ful   to   the light;
Thy name can save, Thy name makes free; We con - se - crate our-selves to Thee

MISSION OF THE CHURCH: EVANGELISM AND MISSIONS

So too are we From self and sin made free.
E - ter - nal light, From dark - ness in - to light.
As serv - ants true, As war - riors brave and true. A - men.

1 Die Sach ist dein, Herr Jesu Christ,
   die Sach, an der wir stehn,
und weil es deine Sache ist,
   kann sie nicht untergehn.
Allein das Weizenkorn, bevor
es fruchtbar sprosst zum Licht empor,
muss sterben in der Erde Schoss
zuvor vom eignen Wesen los.
   Durch Sterben los,
vom eignen Wesen los.

2 Du gingst, o Jesus, unser Haupt,
   durch Leiden himmelan
und führest jeden, der da glaubt,
   mit dir die gleiche Bahn.
Wohlan, so nimm uns allzugleich
zum Teil am Leiden und am Reich.
Führ uns durch deines Todes Tor
samt deiner Sach zum Licht empor,
   zum Licht empor,
durch Nacht zum Licht empor.

FORGET THEM NOT, O CHRIST 427

ELSENHAM 8.8.

Margaret Sangster, d. 1912

J. D. Macey, 1916

1 For - get them not, O Christ, who stand
2 In flood, in flame, in dark, in dread,
3 Ex - alt them o - ver ev - ery fear,
4 Thine is the work they strive to do,
5 Be with Thine own, Thy loved, who stand,

Thy van - guard in the dis - tant land.
Sus - tain, we pray, each lift - ed head.
In per - il come Thy - self more near.
Their foes so man - y, they so few.
Christ's van - guard in the storm - swept land. A - men.

MISSION OF THE CHURCH: EVANGELISM AND MISSIONS

428 O ZION, HASTE

TIDINGS 11.10.11.10. with Refrain

Mary Ann Thomson, 1868

James Walch, 1875

1 O Zi - on, haste, thy mis - sion high ful - fill - ing,
2 Be - hold how man - y thou - sands still are ly - ing
3 Pro - claim to ev - ery peo - ple, tongue, and na - tion
4 Give of thy sons to bear the mes - sage glo - rious;
5 He comes a - gain: O Zi - on, ere thou meet Him,

To tell to all the world that God is light;
Bound in the dark - some pris - on - house of sin,
That God, in whom they live and move, is love:
Give of thy wealth to speed them on their way;
Make known to ev - ery heart His sav - ing grace;

That He who made all na - tions is not will - ing
With none to tell them of the Sav - ior's dy - ing
Tell how He stooped to save His lost cre - a - tion,
Pour out thy soul for them in prayer vic - to - rious,
Let none whom He hath ran - somed fail to greet Him,

REFRAIN

One soul should per - ish, lost in shades of night.
Or of the life He died for them to win.
And died on earth that man might live a - bove. Pub - lish glad ti - dings,
And all thou spend - est Je - sus will re - pay.
Through thy neg - lect, un - fit to see His face.

MISSION OF THE CHURCH: EVANGELISM AND MISSIONS

ti - dings of peace, Ti - dings of Je - sus, re - demp-tion and re - lease.

THOU, WHOSE ALMIGHTY WORD 429

SERUG 6.6.4.6.6.6.4.

John Marriott†, c. 1813

S. S. Wesley's *European Psalmist*, 1872

1 Thou, whose al - might - y word Cha - os and dark - ness heard,
2 Thou who didst come to bring On Thy re - deem - ing wing,
3 Spir - it of truth and love, Life - giv - ing, ho - ly dove,
4 Ho - ly and bless - ed Three, Glo - ri - ous Trin - i - ty,

And took their flight; Hear us, we hum - bly pray, And where the
Heal - ing and sight, Health to the sick in mind, Sight to the
Speed forth Thy flight; Move o'er the wa - ters' face Bear - ing the
Wis - dom, love, might; Bound-less as o - cean's tide Roll - ing in

gos - pel day Sheds not its glo - rious ray, Let there be light!
in - ly blind; O now, to all man-kind, Let there be light!
lamp of grace; And in earth's dark - est place, Let there be light!
full - est pride, Through the world far and wide, Let there be light! A - men.

MISSION OF THE CHURCH: EVANGELISM AND MISSIONS

430 FORTH IN THY NAME

INTERCESSION L.M.

Charles Wesley, 1749

Easy Music for Church Choirs, 1853

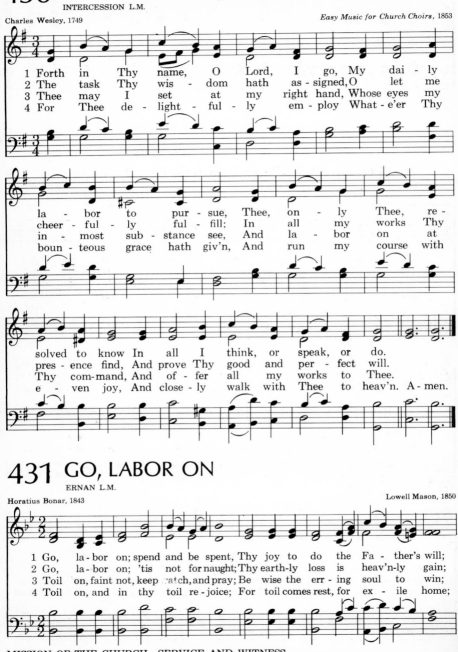

1 Forth in Thy name, O Lord, I go, My dai - ly
2 The task Thy wis - dom hath as - signed, O let me
3 Thee may I set at my right hand, Whose eyes my
4 For Thee de - light - ful - ly em - ploy What - e'er Thy

la - bor to pur - sue, Thee, on - ly Thee, re -
cheer - ful - ly ful - fill; In all my works Thy
in - most sub - stance see, And la - bor on at
boun - teous grace hath giv'n, And run my course with

solved to know In all I think, or speak, or do.
pres - ence find, And prove Thy good and per - fect will.
Thy com - mand, And of - fer all my works to Thee.
e - ven joy, And close - ly walk with Thee to heav'n. A - men.

431 GO, LABOR ON

ERNAN L.M.

Horatius Bonar, 1843

Lowell Mason, 1850

1 Go, la - bor on; spend and be spent, Thy joy to do the Fa - ther's will;
2 Go, la - bor on; 'tis not for naught; Thy earth - ly loss is heav'n - ly gain;
3 Toil on, faint not, keep watch, and pray; Be wise the err - ing soul to win;
4 Toil on, and in thy toil re - joice; For toil comes rest, for ex - ile home;

MISSION OF THE CHURCH: SERVICE AND WITNESS

It   is the way the   Mas-ter went; Should not the serv - ant tread it   still?
Men heed thee, love thee, praise thee not; The   Mas-ter prais - es: what are men?
Go   forth in - to the world's high-way, Com - pel the wan - derer to   come in.
Soon shalt thou hear the bride-groom's voice, The mid-night peal, "Be - hold, I come!"

FORTH IN THY NAME 432

SONG XXXIV L.M.

Charles Wesley, 1749

Orlando Gibbons, 1623

1 Forth in Thy name, O Lord, I   go, My dai - ly
2 The   task Thy wis - dom hath as - signed, O let me
3 Thee may I   set at my right hand, Whose eyes my
4 For   Thee de - light - ful - ly em - ploy What - e'er Thy

la - bor to   pur - sue, Thee, on - ly Thee, re - solved to
cheer - ful - ly ful - fill; In all my works Thy pres - ence
in most sub - stance see, And la - bor on at Thy com -
boun - teous grace hath giv'n, And run my course with e - ven

know In all I think, or speak, or   do.
find, And prove Thy good and per - fect   will.
mand, And of - fer all my works to   Thee.
joy, And close - ly walk with Thee to   heav'n. A - men.

MISSION OF THE CHURCH: SERVICE AND WITNESS

433 JESUS, THOU DIVINE COMPANION

HYFRYDOL 8.7.8.7.D.

Henry van Dyke, 1909

Rowland Hugh Pritchard, c. 1830
Harmony by Ralph Vaughan Williams, 1951

1 Je - sus, Thou di - vine com - pan - ion, By Thy low - ly hu - man birth
2 They who tread the path of la - bor Fol - low where Thy feet have trod;
3 Ev - ery task, how - ev - er sim - ple, Sets the soul that does it free;

Thou hast come to join the work - ers, Bur - den - bear - ers of the earth.
They who work with - out com - plain - ing Do the ho - ly will of God.
Ev - ery deed of love and kind - ness Done to man is done to Thee.

Thou, the car - pen - ter of Nazareth, Toil - ing for Thy dai - ly food,
Thou, the peace that pass - eth knowl - edge, Dwell - est in the dai - ly strife;
Je - sus, Thou di - vine com - pan - ion, Help us all to work our best;

By Thy pa - tience and Thy cour - age, Thou hast taught us toil is good.
Thou, the bread of heav'n, art bro - ken In the sac - ra - ment of life.
Bless us in our dai - ly la - bor, Lead us to our Sab - bath rest. A - men.

MISSION OF THE CHURCH: SERVICE AND WITNESS

GOD OF GRACE AND GOD OF GLORY 434

CWM RHONDDA 8.7.8.7.8.7.

Harry Emerson Fosdick, 1930

John Hughes, 1907

1 God of grace and God of glo - ry, On Thy peo - ple
2 Lo! the hosts of e - vil round us Scorn Thy Christ, as -
3 Cure Thy chil - dren's war - ring mad - ness; Bend our pride to
4 Set our feet on loft - y plac - es; Gird our lives that
5 Save us from weak res - ig - na - tion To the e - vils

pour Thy power; Crown Thine an - cient church's sto - ry; Bring her bud to
sail His ways! From the fears that long have bound us, Free our hearts to
Thy con - trol; Shame our wan - ton, self - ish glad - ness, Rich in things and
they may be Ar - mored with all Christ-like grac - es In the fight to
we de - plore; Let the search for Thy sal - va - tion Be our glo - ry

glo - rious flower. Grant us wis - dom, Grant us cour - age,
faith and praise. Grant us wis - dom, Grant us cour - age,
poor in soul. Grant us wis - dom, Grant us cour - age,
set men free. Grant us wis - dom, Grant us cour - age,
ev - er - more. Grant us wis - dom, Grant us cour - age,

For the fac - ing of this hour, For the fac - ing of this hour.
For the liv - ing of these days, For the liv - ing of these days.
Lest we miss Thy king-dom's goal, Lest we miss Thy king-dom's goal.
That we fail not man nor Thee, That we fail not man nor Thee.
Serv - ing Thee whom we a - dore, Serv - ing Thee whom we a - dore. A-men.

MISSION OF THE CHURCH: SERVICE AND WITNESS

435 O BROTHER MAN, FOLD TO THY HEART

INTERCESSOR 11.10.11.10.

John Greenleaf Whittier, 1847

Charles Hubert Hastings Parry, 1904

1 O broth - er man, fold to thy heart thy broth - er:
2 For he whom Je - sus loved hath tru - ly spo - ken;
3 Fol - low with rev - erent steps the great ex - am - ple
4 Then shall all shack - les fall: the storm - y clan - gor

Where pit - y dwells, the peace of God is there;
The ho - lier wor - ship which He deigns to bless
Of Him whose ho - ly work was do - ing good:
Of wild war mu - sic o'er the earth shall cease;

To wor - ship right - ly is to love each oth - er,
Re - stores the lost, and binds the spir - it bro - ken,
So shall the wide earth seem our Fa - ther's tem - ple,
Love shall tread out the bale - ful fire of an - ger,

Each smile a hymn, each kind - ly deed a prayer.
And feeds the wid - ow and the fa - ther - less!
Each lov - ing life a psalm of grat - i - tude.
And in its ash - es plant the tree of peace. A - men.

MISSION OF THE CHURCH: SERVICE AND WITNESS

LORD OF LIGHT, WHOSE NAME 436

TANTUM ERGO 8.7.8.7.D.

Howell Elvet Lewis, 1916

S. Webbe's *Essay on the Church*
Plain-Chant, 1782

1 Lord of light, whose name out-shin-eth All the stars and suns of space,
2 By the toil of low-ly work-ers In some far out-ly-ing field;
3 Grant that knowl-edge, still in-creas-ing, At Thy feet may low-ly kneel:
4 By the prayers of faith-ful watch-men, Nev-er si-lent day or night;

Deign to make us Thy co-work-ers In the king-dom of Thy grace;
By the cour-age where the ra-diance Of the cross is still re-vealed;
With Thy grace our tri-umphs hal-low, With Thy char-i-ty our zeal;
By the cross of Je-sus bring-ing Peace to men, and heal-ing light;

Use us to ful-fill Thy pur-pose In the gift of Christ Thy Son:
By the vic-to-ries of meek-ness Through re-proach and suf-f'ring won:
Lift the na-tions from the shad-ows To the glad-ness of the sun:
By the love that pass-eth knowl-edge, Mak-ing all Thy chil-dren one:

Fa-ther, as in high-est heav-en So on earth Thy will be done.
Fa-ther, as in high-est heav-en So on earth Thy will be done.
Fa-ther, as in high-est heav-en So on earth Thy will be done.
Fa-ther, as in high-est heav-en So on earth Thy will be done. A-men.

MISSION OF THE CHURCH: SERVICE AND WITNESS

437 THOU, LORD OF LIFE

HESPERUS L.M.

Samuel Longfellow, c. 1886

Henry Baker, 1854

1 Thou, Lord of life, our sav-ing health, Who mak'st Thy suf-f'ring ones our care, Our gifts are still our tru-est wealth, To serve Thee our sin-cer-est prayer.

2 As on the riv-er's ris-ing tide Flow strength and cool-ness from the sea, So through the ways our hands pro-vide, May quick-'ning life flow in from Thee;

3 To heal the wound, to still the pain, And strength to fail-ing puls-es bring, Till the lame feet shall leap a-gain, And the parched lips with glad-ness sing.

4 Bless Thou the gifts our hands have brought! Bless Thou the work our hearts have planned, Ours is the faith, the will, the thought; The rest, O God, is in Thy hand. A-men.

438 TEACH ME THY TRUTH, O MIGHTY ONE

GOSHEN C.M.

Edith Witmer, 1937

Walter E. Yoder, 1938

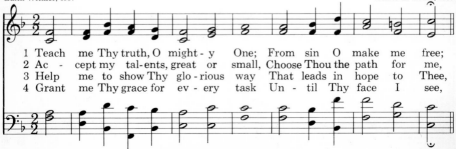

1 Teach me Thy truth, O might-y One; From sin O make me free;

2 Ac-cept my tal-ents, great or small, Choose Thou the path for me,

3 Help me to show Thy glo-rious way That leads in hope to Thee;

4 Grant me Thy grace for ev-ery task Un-til Thy face I see,

MISSION OF THE CHURCH: SERVICE AND WITNESS

Pre - pare my life to fill its place In ser - vice, Lord, for Thee.
Where I shall la - bor joy - ous - ly In ser - vice, Lord, for Thee.
Till oth - er souls their joy shall find, In ser - vice, Lord, for Thee.
Then ev - er new shall be that joy In ser - vice, Lord, for Thee. A - men.

WHERE CROSS THE CROWDED WAYS 439

GERMANY L.M.

Frank Mason North, 1903

W. Gardiner's *Sacred Melodies*, 1815

1 Where cross the crowd - ed ways of life, Where sound the
2 In haunts of wretch - ed - ness and need, On shad - owed
3 From ten - der child - hood's help - less - ness, From wom - an's
4 The cup of wa - ter given for Thee Still holds the
5 O Mas - ter, from the moun - tain side, Make haste to
6 Till sons of men shall learn Thy love, And fol - low

cries of race and clan, A - bove the noise of
thresh - olds dark with fears, From paths where hide the
grief, man's bur - dened toil, From fam - ished souls, from
fresh - ness of Thy grace; Yet long these mul - ti -
heal these hearts of pain; A - mong these rest - less
where Thy feet have trod; Till glo - rious from Thy

self - ish strife, We hear Thy voice, O Son of man!
lures of greed, We catch the vi - sion of Thy tears.
sor - row's stress, Thy heart has nev - er known re - coil.
tudes to see The sweet com - pas - sion of Thy face.
throngs a - bide, O tread the cit - y's streets a - gain;
heav'n a - bove Shall come the cit - y of our God. A - men.

MISSION OF THE CHURCH: SERVICE AND WITNESS

440 O MASTER, LET ME WALK WITH THEE

MARYTON L.M.

Washington Gladden, 1879

Henry Percy Smith, 1874

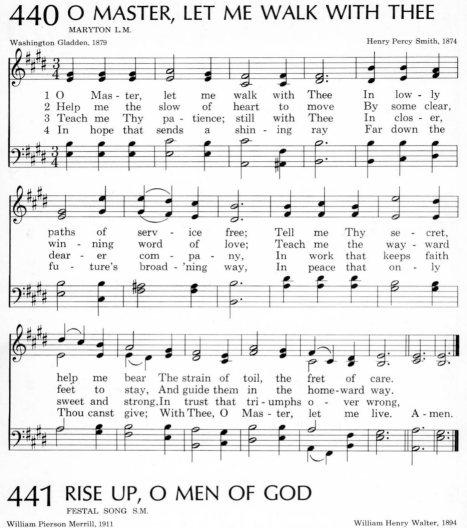

1 O Mas-ter, let me walk with Thee In low-ly
2 Help me the slow of heart to move By some clear,
3 Teach me Thy pa-tience; still with Thee In clos-er,
4 In hope that sends a shin-ing ray Far down the

paths of serv-ice free; Tell me Thy se-cret,
win-ning word of love; Teach me the way-ward
dear-er com-pa-ny, In work that keeps faith
fu-ture's broad-'ning way, In peace that on-ly

help me bear The strain of toil, the fret of care.
feet to stay, And guide them in the home-ward way.
sweet and strong, In trust that tri-umphs o-ver wrong,
Thou canst give; With Thee, O Mas-ter, let me live. A-men.

441 RISE UP, O MEN OF GOD

FESTAL SONG S.M.

William Pierson Merrill, 1911

William Henry Walter, 1894

1 Rise up, O men of God! Have done with less-er things;
2 Rise up, O men of God! His king-dom tar-ries long;
3 Rise up, O men of God! The church for you doth wait,
4 Lift high the cross of Christ! Tread where His feet have trod;

MISSION OF THE CHURCH: SERVICE AND WITNESS

Give heart and soul and mind and strength To serve the King of kings.
Bring in the day of broth-er-hood, And end the night of wrong.
Her strength un-e-qual to her task, Rise up, and make her great!
As broth-ers of the Son of man, Rise up O men of God!

STRONG SON OF GOD 442

ROCKINGHAM OLD L.M.

Alfred Tennyson, 1850

A. Williams' *Supplement to Psalmody*, c. 1780
Adapted by Edward Miller, 1790

1 Strong Son of God, im-mor-tal love, Whom we, that
2 Thou seem-est hu-man and di-vine, The high-est,
3 Our lit-tle sys-tems have their day; They have their
4 Let knowl-edge grow from more to more, But more of

have not seen Thy face, By faith, and faith a-lone, em-
ho-liest man-hood, Thou: Our wills are ours, we know not
day and cease to be; They are but bro-ken lights of
rev-'rence in us dwell; That mind and soul, ac-cord-ing

brace, Be-liev-ing where we can-not prove.
how; Our wills are ours, to make them Thine.
Thee, And Thou, O Lord, art more than they.
well, May make one mu-sic as be-fore. A-men.

MISSION OF THE CHURCH: EDUCATION

443 LEAD ON, O KING ETERNAL

LANCASHIRE 7.6.7.6.D.

Ernest Warburton Shurtleff, 1887

Henry Thomas Smart, 1835

1 Lead on, O King e - ter - nal, The day of march has come;
2 Lead on, O King e - ter - nal, Till sin's fierce war shall cease,
3 Lead on, O King e - ter - nal, We fol - low, not with fears,

Hence - forth in fields of con - quest Thy tents shall be our home:
And ho - li - ness shall whis - per The sweet a - men of peace;
For glad - ness breaks like morn - ing Wher - e'er Thy face ap - pears:

Through days of prep - a - ra - tion Thy grace has made us strong,
For not with swords, loud clash - ing, Nor roll of stir - ring drums,
Thy cross is lift - ed o'er us; We jour - ney in its light;

And now, O King e - ter - nal, We lift our bat - tle song.
But deeds of love and mer - cy, The heav'n - ly king - dom comes.
The crown a - waits the con - quest; Lead on, O God of might. A - men.

MISSION OF THE CHURCH: EDUCATION

O GRANT US LIGHT 444

CANONBURY L.M.

Lawrence Tuttiett, 1885

Arranged from Robert Schumann, 1839

1 O grant us light, that we may know The wis-dom Thou a - lone canst give;
2 O grant us light, that we may see Where er - ror lurks in hu - man lore,
3 O grant us light, that we may learn How dead is life from Thee a - part,

That truth may guide wher-e'er we go, And vir - tue bless wher-e'er we live.
And turn our doubt-ing minds to Thee, And love Thy sim - ple Word the more.
How sure is joy for all who turn To Thee an un - di - vid - ed heart. A-men.

COME, MY WAY, MY TRUTH, MY LIFE 445

FREUEN WIR UNS ALL IN EIN 7.7.7.7.

Bohemian Melody, 15th century
Michael Weisse, 1531
Harmony by George Ratcliffe Woodward, 1910

George Herbert, 1633

1 Come, my Way, my Truth, my Life: Such a way as gives us breath:
2 Come, my Light, my Feast, my Strength: Such a light as shows a feast:
3 Come, my Joy, my Love, my Heart: Such a joy as none can move:

Such a truth as ends all strife: Such a life as kill - eth death.
Such a feast as mends in length: Such a strength as makes his guest.
Such a love as none can part: Such a heart as joys in love.

MISSION OF THE CHURCH: EDUCATION

446 JUDGE ETERNAL, THRONED

ZEUCH MICH, ZEUCH MICH (ALL SAINTS)   8.7.8.7.8.7.

Henry Scott Holland†, 1902

Geistreiches Gesangbuch, Darmstadt, 1698

1 Judge e - ter - nal, throned in splen - dor, Lord of lords and
2 Still the wea - ry folk are pin - ing For the hour that
3 Crown, O God, Thine own en - deav - or; Cleave our dark - ness

King of kings, With Thy liv - ing fire of judg - ment
brings re - lease; And the cit - y's crowd - ed clan - gor
with Thy sword; Feed the faint and hun - gry peo - ples

Purge this land of bit - ter things; Sol - ace all its
Cries a - loud for sin to cease; And the home - steads
With the rich - ness of Thy Word; Cleanse the bod - y

wide do - min - ion With the heal - ing of Thy wings.
and the wood-lands Plead in si - lence for their peace.
of this na - tion Through the glo - ry of the Lord. A - men.

MISSION OF THE CHURCH: CHRISTIAN CITIZENSHIP

FATHER ETERNAL, RULER OF CREATION 447

GENEVA 124 11.10.11.10.10.

Laurence Housman, 1919

Pseaumes octante trois . . ., Geneva, 1551

1 Fa - ther e - ter - nal, rul - er of cre - a - tion, Spir - it of
2 Rac - es and peo - ples, lo we stand di - vid - ed, And shar - ing
3 En - vious of heart, blind - eyed, with tongues con - found - ed, Na - tion by
4 Lust of pos - ses - sion work - eth des - o - la - tions; There is no
5 How shall we love Thee, ho - ly hid - den Be - ing, If we love

life, which moved ere form was made; Through the thick dark - ness
not our griefs, no joys can share; By wars and tu - mults
na - tion still goes un - for - giv'n; In wrath and fear, by
meek - ness in the sons of earth; Led by no star, the
not the world which Thou hast made? O give us broth - er -

cov - 'ring ev - 'ry na - tion Light to man's blind - ness, O be Thou our
love is mocked, de - rid - ed, His con - qu'ring cross no king - dom wills to
jeal - ous - ies sur - round - ed, Build - ing proud tow'rs which shall not reach to
rul - ers of the na - tions Still fail to bring us to the bliss - ful
love for bet - ter see - ing Thy Word made flesh, and in a man - ger

aid: Thy king - dom come, O Lord, Thy will be done.
bear; Thy king - dom come, O Lord, Thy will be done.
heav'n: Thy king - dom come, O Lord, Thy will be done.
birth. Thy king - dom come, O Lord, Thy will be done.
laid: Thy king - dom come, O Lord, Thy will be done. A - men.

MISSION OF THE CHURCH: CHRISTIAN CITIZENSHIP

448 GOD OF OUR FATHERS

NATIONAL HYMN 10.10.10.10.

Daniel Crane Roberts, 1876

George William Warren, c. 1892

1 God of our fa - thers, whose al - might - y hand
2 Thy love di - vine hath led us in the past,
3 From war's a - larms, from dead - ly pes - ti - lence,
4 Re - fresh Thy peo - ple on their toil - some way,

Leads forth in beau - ty all the star - ry band
In this free land by Thee our lot is cast;
Be Thy strong arm - our ev - er sure de - fense;
Lead us from night to nev - er - end - ing day;

Of shin - ing worlds in splen - dor through the skies,
Be Thou our rul - er, guard - ian, guide and stay,
Thy true re - li - gion in our hearts in - crease,
Fill all our lives with love and grace di - vine,

Our grate - ful songs be - fore Thy throne a - rise.
Thy Word our law, Thy paths our cho - sen way.
Thy boun - teous good - ness nour - ish us in peace.
And glo - ry, laud and praise be ev - er Thine. A - men.

MISSION OF THE CHURCH. CHRISTIAN CITIZENSHIP

PEACE IN OUR TIME, O LORD 449

DIADEMATA S.M.D.

John Oxenham, 1936

George Job Elvey, 1868

1 Peace in our time, O Lord, To all the peo - ples, Peace!
2 Too long mis-trust and fear Have held our souls in thrall;
3 O shall we nev - er learn The truth all time has taught,

Peace sure - ly based up - on Thy will And built in right-eous - ness.
Sweep through the earth, keen breath of heav'n, And sound a no - bler call!
That with-out God as ar - chi - tect Our build-ing comes to naught?

Thy power a - lone can break The fet - ters that en - chain
Come, as Thou didst of old, In love so great that men
O liv - ing Christ, who still Dost all our bur - dens share,

The sore - ly strick-en soul of life, And make it live a - gain.
Shall cast a - side all oth - er gods And turn to Thee a - gain!
Come now and dwell with-in the hearts Of all men ev - ery - where! A - men.

MISSION OF THE CHURCH: PEACE AND NON-RESISTANCE

450 O HOLY CITY, SEEN OF JOHN

CONSOLATION (MORNING SONG) 8.6.8.6.8.6.

Walter Russell Bowie, 1909

Folk Hymn
J. Wyeth's *Repository of Sacred Music,*
Part Second, 1813

1 O ho-ly cit-y, seen of John, Where Christ, the Lamb, doth reign,
2 O shame to us who rest con-tent While lust and greed for gain
3 Give us, O God, the strength to build The cit-y that hath stood
4 Al-read-y in the mind of God That cit-y ris-eth fair:

With-in whose four-square walls shall come No night, nor need, nor pain,
In street and shop and ten-e-ment Wring gold from hu-man pain,
Too long a dream, whose laws are love, Whose ways are broth-er-hood,
Lo, how its splen-dor chal-len-ges The souls that great-ly dare,

And where the tears are wiped from eyes That shall not weep a-gain,
And bit-ter lips in blind de-spair Cry, "Christ hath died in vain!"
And where the sun that shin-eth is God's grace for hu-man good.
Yea, bids us seize the whole of life And build its glo-ry there.

451 LORD, AS TO THY DEAR CROSS WE FLEE

GREEN HILL C.M.

John Hampden Gurney‡, 1838

Albert Lister Peace, 1885

1 Lord, as to Thy dear cross we flee, And plead to be for-giv'n;
2 Let grace our self-ish-ness ex-pel, Our earth-li-ness re-fine;
3 Should friends mis-judge, or foes de-fame, Or breth-ren faith-less prove,
4 Kept peace-ful in the midst of strife, For-giv-ing and for-giv'n,

MISSION OF THE CHURCH: PEACE AND NONRESISTANCE

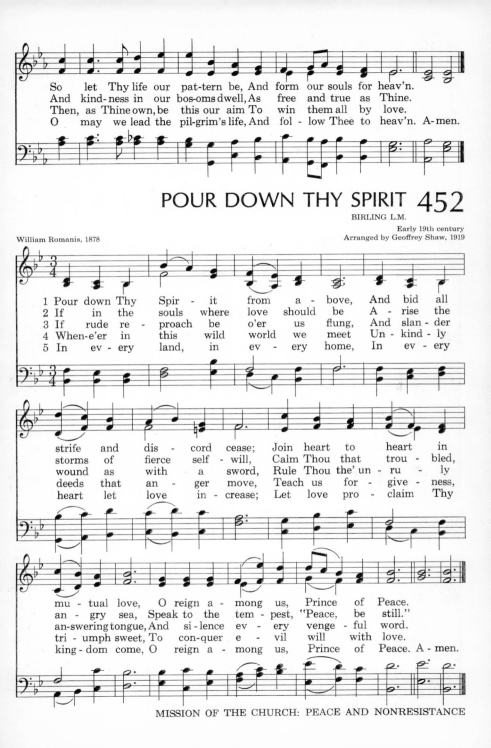

So let Thy life our pat-tern be, And form our souls for heav'n.
And kind-ness in our bos-oms dwell, As free and true as Thine.
Then, as Thine own, be this our aim To win them all by love.
O may we lead the pil-grim's life, And fol - low Thee to heav'n. A-men.

POUR DOWN THY SPIRIT 452

BIRLING L.M.

Early 19th century
Arranged by Geoffrey Shaw, 1919

William Romanis, 1878

1 Pour down Thy Spir - it from a - bove, And bid all
2 If in the souls where love should be A - rise the
3 If rude re - proach be o'er us flung, And slan - der
4 When-e'er in this wild world we meet Un - kind - ly
5 In ev - ery land, in ev - ery home, In ev - ery

strife and dis - cord cease; Join heart to heart in
storms of fierce self - will, Calm Thou that trou - bled,
wound as with a sword, Rule Thou the' un - ru - ly
deeds that an - ger move, Teach us for - give - ness,
heart let love in - crease; Let love pro - claim Thy

mu - tual love, O reign a - mong us, Prince of Peace.
an - gry sea, Speak to the tem - pest, "Peace, be still."
an-swering tongue, And si - lence ev - ery venge - ful word.
tri - umph sweet, To con-quer e - vil will with love.
king - dom come, O reign a - mong us, Prince of Peace. A - men.

MISSION OF THE CHURCH: PEACE AND NONRESISTANCE

453 DEAR FATHER, WHOM WE CANNOT SEE

LOBT GOTT, IHR CHRISTEN 8.6.8.8.6.

Roderic Dunkerley

Nicolaus Herman, 1554
Harmony by Johann Sebastian Bach, c. 1735-1740

1 Dear Fa - ther, whom we can - not see, We know that Thou art near;
2 Dear Fa - ther, King of love and peace, We know that Thou art strong;
3 Dear Fa - ther, Lord of sea and land, We know that Thou art wise;

With long - ing hearts we turn to Thee, And ask that Thou wilt
Make con - flicts ev - ery - where to cease, Let mer - cy ev - ery -
O make the na - tions un - der-stand That on - ly by Thy

set us free From war and hate and fear.
where in - crease, And kind - ness con - quer wrong.
guid - ing hand Can last - ing peace a - rise. A - men.

454 O GOD OF LOVE, O KING OF PEACE

ROCKINGHAM OLD L.M.

A. Williams' *Supplement to
Psalmody*, c. 1780
Adapted by Edward Miller, 1790

Henry Williams Baker, 1860

1 O God of love, O King of peace, Make wars through-out the world to cease;
2 Re - mem-ber, Lord, Thy works of old, The won-ders that our fa - thers told;
3 Whom shall we trust but Thee, O Lord? Where rest but on Thy faith - ful Word?
4 Where saints and an - gels dwell a-bove, All hearts are knit in ho - ly love;

MISSION OF THE CHURCH: PEACE AND NONRESISTANCE

The wrath of sin-ful man re-strain; Give peace, O God, give peace a-gain!
Re-mem-ber not our sin's dark stain; Give peace, O God, give peace a-gain!
None ev-er called on Thee in vain; Give peace, O God, give peace a-gain!
O bind us in that heav'n-ly chain; Give peace, O God, give peace a-gain! A-men.

LET THERE BE LIGHT 455

MISSIONARY CHANT L.M.

William Merrill Vories, 1908

Charles Zeuner, 1832

1 Let there be light, Lord God of hosts! Let there be
2 With-in our pas-sioned hearts in-still The calm that
3 Give us the peace of vi-sion clear To see our
4 Let woe and waste of war-fare cease, That use-ful

wis-dom on the earth! Let broad hu-man-i
end-eth strain and strife; Make us Thy min-is-
broth-ers' good our own, To joy and suf-fer
la-bor yet may build Its homes with love and

ty have birth! Let there be deeds, in-stead of boasts.
ters of life; Purge us from lusts that curse and kill!
not a-lone: The love that cast-eth out all fear!
laugh-ter filled! God, give Thy way-ward chil-dren peace! A-men.

MISSION OF THE CHURCH: PEACE AND NONRESISTANCE

456 LORD OF OUR LIFE, AND GOD

ISTE CONFESSOR (ROUEN) 11.11.11.5.

Matthäus Apelles von Löwenstern, 1644
Christe, du Beistand deiner Kreuzgemeine
Paraphrase by Philip Pusey, 1834

Poitiers Antiphoner, 1746

1 Lord of our life, and God of our sal - va - tion, Star of our
2 Lord, Thou canst help when earth - ly ar - mor fail - eth; Lord, Thou canst
3 Peace, in our hearts, our e - vil thoughts as - suag - ing; Peace, in Thy

night, and hope of ev - ery na - tion, Hear and re - ceive Thy
save when sin it - self as - sail - eth; Lord, o'er Thy rock nor
church, where broth - ers are en - gag - ing; Peace, when the world its

church's sup - pli - ca - tion, Lord God al - might - y.
death nor hell pre - vail - eth; Grant us Thy peace, Lord:
bus - y war is wag - ing; Calm Thy foes' rag - ing! A - men.

4 Grant us Thy help till backward they are driven;
   Grant them Thy truth, that they may be forgiven;
   Grant peace on earth, or after we have striven,
      Peace in Thy heaven.

MISSION OF THE CHURCH: PEACE AND NONRESISTANCE

O GOD OF EARTH AND ALTAR 457

KING'S LYNN 7.6.7.6.D.

English Traditional Melody
Harmony by Ralph Vaughan Williams, 1906
Arrangement Altered

Gilbert Keith Chesterton, c. 1906

1 O God of earth and al - tar, Bow down and hear our cry,
2 From all that ter - ror teach - es, From lies of tongue and pen,
3 Tie in a liv - ing teth - er The prince and priest and thrall,

Our earth - ly rul - ers fal - ter, Our peo - ple drift and die;
From all the eas - y speech - es That com - fort cru - el men,
Bind all our lives to - geth - er, Smite us and save us all;

The walls of gold en - tomb us, The swords of scorn di - vide,
From sale and prof - a - na - tion Of hon - or, and the sword,
In ire and ex - ul - ta - tion A - flame with faith, and free,

Take not Thy thun - der from us, But take a - way our pride.
From sleep and from dam - na - tion, De - liv - er us, good Lord!
Lift up a liv - ing na - tion, A sin - gle sword to Thee.

MISSION OF THE CHURCH: SOCIAL JUSTICE

458 O MASTER WORKMAN OF THE RACE

BETHLEHEM C.M.D.

Jay T. Stocking, 1912

Gottfried Wilhelm Fink, 1842

1 O mas-ter Work-man of the race, Thou Man of Gal-i-lee,
2 O Car-pen-ter of Naz-a-reth, Build-er of life di-vine,
3 O Thou who didst the vi-sion send And gives to each his task,

Who with the eyes of ear-ly youth E-ter-nal things did see:
Who shap-est man to God's own law, Thy-self the fair de-sign;
And with the task suf-fi-cient strength: Show us Thy will, we ask;

We thank Thee for Thy boy-hood faith That shone Thy whole life through;
Build us a tower of Christ-like height, That we the land may view,
Give us a con-science bold and good, Give us a pur-pose true,

"Did ye not know it is My work, My Fa-ther's work to do?"
And see, like Thee, our no-blest work, Our Fa-ther's work to do.
That it may be our high-est joy, Our Fa-ther's work to do. A-men.

MISSION OF THE CHURCH: SOCIAL JUSTICE

O YOUNG AND FEARLESS PROPHET 459

LLANGLOFFAN 7.6.7.6.D.

S. Ralph Harlow, 1930 and 1935

Welsh Hymn Melody
Hymnau a Thonau, 1865

1 O young and fear-less Proph-et of an-cient Gal-i-lee:
2 We mar-vel at the pur-pose that held Thee to Thy course
3 O help us stand un-swerv-ing a-gainst war's blood-y way,
4 Cre-ate in us the splen-dor that dawns when hearts are kind,
5 O young and fear-less Proph-et, we need Thy pres-ence here,

Thy life is still a sum-mons to serve hu-man-i-ty,
While ev-er on the hill-top be-fore Thee loomed the cross;
Where hate and lust and false-hood hold back Christ's ho-ly sway;
That knows not race nor col-or as boun-daries of the mind;
A-mid our pride and glo-ry to see Thy face ap-pear;

To make our thoughts and ac-tions less prone to please the crowd,
Thy stead-fast face set for-ward where love and du-ty shone,
For-bid false love of coun-try, that blinds us to His call
That learns to val-ue beau-ty, in heart, or brain, or soul,
Once more to hear Thy chal-lenge a-bove our nois-y day,

To stand with hum-ble cour-age for truth with hearts un-cowed.
While we be-tray so quick-ly and leave Thee there a-lone.
Who lifts a-bove the na-tion the broth-er-hood of all.
And longs to bind God's chil-dren in-to one per-fect whole.
A-gain to lead us for-ward a-long God's ho-ly way. A-men.

MISSION OF THE CHURCH: SOCIAL JUSTICE

460 GRACIOUS SAVIOR, WHO DIDST HONOR

KOMM, O KOMM 8.7.8.7.7.7.

Emily L. Shirreff

Neu-vermehrtes . . . Gesangbuch,
Meiningen, 1693

1 Gra - cious Sav - ior, who didst hon - or Wom - an - kind as wom - an's son;
2 Je - sus, Son of hu - man moth - er, Bless our moth - er - hood, we pray;
3 Thou who didst with Jo - seph la - bor, Nor didst hum - ble work dis - dain,
4 Thou who didst go forth in sor - row, Toil - ing for the souls of men,

Ver - y man, though God be - got - ten, And with God the Fa - ther one,
Give us grace to lead our chil - dren, Draw them to Thee day by day;
Grant we may Thy foot - steps fol - low Pa - tient - ly through toil or pain;
Thou who shalt draw all men to Thee, Though de - spised, re - ject - ed then;

Grant that wom - an - hood may be Con - se - crat - ed, Lord, to Thee.
May our sons and daugh - ters be Ded - i - cat - ed, Lord, to Thee.
May our qui - et home - life be Lived, O Lord, in Thee, to Thee.
Hum - ble though our in - fluence be, Use it in the world for Thee. A - men.

461 HAPPY THE HOME WHEN GOD

ST. AGNES C.M.

Henry Ware, 1846

John Bacchus Dykes, 1866

1 Hap - py the home when God is there, And love fills ev - ery breast;
2 Hap - py the home where Je - sus' name Is sweet to ev - ery ear;
3 Hap - py the home where prayer is heard, And praise is wont to rise;
4 Lord, let us in our homes a - gree This bless - ed peace to gain;

HOME AND FAMILY: THE CHRISTIAN HOME

When one their wish, and one their prayer, And one their heav'n-ly rest.
Where chil-dren ear - ly lisp His fame, And par-ents hold Him dear.
Where par-ents love the sa - cred Word And all its wis - dom prize.
U - nite our hearts in love to Thee, And love to all will reign. A-men.

LORD OF THE HOME 462

PHILIPPINE L.M.

Robert Edwin Roberts, 1925
Arrangement Altered

Albert Frederick Bayly, 1947

1 Lord of the home, Thine on - ly Son Re - ceived a
2 Help us, O Lord, our homes to make Thy Ho - ly
3 Pray we that all who with us dwell, Thy love and
4 Teach us to keep our homes so fair, That were our
5 Lord, may Thy Spir - it sanc - ti - fy Each house - hold

moth - er's ten - der love; And from an earth - ly
Spir - it's dwell - ing place; Our hands and hearts' de -
joy and peace may know; And while our lips Thy
Lord a child once more, He might be glad our
du - ty we ful - fill, May we our Mas - ter

fa - ther won His vi - sion of Thy home a - bove.
vo - tion take To be the ser - vants of Thy grace.
prais - es tell, May faith - ful lives Thy glo - ry show.
hearth to share, And find a wel - come at our door.
glo - ri - fy In glad o - be - dience to Thy will. A - men.

HOME AND FAMILY: THE CHRISTIAN HOME

463 O HAPPY HOME, WHERE THOU ART

HENLEY 11.10.11.10.

Carl Johann Philipp Spitta, 1833
O selig Haus, wo man dich aufgenommen
Tr. Sarah B. Findlater, 1858, and Others

Lowell Mason, 185

1 O hap - py home, where Thou art loved the dear - est,
2 O hap - py home, where each one serves Thee, low - ly,
3 O hap - py home, where Thou art not for - got - ten
4 Un - til at last, when earth's day's work is end - ed,

Thou lov - ing Friend and Sav - ior of our race,
What - ev - er his ap - point - ed work may be,
When joy is o - ver - flow - ing, full, and free;
All meet Thee in the bless - ed home a - bove,

And where a - mong the guests there nev - er com - eth
Till ev - ery com - mon task seems great and ho - ly,
O hap - py home, where ev - ery wound - ed spir - it
From whence Thou cam - est, where Thou hast as - cend - ed,

One who can hold such high and hon - ored place.
When it is done, O Lord, as un - to Thee.
Is brought, Phy - si - cian, Com - fort - er, to Thee.
Thy ev - er - last - ing home of peace and love! A - men.

HOME AND FAMILY: THE CHRISTIAN HOME

A GLADSOME HYMN OF PRAISE 464

CANAAN 8.7.8.7. with Refrain

Ambrose N. Blatchford, 1876

Composer Unknown

1 A glad-some hymn of praise we sing, And thank-ful-ly we gath - er
2 From shades of night He calls the light, And from the sod the flow - er;
3 Full in His sight His chil-dren stand, By His strong arm de - fend - ed,
4 For noth-ing falls un-known to Him, Or care or joy or sor - row,
5 Then praise the Lord with one ac-cord, To His great name give glo - ry,

To bless the love of God a-bove, Our ev - er - last - ing Fa - ther.
From ev - ery cloud His bless-ings break In sun-shine or in show - er.
And He whose wis - dom guides the world, Our foot-steps hath at - tend - ed.
And He whose mer - cy ruled the past Will be our stay to - mor - row.
And of His nev - er - chang-ing love Re - peat the won-drous sto - ry.

REFRAIN

In Him re - joice with heart and voice Whose glo - ry fad - eth nev - er,

Whose prov - i - dence is our de-fense, Who lives and loves for - ev - er.

HOME AND FAMILY: HYMNS FOR CHILDREN

465 EACH LITTLE FLOWER THAT OPENS

DANISH TUNE   7.6.7.6. with Refrain

Cecil Frances Alexander†, 1848

Danish Traditional Melody

1 Each lit - tle flower that o - pens, Each lit - tle bird that sings:
2 The pur - ple - head - ed moun - tain, The riv - er run - ning by,
3 The cold wind in the win - ter, The pleas - ant sum - mer sun,
4 He gave us eyes to see them, And lips that we might tell

God made their glow - ing col - ors, He made their ti - ny wings.
The sun - set, and the morn - ing That bright-ens up the sky,
The ripe fruits in the gar - den: He made them ev - ery one.
How great is God al - might - y, Who has made all things well.

REFRAIN

Yes, all things bright and beau - ti - ful, All crea-tures great and small,

And all things wise and won - der-ful: The Lord God made them all.

HOME AND FAMILY: HYMNS FOR CHILDREN

ONCE IN ROYAL DAVID'S CITY 466

IRBY 8.7.8.7.7.7.

Cecil Frances Alexander, 1848

Henry John Gauntlett, 1849

1 Once in roy - al Da - vid's cit - y Stood a low - ly
2 He came down to earth from heav - en Who is God and
3 And, through all His won - drous child-hood, He would hon - or
4 And our eyes at last shall see Him, Through His own re -
5 Not in that poor low - ly sta - ble, With the ox - en

cat - tle shed, Where a moth - er laid her Ba - by,
Lord of all, And His shel - ter was a sta - ble,
and o - bey, Love and watch the low - ly maid - en
deem - ing love; For that Child so dear and gen - tle
stand - ing by, We shall see Him; but in heav - en,

In a man - ger for His bed: Mar - y was that moth - er
And His cra - dle was a stall; With the poor, and mean, and
In whose gen - tle arms He lay; Chris - tian chil - dren all must
Is our Lord in heav'n a - bove: And He leads His chil - dren
Set at God's right hand on high: When like stars His chil - dren

mild, Je - sus Christ her lit - tle Child.
low - ly, Lived on earth our Sav - ior ho - ly.
be Mild, o - be - dient good as He.
on To the place where He is gone.
crowned, All in white shall wait a - round.

HOME AND FAMILY: HYMNS FOR CHILDREN

467 I LOVE TO THINK THAT JESUS SAW

CHILDHOOD 8.8.8.6.

Ada Skemp, d. 1927

H. Walford Davies, b. 1869

1 I love to think that Je - sus saw The
2 The same white moon with sil - ver face That
3 The same great God that hears my prayers Heard

same bright sun that shines to - day; It gave Him
sails a - cross the sky at night, He used to
His, when Je - sus knelt to pray; He is my

light to do His work, And smiled up - on His play.
see in Gal - i - lee, And watch it with de - light.
Fa - ther, who will keep His child through ev - ery day.

468 WISE MEN SEEKING JESUS

GLENFINLAS 6.5.6.5.

James Thomas East, 1926

Kenneth George Finlay, 1925

1 Wise men seek - ing Je - sus Tra - veled from a - far,
2 But if we de - sire Him, He is close at hand;
3 Prayer-ful souls may find Him By our qui - et lakes,

HOME AND FAMILY: HYMNS FOR CHILDREN

Guid - ed on their jour - ney By a beau - teous star.
For our na - tive coun - try Is our ho - ly land.
Meet Him on our hill - sides When the morn - ing breaks.

4 In our fertile cornfields
   While the sheaves are bound,
  In our busy markets,
   Jesus may be found.

5 Fishermen talk with Him
   By the great north sea,
  As the first disciples
   Did in Galilee.

6 Every peaceful village
   In our land might be
  Made by Jesus' presence
   Like sweet Bethany.

7 He is more than near us,
   If we love Him well;
  For He seeketh ever
   In our hearts to dwell.

LONG AGO WHEN JESUS 469

GLENFINLAS. 6.5.6.5.

Albert Frederick Bayly, 1954

Kenneth George Finlay, 1925

1 Long a - go when Je - sus Walked in Gal - i - lee,
2 Now He gives the chil - dren Born in ev - ery land,
3 Red - skin, white and yel - low, Black and brown draw near.

Chil - dren found a wel - come At the Sav - ior's knee.
Dark and fair, a bless - ing From His lov - ing hand.
Then, since He re - ceives them, We too hold them dear.

HOME AND FAMILY: HYMNS FOR CHILDREN

470 O COME, ALL YE CHILDREN

IHR KINDERLEIN, KOMMET 11.11.11.11.

Christian von Schmid
Ihr Kinderlein kommet
Tr. Unknown

Johann Abraham Peter Schulz, d. 1800

1 O come, all ye chil - dren, O come, one and all,
2 He's born in a sta - ble for you and for me,
3 See Mar - y and Jo - seph with love - beam - ing eyes
4 Kneel down and a - dore Him with shep - herds to - day,
5 Dear Christ Child, what gifts can we chil - dren be - stow
6 Our hearts, then, to Thee we will of - fer to - day,

To Beth - le - hem haste to the man - ger so small,
Draw near by the bright gleam - ing star - light to see,
Are gaz - ing up - on the rude bed where He lies,
Lift up lit - tle hands now and praise Him as they;
By which our af - fec - tion and glad - ness to show?
We of - fer them glad - ly; ac - cept them, we pray,

God's Son for a gift has been sent you this night
In swad - dling clothes ly - ing so meek and so mild,
The shep - herds are kneel - ing with hearts full of love,
Re - joice that a Sav - ior from sin you can boast,
No rich - es and trea - sures of val - ue can be,
And make them so spot - less and pure that we may

To be your Re - deem - er, your joy and de - light.
And pur - er than an - gels the heav - en - ly Child;
While an - gels sing loud al - le - lu - ias a - bove.
And join in the song of the heav - en - ly host.
But hearts that be - lieve are ac - cept - ed with Thee.
A - bide in Thy pres - ence in heav - en for aye.

HOME AND FAMILY: HYMNS FOR CHILDREN

FOR GOD SO LOVED US 471

GOTT IST DIE LIEBE 10.9. with Refrain

August Rische, d. 1906
Gott ist die Liebe
Paraphrase Composite, 1956 and 1960

Thüringer Melody, c. 1840

1 For God so loved us, He sent the Savior: For God so
2 He sent the Savior, The blest Redeemer; He sent the
3 He bade me welcome, O word of mercy; He bade me
4 Glory and honor, O Love eternal, To Thee be

REFRAIN

loved us, And loves me too.
Savior To set me free.
welcome, O voice divine.
given While life shall last.

Love so unending!

I'll sing Thy praises, God loves His children, Loves even me.

1 Gott ist die Liebe, lässt mich erlösen;
Gott ist die Liebe, er liebt auch mich.

2 Ich lag in Banden der schnöden Sünde;
ich lag in Banden und konnt nicht los.

3 Er sandte Jesum, den treuen Heiland;
er sandte Jesum und macht mich los.

4 Jesus, mein Heiland, gab sich zum Opfer;
Jesus, mein Heiland, büsst meine Schuld.

REFRAIN   Drum sag ich noch einmal:
Gott ist die Liebe,
Gott ist die Liebe,
er liebt auch mich.

HOME AND FAMILY: HYMNS FOR CHILDREN

472 AWAY IN A MANGER

AWAY IN A MANGER 11.11.11.11.

Little Children's Book . . . †, 1885, Sts. 1 and 2
St. 3 somewhat later

James R. Murray (?), 1887

1 A - way in a man-ger, no crib for His bed, The lit - tle Lord
2 The cat - tle are low-ing, the poor ba - by wakes, The lit - tle Lord
3 Be near me, Lord Je - sus; I ask Thee to stay Close by me for

Je - sus laid down His sweet head, The stars in the sky looked
Je - sus, no cry - ing He makes. I love Thee, Lord Je - sus, look
ev - er and love me I pray. Bless all the dear chil-dren in

down where He lay, The lit - tle Lord Je - sus, a - sleep on the hay.
down from the sky, And stay by my side un - til morn-ing is nigh.
Thy ten - der care And fit us for heav-en to live with Thee there.

473 THERE IS A GREEN HILL FAR AWAY

MEDITATION C.M.

Cecil Frances Alexander, 1848

John Henry Gower, 1890

1 There is a green hill far a - way, Out - side a cit - y wall,
2 We may not know, we can - not tell, What pains He had to bear,
3 He died that we might be for-giv'n, He died to make us good,
4 There was no oth - er good e - nough To pay the price of sin;
5 O dear - ly, dear - ly has He loved, And we must love Him too,

HOME AND FAMILY: HYMNS FOR CHILDREN

Where the dear Lord was cru - ci - fied, Who died to save us all.
But we be - lieve it was for us He hung and suf - fered there.
That we might go at last to heav'n, Saved by His pre - cious blood.
He on - ly could un - lock the gate Of heav'n, and let us in.
And trust in His re - deem-ing blood, And try His works to do.

WE WELCOME GLAD EASTER 474

ST. DENIO 11.11.11.11.

Anonymous

Welsh Hymn Melody, 1839

1 We wel-come glad Eas - ter when Je - sus a - rose And won a great
2 And tell how three Mar - ys came ear - ly that day And there at the
3 And sing of the an - gel who said: "Do not fear! Your Sav - ior is
4 So think of the prom-ise which Je - sus did give, That he who be -

REFRAIN

vic - to - ry o - ver His foes.
tomb found the stone rolled a - way." Then raise your glad voic - es, ye
ris'n a - gain; He is not here."
lieves in Him al - so shall live.

chil - dren, and sing, Bring sweet Eas - ter prais - es to Je - sus, our King.

HOME AND FAMILY: HYMNS FOR CHILDREN

475 FATHER, WE THANK THEE FOR THE NIGHT

ONSLOW L.M.

Rebecca J. Weston, late nineteenth century

Daniel Batchellor, 1885

1 Fa - ther, we thank Thee for the night, And for the pleas-ant morn-ing light,
2 Help us to do the things we should, To be to oth-ers kind and good;

For rest and food and lov - ing care, And all that makes the day so fair.
In all we do at work or play To grow more lov-ing ev - ery day. A-men.

476 GOD MY FATHER, LOVING ME

INNOCENTS 7.7.7.7.

George Wallace Briggs, 1930

The Parish Choir, 1850

1 God my Fa - ther, lov - ing me, Gave His Son my friend to be;
2 Je - sus still re - mains the same As in days of old He came;
3 How can I re - pay Thy love, Lord of all the hosts a - bove?
4 I have but my - self to give, Let me for Thy ser - vice live;

Gave His Son my form to take, And to suf - fer for my sake.
As my broth-er by my side, Still He seeks my steps to guide.
What have I, a child, to bring Un - to Thee, Thou heav-'nly King?
Let me fol - low, day by day, Where Thou show-est me the way. A-men.

HOME AND FAMILY: HYMNS FOR CHILDREN

COME, MY SOUL, THOU MUST BE 477

HAYDN 8.4.7.D.

Frederich R. L. von Canitz, 1700
Seele, du musst munter werden
Tr. Henry J. Buckoll, 1838

Arranged from Franz Joseph Haydn, 1791

1 Come, my soul, thou must be wak - ing, Now is break - ing O'er the earth an - oth - er day; Come, to Him who made this splen - dor, See thou ren - der All thy fee - ble powers can pay.

2 Thou too hail the light re - turn - ing, Read - y burn - ing Be the in - cense of thy powers! For the night is safe - ly end - ed; God hath tend - ed With His care thy help - less hours.

3 Pray that He may pros - per ev - er Each en - deav - or, When thine aim is good and true; But that He may ev - er thwart thee, And con - vert thee, When thou e - vil wouldst pur - sue.

4 On - ly God's free gifts a - buse not, Light re - fuse not, But His Spir - it's voice o - bey; Thou with Him shalt dwell, be - hold - ing Light en - fold - ing All things in un - cloud - ed day.

TIMES AND SEASONS: MORNING

478 CHRIST, WHOSE GLORY FILLS THE SKIES

LUX PRIMA 7.7.7.7.7.7.

Charles Wesley, 1740

Charles F. Gounod, 1872

1 Christ, whose glo - ry fills the skies, Christ, the true, the on - ly light,
2 Dark and cheer - less is the morn Un - ac - com - pan - ied by Thee;
3 Vis - it, then, this soul of mine; Pierce the gloom of sin and grief;

Sun of right-eous - ness, a - rise, Tri - umph o'er the shades of night;
Joy - less is the day's re - turn Till Thy mer - cy's beams I see
Fill me, ra - dian - cy di - vine; Scat - ter all my un - be - lief;

Day-spring from on high, be near; Day-star, in my heart ap - pear.
Till they in - ward light im - part, Glad my eyes and warm my heart.
More and more Thy - self dis - play, Shin - ing to the per - fect day. A - men.

479 I OWE THE LORD A MORNING SONG

GRATITUDE C.M.

Amos Herr, 1890

Amos Herr, 1890

1 I owe the Lord a morn-ing song Of grat - i - tude and praise,
2 He kept me safe an - oth - er night; I see an - oth - er day;
3 Keep me from dan - ger and from sin: Help me Thy will to do,
4 Keep me till Thou wilt call me hence, Where nev - er night can be;

TIMES AND SEASONS: MORNING

For the kind mer - cy He has shown In length-'ning out my days.
Now may His Spir - it, as the light, Di - rect me in His way.
So that my heart be pure with-in; And I Thy good-ness know.
And save me, Lord, for Je - sus' sake. He shed His blood for me. A-men.

FATHER, WE PRAISE THEE 480

CHRISTE SANCTORUM 11.11.11.5.

Ascribed to Gregory the Great, d. 604
Nocte surgentes vigilemus omnes
Tr. Percy Dearmer, 1906

Paris Antiphoner, 1681

1 Fa - ther, we praise Thee, now the night is o - ver; Ac - tive and
2 Mon-arch of all things, fit us for Thy man - sions; Ban - ish our
3 All - ho - ly Fa - ther, Son and e - qual Spir - it, Trin - i - ty

watch - ful, stand we all be - fore Thee; Sing - ing, we of - fer
weak - ness, health and whole-ness send - ing; Bring us to heav - en,
bless - ed, send us Thy sal - va - tion; Thine is the glo - ry,

prayer and med - i - ta - tion: Thus we a - dore Thee.
where Thy saints u - nit - ed Joy with-out end - ing.
gleam - ing and re - sound-ing Through all cre - a - tion. A-men.

TIMES AND SEASONS: MORNING

481 LORD GOD OF MORNING

MACH'S MIT MIR, L.M.

Francis Turner Palgrave, 1862

Johann Hermann Schein, 1628

1 Lord God of morn - ing and of night, We
2 Fresh hopes have wak - ened in our hearts, Fresh
3 O Lord of lights! 'tis Thou a - lone Canst
4 Praise God, our Mak - er and our Friend! Praise

thank Thee for Thy gift of light; As in the dawn the
en - er - gy to do our parts; Thy thou - sand sleeps our
make our dark - ened hearts Thine own; Though this new day with
Him through time, till time shall end! Till psalm and song His

shad - ows fly, We seem to find Thee now more nigh.
strength re - store, A thou - sand-fold to serve Thee more.
joy we see, O dawn of God! we cry for Thee!
name a - dore Through heav'n's great day of ev - er - more! A - men.

482 LORD, THOU SHALT EARLY HEAR

WARWICK C.M.

Based on Psalm 5
Scottish Psalter‡, 1650

Samuel Stanley, 1802

1 Lord, Thou shalt ear - ly hear my voice: I ear - ly will di - rect
2 For Thou art not a God that doth In wick - ed - ness de - light;
3 But I in - to Thy house will come In Thine a - bun - dant grace;
4 Let all that trust in Thee be glad, With joy lift up their voice;

TIMES AND SEASONS: MORNING

My prayer to Thee; and, look-ing up, An an - swer will ex - pect.
Nei - ther shall e - vil dwell with Thee, Nor fools stand in Thy sight.
And I will wor-ship in Thy fear To - ward Thy ho - ly place.
Be - cause Thou sav-est them; let all That love Thy name re - joice. A-men.

NEW EVERY MORNING IS THY LOVE 483

MELCOMBE L.M.

John Keble, 1822   Samuel Webbe, 1782

1 New ev - ery morn-ing is Thy love Our wak-ening and up - ris - ing prove
2 New mer - cies, each re - turn-ing day, Hov - er a - round us while we pray;
3 If on our dai - ly course our mind Be set to hal - low all we find,

Through sleep and dark-ness safe-ly brought, Re-stored to life, and power, and thought.
New per - ils past, new sins for-given, New thoughts of God, new hopes of heav'n.
New trea - sures still, of count-less price, God will pro - vide for sac - ri - fice. A-men.

4 The trivial round, the common task,
   Will furnish all we ought to ask,
   Room to deny ourselves, a road
     To bring us daily nearer God.

5 Only, O Lord, in Thy dear love,
   Fit us for perfect rest above,
   And help us, this and every day,
     To live more nearly as we pray.

TIMES AND SEASONS: MORNING

484 DAYSPRING OF ETERNITY

MORGENGLANZ DER EWIGKEIT 7.8.7.8.7.3.

Christian Knorr von Rosenroth, 1684
Morgenglanz der Ewigkeit
Tr. Catherine Winkworth, 1855 and 1863

Johann Rudolph Ahle, 1662

1 Day - spring of e - ter - ni - ty! Hide no more Thy ra-diant dawn - ing!
2 Let Thy mer-cies' morn-ing dew Rouse our con-science from its blind - ness;
3 Let the glow of love de-stroy Cold o - be-dience faint-ly giv - en,
4 Through this dark and tear - ful place Nev - er be Thy light de - nied us,

Light from light's ex-haust-less sea, Shine on us a-fresh this morn - ing!
Glad - den life's dry plains a - new With the riv - ers of Thy kind - ness;
Wake our hearts to love and joy With the flush-ing east - ern heav - en;
O Thou glo-rious sun of grace, To yon world of glad-ness guide us,

And dis - pel with glo - rious might All our night.
Wa - ter dai - ly us Thy flock From the rock.
Let us tru - ly rise ere yet Life hath set.
When to joys that nev - er end We as - cend! A-men.

485 AWAKE, MY SOUL, AND WITH THE SUN

MORNING HYMN L.M.

Thomas Ken, 1694 and 1707

François Hippolyte Barthélémon, c. 1789

1 A - wake, my soul, and with the sun Thy dai - ly stage of du - ty run;
2 In con - ver - sa - tion be sin-cere, Keep con-science as the noon-day clear;
3 Lord, I my vows to Thee re - new; Dis - perse my sins as morn-ing dew;
4 Di - rect, con-trol, sug - gest, this day All I de - sign, or do, or say,
5 Praise God from whom all bless-ings flow. Praise Him, all crea - tures here be - low,

TIMES AND SEASONS: MORNING

Shake off dull sloth, and joy-ful rise To pay thy morn-ing sac-ri-fice.
Think how all-see-ing God thy ways And all thy se-cret thoughts sur-veys.
Guard my first springs of thought and will And with Thy-self my spir-it fill.
That all my powers, with all their might, In Thy sole glo-ry may u-nite.
Praise Him a-bove, ye heav'n-ly host, Praise Fa-ther, Son, and Ho-ly Ghost. A-men.

LIGHT OF LIGHT, ENLIGHTEN ME 486

MEINEM JESUM (MEINHOLD) 7.8.7.8.7.7.

Benjamin Schmolck, 1714
Licht von Licht, erleuchte mich
Tr. Catherine Winkworth, 1858

Gesangbuch, Lüneburg, 1686

1 Light of light, en-light-en me, Now a-new the day is dawn-ing;
2 Fount of all our joy and peace, To Thy liv-ing wa-ters lead me;
3 Kin-dle Thou the sac-ri-fice That up-on my lips is ly-ing;
4 Let me with my heart to-day, Ho-ly, ho-ly, ho-ly, sing-ing

Sun of grace, the shad-ows flee, Bright-en Thou my Sab-bath morn-ing;
Thou from earth my soul re-lease, And with grace and mer-cy feed me;
Clear the shad-ows from my eyes, That from ev-ery er-ror fly-ing,
Rapt a-while from earth a-way, All my soul to Thee up-spring-ing,

With Thy joy-ous sun-shine blest, Hap-py is my day of rest.
Bless Thy Word, that it may prove Rich in fruits that Thou dost love.
No strange fire may in me glow That Thine al-tar doth not know.
Have a fore-taste in-ly given How they wor-ship Thee in heav'n.

487 THE DUTEOUS DAY NOW CLOSETH

O WELT, ICH MUSS DICH LASSEN (INNSBRUCK) 7.7.6.7.7.8.

Paul Gerhardt, 1648
Nun ruhen alle Wälder
Tr. Robert Bridges, 1899

German Melody; Sacred use by 1505
Harmony by Johann Sebastian Bach, 1729

1 The du - teous day now clos - eth, Each flower and tree re-
2 Now all the heav'n-ly splen - dor Breaks forth in star - light
3 His care he drown-eth yon - der, Lost in th'a - byss of
4 A - while his mor - tal blind - ness May miss God's lov - ing

pos - eth, Shade creeps o'er wild and wood: Let
ten - der From myr - iad worlds un - known: And
won - der; To heav'n his soul doth steal: This
kind - ness, And grope in faith - less strife: But

us, as night is fall - ing, On God our mak - er
man, the mar - vel see - ing, For - gets his self - ish
life he dis - es - teem - eth, The day it is that
when life's day is o - ver Shall death's fair night dis -

call - ing, Give thanks to Him the giv - er good.
be - ing, For joy of beau - ty not his own.
dream - eth, That doth from truth his vi - sion seal.
cov - er The fields of ev - er - last - ing life.

TIMES AND SEASONS: EVENING

THE DAY THOU GAVEST, LORD 488

LES COMMANDEMENS DE DIEU 9.8.9.8.

La forme des prieres . . . , Strasbourg, 1545
Harmony adapted from Claude Goudimel, 1565

John Ellerton, 1870

1 The day Thou gav - est, Lord, is end - ed,
2 We thank Thee that Thy church, un - sleep - ing
3 As o'er each con - ti - nent and is - land
4 The sun that bids us rest is wak - ing
5 So be it, Lord; Thy throne shall nev - er,

The dark - ness falls at Thy be - hest;
While earth rolls on - ward in - to light,
The dawn leads on an - oth - er day,
Our breth - ren 'neath the west - ern sky,
Like earth's proud em - pires, pass a - way;

To Thee our morn - ing hymns as - cend - ed,
Through all the world her watch is keep - ing,
The voice of prayer is nev - er si - lent,
And hour by hour fresh lips are mak - ing
Thy king - dom stands, and grows for - ev - er,

Thy praise shall sanc - ti - fy our rest.
And rests not now by day or night.
Nor dies the strain of praise a - way.
Thy won - drous do - ings heard on high.
Till all Thy crea - tures own Thy sway. A - men.

489 O GLADSOME LIGHT, O GRACE

NUNC DIMITTIS 6.6.7.D.

Anonymous, 3rd century (?)
Φῶς ἱλαρὸν ἁγίας δόξης
Tr. Robert Bridges, 1899

Pseaumes octante trois, Geneva, 1551
Harmony adapted from Claude Goudimel, 1565

1 O glad-some light, O grace Of God the Fa-ther's face, Th'e-
2 Now, ere day fad - eth quite, We see the eve - ning light, Our
3 To Thee of right be - longs All praise of ho - ly songs, O

ter - nal splen-dor wear - ing; Ce - les-tial, ho - ly, blest, Our
wont-ed hymn out - pour - ing; Fa - ther of might un - known, Thee,
Son of God, life - giv - er; Thee there-fore, O Most High, The

Sav - ior Je - sus Christ, Joy - ful in Thine ap - pear - ing.
His in - car - nate Son, And Ho - ly Spirit a - dor - ing.
world doth glo - ri - fy, And shall ex - alt for - ev - er.

490 NOW THE DAY IS OVER

MERRIAL 6.5.6.5.

Sabine Baring-Gould, 1865

Joseph Barnby, 1868

1 Now the day is o - ver, Night is draw-ing nigh;
2 Je - sus, give the wea - ry Calm and sweet re - pose;
3 Grant to lit - tle chil - dren Vi - sions bright of Thee;
4 Through the long night watch - es May Thine an - gels spread
5 When the morn - ing wak - ens, Then may I a - rise

TIMES AND SEASONS: EVENING

Shad - ows of the eve - ning Steal a - cross the sky.
With Thy ten - d'rest bless - ing May our eye - lids close.
Guard the sail - ors toss - ing On the deep, blue sea.
Their white wings a - bove me, Watch - ing round my bed.
Pure, and fresh, and sin - less In Thy ho - ly eyes. A - men.

SUN OF MY SOUL, THOU SAVIOR DEAR 491

HURSLEY L.M.

Arranged from *Grosser Gott, wir loben dich*
From *Katholisches Gesangbuch*, Vienna, 1776

John Keble, 1820

1 Sun of my soul, Thou Sav - ior dear, It is not
2 A - bide with me, from morn till eve, For with - out
3 Watch by the sick; en - rich the poor With bless - ings
4 Come near and bless us when we wake, Ere through the

night if Thou be near; O may no earth - born cloud a - rise
Thee I can - not live; A - bide with me when night is nigh,
from Thy bound-less store; Be ev - ery mourn - er's sleep to - night,
world our way we take, Till in the o - cean of Thy love

To hide Thee from Thy ser - vant's eyes.
For with - out Thee I dare not die.
Like in - fants' slum - bers, pure and light.
We lose our - selves in heav'n a - bove. A - men.

492 NOW, ON LAND AND SEA DESCENDING

VESPER HYMN 8.7.8.7.8.6.8.7.

Samuel Longfellow‡, 1859

John Andrew Stevenson, 1818

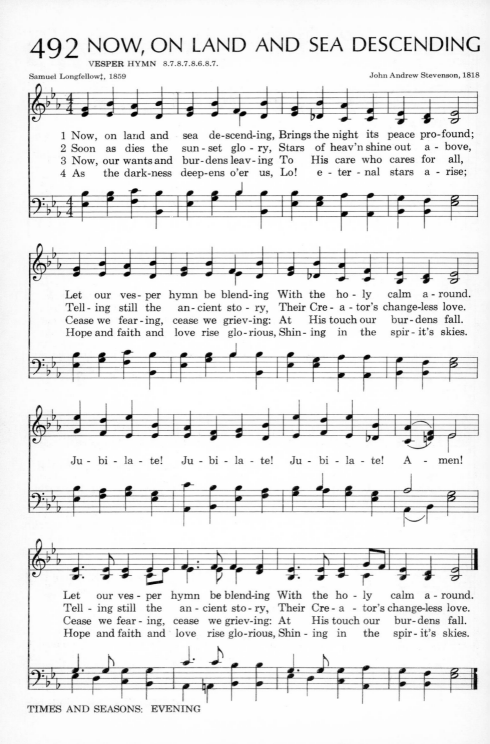

1 Now, on land and sea de-scend-ing, Brings the night its peace pro-found;
2 Soon as dies the sun-set glo - ry, Stars of heav'n shine out a - bove,
3 Now, our wants and bur-dens leav-ing To His care who cares for all,
4 As the dark-ness deep-ens o'er us, Lo! e - ter - nal stars a - rise;

Let our ves-per hymn be blend-ing With the ho - ly calm a - round.
Tell-ing still the an-cient sto - ry, Their Cre - a - tor's change-less love.
Cease we fear-ing, cease we griev-ing: At His touch our bur-dens fall.
Hope and faith and love rise glo-rious, Shin - ing in the spir - it's skies.

Ju - bi - la - te! Ju - bi - la - te! Ju - bi - la - te! A - men!

Let our ves - per hymn be blend-ing With the ho - ly calm a - round.
Tell - ing still the an - cient sto - ry, Their Cre - a - tor's change-less love.
Cease we fear - ing, cease we griev-ing: At His touch our bur-dens fall.
Hope and faith and love rise glo-rious, Shin - ing in the spir - it's skies.

TIMES AND SEASONS: EVENING

DAY IS DYING IN THE WEST 493

CHAUTAUQUA 7.7.7.7.4. with Refrain

Mary A. Lathbury†, 1877 and 1890

William F. Sherwin, 1877

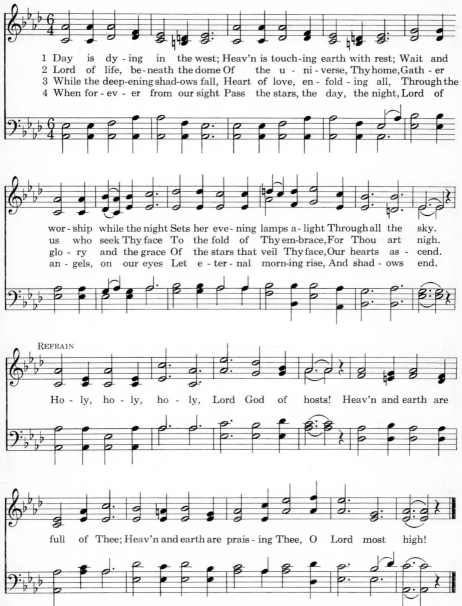

1 Day is dy-ing in the west; Heav'n is touch-ing earth with rest; Wait and
2 Lord of life, be-neath the dome Of the u-ni-verse, Thy home, Gath-er
3 While the deep-ening shad-ows fall, Heart of love, en-fold-ing all, Through the
4 When for-ev-er from our sight Pass the stars, the day, the night, Lord of

wor-ship while the night Sets her eve-ning lamps a-light Through all the sky.
us who seek Thy face To the fold of Thy em-brace, For Thou art nigh.
glo-ry and the grace Of the stars that veil Thy face, Our hearts as-cend.
an-gels, on our eyes Let e-ter-nal morn-ing rise, And shad-ows end.

REFRAIN

Ho-ly, ho-ly, ho-ly, Lord God of hosts! Heav'n and earth are

full of Thee; Heav'n and earth are prais-ing Thee, O Lord most high!

TIMES AND SEASONS: EVENING

494 AT EVEN, ERE THE SUN WAS SET

ANGELUS L.M.

Henry Twells, 1868

Scheffler's *Heilige Seelenlust*, 1657

1 At e - ven, ere the sun was set, The sick, O
  Lord, a - round Thee lay; O in what di - vers pains they met!
  O with what joy they went a - way!

2 Once more 'tis e - ven - tide, and we, Op - pressed with
  va - rious ills, draw near; What if Thy form we can - not see?
  We know and feel that Thou art here.

3 O Sav - ior Christ, our woes dis - pel: For some are
  sick, and some are sad, And some have nev - er loved Thee well,
  And some have lost the love they had.

4 And none, O Lord, have per - fect rest, For none are
  whol - ly free from sin; And they who fain would serve Thee best
  Are con - scious most of wrong with - in. A - men.

5 O Savior Christ, Thou too art man;
  Thou hast been troubled, tempted, tried;
  Thy kind but searching glance can scan
  The very wounds that shame would hide.

6 Thy touch has still its ancient power;
  No word from Thee can fruitless fall:
  Hear in this solemn evening hour,
  And in Thy mercy heal us all.

TIMES AND SEASONS: EVENING

ABIDE WITH ME 495

EVENTIDE 10.10.10.10.

Henry Francis Lyte, 1847

William Henry Monk, 1861

1 A - bide with me: fast falls the e - ven - tide; The dark - ness
2 Swift to its close ebbs out life's lit - tle day; Earth's joys grow
3 I need Thy pres - ence ev - ery pass - ing hour; What but Thy
4 I fear no foe, with Thee at hand to bless: Ills have no

deep - ens; Lord, with me a - bide: When oth - er help - ers fail, and
dim, its glo - ries pass a - way; Change and de - cay in all a -
grace can foil the temp-ter's power? Who like Thy - self my guide and
weight, and tears no bit - ter - ness. Where is death's sting? where, grave, thy

com - forts flee, Help of the help-less, O a - bide with me.
round I see; O Thou who chang-est not, a - bide with me.
stay can be? Through cloud and sun-shine, O a - bide with me.
vic - to - ry? I tri - umph still, if Thou a - bide with me. A - men.

5 Hold then Thy cross before my closing eyes;
   Shine through the gloom, and point me to the skies:
   Heav'n's morning breaks, and earth's vain shadows flee:
   In life and death, O Lord, abide with me.

TIMES AND SEASONS: EVENING

496 ALL PRAISE TO THEE, MY GOD

TALLIS' CANON L.M.

Thomas Ken, 1709

Thomas Tallis, c. 1567

1 All praise to Thee, my God, this night, For all the
2 For - give me, Lord, for Thy dear Son, The ill that
3 O may my soul on Thee re - pose, And with sweet

bless - ings of the light: Keep me, O keep me, King of
I this day have done; That with the world, my - self, and
sleep my eye - lids close; Sleep that shall me more vig - 'rous

kings, Be - neath Thine own al - might - y wings.
Thee, I, ere I sleep, at peace may be.
make To serve my God when I a - wake. A - men.

*Tenor is in canon beginning here.

4 When in the night I sleepless lie,
My soul with heav'nly thoughts supply!
Let no ill dreams disturb my rest,
No powers of darkness me molest!

5 Praise God, from whom all blessings flow;
Praise Him, all creatures here below;
Praise Him above, ye heav'nly host:
Praise Father, Son, and Holy Ghost.

TIMES AND SEASONS: EVENING

O DAY OF SACRED REST 497

LISCHER 6.6.6.6.8.8.

"Hayward" in John Dobell's, *Collection*, 1806, and Others

Friedrich Schneider, d. 1853
Arranged by Lowell Mason, 1841

1 O day of sa - cred rest, We wel - come thee a - new;
2 To heav'n our prayers we send, O Son of God most high;
3 De - scend, cel - es - tial Dove, With all Thy quick -'ning powers;

Lord, make these mo - ments blest, Send Thy re - fresh - ing dew;
Thy scep - ter, Lord, ex - tend, As hum - bly we draw nigh;
Dis - close a Sav - ior's love, And bless the sa - cred hours:

From fleet - ing plea - sures and de - lights, I soar to reach im -
May sin - ful hearts now con - trite be, Teach all to know and
Then shall my soul new life ob - tain, Nor Sab - baths be en -

mor - tal heights, I soar to reach im - mor - tal heights.
fol - low Thee, Teach all to know and fol - low Thee.
joyed in vain, Nor Sab - baths be en - joyed in vain.

TIMES AND SEASONS: THE LORD'S DAY

498 PRAISE OUR FATHER FOR THIS SUNDAY

P'UT'O 8.8.7.8.

Tzu-ch'en Chao, 1931
Tr. Frank W. Price, 1952

Chinese Melody
Hymns of Universal Praise, 1936

1 Praise our Fa-ther for this Sun-day, Praise His good-ness now and al-way.
2 Aft-er toil-ing through the long week Now we gath-er to hear Thee speak.
3 Some-times we bear pain and sor-row, Some-times dark-ness hides the mor-row;
4 Some-times we find peace and glad-ness, Calm and hope in joy and sad-ness;
5 Here we come our lives to of-fer, Hearts and minds we hum-bly prof-fer.

Praise His grace that loves men thus, Praise His mer-cy that for-gives us.
In Thy house may all be blest, Here may all gain strength and find rest.
Fa-ther, Fa-ther, leave us not When sore trou-ble be-comes our lot.
On our way God sheds His light, Loves us ev-er, day and dark night.
Fa-ther, hear us while we pray, And re-ceive us, now and for aye. A-men.

499 THIS IS THE DAY THE LORD HATH MADE

ARLINGTON C.M.

Based on Psalm 118
Isaac Watts, 1719

Thomas Augustine Arne, 1762
Arranged by Ralph Harrison, 1784

1 This is the day the Lord hath made; He calls the hours His own;
2 To-day He rose and left the dead, And Sa-tan's em-pire fell;
3 Blest be the Lord who comes to men With mes-sag-es of grace;
4 Ho-san-na in the high-est strains The church on earth can raise!

Let heav'n re-joice, let earth be glad, And praise sur-round the throne.
To-day the saints His tri-umphs spread, And all His won-ders tell.
Who comes in God His Fa-ther's name To save our sin-ful race.
The high-est heav'ns in which He reigns Shall give Him no-bler praise. A-men.

TIMES AND SEASONS: THE LORD'S DAY

THIS IS THE DAY OF LIGHT 500

FRANCONIA S.M.

J. B. König's, *Harmonischer Liederschatz*, 1738
Arranged by William Henry Havergal, 1847

John Ellerton, 1867

1 This is the day of light: Let there be light to - day; O
2 This is the day of rest: Our fail - ing strength re - new; On
3 This is the day of peace: Thy peace our spir - its fill; Bid
4 This is the day of pray'r: Let earth to heav'n draw near; Lift
5 This is the first of days: Send forth Thy quick-'ning breath, And

Day-spring, rise up - on our night, And chase its gloom a - way.
wea - ry brain and trou-bled breast Shed Thou Thy fresh-'ning dew.
Thou the blasts of dis - cord cease, The waves of strife be still.
up our hearts to seek Thee there, Come down to meet us here.
wake dead souls to love and praise, O Van-quish-er of death! A-men.

COME, LET US JOIN WITH ONE ACCORD 501

RICHMOND C.M.

Charles Wesley, 1763

Thomas Haweis, 1792

1 Come, let us join with one ac - cord In hymns a - round the throne!
2 This is the day which God hath blest, The bright-est of the sev'n,
3 Then let us in His name sing on, And has - ten to that day
4 Not one, but all our days be - low, Let us in hymns em - ploy;

This is the day our ris - ing Lord Hath made and called His own.
Type of that ev - er - last - ing rest The saints en - joy in heav'n.
When our Re - deem - er shall come down, And shad - ows pass a - way.
And in our Lord re - joic - ing, go To His e - ter - nal joy.

TIMES AND SEASONS: THE LORD'S DAY

502 LORD, DISMISS US WITH THY BLESSING

SICILIAN MARINERS 8.7.8.7.8.7.

Attributed to John Fawcett‡, 1773

Tattersall's *Psalmody*, 1794

1 Lord, dis - miss us with Thy bless - ing; Fill our hearts with
2 Thanks we give and ad - o - ra - tion For Thy gos - pel's
3 So that when Thy love shall call us, Sav - ior, from the

joy and peace; Let us each, Thy love pos - sess - ing,
joy - ful sound: May the fruits of Thy sal - va - tion
world a - way, Let no fear of death ap - pall us,

Tri - umph in re - deem - ing grace: O re - fresh us,
In our hearts and lives a - bound: Ev - er faith - ful,
Glad Thy sum - mons to o - bey: May we ev - er,

O re - fresh us, Trav - 'ling through this wil - der - ness.
Ev - er faith - ful To the truth may we be found;
May we ev - er Reign with Thee in end - less day. A - men.

TIMES AND SEASONS: CLOSE OF WORSHIP

GOD BE WITH YOU TILL WE MEET 503

RANDOLPH 9.8.8.9.

Ralph Vaughan Williams, 1906
Arrangement Altered

Jeremiah Eames Rankin†, 1880

1 God be with you till we meet a-gain; By His coun-sels guide, up - hold you,
2 God be with you till we meet a-gain; 'Neath His wings pro - tect - ing hide you,
3 God be with you till we meet a-gain; When life's per - ils thick con-found you,
4 God be with you till we meet a-gain; Keep love's ban - ner float - ing o'er you,

With His sheep se - cure - ly fold you: God be with you till we meet a-gain.
Dai - ly man - na still pro-vide you: God be with you till we meet a-gain.
Put His arms un - fail - ing round you: God be with you till we meet a-gain.
Smite death's threat-'ning wave be-fore you: God be with you till we meet a gain. A-men.

GOD BE WITH YOU TILL WE MEET 504

GOD BE WITH YOU 9.8.8.9.

Jeremiah Eames Rankin†, 1880

William Gould Tomer, 1880

1 God be with you till we meet a - gain; By His coun-sels guide, up-hold you,
2 God be with you till we meet a - gain; 'Neath His wings pro-tect-ing hide you,
3 God be with you till we meet a - gain; When life's per - ils thick con-found you,
4 God be with you till we meet a - gain; Keep love's ban-ner float-ing o'er you,

With His sheep se-cure-ly fold you: God be with you till we meet a - gain.
Dai - ly man-na still pro-vide you: God be with you till we meet a - gain.
Put His arms un-fail-ing round you: God be with you till we meet a - gain.
Smite death's threat-'ning wave be-fore you: God be with you till we meet a - gain. A-men.

TIMES AND SEASONS: CLOSE OF WORSHIP

505 SAVIOR, AGAIN TO THY DEAR NAME

ELLERS 10.10.10.10.

John Ellerton, 1868

Edward John Hopkins, 1869

1 Sav - ior, a - gain to Thy dear name we raise
2 Grant us Thy peace up - on our home - ward way;
3 Grant us Thy peace, Lord, through the com - ing night;
4 Grant us Thy peace through - out our earth - ly life,

With one ac - cord our part - ing hymn of praise;
With Thee be - gan, with Thee shall end the day:
Turn Thou for us its dark - ness in - to light;
Our balm in sor - row, and our stay in strife;

We stand to bless Thee ere our wor - ship cease;
Guard Thou the lips from sin, the hearts from shame,
From harm and dan - ger keep Thy chil - dren free,
Then, when Thy voice shall bid our con - flict cease,

Then, low - ly kneel - ing, wait Thy word of peace.
That in this house have called up - on Thy name.
For dark and light are both a - like to Thee.
Call us, O Lord, to Thine e - ter - nal peace. A - men.

TIMES AND SEASONS: CLOSE OF WORSHIP

NOW MAY HE, WHO FROM THE DEAD 506

INNOCENTS 7.7.7.7.

John Newton, 1779

The Parish Choir, 1850

1 Now may He, who from the dead Brought the shep-herd of the sheep,
2 May He teach us to ful - fill What is pleas-ing in His sight;
3 To that dear Re - deem - er's praise, Who the cov-enant sealed with blood,

Je - sus Christ, our king and head, All our souls in safe - ty keep.
Per - fect us in all His will, And pre-serve us day and night.
Let our hearts and voic - es raise Loud thanks-giv-ings to our God. A-men.

TO GOD THE ONLY WISE 507

ST. MICHAEL (OLD 134) S.M.

From *Pseaumes octante trois*, Geneva, 1551
Adapted by William Crotch, 1836

Isaac Watts, 1707

1 To God the on - ly wise, Our Sav - ior, and our King, Let all the
2 'Tis His al-might - y love, His coun - sel, and His care, Pre - serve us

saints be - low the skies Their hum - ble prais - es bring.
safe from sin and death, And ev - ery hurt - ful snare. A - men.

TIMES AND SEASONS: CLOSE OF WORSHIP

508 GREAT GOD, WE SING THAT MIGHTY

WAREHAM L.M.

Philip Doddridge, 1755

William Knapp, 1738

1 Great God, we sing that might - y hand By which sup -
2 By day, by night, at home, a - broad, Still are we
3 With grate - ful hearts the past we own; The fu - ture,
4 In scenes ex - alt - ed or de - pressed, Thou art our

port - ed still we stand; The ope - ning year Thy mer - cy
guard - ed by our God; By His in - ces - sant boun - ty
all to us un - known, We to Thy guard - ian care com -
joy, and Thou our rest; Thy good - ness all our hopes shall

shows; That mer - cy crowns it, till it close.
fed, By His un - err - ing coun - sel led.
mit, And, peace - ful, leave be - fore Thy feet.
raise, A - dored through all our chang - ing days. A - men.

509 FOR THY MERCY AND THY GRACE

UNIVERSITY COLLEGE 7.7.7.7.

Henry Downton, 1841

Henry John Gauntlett, 1852

1 For Thy mer - cy and Thy grace, Con - stant through an - oth - er year,
2 Lo! our sins on Thee we cast, Thee our per - fect sac - ri - fice,
3 In our weak - ness and dis - tress, Rock of strength, be Thou our stay;
4 Keep us faith - ful, keep us pure, Keep us ev - er - more Thine own,

TIMES AND SEASONS: OLD AND NEW YEAR

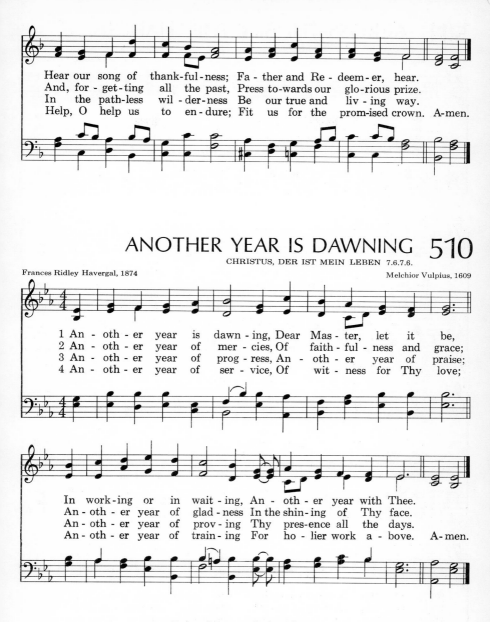

Hear our song of thank-ful-ness; Fa - ther and Re - deem- er, hear.
And, for - get - ting all the past, Press to-wards our glo-rious prize.
In the path-less wil - der-ness Be our true and liv - ing way.
Help, O help us to en-dure; Fit us for the prom-ised crown. A-men.

ANOTHER YEAR IS DAWNING 510

CHRISTUS, DER IST MEIN LEBEN 7.6.7.6.

Frances Ridley Havergal, 1874

Melchior Vulpius, 1609

1 An - oth - er year is dawn - ing, Dear Mas - ter, let it be,
2 An - oth - er year of mer - cies, Of faith - ful - ness and grace;
3 An - oth - er year of prog - ress, An - oth - er year of praise;
4 An - oth - er year of ser - vice, Of wit - ness for Thy love;

In work-ing or in wait - ing, An - oth - er year with Thee.
An - oth - er year of glad - ness In the shin-ing of Thy face.
An - oth - er year of prov - ing Thy pres-ence all the days.
An - oth - er year of train - ing For ho - lier work a - bove. A- men.

5 Another year is dawning,
Dear Master, let it be,
On earth, or else in heaven,
Another year for Thee!

TIMES AND SEASONS: OLD AND NEW YEAR

511 ACROSS THE SKY THE SHADES

NUN FREUT EUCH 8.7.8.7.8.8.7.

James Hamilton†, 1882

J. Klug's *Geistliche Lieder*, 1535

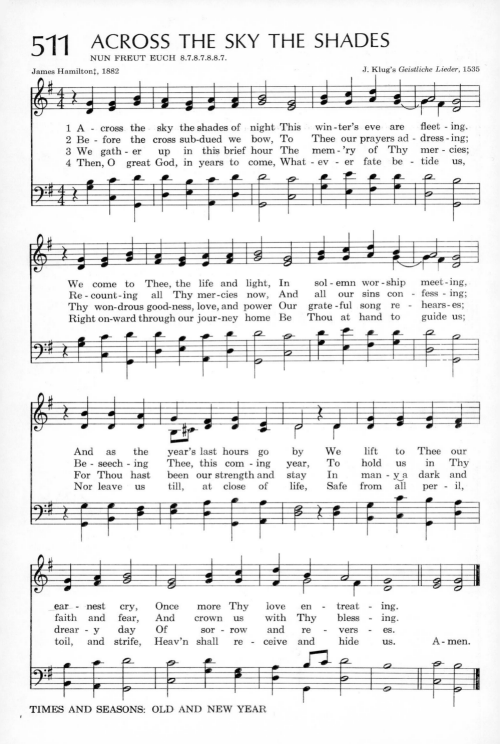

1 A - cross the sky the shades of night This win-ter's eve are fleet-ing.
2 Be - fore the cross sub-dued we bow, To Thee our prayers ad - dress-ing;
3 We gath - er up in this brief hour The mem - 'ry of Thy mer - cies;
4 Then, O great God, in years to come, What - ev - er fate be - tide us,

We come to Thee, the life and light, In sol - emn wor-ship meet-ing,
Re - count-ing all Thy mer-cies now, And all our sins con - fess-ing;
Thy won-drous good-ness, love, and power Our grate-ful song re - hears-es;
Right on-ward through our jour-ney home Be Thou at hand to guide us;

And as the year's last hours go by We lift to Thee our
Be - seech - ing Thee, this com - ing year, To hold us in Thy
For Thou hast been our strength and stay In man - y a dark and
Nor leave us till, at close of life, Safe from all per - il,

ear - nest cry, Once more Thy love en - treat - ing.
faith and fear, And crown us with Thy bless - ing.
drear - y day Of sor - row and re - vers - es.
toil, and strife, Heav'n shall re - ceive and hide us. A - men.

TIMES AND SEASONS: OLD AND NEW YEAR

'TIS WINTER NOW 512

MELROSE L.M.

Samuel Longfellow, 1864

Frederick Charles Maker, d. 1927

1 'Tis win - ter now; the fall - en snow
2 And yet God's love is not with - drawn;
3 And though a - broad the sharp winds blow,
4 O God! who giv'st the win - ter's cold,

Has left the heav'ns all cold - ly clear;
His life with - in the keen air breathes,
And skies are chill, and frosts are keen,
As well as sum - mer's joy - ous rays,

Through leaf - less boughs the sharp winds blow,
His beau - ty paints the crim - son dawn,
Home clos - er draws her cir - cle now,
Us warm - ly in Thy love en - fold,

And all the earth lies dead and drear.
And clothes the boughs with glit - tering wreaths.
And warm - er glows her light with - in.
And keep us through life's win - try days. A - men.

TIMES AND SEASONS: THE SEASONS

513 THE GLORY OF THE SPRING

KING'S LANGLEY C.M.

Thomas Hornblower Gill, 1867

Melody, Lucy Broadwood
Arranged and harmonized by
Ralph Vaughan Williams, 1906

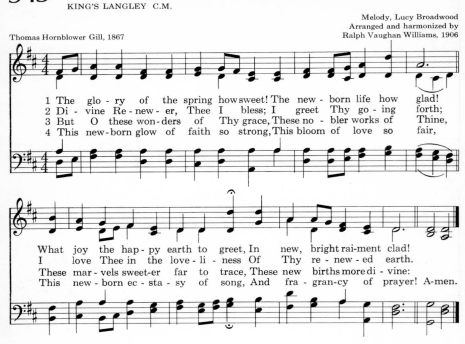

1 The glo - ry of the spring how sweet! The new - born life how glad!
2 Di - vine Re - new - er, Thee I bless; I greet Thy go - ing forth;
3 But O these won-ders of Thy grace, These no - bler works of Thine,
4 This new-born glow of faith so strong, This bloom of love so fair,

What joy the hap - py earth to greet, In new, bright rai - ment clad!
I love Thee in the love - li - ness Of Thy re - new - ed earth.
These mar - vels sweet-er far to trace, These new births more di - vine:
This new - born ec - sta - sy of song, And fra - gran-cy of prayer! A-men.

5 Creator Spirit, work in me
   These wonders sweet of Thine;
   Divine Renewer, graciously
   Renew this heart of mine.

6 Still let new life and strength upspring,
   Still let new joy be giv'n;
   And grant the glad new song to ring
   Through the new earth and heav'n.

514 KINDLY SPRING AGAIN IS HERE

ORIENTIS PARTIBUS 7.7.7.7.

John Newton‡, 1779

13th century French Melody
Harmony by Richard Redhead, 1853

1 Kind - ly spring a - gain is here, Trees and fields in bloom ap - pear;
2 Where in win - ter all was snow, Now the flowers in clus - ters grow;
3 Lord, af - ford a spring to me, Let me feel like what I see;
4 On Thy gar - den deign to smile, Raise the plants, en - rich the soil;

TIMES AND SEASONS: THE SEASONS

Hark! the birds with art - less lays War - ble their Cre - a - tor's praise.
And the corn in green ar - ray Prom - is - es a har - vest day.
Speak, and by Thy gra - cious voice Make my droop-ing heart re - joice.
Soon Thy pres-ence will re - store Life to what seemed dead be - fore.

WITH SONGS AND HONORS 515

BROMSGROVE C.M.

Based on Psalm 147
Isaac Watts, 1719

Psalmodia Evangelica, 1789

1 With songs and hon - ors sound-ing loud, Ad - dress the Lord on
2 He sends His showers of bless - ing down To cheer the plains be -
3 His hoar - y frost, His fleec - y snow, De - scend and clothe the
4 He sends His word, and melts the snow; The fields no lon - ger
5 The chang-ing wind, the fly - ing cloud, O - bey His might-y

high; O - ver the heav'ns He spreads His cloud, And
low; He makes the grass the moun - tains crown, And
ground; The liq - uid streams for - bear to flow, In
mourn; He calls the warm - er gales to blow, And
word: With songs and hon - ors sound - ing loud Praise

wa - ters veil the sky, And wa - ters veil the sky.
corn in val - leys grow, And corn in val - leys grow.
i - cy fet - ters bound, In i - cy fet - ters bound.
bids the spring re - turn, And bids the spring re - turn.
ye the sov - 'reign Lord, Praise ye the sov - 'reign Lord.

TIMES AND SEASONS: THE SEASONS

516 SUMMER SUNS ARE GLOWING

RUTH 6.5.6.5.D.

William Walsham How, 1871

Samuel Smith, 1865

1 Sum - mer suns are glow - ing O - ver land and sea,
2 God's free mer - cy stream - eth O - ver all the world,
3 Lord, up - on our blind - ness Thy pure ra - diance pour;
4 We will nev - er doubt Thee Though Thou veil Thy light;

Hap - py light is flow - ing Boun - ti - ful and free;
And His ban - ner gleam - eth Ev - ery-where un - furled:
For Thy lov - ing - kind - ness Make us love Thee more:
Life is dark with - out Thee; Death with Thee is bright.

Ev - ery-thing re - joic - es In the mel - low rays:
Broad and deep and glo - rious, As the heav'n a - bove,
And when clouds are drift - ing, Dark a - cross our sky,
Light of light! shine o'er us On our pil - grim way,

All earth's thou-sand voic - es Swell the psalm of praise.
Shines in might vic - to - rious His e - ter - nal love.
Then, the veil up - lift - ing, Fa - ther, be Thou nigh.
Go Thou still be - fore us To the end - less day. A - men.

TIMES AND SEASONS: THE SEASONS

THE YEAR IS SWIFTLY WANING 517

WAS KANN ES SCHÖN'RES GEBEN 7.6.7.6.

German Folk Melody
Gesangbuch mit Noten, Berne, Indiana, 1890

William Walsham How, 1871

1 The year is swift - ly wan - ing, The sum - mer days are past;
2 The ev - er-chang - ing sea - sons In si - lence come and go;
3 O pour Thy grace up - on us, That we may wor - thier be,
4 O by each mer - cy sent us, And by each grief and pain,
5 Our bar - ren hearts make fruit - ful With ev - ery good - ly grace,

And life, brief life, is speed - ing; The end is near - ing fast.
But Thou, e - ter - nal Fa - ther, No time or change canst know.
Each year that pass - es o'er us, To dwell in heav'n with Thee.
By bless - ings like the sun - shine, And sor - rows like the rain,
That we Thy name may hal - low, And see at last Thy face. A - men.

TIMES AND SEASONS: THE SEASONS:

PRAISE, O PRAISE OUR GOD AND KING 518

MONKLAND 7.7.7.7.

Henry Williams Baker, 1861

John Bernard Wilkes, 1861

1 Praise, O praise our God and King! Hymns of ad - o - ra - tion sing;
2 Praise Him that He made the sun Day by day his course to run;
3 Praise Him that He gave the rain To ma - ture the swell - ing grain;
4 And hath bid the fruit - ful field Crops of pre - cious in - crease yield;
5 Glo - ry to our boun - teous King! Glo - ry let cre - a - tion sing!

For His mer - cies still en - dure Ev - er faith - ful, ev - er sure.
For His mer - cies still en - dure Ev - er faith - ful, ev - er sure.
For His mer - cies still en - dure Ev - er faith - ful, ev - er sure.
For His mer - cies still en - dure Ev - er faith - ful, ev - er sure.
Glo - ry to the Fa - ther, Son, And blest Spir - it, three in One. A - men.

TIMES AND SEASONS: HARVEST AND THANKSGIVING

519 COME, YE THANKFUL PEOPLE, COME

ST. GEORGE'S WINDSOR 7.7.7.7.D.

Henry Alford, 1844
Altered in *Hymns Ancient and Modern*, 1861

George Job Elvey, 1858

1 Come, ye thank-ful peo-ple, come, Raise the song of har-vest-home:
2 All the world is God's own field, Fruit un-to His praise to yield;
3 For the Lord our God shall come, And shall take His har-vest home;
4 E - ven so, Lord, quick-ly come To Thy fi - nal har-vest home;

All is safe-ly gath-ered in, Ere the win-ter storms be-gin;
Wheat and tares to - geth-er sown, Un - to joy or sor - row grown;
From His field shall in that day All of-fens-es purge a - way;
Gath - er Thou Thy peo-ple in, Free from sor-row, free from sin;

God, our Mak-er, doth pro-vide For our wants to be sup-plied:
First the blade, and then the ear, Then the full corn shall ap-pear:
Give His an-gels charge at last In the fire the tares to cast,
There for-ev-er pu-ri-fied, In Thy pres-ence to a-bide:

Come to God's own tem-ple, come, Raise the song of har-vest-home.
Lord of har-vest, grant that we Whole-some grain and pure may be.
But the fruit-ful ears to store In His gar-ner ev-er-more.
Come, with all Thine an-gels, come, Raise the glo-rious har-vest-home. A-men.

TIMES AND SEASONS: HARVEST AND THANKSGIVING

SING TO THE LORD OF HARVEST 520

WIE LIEBLICH IST DER MAIEN 7.6.7.6.D.

John Samuel Bewley Monsell, 1866

German Folk Melody, 1581
Setting by Healey Willan, 1959

1 Sing to the Lord of har-vest, Sing songs of love and praise;
2 By Him the clouds drop fat-ness, The des-erts bloom and spring,
3 Heap on His sa-cred al-tar The gifts His good-ness gave,
4 To God the gra-cious Fa-ther, Who made us "ver-y good,"

With joy-ful hearts and voic - es Your al - le - lu - ias raise!
The hills leap up in glad - ness, The val - leys laugh and sing.
The gold - en sheaves of har - vest, The souls He died to save.
To Christ, who, when we wan - dered, Re - stored us with His blood,

By Him the roll - ing sea - sons In fruit-ful or - der move;
He fill - eth with His full - ness All things with large in - crease;
Your hearts lay down be - fore Him When at His feet ye fall,
And to the Ho - ly Spir - it, Who doth up - on us pour

Sing to the Lord of har - vest A song of hap-py love.
He crowns the year with good - ness, With plen - ty, and with peace.
And with your lives a - dore Him Who gave His life for all.
His bless - ed dews and sun - shine, Be praise for - ev - er - more. A-men.

TIMES AND SEASONS: HARVEST AND THANKSGIVING

521 WE PLOW THE FIELDS, AND SCATTER

WIR PFLÜGEN 7.6.7.6.D. with Refrain

Matthias Claudius, 1782
Wir pflügen und wir streuen
Tr. Jane Montgomery Campbell, 1861

Lieder für Volksschulen mit
Musik, Hannover, 1800

1 We plow the fields, and scat-ter The good seed on the land,
2 He on-ly is the Mak-er Of all things near and far;
3 We thank Thee, then, O Fa-ther, For all things bright and good,

But it is fed and wa-tered By God's al-might-y hand;
He paints the way-side flow-er, He lights the eve-ning star;
The seed-time and the har-vest, Our life, our health, our food;

He sends the snow in win-ter, The warmth to swell the grain,
The winds and waves o-bey Him, By Him the birds are fed;
No gifts have we to of-fer, For all Thy love im-parts,

The breez-es and the sun-shine, And soft re-fresh-ing rain.
Much more to us, His chil-dren, He gives our dai-ly bread.
But that which Thou de-sir-est, Our hum-ble, thank-ful hearts.

REFRAIN

All good gifts a-round us Are sent from heav'n a-bove;

TIMES AND SEASONS: HARVEST AND THANKSGIVING

Then thank the Lord, O thank the Lord For all His love.

THE GOD OF HARVEST PRAISE 522

PERKINS 6.6.4.6.6.6.6.4.

James Montgomery†, 1840

Edward A. Perkins, mid 19th century

1 The God of har - vest praise; In loud thanks-giv - ing raise
2 Yes, bless His ho - ly name, And pur - est thanks pro-claim
3 The God of har - vest praise; Hands, hearts, and voic - es raise

Hand, heart and voice; The val - leys smile and sing, For - ests and
Through all the earth; To glo - ry in your lot Is come - ly,
With one ac - cord; From field to gar - ner throng, Bear - ing your

moun-tains ring; The plains their trib - ute bring; The streams re - joice.
but be not God's ben - e - fits for-got, A - midst your mirth.
sheaves a-long, And, in your har - vest song, Bless ye the Lord. A-men.

TIMES AND SEASONS: HARVEST AND THANKSGIVING

523 O LORD OF HEAVEN AND EARTH

ES IST KEIN TAG 8.8.8.4.

Christopher Wordsworth‡, 1863

J. D. Meyer's *Geistliche Seelenfreud*, 1692

1 O Lord of heav'n and earth and sea, To Thee all
2 The gold-en sun-shine, ver-nal air, Sweet flowers and
3 For peace-ful homes and health-ful days, For all the
4 Thou didst not spare Thine, on-ly Son, But gav'st Him

praise and glo-ry be; How shall we show our
fruit Thy love de-clare; When har-vests rip-en,
bless-ings earth dis-plays, We owe Thee thank-ful-
for a world un-done, And free-ly with that

love to Thee, Who giv-est all?
Thou art there, Who giv-est all.
ness and praise, Who giv-est all.
bless-ed One, Thou giv-est all. A-men.

5 Thou giv'st the Spirit's blessed dower,
   Spirit of life and love and power,
   And dost His sevenfold graces shower
        Upon us all.

6 For souls redeemed, for sins forgiven,
   For means of grace and hopes of heaven,
   Father, all praise to Thee be given,
        Who givest all. Amen.

TIMES AND SEASONS: HARVEST AND THANKSGIVING

PRAISE TO GOD, IMMORTAL PRAISE 524

PRAYER 7.7.7.7.

Anna L. Barbauld†, 1773   PART I   Asahel Abbot, c. 1852

1 Praise to God, im - mor - tal praise, For the love that crowns our days;
2 For the bless - ings of the field, For the stores the gar - dens yield,
3 Clouds that drop re - fresh - ing dews; Suns that gen - ial heat dif - fuse;
4 All that spring with boun - teous hand, Scat - ters o'er the smil - ing land;
5 These, great God, to Thee we owe, Source whence all our bless - ings flow;

Boun - teous source of ev - ery joy, Let Thy praise our tongues em - ploy.
For the joy which har - vests bring, Grate - ful prais - es now we sing.
Flocks that whit - en all the plain, Yel - low sheaves of rip - ened grain.
All that lib - 'ral au - tumn pours From her o - ver - flow - ing stores.
And for these our souls shall raise Grate - ful vows and sol - emn praise.

LORD, SHOULD RISING WHIRLWINDS 525

ORIENTIS PARTIBUS 7.7.7.7

13th century French Melody
Harmony by Richard Redhead, 1853

Anna L. Barbauld†, 1773   PART II

6 Lord, should ris - ing whirl-winds tear From its stem the rip - ening ear;
7 Should the vine put forth no more, Nor the o - live yield her store;
8 Should Thine al - tered hand re - strain Th' ear - ly and the lat - ter rain
9 Yet to Thee my soul should raise Grate - ful vows and sol - emn praise;

Should the fig - tree's blast - ed shoot Drop her green un - time - ly fruit;
Though the sick - 'ning flocks should fall, And the herds de - sert the stall;
Blast each o - p'ning bud of joy, And the ris - ing year de - stroy;
And, when ev - ery bless - ing's flown, Love Thee for Thy - self a - lone!

TIMES AND SEASONS: HARVEST AND THANKSGIVING

526 WE THANK THEE, LORD

SONG XXXIV L.M.

George Edward Lynch Cotton, 1856

Orlando Gibbons, 1623

1 We thank Thee, Lord, for this fair earth, The glit-tering
2 Thine are the flowers that clothe the ground, The trees that
3 Yet teach us still how far more fair, More glo-rious,
4 So, while we gaze with thought-ful eye On all the

sky, the sil - ver sea; For all their beau-ty, all their
wave their arms a - bove, The hills that gird our dwell-ings
Fa - ther, in Thy sight, Is one pure deed, one ho - ly
gifts Thy love has giv'n, Help us in Thee to live and

worth, Their light and glo - ry, come from Thee.
round, As Thou dost gird Thine own with love.
prayer, One heart that owns Thy Spir - it's might.
die, By Thee to rise from earth to heav'n.

TIMES AND SEASONS: HARVEST AND THANKSGIVING

WE PRAISE THEE, O GOD 527

REVIVE US AGAIN 11.11. with Refrain

William Paton Mackay, 1863 and 1867

"English Melody" in Bliss and
Sankey's *Gospel Hymns* ..., 1875

1 We praise Thee, O God, for the Son of Thy love,
2 We praise Thee, O God, for Thy Spir - it of light,
3 All glo - ry and praise to the Lamb that was slain,
4 We praise Thee, O God, for the joy Thou hast giv'n
5 Re - vive us a - gain, fill each heart with Thy love;

For Je - sus who died, and is now gone a - bove.
Who has shown us our Sav - ior and scat - tered our night.
Who has borne all our sins, and doth cleanse ev - ery stain.
To Thy saints in com - mu - nion these fore - tastes of heav'n.
May each soul be re - kin - dled with fire from a - bove.

REFRAIN

Hal - le - lu - jah! Thine the glo - ry, Hal - le - lu - jah! A - men!

Hal - le - lu - jah! Thine the glo - ry, Re - vive us a - gain.

GOSPEL SONGS

528 COME, LET US ALL UNITE

GOD IS LOVE 8.3.8.3.8.8.8.4. with Refrain

Ascribed to Howard Kingsbury

Edmund S. Lorenz, 1886

1 Come, let us all u - nite to sing, God is love;
Let heav'n and earth their prais - es bring, God is love;
Let ev - ery soul from sin a - wake, Each in his heart sweet mu - sic make, And sing with
us for Je - sus' sake, For God is love.

2 O tell to earth's re - mot - est bound, God is love;
In Christ we have re - demp - tion found, God is love;
His blood has washed our sins a - way, His Spir - it turned our night to day, And now we
can re - joice to say, That God is love.

3 How hap - py is our por - tion here, God is love;
His prom - is - es our spir - its cheer, God is love;
He is our sun and shield by day, Our help, our hope, our strength and stay, He will be
with us all the way, Our God is love.

REFRAIN

God is love! God is love! God is love! God is love!
Come, let us all u - nite to sing That God is love.

GOSPEL SONGS

COME, WE THAT LOVE THE LORD 529

WE'RE MARCHING TO ZION S.M. with Refrain

Isaac Wattst, 1707
Refrain added by Robert Lowry

Robert Lowry, 1867

1 Come, we that love the Lord, And let our joys be known; Join
2 Let those re - fuse to sing Who nev - er knew our God; But
3 The hill of Zi - on yields A thou - sand sa - cred sweets, Be -
4 Then let our songs a - bound, And ev - ery tear be dry; We're

in a song with sweet ac - cord, Join in a song with sweet ac - cord,
chil - dren of the heav'n - ly King, But chil - dren of the heav'n - ly King
fore we reach the heav'n - ly fields, Be - fore we reach the heav'n - ly fields,
march-ing through Im - man - uel's ground, We're march-ing through Im - man - uel's ground,

And thus sur - round the throne, And thus sur-round the throne.
May speak their joys a - broad, May speak their joys a - broad,
Or walk the gold - en streets, Or walk the gold - en streets.
To fair - er worlds on high, To fair - er worlds on high.

1 And thus sur-round the throne, And thus sur-round the throne.

REFRAIN

We're march - ing to Zi - on, Beau - ti - ful, beau - ti - ful Zi - on; We're
We're march-ing on to Zi - on,

march - ing up-ward to Zi - on, The beau - ti - ful cit - y of God.
Zi - on, Zi - on,

GOSPEL SONGS

530 PRAISE HIM! PRAISE HIM!

ALLEN Irregular with Refrain

Fanny Crosby, 1869, and Others

Chester G. Allen, 186

1 Praise Him! praise Him! Je-sus, our bless-ed Re-deem-er! Sing, O earth, His
2 Praise Him! praise Him! Je-sus, our bless-ed Re-deem-er! For our sins He
3 Praise Him! praise Him! Je-sus, our bless-ed Re-deem-er! Heav'n-ly por-tals,

won-der-ful love pro-claim! Hail Him! hail Him! high-est arch-an-gels in glo-ry;
suf-fered, and bled, and died; He our Rock, our hope of e-ter-nal sal-va-tion,
loud with ho-san-nas ring! Je-sus, Sav-ior, reign-eth for-ev-er and ev-er;

REFRAIN: Praise Him! praise Him! tell of His ex-cel-lent great-ness.

Fine

Strength and hon-or give to His ho-ly name! Like a shep-herd, Je-sus will
Hail Him! hail Him! Je-sus the cru-ci-fied. Sound His prais-es! Je-sus who
Crown Him! crown Him! Proph-et, and Priest, and King! Christ is com-ing, o-ver the

Praise Him! praise Him! ev-er in joy-ful song.

D.S.

guard His chil-dren, In His arms He car-ries them all day long:
bore our sor-rows, Love un-bound-ed, won-der-ful, deep and strong:
world vic-to-rious; Power and glo-ry un-to the Lord be-long:

GOSPEL SONGS

O MY SOUL, BLESS THOU JEHOVAH 531

CLOSE TO THEE 8.7.8.7. with Refrain

Based on Psalm 103
United Presbyterian Book of Psalms, 1871

Silas Jonas Vail, 1874

1 O my soul, bless thou Je - ho - vah, All with - in me bless His name;
2 Who for - gives all thy trans-gres - sions, Thy dis - eas - es all who heals;
3 Who with ten - der mer - cies crowns thee, Who with good things fills thy mouth,
4 In His right - eous-ness, Je - ho - vah Will de - liv - er those dis-tressed;
5 For as high as is the heav - en, Far a - bove the earth be - low,

Bless Je - ho - vah, and for - get not All His mer - cies to pro - claim.
Who re - deems thee from de - struc - tion, Who with thee so kind - ly deals;
So that e - ven like the ea - gle Thou hast been re - stored to youth.
He will ex - e - cute just judg - ment In the cause of all op-pressed.
Ev - er great to them that fear Him Is the mer - cy He will show.

REFRAIN

Bless Je - ho - vah, all His crea - tures Ev - er un - der His con - trol,

All through-out His vast do - min - ion; Bless Je - ho - vah, O my soul.

GOSPEL SONGS

532 TO GOD BE THE GLORY

TO GOD BE THE GLORY 11.11.11.11. with Refrain

Fanny Crosby, 1875

William Howard Doane, 1875

1 To God be the glo - ry, great things He hath done, So loved He the
2 O per - fect re - demp - tion, the pur-chase of blood, To ev - ery be -
3 Great things He hath taught us, great things He hath done, And great our re -

world that He gave us His Son, Who yield - ed His life an a -
liev - er the prom - ise of God; The vil - est of - fend - er who
joic - ing through Je - sus the Son; But pur - er, and high - er, and

tone-ment for sin, And o-pened the Life-gate that all may go in.
tru - ly be - lieves, That mo-ment from Je - sus a par - don re - ceives.
great - er will be Our won-der, our trans-port, when Je - sus we see.

REFRAIN

Praise the Lord, praise the Lord, Let the earth hear His voice! Praise the

Lord, praise the Lord, Let the peo - ple re - joice! O come to the Fa - ther, through

GOSPEL SONGS

Je - sus the Son, And give Him the glo - ry, great things He hath done.

GOD OF OUR STRENGTH 533

GOD OF OUR STRENGTH L.M. with Refrain

Fanny Crosby, 1882   William Howard Doane, 1883

1 God of our strength, en-throned a-bove, The source of life, the fount of love;
2 To Thee we lift our joy - ful eyes, To Thee on wings of faith we rise,
3 God of our strength, from day to day Di - rect our thoughts and guide our way;
4 God of our strength, on Thee we call; God of our hope, our light, our all,

O let de - vo - tion's sa - cred flame Our souls a - wake to praise Thy name.
Come Thou, and let Thy courts on earth Ring out Thy praise in days of mirth.
O may our hearts u - nit - ed be In sweet com-mun - ion, Lord, with Thee.
Thy name we praise, Thy love a - dore, Our rock, our shield, for - ev - er - more.

REFRAIN

God of our strength, we wait on Thee, Our sure de - fense for - ev - er be.

GOSPEL SONGS

534 GREAT IS THY FAITHFULNESS

FAITHFULNESS 11.10.11.10. with Refrain

Thomas O. Chisholm, 1923

William M. Runyan, 1923

1 Great is Thy faith-ful-ness, O God my Fa-ther, There is no
2 Sum-mer and win-ter, and spring-time and har-vest, Sun, moon, and
3 Par-don for sin and a peace that en-dur-eth, Thy own dear

shad-ow of turn-ing with Thee; Thou chang-est not, Thy com-
stars in their cours-es a-bove, Join with all na-ture in
pres-ence to cheer and to guide; Strength for to-day and bright

pas-sions, they fail not; As Thou hast been Thou for-ev-er wilt be.
man-i-fold wit-ness To Thy great faith-ful-ness, mer-cy, and love.
hope for to-mor-row, Bless-ings all mine, with ten thou-sand be-side!

REFRAIN

Great is Thy faith-ful-ness! Great is Thy faith-ful-ness! Morn-ing by morn-ing new mer-cies I see;

All I have need-ed Thy hand hath pro-vid-ed, Great is Thy faith-ful-ness! Lord un-to me!

GOSPEL SONGS

HOW GREAT THOU ART 535

O STORE GUD 11.10.11.10. with Refrain

Carl Boberg, 1859-1940
Tr. by Stuart K. Hine, b. 1899

Swedish Folk Melody
Arranged by Manna Music, Inc.

1 O Lord my God! When I in awe-some won-der Con-sid-er
2 When through the woods and for-est glades I wan-der And hear the
3 And when I think that God, his Son not spar-ing, Sent him to
4 When Christ shall come with shout of ac-cla-ma-tion And take me

all the worlds thy hands have made, I see the stars, I hear the roll-ing
birds sing sweet-ly in the trees; When I look down from loft-y moun-tain
die, I scarce can take it in; That on the cross, my bur-den glad-ly
home, what joy shall fill my heart! Then I shall bow in hum-ble ad-o-

REFRAIN

thun-der, thy pow'r through-out the un-i-verse dis-played,
gran-deur And hear the brook and feel the gen-tle breeze; Then sings my
bear-ing, He bled and died to take a-way my sin;
ra-tion And there pro-claim, my God, how great thou art!

soul, my Sav-ior God to thee; How great thou art, how great thou art! Then sings my

soul, my Sav-ior God to thee; How great thou art, How great thou art!

GOSPEL SONGS

536 HOLY, HOLY, HOLY IS THE LORD

HOLY IS THE LORD 9.10.9.9.10.9. with Refrain

Fanny Crosby, 1869

William Batchelder Bradbury, 1869

1 Ho - ly, ho - ly, ho - ly is the Lord! Sing, O ye peo - ple,
2 Praise Him, praise Him, shout a - loud for joy! Watch - man of Zi - on,
3 King e - ter - nal, bless - ed be His name! So may His chil - dren

glad - ly a - dore Him; Let the moun - tains trem - ble at His Word,
her - ald the sto - ry; Sin and death, His king - dom shall de - stroy,
glad - ly a - dore Him; When in heav'n we join the hap - py strain,

Let the hills be joy - ful be - fore Him; Might - y in wis - dom,
All the earth shall sing of His glo - ry; Praise Him, ye an - gels,
When we cast our bright crowns be - fore Him; There in His like - ness,

bound - less in mer - cy, Great is Je - ho - vah, King o - ver all.
ye who be - hold Him Robed in His splen - dor, match - less, di - vine.
joy - ful a - wak - ing, There we shall see Him, there we shall sing.

GOSPEL SONGS

Ho - ly, ho - ly, ho - ly is the Lord, Let the hills be joy - ful be - fore Him.

'TIS THE PROMISE OF GOD 537

HALLELUJAH, 'TIS DONE 12.12. with Refrain

Philip Paul Bliss, 1874

Philip Paul Bliss, 1874

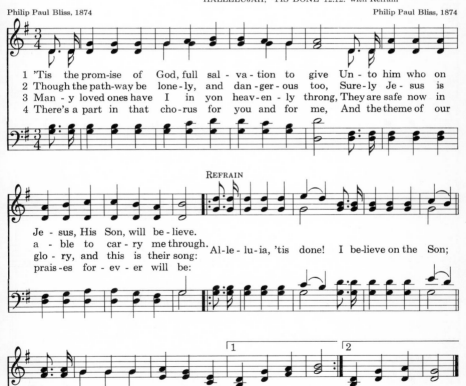

1 'Tis the prom-ise of God, full sal - va - tion to give Un - to him who on
2 Though the path-way be lone - ly, and dan - ger - ous too, Sure - ly Je - sus is
3 Man - y loved ones have I in yon heav - en - ly throng, They are safe now in
4 There's a part in that cho - rus for you and for me, And the theme of our

Je - sus, His Son, will be - lieve.
a - ble to car - ry me through.
glo - ry, and this is their song:
prais - es for - ev - er will be:

REFRAIN

Al - le - lu - ia, 'tis done! I be - lieve on the Son;

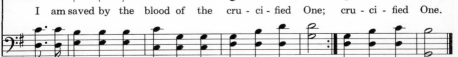

I am saved by the blood of the cru - ci - fied One; cru - ci - fied One.

GOSPEL SONGS

538 THE LOVE OF GOD

LOVE OF GOD   8.8.8.8.8.8.6.8.6. with Refrain

F. M. Lehman, c. 1917

F. M. Lehman, c. 1917
Arranged by Claudia Lehman Mays

1 The love of God   is great-er   far   Than tongue or pen   can ev-er tell;
2 When hoar-y time   shall pass a-way, And earth-ly thrones and king-doms fall;
3 Could we with ink   the o-cean   fill And were the skies   of parch-ment made;

It   goes be-yond   the high-est   star, And reach-es to   the low-est hell.
When men who here   re-fuse to   pray, On rocks and hills   and moun-tains call;
Were ev-ery stalk   on earth a   quill, And ev-ery man   a scribe by trade;

The guilt-y   pair, bowed down with care, God gave His   Son   to   win;
God's love, so   sure, shall still en-dure, All meas-ure-less   and strong;
To write the love   of God a-bove Would drain the o-cean dry;

His err-ing child   He rec-on-ciled, And par-doned from   his   sin.
Re-deem-ing grace   to Ad-am's race   The saints' and an-gels' song.
Nor could the scroll con-tain the   whole, Though stretched from sky to   sky.

REFRAIN

O love of God,   how rich and   pure! How meas-ure-less   and strong!

GOSPEL SONGS

It shall for - ev - er - more en - dure The saints' and an - gels' song.

MORE LOVE TO THEE, O CHRIST 539

MORE LOVE TO THEE 6.4.6.4.6.6.4.4.

Elizabeth Payson Prentiss, 1856

William Howard Doane, 1870

1 More love to Thee, O Christ, More love to Thee! Hear Thou the
2 Once earth - ly joy I craved, Sought peace and rest; Now Thee a -
3 Let sor - row do its work, Send grief and pain; Sweet are Thy
4 Then shall my lat - est breath Whis - per Thy praise; This be the

prayer I make, On bend - ed knee; This is my ear - nest plea,
lone I seek, Give what is best: This all my prayer shall be,
mes - sen-gers, Sweet their re - frain, When they can sing with me,
part - ing cry My heart shall raise, This still its prayer shall be,

More love, O Christ, to Thee, More love to Thee, More love to Thee!

GOSPEL SONGS

540 I STAND AMAZED IN THE PRESENCE

HOW MARVELOUS 8.7.8.7. with Refrain

Charles H. Gabriel, 1905
Source of St. 4 unknown

Charles H. Gabriel, 1905

1 I stand a-mazed in the pres-ence Of Je-sus the Naz-a-rene,
2 For me it was in the gar-den He prayed,"Not My will, but Thine;"
3 In pit-y an-gels be-held Him, And came from the world of light
4 He took my sins and my sor-rows, He made them His ver-y own;
5 When with the ran-somed in glo-ry His face I at last shall see,

And won-der how He could love me, A sin-ner con-demned, un-clean.
He had no tears for His own griefs, But sweat drops of blood for mine.
To com-fort Him in the sor-row He bore for my soul that night.
He bore the bur-den to Cal-vary, And suf-fered and died a-lone.
'Twill be my joy through the a-ges To sing of His love for me.

REFRAIN

How mar-vel-ous! How won-der-ful!

O how mar-vel-ous! O how won-der-ful! And my song shall ev-er be:

How mar-vel-ous! How won-der-ful!

O how mar-vel-ous! O how won-der-ful Is my Sav-ior's love for me!

GOSPEL SONGS

MARVELOUS GRACE 541

MARVELOUS GRACE 9.9.9.9. with Refrain

Julia H. Johnson, c. 1910

Daniel Brink Towner, 1910

1 Mar - vel-ous grace of our lov - ing Lord, Grace that ex - ceeds our
2 Sin and de-spair like the sea waves cold, Threat-en the soul with
3 Dark is the stain that we can-not hide, What can a - vail to
4 Mar - vel-ous, in - fi - nite, match-less grace, Free - ly be-stowed on

sin and our guilt, Yon - der on Cal - va - ry's mount out - poured,
in - fi - nite loss; Grace that is great - er, yes, grace un - told,
wash it a - way? Look! there is flow - ing a crim - son tide;
all who be - lieve; You that are long - ing to see His face,

REFRAIN

There where the blood of the Lamb was spilt. Grace, grace,
Points to the re - fuge, the might - y cross.
Whit - er than snow you may be to - day.
Will you this mo - ment His grace re - ceive? Mar - vel-ous grace,

God's grace, Grace that will par - don and cleanse with - in; Grace,
in - fi - nite grace, Mar - vel-ous

grace, God's grace, Grace that is great - er than all our sin.
grace, in - fi - nite grace,

GOSPEL SONGS

542 I'VE FOUND A FRIEND

FRIEND 8.7.8.7.D.

James G. Small, 1863

George C. Stebbins, 1878

1 I've found a Friend, O such a Friend! He loved me ere I knew Him;
2 I've found a Friend, O such a Friend! He bled, He died to save me;
3 I've found a Friend, O such a Friend! So kind, and true, and ten - der,

He drew me with the cords of love, And thus He bound me to Him.
And not a - lone the gift of life, But His own self He gave me.
So wise a coun - se - lor and guide, So might - y a de - fend - er!

And 'round my heart still close - ly twine Those ties which naught can sev - er,
Naught that I have my own I call, I hold it for the giv - er;
From Him who loves me now so well, What power my soul can sev - er?

For I am His, and He is mine, For - ev - er and for - ev - er.
My heart, my strength, my life, my all Are His, and His for - ev - er.
Shall life or death, shall earth or hell? No! I am His for - ev - er.

GOSPEL SONGS

HE LEADETH ME, O BLESSED THOUGHT 543

HE LEADETH ME L.M. with Refrain

Joseph H. Gilmore†, 1862

William Batchelder Bradbury, 1864

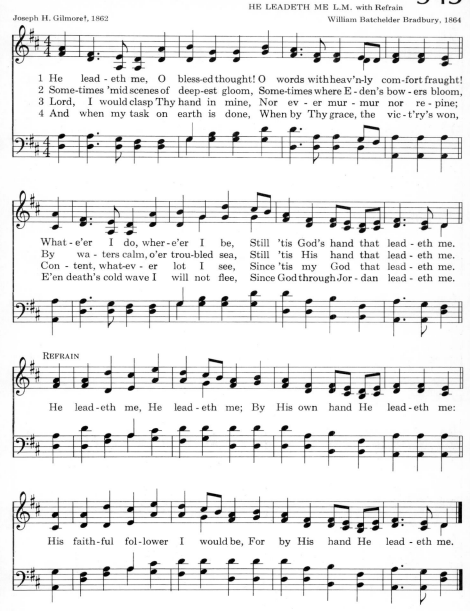

1 He lead-eth me, O bless-ed thought! O words with heav'n-ly com-fort fraught!
2 Some-times 'mid scenes of deep-est gloom, Some-times where E - den's bow - ers bloom,
3 Lord, I would clasp Thy hand in mine, Nor ev - er mur - mur nor re - pine;
4 And when my task on earth is done, When by Thy grace, the vic - t'ry's won,

What - e'er I do, wher - e'er I be, Still 'tis God's hand that lead - eth me.
By wa - ters calm, o'er trou-bled sea, Still 'tis His hand that lead - eth me.
Con - tent, what-ev - er lot I see, Since 'tis my God that lead - eth me.
E'en death's cold wave I will not flee, Since God through Jor - dan lead - eth me.

REFRAIN

He lead-eth me, He lead-eth me; By His own hand He lead-eth me:

His faith-ful fol-lower I would be, For by His hand He lead - eth me.

544 BLESSED ASSURANCE

BLESSED ASSURANCE 9.10.9.9. with Refrain

Fanny Crosby, 1873

Mrs. Joseph F. Knapp, 1873

1 Bless - ed as - sur - ance, Je - sus is mine! O what a fore - taste of
2 Per - fect sub - mis - sion, per - fect de - light, Vi - sions of rap - ture
3 Per - fect sub - mis - sion, all is at rest, I in my Sav - ior am

glo - ry di - vine! Heir of sal - va - tion, pur - chased of God,
burst on my sight; An - gels de - scend - ing bring from a - bove
hap - py and blest; Watch - ing and wait - ing, look - ing a - bove,

REFRAIN

Born of His Spir - it, washed in His blood; This is my sto - ry,
Ech - oes of mer - cy, whis - pers of love.
Filled with His good - ness, lost in His love.

this is my song, Prais - ing my Sav - ior all the day long; This is my

sto - ry, this is my song, Prais - ing my Sav - ior all the day long.

GOSPEL SONGS

BLESSED SAVIOR, WE ADORE THEE 545

GLORIOUS NAME 8.7.8.7. with Refrain

Benjamin Baylus McKinney, 1942

Benjamin Baylus McKinney, 1942

1 Bless - ed Sav - ior, we a - dore Thee, We Thy love and grace pro-claim;
2 Great Re - deem - er, Lord and Mas - ter, Light of all e - ter - nal days;
3 From the throne of heav - en's glo - ry To the cross of sin and shame,
4 Come, O come, im - mor - tal Sav - ior, Come and take Thy roy - al throne;

Thou art might - y, Thou art ho - ly, Glo - rious is Thy match - less name!
Let the saints of ev - ery na - tion Sing Thy just and end - less praise!
Thou didst come to die a ran - som, Guilt - y sin - ners to re - claim!
Come, and reign, and reign for - ev - er. Be the king - dom all Thine own!

REFRAIN

Glo - - - ri - ous, Glo - - - ri - ous,

Glo - rious is Thy name, O Lord! Glo - rious is Thy name, O Lord!

Glo - rious is Thy name, O Lord! Glo - - - ri - ous,

Glo - rious is Thy name, O Lord!

Glo - - - ri - ous, Glo - rious is Thy name, O Lord!

Glo - rious is Thy name, O Lord!

GOSPEL SONGS

546 A WONDERFUL SAVIOR IS JESUS

KIRKPATRICK 11.8.11.8. Refrain

Fanny Crosby, 1890

William J. Kirkpatrick, 1890

1 A won-der-ful Sav-ior is Je-sus my Lord, A won-der-ful
2 A won-der-ful Sav-ior is Je-sus my Lord, He tak-eth my
3 With num-ber-less bless-ings each mo-ment He crowns, And filled with His
4 When clothed in His bright-ness, trans-port-ed I rise To meet Him in

Sav-ior to me; He hid-eth my soul in the cleft of the rock, Where
bur-den a-way; He hold-eth me up, and I shall not be moved, He
full-ness di-vine, I sing in my rap-ture, O glo-ry to God For
clouds of the sky, His per-fect sal-va-tion, His won-der-ful love I'll

REFRAIN

riv-ers of plea-sure I see.
giv-eth me strength as my day.   He hid-eth my soul in the cleft of the rock
such a Re-deem-er as mine!
shout with the mil-lions on high.

That shad-ows a dry, thirst-y land; He hid-eth my life in the depths of His love,

And cov-ers me there with His hand, And cov-ers me there with His hand.

GOSPEL SONGS

IN LOVING KINDNESS JESUS CAME 547

HE LIFTED ME 8.8.8.6. with Refrain

Charles H. Gabriel, 1905

Charles H. Gabriel, 1905

1 In lov-ing kind-ness Je-sus came My soul in mer-cy to re-claim,
2 He called me long be-fore I heard, Be-fore my sin-ful heart was stirred,
3 His brow was pierced with man-y a thorn, His hands by cru-el nails were torn,
4 Now on a high-er plane I dwell, And with my soul I know 'tis well;

And from the depths of sin and shame Through grace He lift-ed me.
But when I took Him at His word, For-giv'n, He lift-ed me.
When from my guilt and grief, for-lorn, In love He lift-ed me.
Yet how or why I can-not tell He should have lift-ed me.

He lift-ed me.

Refrain

From sink-ing sand He lift-ed me, With ten-der hand He lift-ed me,

From shades of night to plains of light, O praise His name. He lift-ed me!

GOSPEL SONGS

548 COME WITH THY SINS

COME TO THE FOUNTAIN 8.7.8.7. with Refrain

Fanny Crosby, 1883

George C. Stebbins, 1883

1 Come with thy sins to the Foun - tain, Come with thy bur - den of grief;
2 Come as thou art to the Foun - tain, Je - sus is wait-ing for thee;
3 These are the words of the Sav - ior; They who re-pent and be - lieve,
4 Come and be healed at the Foun - tain, List to the peace-speak-ing voice;

Bur - y them deep in its wa - ters, There thou wilt find a re - lief.
What though thy sins be like crim - son, White as the snow they shall be.
They who are will - ing to trust Him, Life at His hand shall re-ceive.
O - ver a sin - ner re-turn - ing Now let the an - gels re-joice.

REFRAIN

Haste thee a - way, why wilt thou stay? Risk not thy soul on a mo-ment's de-lay;

Je - sus is wait - ing to save thee, Mer - cy is plead-ing to - day.

GOSPEL SONGS

I HEAR THY WELCOME VOICE 549

WELCOME VOICE S.M. with Refrain

Lewis Hartsough, 1872

Lewis Hartsough, 1872

1 I hear Thy wel - come voice, That calls me, Lord, to Thee,
2 Though com - ing weak and vile, Thou dost my strength as - sure;
3 'Tis Je - sus calls me on To per - fect faith and love,

For cleans - ing in Thy pre-cious blood That flowed on Cal - va - ry.
Thou dost my vile-ness ful - ly cleanse, Till spot - less all and pure.
To per - fect hope, and peace, and trust, For earth and heav'n a - bove.

REFRAIN

I am com - ing, Lord! Com - ing now to Thee! Wash me,

cleanse me in the blood That flowed on Cal - va - ry.

GOSPEL SONGS

550 SINNERS JESUS WILL RECEIVE

NEUMEISTER 7.7.7.7. with Refrain

Erdmann Neumeister, 1718
Jesus nimmt die Sünder an!
Tr. Emma F. Bevan, 1858
Arranged by James McGranahan

James McGranahan, 1883

1 Sin - ners Je - sus will re - ceive: Sound this word of grace to all
2 Come, and He will give you rest; Trust Him, for His word is plain;
3 Now my heart con-demns me not, Pure be - fore the law I stand;
4 Christ re - ceiv - eth sin - ful men, E - ven me with all my sin;

Who the heav'n - ly path - way leave, All who lin - ger, all who fall.
He will take the sin - ful - est; Christ re - ceiv - eth sin - ful men.
He who cleansed me from all spot. Sat - is - fied His last de - mand.
Purged from ev - ery spot and stain, Heav'n with Him I en - ter in.

REFRAIN

Sing it o'er and o'er a - gain: Christ re -
Sing it o'er a - gain, Sing it o'er a - gain: Christ re -

ceiv - eth sin - ful men; Make the mes - sage
ceiv-eth sin - ful men, Christ re-ceiv-eth sin-ful men; Make the mes-sage plain,

clear and plain: Christ re - ceiv - eth sin - ful men.

Make the mes-sage plain:

GOSPEL SONGS

I WILL SING THE WONDROUS STORY 551

WONDROUS STORY 8.7.8.7. with Refrain

Francis H. Rowley, 1886
Altered by Ira D. Sankey, 1887

Peter P. Bilhorn, 1886

1 I will sing the won-drous sto - ry Of the Christ who died for me,
2 I was lost, but Je - sus found me, Found the sheep that went a - stray,
3 I was bruised, but Je - sus healed me; Faint was I from man-y a fall;
4 Days of dark - ness still come o'er me, Sor - row's paths I of - ten tread,
5 He will keep me till the riv - er Rolls its wa - ters at my feet;

How He left His home in glo - ry For the cross of Cal - va - ry.
Threw His lov - ing arms a - round me, Drew me back in - to His way.
Sight was gone, and fears pos-sessed me, But He freed me from them all.
But the Sav - ior still is with me; By His hand I'm safe - ly led.
Then He'll bear me safe - ly o - ver, Where the loved ones I shall meet.

REFRAIN

Yes, I'll sing the won-drous sto - ry Of the
Yes, I'll sing the won-drous sto - ry

Christ who died for me, Sing it with the saints in
Of the Christ who died for me, Sing it with

glo - ry, Gath-ered by the crys-tal sea.
the saints in glo - ry, Gath-ered by the crys-tal sea.

GOSPEL SONGS

552 THERE WERE NINETY AND NINE

NINETY AND NINE Irregular

Elizabeth C. Clephane, 1868

Ira D. Sankey, 1874

1 There were nine - ty and nine that safe - ly lay In the
2 "Lord, Thou hast here Thy nine - ty and nine; Are
3 But none of the ran - somed ev - er knew How
4 "Lord, whence are those blood - drops all the way That
5 But all through the moun - tains, thun - der - riv'n, And

shel - ter of the fold, But one was out on the
they not e - nough for Thee?" But the Shep-herd made an - swer:
deep were the wa - ters crossed; Nor how dark was the night that the
mark out the moun-tain's track?" "They were shed for one who had
up from the rock - y steep, There a - rose a glad cry to the

hills a - way, Far off from the gates of gold, A -
"This of Mine Has wan - dered a - way from Me; And al-
Lord passed through Ere He found His sheep that was lost.
gone a - stray Ere the Shep - herd could bring him back." "Lord,
gate of heav'n, "Re - joice! I have found My sheep!" And the

way on the moun - tains wild and bare, A - way from the ten - der
though the road be rough and steep I go to the des - ert to
Out in the des - ert He heard its cry, Sick and so help-less and
whence are Thy hands so rent and torn?" "They are pierced to - night by
an - gels ech-oed a - round the throne, "Re - joice, for the Lord brings

GOSPEL SONGS

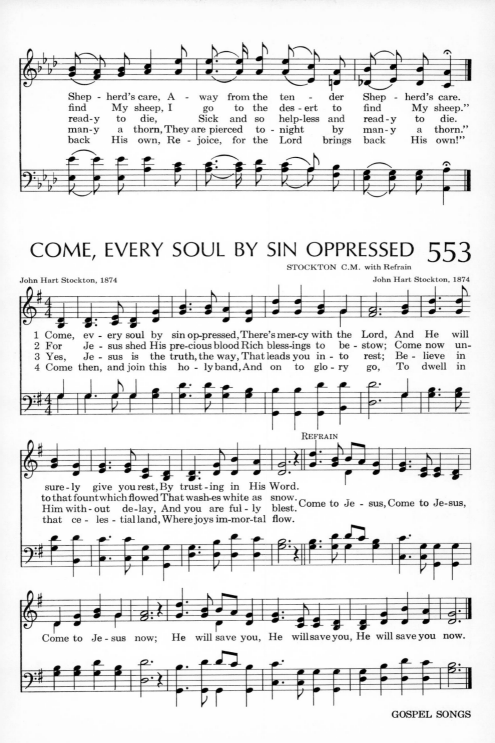

Shep - herd's care, A - way from the ten - der Shep - herd's care.
find My sheep, I go to the des - ert to find My sheep."
read-y to die, Sick and so help-less and read-y to die.
man-y a thorn, They are pierced to-night by man-y a thorn."
back His own, Re - joice, for the Lord brings back His own!"

COME, EVERY SOUL BY SIN OPPRESSED 553

STOCKTON C.M. with Refrain

John Hart Stockton, 1874   John Hart Stockton, 1874

1 Come, ev - ery soul by sin op-pressed, There's mer-cy with the Lord, And He will
2 For Je - sus shed His pre-cious blood Rich bless-ings to be - stow; Come now un-
3 Yes, Je - sus is the truth, the way, That leads you in - to rest; Be - lieve in
4 Come then, and join this ho - ly band, And on to glo - ry go, To dwell in

REFRAIN

sure - ly give you rest, By trust-ing in His Word.
to that fount which flowed That wash-es white as snow.
Him with-out de-lay, And you are ful - ly blest. Come to Je - sus, Come to Je-sus,
that ce - les - tial land, Where joys im-mor-tal flow.

Come to Je - sus now; He will save you, He will save you, He will save you now.

GOSPEL SONGS

554 I WILL SING OF MY REDEEMER

MY REDEEMER 8.7.8.7. with Refrain

Philip Paul Bliss, 1876

James McGranahan, 1877

1 I will sing of my Re-deem-er And His won-drous love to me;
2 I will tell the won-drous sto-ry, How my lost es-tate to save,
3 I will praise my dear Re-deem-er, His tri-um-phant power I'll tell,
4 I will sing of my Re-deem-er, And His heav'n-ly love to me;

On the cru-el cross He suf-fered From the curse to set me free.
In His bound-less love and mer-cy, He the ran-som free-ly gave.
How the vic-to-ry He giv-eth O-ver sin and death and hell.
He from death to life hath brought me, Son of God, with Him to be.

REFRAIN

Sing, O sing of my Re-deem-er, With His

Sing, O sing of my Re-deem-er, Sing, O sing of my Re-deem-er, With His

blood He pur-chased me; On the cross He sealed my

blood He purchased me, With His blood He purchased me; On the cross He sealed my pardon, On the

par-don, Paid the debt and made me free.

cross He sealed my par-don, Paid the debt and made me free, and made me free.

GOSPEL SONGS

WOULD YOU BE FREE 555

THERE IS POWER IN THE BLOOD 10.9.10.8. with Refrain

Lewis E. Jones, c. 1899

Lewis E. Jones, 1899

1 Would you be free from your bur-den of sin? There's power in the blood,
2 Would you be free from your pas-sion and pride? There's power in the blood,
3 Would you be whit-er, much whit-er than snow? There's power in the blood,
4 Would you do ser-vice for Je-sus your King? There's power in the blood,

power in the blood; Would you o'er e-vil a vic-to-ry win? There's
power in the blood; Come for a cleans-ing to Cal-va-ry's tide: There's
power in the blood; Sin-stains are lost in its life-giv-ing flow; There's
power in the blood; Would you live dai-ly His prais-es to sing? There's

REFRAIN

won-der-ful power in the blood. There is power, power, Won-der-work-ing power
there is

In the blood of the Lamb; There is power, power,
In the blood of the Lamb; there is

Won-der-work-ing power In the pre-cious blood of the Lamb.

GOSPEL SONGS

556 O HAVE YOU NOT HEARD

THE BEAUTIFUL RIVER 11.7.11.7. with Refrain

R. Torry, Jr.†, c. 1862

Asa Hull, c. 1862

1 O have you not heard of that beau-ti-ful stream That flows through our Fa-ther's
2 Its foun-tains are deep and its wa-ters are pure; And sweet to the wea-ry
3 This beau-ti-ful stream is the riv-er of life! It flows for all na-tions
4 O will you not drink of this beau-ti-ful stream, And dwell on its peace-ful

land? Its wa-ters gleam bright in the heav-en-ly light, And rip-ple o'er gold-en
soul; It flows from the throne of Je-ho-vah a-lone! O come where its bright waves
free! A balm for each wound in its wa-ter is found; O sin-ner, it flows for
shore? The Spir-it says, Come, all ye wea-ry ones, home, And wan-der in sin no

REFRAIN

sand.
roll.
thee! O seek that beau-ti-ful stream, O seek that beau-ti-ful stream; Its
more.

wa-ters, so free, are flow-ing for thee, O seek that beau-ti-ful stream.

GOSPEL SONGS

1 Ich weiss einen Strom, dessen herrliche Flut
　 fliesst wunderbar stille durchs Land,
　doch strahlet und glänzt er wie feurige Glut,
　 wem ist dieses Wässer bekannt?

2 Wohin dieser Strom sich nur immer ergiesst,
　 da jubelt und jauchzet das Herz,
　das nunmehr den köstlichsten Segen geniesst,
　 erlöset von Sorgen und Schmerz.

3 Der Strom ist gar tief und sein Wasser ist klar,
　 es schmecket so lieblich und fein;
　es heilet die Kranken und stärkt wunderbar,
　 ja machet die Unreinsten rein.

4 Wen dürstet, der komme und trinke sich satt,
　 so rufet der Geist und die Braut,
　nur wer in dem Strome gewaschen sich hat,
　 das Angesicht Gottes einst schaut.

REFRAIN: 　O Seele, ich bitte dich: Komm!
　　　　　Und such diesen herrlichen Strom!
　　　　　Sein Wasser fliesst frei und mächtiglich,
　　　　　o glaub's, es fliesset für dich!

THY LIFE WAS GIVEN FOR ME 557

SACRIFICE 6.6.6.6.6.6.

Frances Ridley Havergal, 1871

Philip Paul Bliss, 1874

1 Thy life was given for me; Thy blood, O Lord, was shed.
2 Long years were spent for me In wea - ri - ness and woe,
3 And Thou hast brought to me, Down from Thy home a - bove,
4 O let my life be given, My years for Thee be spent,

That I might ran - somed be, And quick - ened from the dead:
That through e - ter - ni - ty Thy glo - ry I might know:
Sal - va - tion full and free, Thy par - don and Thy love:
World fet - ters all be riven, And joy with suf - fering blent!

Thy life, Thy life was given for me; What have I given for Thee?
Long years, long years were spent for me; Have I spent one for Thee?
Great gifts, great gifts Thou brought-est me; What have I brought to Thee?
Thou gav'st, Thou gav'st Thy - self for me; I give my - self to Thee.

GOSPEL SONGS

558 MY HOPE IS BUILT ON NOTHING LESS

SOLID ROCK L.M. with Refrain

Edward Mote, c. 1834

William Batchelder Bradbury, 1863

1 My hope is built on noth-ing less Than Je - sus' blood and
2 When dark-ness seems to veil His face, I rest on His un -
3 His oath, His cov - e - nant, and blood, Sup - port me in the
4 When He shall come with trum-pet sound, O may I then in

right-eous-ness; I dare not trust the sweet-est frame, But whol - ly
chang-ing grace; In ev - er-y high and storm - y gale, My an - chor
whelm-ing flood; When all a - round my soul gives way, He then is
Him be found; Clad in His right-eous - ness a - lone, Fault-less to

REFRAIN

lean on Je - sus' name.
holds with - in the vail. On Christ, the sol - id rock, I stand; All
all my hope and stay.
stand be - fore the throne.

oth - er ground is sink-ing sand, All oth - er ground is sink-ing sand.

GOSPEL SONGS

WONDERFUL SAVIOR, REDEEMER 559

WONDERFUL SAVIOR 8.5.8.5. with Refrain

Wellington K. Jacobs, 1902

Wellington K. Jacobs, 1902

1 Won - der - ful Sav - ior, Re - deem - er, Thou in ten - d'rest love
2 Thou hast in great - est com - pas - sion Died our souls to save:
3 O - pen my heart e'er to hear Thee, Quick to hear Thy voice;

Watch - est o'er ev - ery be - liev - er, From Thy throne a - bove.
Pur - chased for us our re - demp - tion, Hope be - yond the grave.
Fill Thou my soul with Thy prais - es, Let my heart re - joice.

REFRAIN

Won - der - ful Sav - ior! Mer - ci - ful Sav - ior!
Je - sus, won - der - ful Sav - ior! Je - sus, mer - ci - ful Sav - ior!

My hope and Re - deem - er, Who shed His blood for me. (for me.)

GOSPEL SONGS

560 JESUS, KEEP ME NEAR THE CROSS

NEAR THE CROSS 7.6.7.6. with Refrain

Fanny Crosby, 1869

William Howard Doane, 1869

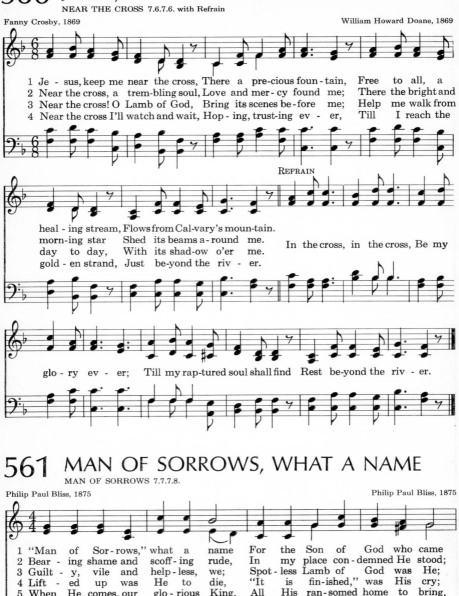

1 Je - sus, keep me near the cross, There a pre-cious foun-tain, Free to all, a
2 Near the cross, a trem-bling soul, Love and mer-cy found me; There the bright and
3 Near the cross! O Lamb of God, Bring its scenes be-fore me; Help me walk from
4 Near the cross I'll watch and wait, Hop-ing, trust-ing ev - er, Till I reach the

REFRAIN

heal - ing stream, Flows from Cal-vary's moun-tain.
morn-ing star Shed its beams a-round me.
day to day, With its shad-ow o'er me.
gold-en strand, Just be-yond the riv - er.

In the cross, in the cross, Be my

glo - ry ev - er; Till my rap-tured soul shall find Rest be-yond the riv - er.

561 MAN OF SORROWS, WHAT A NAME

MAN OF SORROWS 7.7.7.8.

Philip Paul Bliss, 1875

Philip Paul Bliss, 1875

1 "Man of Sor-rows," what a name For the Son of God who came
2 Bear - ing shame and scoff-ing rude, In my place con-demned He stood;
3 Guilt - y, vile and help-less, we; Spot-less Lamb of God was He;
4 Lift - ed up was He to die, "It is fin-ished," was His cry;
5 When He comes, our glo-rious King, All His ran-somed home to bring,

GOSPEL SONGS

Ru - ined sin - ners to re - claim! Al - le - lu - ia! what a Sav - ior!
Sealed my par - don with His blood; Al - le - lu - ia! what a Sav - ior!
"Full a - tone-ment!" can it be? Al - le - lu - ia! what a Sav - ior!
Now in heav'n ex - alt - ed high; Al - le - lu - ia! what a Sav - ior!
Then a new this song we'll sing: Al - le - lu - ia! what a Sav - ior!

CHRIST HAS FOR SIN ATONEMENT MADE 562

BENTON HARBOR (HOFFMAN) 8.7.8.7. with Refrain

Elisha A. Hoffman, 1891   Elisha A. Hoffman, 1891

1 Christ has for sin a-tone-ment made, What a won-der-ful Sav - ior! We are re-
2 I   praise Him for the cleans-ing blood, What a won-der-ful Sav - ior! That rec - on-
3 He cleansed my heart from all its sin, What a won-der-ful Sav - ior! And now He
4 He gives me o - ver-com-ing power, What a won-der-ful Sav - ior! And tri-umph

Refrain

deemed! the price is paid! What a won-der-ful Sav - ior!
ciled my soul to God; What a won-der-ful Sav - ior!   What a won-der-ful Sav - ior
reigns and rules there-in; What a won-der-ful Sav - ior!
in   each try-ing hour; What a won-der-ful Sav - ior!

is Je - sus, my Je - sus! What a won-der-ful Sav - ior is Je - sus, my Lord!

GOSPEL SONGS

563 THOU DIDST LEAVE THY THRONE

ROOM FOR THEE Irregular

Emily E. S. Elliott‡, 1864

Ira David Sankey, 1876

1 Thou didst leave Thy throne, and Thy king - ly crown, When Thou
2 Heav'n's arch - es rang when the an - gels sang, Of Thy
3 Fox - es found their rest, and the birds had their nests, In the
4 Thou cam - est, O Lord, with Thy liv - ing word, That should
5 Heav'n's arch - es shall ring, and its choirs shall sing, At Thy

cam - est to earth for me; But in Beth - le-hem's home there was
birth and Thy roy - al de - cree; But in low - ly birth didst Thou
shade of the ce - dar tree; But Thy couch was the sod, O Thou
set Thy peo - ple free; But with mock - ing and scorn and with
com - ing to vic - to - ry, Thou wilt call me home, say - ing "Yet

found no room, For Thy ho - ly na - tiv - i - ty.
come to earth, And in great - est hu - mil - i - ty.
Son of God, In the des - erts of Gal - i - lee.
crown of thorn, Did they bear Thee to Cal - va - ry.
there is room," There is room at My side for thee.

REFRAIN

O come to my heart, Lord Je - sus! There is room in my heart for Thee.

O come to my heart, Lord Je - sus, come! There is room in my heart for Thee.

GOSPEL SONGS

IF YE THEN WITH CHRIST BE RISEN 564

IF YE THEN BE RISEN 8.5.8.5.8.7.8.7. with Refrain

Grant Colfax Tullar, 1926

I. H. Meredith, 1926

1 If ye then with Christ be ris-en, Seek those things a-bove; Let His glo-ry
2 If ye then with Christ be ris-en, And the vic-t'ry won, Let your thoughts on
3 If ye then with Christ be ris-en, Let thy soul re-joice; Let con-tin-ual

shine a-round thee, Show-ing forth His love. Once up-on the cross He suf-fered,
Him be cen-tered Till the race is run; Let no anx-ious thought per-plex thee,
praise be sound-ing, With glad heart and voice. He who died to be your Sav-ior

Gave His life a ran-som free, Yet the grave could not re-tain Him, And He
Or temp-ta-tion still dis-may, Think when-e'er the clouds sur-round thee, Soon shall
Rose a-gain to be your King; If ye then with Him be ris-en, Let your

REFRAIN

lives e-ter-nal-ly.
dawn a bright-er day.   If ye then be ris-en   With the King of
joy-ous prais-es ring.   ris-en

love, Look not to the things that per-ish, Seek those things a-bove.

GOSPEL SONGS

565 I KNOW THAT MY REDEEMER LIVETH

FILLMORE 9.8.9.8. with Refrain

Jessie Brown Pounds, 1893

James H. Fillmore, 1893

1 I know that my Re-deem-er liv - eth, And on the earth
2 I know His prom-ise nev-er fail - eth, The word He speaks,
3 I know my man-sion He pre - par - eth, That where He is

a - gain shall stand; I know e - ter - nal life He
it can-not die; Though cru - el death my flesh as -
there I may be; O won - drous thought, for me He

giv - eth, That grace and power are in His hand.
sail - eth, Yet I shall see Him by and by.
car - eth, And He at last will come for me.

REFRAIN

I know, I know that Je - sus liv - eth, And on the

earth a - gain shall stand; I know, I know that life He

GOSPEL SONGS

giv - eth, That grace and power are in His hand.

That grace and power

CHRIST WHO LEFT HIS HOME IN GLORY 566

CHRIST IS RISEN 8.7.8.7. with Refrain

Abram Bowman Kolb, 1896   Abram Bowman Kolb, 1896

1 Christ who left His home in glo - ry, And up - on the cross was slain,
2 While the world in peace was sleep-ing, Ear - ly on that East - er day,
3 Christ, our lov - ing Me - di - a - tor, Now with God for you and me

Now is ris'n! O tell the sto - ry That the Sav - ior lives a - gain.
Came the faith - ful wom - en, weep-ing, But the stone was rolled a - way.
In - ter-cedes, and our Cre - a - tor Hears and an - swers ev - ery plea.

REFRAIN

Hail Him! Hail Him! Tell the sto - ry;
Hail to the King, the might-y Re-deem-er! Hail Him who robbed the grave of its power!

Hail! all hail! Je - sus lives for - ev - er - more.
Tell ev - ery na - tion, all is well,

GOSPEL SONGS

567 LOW IN THE GRAVE HE LAY

CHRIST AROSE 11.10. with Refrain

Robert Lowry, 1874

Robert Lowry, 1874

1 Low in the grave He lay, Je - sus, my Sav - ior! Wait - ing the com - ing day,
2 Vain - ly they watch His bed, Je - sus, my Sav - ior! Vain - ly they seal the dead,
3 Death can-not keep his prey, Je - sus, my Sav - ior! He tore the bars a - way,

REFRAIN

Je - sus, my Lord! Up from the grave He a - rose, With a
He a - rose,

might - y tri-umph o'er His foes! He a - rose a vic - tor from the
He a - rose!

dark do - main, And He lives for - ev - er with His saints to reign; He a -

rose! He a - rose! Al - le - lu - ia! Christ a - rose!
He a-rose! He a-rose!

GOSPEL SONGS

AS LIVES THE FLOWER WITHIN THE SEED 568

CHRIST LIVETH IN ME C.M. with Refrain

Daniel Webster Whittle, c. 1891

James McGranahan, 1891

1 As lives the flower with-in the seed, As in the cone the tree,
2 Once far from God and dead in sin, No light my heart could see;
3 As rays of light from yon-der sun The flowers of earth set free,
4 With long-ing all my heart is filled, That like Him I may be,

So, praise the God of truth and grace, His Spir-it dwell-eth in me.
But in God's Word the light I found, Now Christ liv-eth in me.
So life and light and love came forth From Christ liv-ing in me.
As on the won-drous thought I dwell, That Christ liv-eth in me.

REFRAIN

Christ liv-eth in me, Christ liv-eth in me,
Christ liv-eth in me, Christ liv-eth in
me, O

O what a sal - va - tion this, That Christ liv-eth in me!

GOSPEL SONGS

569 HE IS COMING, THE MAN OF SORROWS

NEWCASTLE 9.6.9.6. with Refrain

Fanny Crosby, 1887

Ira David Sankey, 1887

1 He is com - ing, the Man of Sor - rows, Now ex - alt - ed on high;
2 He is com - ing, our lov - ing Sav - ior, Bless-ed Lamb that was slain;
3 He is com - ing, our Lord and Mas - ter, Our Re - deem - er and King;
4 He shall gath - er His cho-sen peo - ple, Who are called by His name;

He is com - ing with loud ho - san - nas, In the clouds of the sky.
In the glo - ry of God the Fa - ther, On the earth He shall reign.
We shall see Him in all His beau - ty, And His praise we shall sing.
And the ran-somed of ev - ery na - tion For His own He shall claim.

REFRAIN

Al - le - lu - ia! Al - le - lu - ia! He is com - ing a - gain;

And with joy we shall gath-er round Him, At His com - ing to reign.

GOSPEL SONGS

IT MAY BE AT MORN 570

CHRIST RETURNETH 12.12.12.7. with Refrain

H. L. Turner, 1878

James McGranahan, 1878

1 It may be at morn, when the day is a - wak - ing, When
2 It may be at mid - day, it may be at twi - light, It
3 While its hosts cry, "Ho - san - na," from heav - en de - scend - ing, With
4 O joy! O de - light! should we go with - out dy - ing, No

sun - light through dark - ness and shad - ow is break - ing, That Je - sus will
may be, per - chance, that the black - ness of mid - night Will burst in - to
glo - ri - fied saints and the an - gels at - tend - ing, With grace on His
sick - ness, no sad - ness, no dread and no cry - ing, Caught up through the

come in the full - ness of glo - ry, To re - ceive from the world "His own."
light in the blaze of His glo - ry, When Je - sus re - ceives "His own."
brow, like a ha - lo of glo - ry, Will Je - sus re - ceive "His own."
clouds with our Lord in - to glo - ry, When Je - sus re - ceives "His own."

REFRAIN

O Lord Je - sus, how long, How long ere we shout the glad song, Christ re -

turn - eth! Al - le - lu - ia! Al - le - lu - ia! A - men, Al - le - lu - ia! A - men.

GOSPEL SONGS

571 JUDGE ME, GOD OF MY SALVATION

AMARA 8.7.8.7. with Refrain

Based on Psalm 43
Psalter, 1912

William O. Perkins, d. 1902

1 Judge me, God of my sal - va - tion, Plead my cause, for Thee I trust;
2 On Thy strength a - lone re - ly - ing, Why am I cast off by Thee,
3 Light and truth, my way at - tend - ing, Send Thou forth to be my guide;
4 At Thy sa - cred al - tar bend - ing, God, my God, my bound-less joy,

Hear my ear - nest sup - pli - ca - tion, Save me from my foes un - just.
In my help - less sor - row sigh - ing, While the foe op - press - es me?
Till Thy ho - ly mount as-cend - ing, I with - in Thy house a - bide.
Harp and voice, in wor-ship blend-ing, For Thy praise will I em - ploy.

REFRAIN

O my soul, why art thou griev-ing? What dis - qui - ets and dis-mays?

Hope in God; His help re - ceiv - ing, I shall yet my Sav - ior praise.

GOSPEL SONGS

SAVIOR, LIKE A SHEPHERD LEAD US 572

BRADBURY 8.7.8.7.8.7.

D. Thrupp's *Hymns for the Young*. 1836

William Batchelder Bradbury, 1859

1 Sav - ior, like a shep-herd lead us, Much we need Thy ten-d'rest care;
2 We are Thine, do Thou be - friend us, Be the guard-ian of our way;
3 Thou hast prom-ised to re - ceive us, Poor and sin - ful though we be;
4 Ear - ly let us seek Thy fa - vor, Ear - ly let us do Thy will;

In Thy pleas-ant pas-tures feed us, For our use Thy folds pre - pare;
Keep Thy flock, from sin de - fend us, Seek us when we go a - stray:
Thou hast mer - cy to re - lieve us, Grace to cleanse, and power to free:
Bless - ed Lord and on - ly Sav - ior, With Thy love our bos-oms fill:

Bless - ed Je - sus! Bless-ed Je - sus! Thou hast bought us, Thine we are,
Bless - ed Je - sus! Bless-ed Je - sus! Hear, O hear us, when we pray,
Bless - ed Je - sus! Bless-ed Je - sus! We will ear - ly turn to Thee,
Bless - ed Je - sus! Bless-ed Je - sus! Thou hast loved us, love us still,

Bless-ed Je - sus! Bless-ed Je - sus! Thou hast bought us, Thine we are.
Bless-ed Je - sus! Bless-ed Je - sus! Hear, O hear us, when we pray.
Bless-ed Je - sus! Bless-ed Je - sus! We will ear - ly turn to Thee.
Bless-ed Je - sus! Bless-ed Je - sus! Thou hast loved us, love us still. A-men.

GOSPEL SONGS

573 ALL THE WAY MY SAVIOR LEADS ME

ALL THE WAY 8.7.8.7.D.

Fanny Crosby, 1875

Robert Lowry, 1875

1 All the way my Sav-ior leads me; What have I to ask be-side?
2 All the way my Sav-ior leads me; Cheers each wind-ing path I tread;
3 All the way my Sav-ior leads me; O the full-ness of His love!

Can I doubt His ten-der mer-cy, Who through life has been my guide?
Gives me grace for ev-ery tri-al; Feeds me with the liv-ing bread;
Per-fect rest to me is prom-ised In my Fa-ther's house a-bove;

Heav'n-ly peace, di-vin-est com-fort, Here by faith in Him to dwell!
Though my wea-ry steps may fal-ter, And my soul a-thirst may be,
When my spir-it, clothed im-mor-tal, Wings its flight to realms of day,

For I know, what-e'er be-fall me, Je-sus do-eth all things well;
Gush-ing from the rock be-fore me, Lo! a spring of joy I see;
This my song through end-less a-ges, Je-sus led me all the way;

For I know, what-e'er be-fall me, Je-sus do-eth all things well.
Gush-ing from the rock be-fore me, Lo! a spring of joy I see.
This my song through end-less a-ges, Je-sus led me all the way.

GOSPEL SONGS

BE NOT DISMAYED WHATE'ER BETIDE 574

GOD CARES C.M. with Refrain

Civilla D. Martin, 1904   Walter Stillman Martin, 1904

1 Be   not dis - mayed what-e'er   be - tide,   God will take care   of   you;
2 Through days of   toil when heart   doth fail,   God will take care   of   you;
3 All   you may   need He   will   pro - vide,   God will take care   of   you;
4 No   mat - ter what may be   the test,   God will take care   of   you;

Be - neath His wings of   love   a - bide,   God will take care   of   you.
When dan - gers fierce your path as - sail,   God will take care   of   you.
Noth - ing you   ask   will   be   de - nied,   God will take care   of   you.
Lean, wea - ry one, up - on   His breast, God will take care   of   you.

REFRAIN

God   will   take   care   of   you, Through ev - er - y   day,   O'er all   the way;

He   will   take   care   of   you,   God will take care   of   you.

GOSPEL SONGS

575 UNDER HIS WINGS I AM SAFELY ABIDING

UNDER HIS WINGS 11.10.11.10. with Refrain

William Orcutt Cushing, c. 1896

Ira David Sankey, 1896

1 Un - der His wings I am safe - ly a - bid - ing; Though the night
2 Un - der His wings, what a ref - uge in sor - row! How the heart
3 Un - der His wings, O what pre - cious en - joy - ment! There will I

deep - ens and tem - pests are wild, Still I can trust Him; I
yearn - ing - ly turns to His rest! Oft - en when earth has no
hide till life's tri - als are o'er; Shel - tered, pro - tect - ed, no

know He will keep me; He has re - deemed me, and I am His child.
balm for my heal - ing, There I find com - fort, and there I am blest.
e - vil can harm me; Rest - ing in Je - sus I'm safe ev - er - more.

REFRAIN

Un - der His wings, un - der His wings, Who from His love can sev - er?

Un - der His wings my soul shall a - bide, Safe - ly a - bide for - ev - er.

GOSPEL SONGS

WHEN PEACE, LIKE A RIVER 576

IT IS WELL 11.8.11.9. with Refrain

Horatio G. Spafford, 1873

Philip Paul Bliss, 1876

1 When peace, like a riv - er, at - tend - eth my way, When sor - rows like
2 Though Sa - tan should buf - fet, though tri - als should come, Let this blest as -
3 My sin! O the bliss of this glo - ri - ous thought, My sin! not in
4 And, Lord, haste the day when the faith shall be sight, The clouds be rolled

sea - bil - lows roll; What-ev - er my lot, Thou hast taught me to say,
sur - ance con - trol, That Christ hath re - gard - ed my help - less es - tate,
part, but the whole, Is nailed to His cross and I bear it no more,
back as a scroll, The trump shall re - sound and the Lord shall de - scend,

REFRAIN

It is well, it is well with my soul.
And hath shed His own blood for my soul.
Praise the Lord, praise the Lord, O my soul!
"E - ven so," it is well with my soul.

It is well with my

It is well

soul, It is well, it is well with my soul.

with my soul,

GOSPEL SONGS

577 WHEN WE WALK WITH THE LORD

TRUST AND OBEY 6.6.9.D. with Refrain

John H. Sammis, 1887

Daniel Brink Towner, 1887

1 When we walk with the Lord In the light of His Word, What a glo - ry He
2 Not a bur - den we bear, Not a sor - row we share, But our toil He doth
3 But we nev - er can prove The de-lights of His love, Un -til all on the
4 Then in fel - low- ship sweet We will sit at His feet, Or we'll walk by His

sheds on our way! While we do His good will, He a - bides with us still,
rich - ly re - pay; Not a grief nor a loss, Not a frown nor a cross,
al - tar we lay, For the fa - vor He shows, And the joy He be - stows,
side in the way; What He says we will do, Where He sends we will go,

REFRAIN

And with all who will trust and o - bey.
But is blest if we trust and o - bey.
Are for them who will trust and o - bey.
Nev-er fear, on - ly trust and o - bey.

Trust and o - bey, for there's no oth - er

way To be hap - py in Je - sus, but to trust and o - bey.

GOSPEL SONGS

I NEED THEE EVERY HOUR 578

NEED 6.4.6.4. with Refrain

Annie S. Hawks, 1872

Robert Lowry, 1872

1 I need Thee ev-ery hour, Most gra-cious Lord;
2 I need Thee ev-ery hour, Stay Thou near by;
3 I need Thee ev-ery hour, In joy or pain;
4 I need Thee ev-ery hour, Teach me Thy will;
5 I need Thee ev-ery hour, Most ho-ly One;

No ten - der voice like Thine Can peace af - ford.
Temp - ta - tions lose their power When Thou art nigh.
Come quick - ly and a - bide, Or life is vain.
And Thy rich prom - is - es In me ful - fill.
O make me Thine in - deed, Thou bless - ed Son.

REFRAIN

I need Thee, O I need Thee, Ev - ery hour I need Thee;

O bless me now, my Sav - ior, I come to Thee. A - men.

GOSPEL SONGS

579 NEARER, STILL NEARER

MORRIS 9.10.9.10.

Leila Naylor Morris, 1898   Leila Naylor Morris, 1898

1 Near - er, still near - er, close to Thy heart, Draw me, my
2 Near - er, still near - er, noth - ing I bring, Naught as an
3 Near - er, still near - er, Lord, to be Thine, Sin, with its
4 Near - er, still near - er, while life shall last, Till safe in

Sav - ior, so pre - cious Thou art; Fold me, O fold me
of - f'ring to Je - sus my King, On - ly my sin - ful,
fol - lies, I glad - ly re - sign, All of its plea - sures,
glo - ry my an - chor is cast, Through end - less a - ges,

close to Thy breast, Shel - ter me safe in that
now con - trite heart; Grant me the cleans - ing Thy
pomp and its pride; Give me but Je - sus, my
ev - er to be, Near - er, my Sav - ior, still

ha - ven of rest, Shel - ter me safe in that ha - ven of rest.
blood doth im - part, Grant me the cleans-ing Thy blood doth im - part.
Lord cru - ci - fied, Give me but Je - sus, my Lord cru - ci - fied.
near - er to Thee, Near - er, my Sav - ior, still near - er to Thee.

GOSPEL SONGS

HELP ME TO BE HOLY 580

TOWNER 11.11.11.11.

Adoniram J. Gordon, c. 1894

Daniel Brink Towner, 1894

1 Help me to be ho - ly, O Fa - ther of light;
2 Help me to be ho - ly, O Sav - ior di - vine;
3 Help me to be ho - ly, O Spir - it di - vine;

Guilt - bur - dened and low - ly, I bow in Thy sight;
Why con - quer so slow - ly This na - ture of mine?
Come, sanc - ti - fy whol - ly This tem - ple of Thine;

How shall a stained con - science Dare gaze on Thy face,
Stamp deep - ly Thy like - ness Where Sa - tan's hath been;
Now cast out each i - dol. Here set up Thy throne.

E'en though in Thy pres - ence Thou grant me a place?
Ex - pel with Thy bright - ness My dark - ness and sin!
Reign, reign with - out ri - val, Su - preme and a - lone! A - men.

GOSPEL SONGS

581 I AM THINE, O LORD

DRAW ME NEARER 10.7.10.7. with Refrain

Fanny Crosby, 1875

William Howard Doane, 1875

1 I am Thine, O Lord, I have heard Thy voice, And it
2 Con - se - crate me now to Thy ser - vice, Lord, By the
3 O the pure de - light of a sin - gle hour That be -
4 There are depths of love that I can - not know Till I

told Thy love to me; But I long to rise in the arms of faith,
power of grace di - vine; Let my soul look up with a stead-fast hope,
fore Thy throne I spend, When I kneel in prayer, and with Thee, my God,
cross the nar - row sea; There are heights of joy that I may not reach

And be clos - er drawn to Thee.
And my will be lost in Thine.
I com - mune as friend with friend!
Till I rest in peace with Thee.

REFRAIN

Draw me near - er, near - er, near - er,

near - er, bless - ed Lord, To the cross where Thou hast died; Draw me

near - er, near - er, near-er, bless-ed Lord, To Thy pre - cious bleed - ing side.

GOSPEL SONGS

I'M PRESSING ON THE UPWARD WAY 582

HIGHER GROUND L.M. with Refrain

Johnson Oatman, Jr., d. 1922

Charles H. Gabriel, 1892

1 I'm press-ing on the up-ward way, New heights I'm gain-ing ev-er-y day;
2 My heart has no de-sire to stay Where doubts a-rise and fears dis-may;
3 I want to live a-bove the world, Though Sa-tan's darts at me are hurled;
4 I want to scale the ut-most height, And catch a gleam of glo-ry bright;

Still pray-ing as I on-ward bound, "Lord, plant my feet on high-er ground."
Tho' some may dwell where these a-bound, My prayer, my aim is high-er ground.
For faith has caught the joy-ful sound, The song of saints on high-er ground.
But still I'll pray till heav'n I've found, "Lord, lead me on to high-er ground."

REFRAIN

Lord, lift me up and let me stand, By faith, on heav-en's ta-ble-land,

A high-er plane than I have found; Lord, plant my feet on high-er ground.

GOSPEL SONGS

583 LORD JESUS, I LONG TO BE PERFECTLY

WHITER THAN SNOW 11.11.11.11. with Refrain

James L. Nicholson†, 1872

William Gustavus Fischer, 1872

1 Lord Je - sus, I long to be per - fect - ly whole;
2 Lord Je - sus, come down from Thy throne in the skies,
3 Lord Je - sus, Thou se - est I pa - tient - ly wait;
4 The bless - ing by faith, I re - ceive from a - bove;

I want Thee for - ev - er, to live in my soul;
And help me to make a com - plete sac - ri - fice;
Come now, and with - in me a new heart cre - ate;
O glo - ry! My soul is made per - fect in love;

Break down ev - ery i - dol, cast out ev - ery foe;
I give up my - self and what - ev - er I know,
To those who have sought Thee, Thou nev - er saidst No,
My prayer has pre - vailed, and this mo - ment I know,

REFRAIN

1-3 Now wash me, and I shall be whit - er than snow.
4 The blood is ap - plied, I am whit - er than snow. Whit - er than snow, yes,

whit - er than snow; Now wash me, and I shall be whit - er than snow.

GOSPEL SONGS

O LIFE IN WHOM IS LIFE INDEED 584

BAPTISTE L.M. with Refrain

Jesse Brown Pounds, d. 1921

"From Baptiste," c. 1920

1 O Life in whom is life in - deed, Through whom our
2 O Light be - yond men's high - est thought, Be - yond all
3 O Good be - yond the dreams of men, Who mak - est

best de - sires are freed. Stir Thou that life in
wis - dom seers have wrought, Ne'er yet that light in
stained lives white a - gain, Thou Christ, be - stow Thy

us, we plead; We come to Thee, we come to Thee!
vain was sought; We come to Thee, we come to Thee!
pure - ness when We come to Thee, we come to Thee!

REFRAIN Come to Thee, Come to Thee, Come to Thee, We come to Thee.

We come to Thee, We come to Thee, We come to Thee, We come to Thee.

Come to Thee, Come to Thee, Come to Thee, We come to Thee.

GOSPEL SONGS

585 LORD, I AM FONDLY, EARNESTLY

OPEN THE WELLS 10.9.10.9. with Refrain

Elisha Albright Hoffman, c. 1902

Charles Edward Pollock, c. 1902

1 Lord, I am fond - ly, ear - nest - ly long - ing In - to Thy
2 Dead to the world would I be, O Fa - ther! Dead un - to
3 I would be Thine, and serve Thee for - ev - er, Filled with Thy

ho - ly like - ness to grow; Thirst - ing for more and deep - er com -
sin, a - live un - to Thee; Cru - ci - fy all the earth - ly with -
Spir - it, lost in Thy love; Come to my heart, Lord, come with a -

REFRAIN

mun - ion, Yearn - ing Thy love more ful - ly to know. O - pen the
in me, Emp - tied of sin and self may I be.
noint - ing, Show - ers of grace send down from a - bove. O - pen the

wells of grace and sal - va - tion, Pour the rich
O - pen the wells of grace and sal - va - tion,

streams deep in - to my heart; Cleanse and re - fine my
Pour the rich streams deep in - to my heart; Cleanse and re - fine my

GOSPEL SONGS

thought and af - fec - tion, Seal me and make me pure as Thou art.
thought and af - fec - tion, Seal me and make me pure as Thou art.

I KNOW NOT WHY GOD'S WONDROUS 586

EL NATHAN C.M. with Refrain

Daniel W. Whittle, 1883   James McGranahan, 1883

1 I know not why God's won-drous grace To me He hath made known,
2 I know not how this sav - ing faith To me He did im - part,
3 I know not how the Spir - it moves, Con-vinc - ing men of sin,
4 I know not when my Lord may come, At night or noon - day fair,

Nor why, un - wor - thy, Christ in love Re - deemed me for His own.
Nor how be - liev - ing in His Word Wrought peace with - in my heart.
Re - veal - ing Je - sus through the Word, Cre - at - ing faith in Him.
Nor if I'll walk the vale with Him, Or meet Him in the air.

REFRAIN

But I know whom I have be - liev - ed, and am per - suad - ed that He is

a - ble To keep that which I've com-mit-ted Un-to Him a - gainst that day.

GOSPEL SONGS

587 O WONDERFUL, WONDERFUL WORD

WONDERFUL WORD 11.8.11.8.11.8.12.8.

J. L. Sterling, c. 1886

Ira David Sankey, 1886

1 O won - der - ful, won - der - ful Word of the Lord! True
2 O won - der - ful, won - der - ful Word of the Lord! The
3 O won - der - ful, won - der - ful Word of the Lord! Our
4 O won - der - ful, won - der - ful Word of the Lord! The

wis - dom its pa - ges un - fold; And though we may read them a
lamp that our Fa - ther a - bove So kind - ly has light - ed to
on - ly sal - va - tion is there; It car - ries con - vic - tion down
hope of our friends in the past; Its truth, where so firm - ly they

thou - sand times o'er, They nev - er, no nev - er, grow old!
teach us the way That leads to the arms of His love!
deep in the heart, And shows us our - selves as we are.
an - chored their trust, Through a - ges e - ter - nal shall last.

Each line hath a trea - sure, each prom - ise a pearl, That
Its warn - ings, its coun - sels, are faith - ful and just; Its
It tells of a Sav - ior, and points to the cross, Where
O won - der - ful, won - der - ful Word of the Lord! Un -

all if they will may se - cure; And we know that when time and the
judg - ments are per - fect and pure; And we know that when time and the
par - don we now may se - cure, For we know that when time and the
chang - ing, a - bid - ing and sure; For we know that when time and the

GOSPEL SONGS

world pass a - way, God's Word shall for - ev - er en - dure.

IN THE LAND OF STRANGERS 588

WELCOME, WANDERER, WELCOME 6.5.6.4. with Refrain

Horatius Bonar, 1874
Refrain added by Ira David Sankey

Ira David Sankey, 1884

1 In the land of stran - gers Whith - er thou art gone,
2 From the land of hun - ger, Faint - ing, fam - ished, lone,
3 See the door still o - pen: Thou art still My own;
4 See the well - spread ta - ble, Un - for - got - ten one!
5 Thou art friend - less, hope - less, Hope - less and un - done;

Hear a far voice call - ing, My son, My son!
Come to love and glad - ness, My son, My son!
Eyes of love are on thee, My son, My son!
Here is rest and plen - ty, My son, My son!
Mine is love un - chang - ing, My son, My son!

REFRAIN

Wel - come, wan - d'rer, wel - come, Wel - come back to home;

Thou hast wan - dered far a - way: Come home, come home.

GOSPEL SONGS

589 ENCAMPED ALONG THE HILLS

FAITH IS THE VICTORY C.M.D. with Refrain

John H. Yates, 1891

Ira David Sankey, 1891

1 En-camped a - long the hills of light, Ye Chris-tian sol - diers, rise, And
2 His ban - ner o - ver us is love, Our sword the Word of God; We
3 On ev - ery hand the foe we find Drawn up in dread ar - ray; Let
4 To him that o - ver-comes the foe, White rai - ment shall be giv'n; Be -

press the bat - tle ere the night Shall veil the glow-ing skies. A - gainst the foe in
tread the road the saints a-bove With shouts of tri-umph trod. By faith, they like a
tents of ease be left be-hind, And on-ward to the fray. Sal - va-tion's hel - met
fore the an - gels he shall know His name con-fessed in heav'n. Then on-ward from the

vales be-low Let all our strength be hurled; Faith is the vic - to - ry, we know,
whirl-wind's breath, Swept on o'er ev-ery field; The faith by which they con-quered death
on each head, With truth all girt a - bout, The earth shall trem-ble 'neath our tread,
hills of light, Our hearts with love a - flame; We'll van-quish all the hosts of night,

REFRAIN

That o - ver-comes the world.
Is still our shin-ing shield. Faith is the vic - to - ry! Faith is the
And ech - o with our shout.
In Je-sus' con-qu'ring name. Faith is the vic - to - ry! Faith is the

GOSPEL SONGS

591 ONWARD, CHRISTIAN SOLDIERS

ST. GERTRUDE 6.5.6.5.D. with Refrain

Sabine Baring-Gould, 1865

Arthur Seymour Sullivan, 1871

1 On - ward, Chris-tian sol - diers, March-ing as to war, With the cross of Je - sus
2 Like a might-y ar - my Moves the church of God; Broth-ers, we are tread - ing
3 Crowns and thrones may per-ish, King-doms rise and wane, But the church of Je - sus
4 On - ward, then, ye peo - ple! Join our hap-py throng! Blend with ours your voic-es

Go - ing on be - fore; Christ the roy - al Mas - ter Leads a-gainst the foe;
Where the saints have trod; We are not di - vid - ed, All one bod - y we,
Con - stant will re - main; Gates of hell can nev - er 'Gainst that church pre-vail;
In the tri-umph song; Glo - ry, laud, and hon - or, Un - to Christ the King;

REFRAIN

For - ward in - to bat - tle, See, His ban-ners go.
One in hope and doc - trine, One in char - i - ty.
We have Christ's own prom-ise, And that can-not fail.
This through count-less a - ges Men and an-gels sing.

On-ward, Chris-tian sol - diers,

March-ing as to war, With the cross of Je - sus, Go - ing on be - fore.

GOSPEL SONGS

STAND UP! STAND UP FOR JESUS 592

WEBB 7.6.7.6.D.

George Duffield, Jr., 1858

George James Webb, 1830

1 Stand up! stand up for Je - sus! Ye sol - diers of the cross;
2 Stand up! stand up for Je - sus! The trum - pet call o - bey;
3 Stand up! stand up for Je - sus! Stand in His strength a - lone;
4 Stand up! stand up for Je - sus! The strife will not be long;

Lift high His roy - al ban - ner, It must not suf - fer loss.
Forth to the might - y con - flict, In this His glo - rious day.
The arm of flesh will fail you, Ye dare not trust your own.
This day the noise of bat - tle, The next the vic - tor's song.

From vic - t'ry un - to vic - t'ry His ar - my He shall lead
Ye that are men now serve Him, A - gainst un - num - bered foes;
Put on the gos - pel ar - mor, Each piece put on with prayer;
To him that o - ver - com - eth, A crown of life shall be;

Till ev - ery foe is van - quished, And Christ is Lord in - deed.
Let cour - age rise with dan - ger, And strength to strength op - pose.
Where du - ty calls or dan - ger, Be nev - er want - ing there!
He with the King of glo - ry Shall reign e - ter - nal - ly!

GOSPEL SONGS

593 I LOVE TO TELL THE STORY

HANKEY 7.6.7.6.D. with Refrain

Catherine Hankey, 1866
Refrain by William G. Fischer, 1869

William G. Fischer, 1869

1 I love to tell the sto - ry Of un-seen things a - bove, Of Je - sus
2 I love to tell the sto - ry; More won-der-ful it seems Than all the
3 I love to tell the sto - ry; 'Tis pleas-ant to re - peat What seems, each
4 I love to tell the sto - ry; For those who know it best Seem hun - ger-

and His glo - ry, Of Je - sus and His love. I love to tell the
gold - en fan - cies Of all our gold - en dreams. I love to tell the
time I tell it, More won - der - ful - ly sweet. I love to tell the
ing and thirst-ing To hear it, like the rest. And when, in scenes of

sto - ry, Be - cause I know it's true; It sat - is - fies my long - ings
sto - ry, It did so much for me; And that is just the rea - son
sto - ry, For some have nev - er heard The mes - sage of sal - va - tion
glo - ry, I sing the new, new song, 'Twill be the old, old sto - ry

REFRAIN

As noth - ing else would do.
I tell it now to thee. I love to tell the sto - ry, 'Twill be my theme in
From God's own ho - ly Word.
That I have loved so long.

glo - ry, To tell the old, old sto - ry Of Je - sus and His love.

GOSPEL SONGS

WE HAVE HEARD A JOYFUL SOUND 594

JESUS SAVES 7.6.7.6.7.7.7.6.

Priscilla J. Owens, c. 1882

William J. Kirkpatrick, 1882

1 We have heard a joy - ful sound: Je - sus saves! Je - sus saves!
2 Waft it on the roll - ing tide: Je - sus saves! Je - sus saves!
3 Sing a - bove the bat - tle strife, Je - sus saves! Je - sus saves!
4 Give the winds a might - y voice: Je - sus saves! Je - sus saves!

Spread the ti - dings all a - round: Je - sus saves! Je - sus saves!
Tell to sin - ners far and wide: Je - sus saves! Je - sus saves!
By His death and end - less life, Je - sus saves! Je - sus saves!
Let the na - tions now re - joice, Je - sus saves! Je - sus saves!

Bear the news to ev - ery land; Climb the steeps and cross the waves;
Sing, ye is - lands of the sea; Ech - o back, ye o - cean caves;
Sing it soft - ly through the gloom, When the heart for mer - cy craves;
Shout sal - va - tion full and free, High - est hills and deep - est caves;

On - ward! 'tis our Lord's com - mand: Je - sus saves! Je - sus saves!
Earth shall keep her ju - bi - lee: Je - sus saves! Je - sus saves!
Sing in tri - umph o'er the tomb, Je - sus saves! Je - sus saves!
This our song of vic - to - ry, Je - sus saves! Je - sus saves!

GOSPEL SONGS

595 WHEN MORNING GILDS THE SKIES

GENEVA 3 (O SEIGNEUR) 6.6.7.6.6.7.D.

Katholisches Gesangbuch, Würzburg, 1828
Beim frühen Morgenlicht
Tr. Edward Caswall†, 1854

Pseaumes octante trois . . . , Geneva, 1551
Harmony from *The Yattendon Hymnal*, 1899

1 When morn-ing gilds the skies, My heart a-wak-ing cries: May Je-sus Christ be prais-ed!
2 The night be-comes as day, When from the heart we say; May Je-sus Christ be prais-ed!

A - like at work or prayer To Je-sus I re-pair: May Je-sus Christ be prais-ed!
In heav'n's e-ter-nal bliss, The love-liest strain is this: May Je-sus Christ be prais-ed!

Does sad-ness fill my mind, A sol-ace here I find: May Je-sus Christ be prais-ed!
Be this, while life is mine, My can-ti-cle di-vine, May Je-sus Christ be prais-ed!

Or fades my earth-ly bliss, My com-fort still is this! May Je-sus Christ be prais-ed!
Be this th'e-ter-nal song, Through all the a-ges long: May Je-sus Christ be prais-ed!

CHORAL HYMNS

O PRAISE YE THE LORD 596

OLD 104th 5.5.5.5.6.5.6.5.

Based on Psalm 150
Henry Williams Baker, 1875

Ravenscroft's *Psalter*, 1621

1 O praise ye the Lord! Praise Him in the height; Rejoice in His Word, Ye angels of light; Ye heavens, adore Him By whom ye were made, And worship before Him, In brightness arrayed.

2 O praise ye the Lord! Praise Him upon earth, In tuneful accord, Ye sons of new birth; Praise Him who hath brought you His grace from above, Praise Him who hath taught you To sing of His love.

3 O praise ye the Lord! All things that give sound; Each jubilant chord, Reecho around; Loud organs, His glory Forth tell in deep tone, And sweet harp, the story Of what He hath done.

4 O praise ye the Lord! Thanksgiving and song To Him be outpoured All ages along: For love in creation, For heaven restored, For grace of salvation, O praise ye the Lord!

CHORAL HYMNS

597 EIN FESTE BURG IST UNSER GOTT

EIN FESTE BURG 8.7.8.7.6.5.5.6.7.

Based on Psalm 46
Martin Luther, 1527 or 1528

Martin Luther, 1529

1 Ein fe - ste Burg ist un - ser Gott, ein gu - te Wehr und Waf - fen.
2 Mit un - srer Macht ist nichts ge - tan, wir sind gar bald ver - lo - ren.
3 Und wenn die Welt voll Teu - fel wär und wollt uns gar ver - schling - en,
4 Das Wort sie sol - len las - sen stahn und kein Dank da - zu ha - ben.

Er hilft uns frei aus al - ler Not, die uns jetzt hat be - trof - fen.
Es streit für uns der rech - te Mann, den Gott hat selbst er - ko - ren.
So fürch-ten wir uns nicht so sehr; es soll uns doch ge - ling - en.
Er ist bei uns wohl auf dem Plan mit sei - nem Geist und Ga - ben.

Der alt bö - se Feind mit Ernst er's jetzt meint; gross Macht und viel List
Fragst du, wer der ist? Er heisst Je - sus Christ, der Herr Ze - ba - oth,
Der Fürst die - ser Welt, wie saur er sich stellt, tut er uns doch nichts;
Neh - men sie den Leib, Gut, Ehr, Kind und Weib; lass fah - ren da - hin,

sein grau-sam Rü-stung ist; auf Erd ist nicht seins-glei - chen.
und ist kein an - drer Gott; das Feld muss er be - hal - ten.
das macht, er ist ge - richt, ein Wört - lein kann ihn fäl - len.
sie ha - ben's kein Ge - winn; das Reich muss uns doch blei - ben. A-men.

CHORAL HYMNS

Tr. Thomas Carlyle†, 1831

1 A safe stronghold our God is still,
A trusty shield and weapon;
He'll help us clear from all the ill
That hath us now o'ertaken.
The ancient prince of hell,
Doth show purpose fell;
His mail, craft, and power,
He weareth in this hour,
On earth is not his fellow.

2 With force of arms we nothing can,
Full soon were we down-ridden;
But for us fights the proper man,
Whom God Himself hath bidden.
Ask ye, Who is this same?
Christ Jesus His name,
Lord Sabaoth's Son,
He and no other one
Shall conquer in the battle.

3 And were this world all devils o'er
And watching to devour us,
We lay it not to heart so sore,
Not they can overpower us.
And let the prince of ill
Look grim as he will,
He harms not a whit,
For why? His doom is writ,
A word shall quickly slay him.

4 God's Word, for all their craft and force,
One moment will not linger,
But spite of hell, shall have its course,
'Tis written by His finger.
And though they take our life,
Goods, fame, children, wife,
Their profit is small;
These things shall vanish all,
The city of God remaineth.

NOW PRAISE WE CHRIST 598

Based on Latin of Coelius Sedulius, c. 450   CHRISTUM WIR SOLLEN LOBEN SCHON L.M.
Tr. Martin Luther, 1524
Christum wir sollen loben schon
Tr. Richard Massie†, 1854

Enchiridion, Erfurt, 1524

1 Now praise we Christ, the ho - ly One, The bless - ed vir - gin
2 He who Him - self all things did make A ser - vant's form vouch-
3 The grace and power of God the Lord Up - on the moth - er
4 The heav'n - ly choirs re - joice and raise Their voice to God in
5 All hon - or un - to Christ be paid, Pure off - spring of the

Ma - ry's Son, Far as the glo - rious sun doth shine
safed to take That He as man man - kind might win
was out - poured; A vir - gin pure and un - de - filed
songs of praise. To hum - ble shep - herds is pro - claimed
fa - vored maid, With Fa - ther and with Ho - ly Ghost,

Sts. 1-4 | St. 5

E'en to the world's re - mote con - fine.
And save His crea - tures from their sin.
In won - drous wise con - ceived a child.
The Shep - herd who the world hath framed.
Till time in end - less time be lost. A - men.

CHORAL HYMNS

599 JESUS, JOY OF MAN'S DESIRING

WERDE MUNTER 8.7.8.7.8.8.7.7.

Martin Janus, 1661
Jesu, meiner Seelen Wonne
Tr. Unknown

Johann Schop, 1642
Harmony by Johann Sebastian Bach, c. 1727

1 Je - sus, joy of man's de-sir-ing, Ho - ly wis - dom, love most bright,
2 Through the way, where hope is guid-ing, Hark, what peace-ful mu - sic rings,

Drawn by Thee, our souls as - pir-ing, Soar to un - cre - at - ed light.
Where the flock, in Thee con-fid-ing, Drink of joy from death - less springs.

Word of God, our flesh that fash-ioned, With the fire of life im-pas-sioned,
Theirs is beau - ty's fair - est plea-sure; Theirs is wis-dom's ho - liest trea-sure;

Striv - ing still to truth un - known, Soar-ing, dy - ing round Thy throne.
Thou dost ev - er lead Thine own In the love of joys un - known.

(Numbers in parentheses indicate measures of rest if Bach's accompaniment is used.)

CHORAL HYMNS

JESUS, PRICELESS TREASURE 600

JESU, MEINE FREUDE 6.6.5.6.6.5.7.8.6.

Johann Franck, 1653
Jesu, meine Freude
Tr. Catherine Winkworth, 1853 and 1869

Johann Crüger, 1653
Harmony by Johann Sebastian Bach, 1723

1 Je - sus, price-less trea - sure, Source of pur-est plea - sure, Tru-est friend to me;
2 In Thine arm I rest me; Foes who would mo-lest me Can-not reach me here.
3 Hence, all thoughts of sad-ness! For the Lord of glad-ness, Je - sus, en - ters in:

Long my heart hath pant - ed, Till it well-nigh faint - ed, Thirst-ing af - ter Thee.
Though the earth be shak - ing, Ev - ery heart be quak - ing, Je - sus calms my fear;
Those who love the Fa - ther, Though the storms may gath-er, Still have peace with-in;

Thine I am, O spot - less Lamb, I will suf - fer
Sin and hell in con - flict fell With their heav - iest
Yea, what - e'er we here must bear, Still in Thee lies

naught to hide Thee, Ask for naught be - side Thee.
storms as - sail me: Je - sus will not fail me.
pur - est plea - sure, Je - sus, price - less trea - sure!

CHORAL HYMNS

601 ALL HAIL THE POWER OF JESUS' NAME

DIADEM C.M.

Edward Perronet, 1779 and 1780
Altered by John Rippon

James Ellor, c. 1838

1 All hail the power of Je - sus' name! Let an - gels pros-trate
2 Ye cho - sen seed of Is - rael's race, Ye ran-somed of the
3 Let ev - ery kin - dred, ev - ery tribe, On this ter - res-trial
4 O that with yon - der sa - cred throng We at His feet may

fall, Let an - gels pros-trate fall; Bring forth the roy - al
fall, Ye ran - somed of the fall; Hail Him who saves you
ball, On this ter - res - trial ball, To Him all maj - es -
fall, We at His feet may fall! We'll join the ev - er -

di - a - dem, And crown Him,
by His grace,
ty as - cribe,
last - ing song, And crown Him, crown Him, crown Him, crown Him,

crown

crown Him, crown Him, crown Him, And crown Him Lord of all. A-men.

Him,

Another setting of this hymn may be found at No. 95.

CHORAL HYMNS

GOD, THE LORD, A KING REMAINETH 602

Based on Psalm 93
John Keble, 1839

BRYN CALFARIA 8.7.8.7.4.7.

William Owen, 1850

1 God, the Lord, a King re-main-eth, Robed in His own glo-rious light;
2 In her ev-er-last-ing sta-tion Earth is poised, to swerve no more;
3 With all tones of wa-ters blend-ing, Glo-rious is the break-ing deep;
4 Lord, the words Thy lips are tell-ing Are the per-fect ver-i-ty;

God hath robed Him and He reign-eth; He hath gird-ed Him with might.
Thou hast laid Thy throne's foun-da-tion From all time where thought can soar.
Glo-rious, beau-teous, with-out end-ing, God, who reigns on heav'n's high steep.
Of Thine high e-ter-nal dwell-ing, Ho-li-ness shall in-mate be:

Al-le-lu-ia! Al-le-lu-ia! Al-le-lu-ia!
Al-le-lu-ia! Al-le-lu-ia! Al-le-lu-ia!
Al-le-lu-ia! Al-le-lu-ia! Al-le-lu-ia!
Al-le-lu-ia! Al-le-lu-ia! Al-le-lu-ia!

God is King in depth and height! God is King in depth and height!
Lord, Thou art for-ev-er-more! Lord, Thou art for-ev-er-more!
Songs of o-cean nev-er sleep. Songs of o-cean nev-er sleep.
Pure is all that lives with Thee. Pure is all that lives with Thee. A-men.

CHORAL HYMNS

603 GOD OF OUR LIFE

YATTENDON 11 10.4.10.4.10.10.

Hugh Thomson Kerr, 1916

H. Ellis Wooldridge, 1890

1 God of our life, through all the cir - cling years, We trust in
2 God of the past, our times are in Thy hand; With us a -
3 God of the com - ing years, through paths un - known We fol - low

Thee; In all the past, through all our hopes and
bide. Lead us by faith to hope's true prom - ised
Thee; When we are strong, Lord, leave us not a -

fears, Thy hand we see. With each new day, when morn - ing lifts the
land; Be thou our guide. With Thee to bless, the dark - ness shines as
lone; Our ref - uge be. Be Thou for us in life our dai - ly

veil, We own Thy mer - cies, Lord, which nev - er fail.
light. And faith's fair vi - sion chang - es in - to sight.
bread, Our heart's true home when all our years have sped.

CHORAL HYMNS

LOVE OF THE FATHER 604

SONG XXII 10.10.10.10.

Anonymous, 12th century
Amor patris et filii
Tr. Robert Bridges, 1899

Orlando Gibbons, 1623
Harmony from *The Yattendon Hymnal*, 1899

1 Love of the Fa - ther, love of God the Son,
2 Thou the all ho - ly, Thou su - preme in might,
3 E - ter - nal glo - ry, all men Thee a - dore,

From whom all came, in whom was all be - gun;
Thou dost give peace, Thy pres - ence mak - eth right;
Who art and shalt be wor - shiped ev - er - more.

Who form - est heav'n - ly beau - ty out of strife,
Thou with Thy fa - vor all things dost en - fold,
Us whom Thou mad - est, com - fort with Thy might,

Cre - a - tion's whole de - sire and breath of life.
With Thine all - kind - ness free from harm wilt hold.
And lead us to en - joy Thy heav'n - ly light. A - men.

CHORAL HYMNS

605 GOD IS WORKING HIS PURPOSE OUT

PURPOSE Irregular

Arthur Campbell Ainger, 1894

Martin Shaw, 1931

Octaves to the end

1 God is work - ing His pur - pose out As year suc -
2 From ut - most east to ut - most west, Wher - e'er man's
3 March we forth in the strength of God, With the ban - ner of
4 All we can do is noth - ing worth Un - less God

ceeds to year: God is work - ing His
foot hath trod, By the mouth of man - y
Christ un - furled, That the light of the glo - rious
bless - es the deed; Vain - ly we hope for the

pur - pose out, And the time is draw - ing near; Near - er and
mes - sen - gers Goes forth the voice of God; Give ear to
gos - pel of truth May shine through-out the world: Fight we the
har - vest - tide Till God gives life to the seed; Yet near - er and

CHORAL HYMNS

near - er draws the time, The time that shall sure - ly be,
me, ye con - ti - nents, Ye isles, give ear to me,
fight with sor - row and sin To set their cap - tives free,
near - er draws the time, The time that shall sure - ly be,

When the earth shall be filled with the glo - ry of God
That the earth may be filled with the glo - ry of God
That the earth may be filled with the glo - ry of God
When the earth shall be filled with the glo - ry of God

Sts. 1-3 | St. 4

As the wa - ters cov - er the sea.
As the wa - ters cov - er the sea.
As the wa - ters cov - er the sea.
As the wa - ters cov - er the sea.

CHORAL HYMNS

606 PRAISE GOD FROM WHOM

DOXOLOGY (DEDICATION ANTHEM)

Thomas Ken, 1709

Lowell Mason's *Boston Handel and Haydn Society* . . . , 1830
Possibly Samuel Stanley, d. 1822

Praise God from whom all bless - ings flow,
Praise Him all crea - tures here be - low,
Praise Him a - bove,

CHORAL HYMNS

Soprano and tenor voices exchanged as in *Harmonia Sacra*, 1876

CHORAL HYMNS

Father, Son, and Holy Ghost, Hal - le - lu - jah, hal - le - lu - jah, hal - le - lu - jah, A - men, A - men, Hal - le - lu - jah, hal - le - lu - jah, hal - le - lu - jah, hal - le - Hal - le - lu - jah, lu - jah, hal - le - lu - jah, hal - le - lu - jah, hal - le - lu - jah, hal - le - lu - jah, A - men, A - men, Hal - le - lu - jah, A - men, Hal - le - lu - jah, A - men.

CHORAL HYMNS

BREAD OF THE WORLD 607

GENEVA 118 (RENDEZ A DIEU) 9.8.9.8.D.

Reginald Heber, 1827

La forme des prieres . . . , Strasbourg, 1545
(Second line, Geneva, 1551)
Harmony adapted from Claude Goudimel, 1565

Bread of the world in mer-cy bro - ken, Wine of the soul in mer - cy shed,

By whom the words of life were spo - ken, And in whose death our sins are dead;

Look on the heart by sor-row bro- ken, Look on the tears by sin - ners shed;

And be Thy feast to us a to - ken That by Thy grace our souls are fed.

Another setting of this text may be found at No. 407.

CHORAL HYMNS

608 LORD, ALL MY HEART IS FIXED ON THEE

HERZLICH LIEB HAB' ICH DICH, O HERR 8.8.7 8.8.7.8.8.8.8.4.8.8.

Martin Schalling, 1567
Herzlich Lieb hab' ich dich, O Herr
Tr. Catherine Winkworth, 1863

B. Schmid's *Orgeltabulatur-Buch*, 1577
Harmony from *Chorale Book for England*, 1863

1 Lord, all my heart is fixed on Thee, I pray Thee, be not far from me, With ten-der grace up-hold me. The whole wide world de-lights me not, Of heav'n or earth, Lord, ask I not, If but Thy love en-fold me.

2 Rich are Thy gifts! 'Twas God that gave Bod-y and soul and all I have In this poor life of la-bor; O grant that I may through Thy grace Use all my powers to show Thy praise, And serve and help my neigh-bor;

CHORAL HYMNS

Yea, though my heart be like to break, Thou art my trust that
From all false doc-trine keep me, Lord; All lies and mal-ice

nought can shake, My por-tion and my hid-den joy, Whose cross could all my
from me ward; In ev-ery cross up-hold Thou me, That I may bear it

bonds de-stroy; Lord Je-sus Christ! My God and Lord! My
pa-tient-ly; Lord Je-sus Christ! My God and Lord! My

God and Lord! For-sake me not who trust Thy Word!
God and Lord! In death Thy com-fort still af-ford. A-men.

CHORAL HYMNS

609 BREAK FORTH, O BEAUTEOUS HEAVENLY LIGHT

ERMUNTRE DICH 8.7.8.7.8.8.7.7.

Johann Rist, 1641
Ermuntre dich, mein schwacher Geist
Tr. St. 1 composite
Sts. 2, 3 Arthur Tozer Russell, 1851

Johann Schop, 1641
Harmony by Johann Sebastian Bach, 1734

1 Break forth, O beau-teous heav'n-ly light, And ush - er in the morn - ing;
2 O won-drous work! O won-drous night, All else so far ex - cell - ing!
3 All bless - ing, thanks, and praise to Thee, Lord Je - sus Christ, be giv - en:

Ye shep-herds, shrink not with af-fright, But hear the an - gel's warn - ing.
The Sav - ior now, un - veiled to sight, On earth as man is dwell - ing:
Our broth - er Thou hast deign'd to be, Our foes in sun - der riv - en.

This Child, now born in in - fan - cy, Our con - fi - dence and
That man to whom a - lone is given Power o'er the lights, the
O grant us through our day of grace With con - stant praise to

joy shall be, The power of Sa - tan break - ing, Our
clouds of heav'n! The trem-bling heav'ns a - dore Him! The
seek Thy face. Grant us ere long in glo - ry With

peace   e - ter - nal   mak - ing.
moun - tains   shake   be - fore   Him!
prais - es   to   a - dore   Thee. A - men.

O SONS AND DAUGHTERS, LET US SING 610

GELOBT SEI GOTT 8.8.8. with Alleluia

Jean Tisserand (?), 15th century
O Filii et Filiae
Tr. John Mason Neale, 1851
Altered by Compilers of *Hymns Ancient and Modern*, 1861

Melchior Vulpius, 1609

1 O   sons and daugh-ters, let   us   sing!   The King of heav'n, the
2 That Sun-day morn, at break   of   day,   The faith-ful wom - en
3 An   an - gel   clad   in   white   they   see,   Who sat and spake un-
4 How blest are   they who have   not   seen,   And yet whose faith   hath
5 On   this most ho - ly   day   of   days,   To God your hearts and

glo - rious King,   O'er death to - day   rose   tri - umph - ing.
went   their   way   To   seek the   tomb where Je - sus   lay.
to   the   three,   "Your Lord doth   go   to   Gal - i - lee."
con - stant been;   For they e - ter - nal   life   shall win.
voic - es   raise   In   laud, and   ju - bi - lee,   and praise.

Al - le - lu - ia!   Al - le - lu - ia!   Al - le - lu - ia!

CHORAL HYMNS

611 CHRIST LAY AWHILE IN DEATH'S STRONG BANDS

CHRIST LAG IN TODESBANDEN 8.7.8.7.7.7.8.7.4.

Martin Luther, 1524
Christ lag in Todesbanden
Tr. Richard Massie, 1854

Melody adapted from *Christ ist erstanden* in 1524
Version of Johann Sebastian Bach, c. 1740

1 Christ lay a-while in death's strong bands, For our of - fenc - es giv — en;
2 It was a strange and dread-ful strife, When life and death con - tend — ed;
3 So let us keep the fes - ti - val, Where-to the Lord in - vites us;
4 Then let us feast this Ea - ster day On the true bread of heav — en;

But now at God's right hand He stands, And brings us life from heav — en:
The vic - to - ry re-mained with life, The reign of death was end — ed:
Christ is Him-self the joy of all, The sun which warms and lights us;
The Word of grace hath purged a - way The old and wick - ed leav — en:

Where-fore let us joy - ful be, And sing to God right thank-ful - ly
Ho - ly Scrip - tures plain-ly saith, That death is swal - lowed up by death,
By His grace He doth im - part E - ter - nal sun - shine to the heart;
Christ a - lone our souls will feed, He is our meat and drink in - deed;

Loud songs of Al - le - lu - ia! Al - le - lu - ia!
Made hence-forth a de - ri - sion. Al - le - lu - ia!
The night of sin is end - ed. Al - le - lu - ia!
Faith lives up - on no oth - er. Al - le - lu - ia!

CHORAL HYMNS

CHRIST IS ARISEN 612

CHRIST IST ERSTANDEN

German Hymn, c. 1100
Christ ist erstanden, von der Marter alle
Tr. William Gustave Polack, 1939

Germany Melody, 12th century
Version, Wittenberg, 1529

Christ is a - ris - en From the grave's dark pris-on. We now re-joice with glad-ness;

Christ will end all sad - ness. Lord, have mer - cy. All our hopes were end - ed

Had Je - sus not as - cend - ed From the grave tri-um-phant-ly. For this, Lord Christ,

we wor-ship Thee. Lord, have mer-cy. Al-le - lu - ia! Al-le - lu - ia! Al - le - lu - ia!

We now re-joice with glad-ness; Christ will end all sad-ness. Lord, have mer-cy. A-men.

CHORAL HYMNS

613 THE LORD IS RISEN INDEED

EASTER ANTHEM

"Words from Scripture and Dr. Young"

William Billings, 1786

CHORAL HYMNS

CHORAL HYMNS

CHORAL HYMNS

THIS JOYFUL EASTERTIDE 614

VRUECHTEN 6.7.6.7. with Refrain

David's Psalmen, Amsterdam, 1685
Harmony by Alice Parker, 1966

George Ratcliffe Woodward, 1902

1 This joy-ful East-er-tide A - way with sin and sor - - - row!
  My love, the Cru-ci-fied, Hath sprung to life this mor - - - row.
2 My flesh in hope shall rest, And for a sea-son slum - - - ber:
  Till trump from east to west Shall wake the dead in num - - - ber,
3 Death's flood hath lost its chill, Since Je - sus crossed the riv - - - er:
  Lov - er of souls, from ill My pass - ing soul de - liv - - - er.

Had Christ, that once was slain, Ne'er burst His three - day pris - on,

Our faith had been in vain: But now hath Christ a - ris - en, a -

ris - en, a - ris - en, a - ris - - - - en.

CHORAL HYMNS

615 BUILT ON THE ROCK

KIRKEN DEN ER ET 8.8.8.8.8.8.8.8.

Nicolai F. S. Grundtvig, 1837
Kirken den er et gammelt Hus
Tr. Carl Döving†, 1909

Ludvig M. Lindeman, 1840

1 Built on the Rock the church doth stand, E - ven when stee - ples are
2 Sure - ly in tem - ples made with hands, God, the most high, is not
3 Now we may gath - er with our King E'en in the low - li - est

fall - ing; Crum-bled have spires in ev - ery land, Bells still are
dwell - ing; High a - bove earth His tem - ple stands, All earth - ly
dwell - ing; Prais - es to Him we there may bring, His won-drous

chim - ing and call - ing, Call - ing the young and old to rest,
tem - ples ex - cell - ing. Yet He whom heav'ns can - not con - tain
mer - cy forth - tell - ing. Je - sus His grace to us ac - cords;

But a - bove all the soul dis - trest, Long-ing for rest ev - er - last - ing.
Chose to a - bide on earth with men, Built in our bod - ies His tem - ple.
Spir - it and life are all His words; His truth doth hal - low the tem - ple.

CHORAL HYMNS

O JESUS CHRIST, TO THEE MAY HYMNS 616

CITY OF GOD 11.10.11.10.

Bradford Gray Webster, 1954

Daniel Moe, 1957

1 O Je - sus Christ, to Thee may hymns be ris - ing,
2 Grant us new cour - age, sac - ri - fi - cial, hum - ble,
3 Show us Thy Spir - it, brood - ing o'er each cit - y,

In ev - ery cit - y for Thy love and care;
Strong in Thy strength to ven - ture and to dare;
As Thou didst weep a - bove Je - ru - sa - lem,

In - spire our wor - ship, grant the glad sur - pris - ing
To lift the fall - en, guide the feet that stum - ble,
Seek - ing to gath - er all in love and pit - y,

That Thy blest Spir - it brings men ev - ery - where.
Seek out the lone - ly and God's mer - cy share.
And heal - ing those who touch Thy gar - ment's hem.

CHORAL HYMNS

617 I LOVE THE LORD

GELINEAU 114

Based on Psalm 116
Gelineau *Psalms*, 1953
Tr. Ladies of the Grail, 1955

Joseph Gelineau, 1953, and Others

1　　I love　　　the　Lord, for He has **heard**　　　the **cry** of my ap - **peal**;
2　They sur - **round**ed me, the **snares**　　of　**death**, with the anguish of the **tomb**;
3　　How **gracious** is the **Lord**,　　and　**just**;　　　our **God** has com - **passion**.
4　　Turn **back**,　　my　**soul**, to your **rest**　　for the **Lord** has been **good**,
5　I will **walk**　in　　the **presence** of the **Lord**　in the **land** of　the　**living**.

1　　for He **turned** His **ear**　　　to　　**me**,　　in the **day** when　　I **called** Him.
2　　they **caught** me, **sorrow** and dis - **tress**.　　　I **called** on　　the **Lord's** name.
3　　The **Lord** pro - **tects** the simple **hearts**,　　I was **helpless**, so　He **saved** me.
4　　He has **kept**　my **soul**　from　**death**,　　and my **feet**　　from **stum** - bling.
5 Praise the **Father**, the **Son**, and Holy **Spirit**,　　for - **ever**　　and ev - er.

Antiphon 1
Obligatory
after verse 2

O Lord, my God, de - liv - er me!

A. G. Murray

Antiphon 2

When I cry to the Lord, He hears my prayer.

C. W. Howell

Antiphon 3

I will walk in the pres-ence of the Lord in the land of the liv - ing.

One Antiphon should be sung following each stanza. The Psalm may be sung by a
soloist (soloists) and the Antiphon by choir or congregation.

CHORAL HYMNS

CRY OUT WITH JOY 618

GELINEAU 99

Based on Psalm 100
Gelineau *Psalms*, 1953
Tr. Ladies of the Grail, 1955

Joseph Gelineau, 1953
and A. Gregory Murray

1 Cry out with joy to the Lord, all the earth.
2 Know that He, the Lord, is God.
3 Go within His gates, giving thanks.
4 In - deed, how good is the Lord,
5 Give glory to the Father Al - mighty,

1 Serve the Lord with gladness.
2 He made us, we be - long to Him,
3 Enter His courts with songs of praise.
4 e - ternal His merciful love;
5 to His Son, Jesus Christ, the Lord,

1 Come be - fore Him, singing for joy.
2 we are His people, the sheep of His flock.
3 Give thanks to Him and bless His name.
4 He is faithful from age to age.
5 to the Spirit who dwells in our hearts.

Antiphon 1

A - rise, come to your God, sing Him your songs of re-joic - ing.

Antiphon 2

Glo - ry to You, O God!

A. G. Murray

Antiphon 3

Al - le - lu - ia, al - le - lu - ia, al - le - lu - ia.

One Antiphon should be sung following each stanza. The Psalm may be sung by a
soloist (soloists) and the Antiphon by choir or congregation.

CHORAL HYMNS

619 LORD, THOU HAST SEARCHED ME

TENDER THOUGHT L.M.

Based on Psalm 139
The Psalter Hymnal, 1927

Folk Hymn
A. Davisson's *Kentucky Harmony*, 1816

1 Lord, Thou hast searched me and dost know
2 My words from Thee I can - not hide;
3 Where can I go a - part from Thee,
4 If I the wings of morn - ing take,
5 If deep - est dark - ness cov - er me,

Wher - e'er I rest, wher - e'er I go;
I feel Thy power on ev - ery side;
Or whith - er from Thy pres - ence flee?
And far a - way my dwell - ing make,
The dark - ness hid - eth not from Thee;

Thou know - est all that I have planned,
O won - drous knowl - edge, aw - ful might,
In heav'n? It is Thy dwell - ing fair;
The hand that lead - eth me is Thine,
To Thee both night and day are bright,

And all my ways are in Thy hand.
Un - fath - omed depth, un - mea - sured height!
In death's a - bode? Lo, Thou art there.
And my sup - port Thy power di - vine.
The dark - ness shin - eth as the light.

CHORAL HYMNS

THE LORD IS IN HIS HOLY TEMPLE 620

Habakkuk 2:20

George Frederick Root, d. 1895

The Lord is in His ho-ly tem - ple, The Lord is in His ho-ly tem - ple, Let all the earth keep si - lence, Let all the earth keep si - lence be - fore Him, Keep si-lence, keep si- lence be - fore Him. A - men.

THE LORD IS IN HIS HOLY TEMPLE 621

Habakkuk 2:20

Edwin Othello Excell, c. 1902

The Lord is in His ho - ly tem - ple, Let all the earth keep si - lence, keep si - lence be - fore Him. A - men.

MUSICAL AIDS TO WORSHIP

622 HOLY, HOLY, HOLY, LORD GOD

Samuel Sebastian Wesley, c. 1865

Ho - ly, ho - ly, ho - ly, Lord God of hosts, Heav'n and earth are full of Thy glo - ry: Glo - ry be to Thee, O Lord most high. A - men.

623 NOW TO THE KING OF HEAVEN

ST. JOHN 6.6.6.6.8.8.

Philip Doddridge, 1755
and Isaac Watts, 1719

The Parish Choir, 1851

Now to the King of heav'n Your cheer - ful voic - es raise; To Him be glo - ry giv'n, Power, maj - es - ty and praise; Wide as He reigns His name be sung By ev - ery tongue in end - less strains. A - men.

MUSICAL AIDS TO WORSHIP

JESUS, STAND AMONG US 624

WEM IN LEIDENSTAGEN 6.5.6.5.

William Pennefather, 1855

Friedrich Filitz, 1847

1 Je - sus, stand a - mong us In Thy ris - en power;
2 Breathe the Ho - ly Spir - it In - to ev - ery heart;

Let this time of wor - ship Be a hal - lowed hour.
Bid the fears and sor - rows From each soul de - part. A - men.

O LORD OF LOVE, THOU LIGHT DIVINE 625

VICTORY 8.8.8. with Alleluia

Giovanni Pierluigi da Palestrina, 1591
Adapted by William Henry Monk, 1861

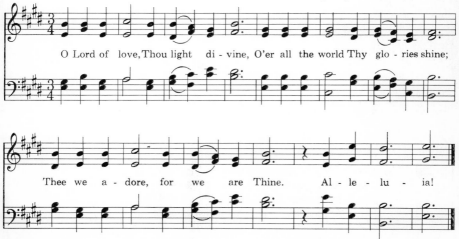

O Lord of love, Thou light di - vine, O'er all the world Thy glo - ries shine;

Thee we a - dore, for we are Thine. Al - le - lu - ia!

MUSICAL AIDS TO WORSHIP

626 O COME, LET US WORSHIP

Psalm 95: 6,7

J. Harold Moyer, 1964

O come, let us wor-ship and bow down; Let us kneel be-fore the

For He is our God,

Lord our Mak-er. For He is our God, And we are the

peo-ple of His pas-ture and the sheep of His hand.

627 OUR FATHER WHO ART IN HEAVEN

Matthew 6: 9-13

1 Our Father who art in heaven, Hallowed be Thy name.
2 Give us this day our dai - ly bread.
3 And lead us not into temptation, but deliver us from evil:

Thy kingdom come. Thy will be done in earth, as it is in heaven.
And forgive us our trespasses, as we forgive them that trespass a - gainst us.
For Thine is the kingdom, and the power, and the glory, for - ever. A - men.

MUSICAL AIDS TO WORSHIP

CREATE IN ME A CLEAN HEART 628

Psalm 51: 10-12

1 Create in me a clean heart, O God;
2 Cast me not away from Thy pres - ence;
3 Restore unto me the joy of Thy sal - va - tion;

and renew a right spirit with - in me.
and take not Thy Ho - ly Spir - it from me.
and uphold me with Thy free spir - it.

ALMIGHTY FATHER, HEAR OUR PRAYER 629

Arranged from Felix Mendelssohn, 1846

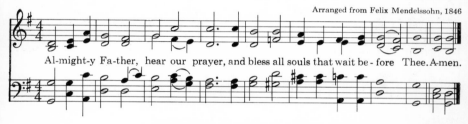

Al-might-y Fa-ther, hear our prayer, and bless all souls that wait be - fore Thee. A-men.

HEAR THOU OUR PRAYER 630

Nelson T. Huffman, b. 1901

Nelson T. Huffman, b. 1901

Hear Thou our prayer, Lord, and bless all

souls that wait be - fore Thee. A - men.

MUSICAL AIDS TO WORSHIP

631 SEND OUT THY LIGHT AND THY TRUTH

LUX FIAT

Psalm 43: 3

Charles F. Gounod, d. 1893

Send out Thy light and Thy truth, let them lead me; O let them bring me to Thy ho - ly hill. Send out Thy light and Thy truth, let them lead me; O let them bring me to Thy ho - ly hill. O let them lead me, O let them lead me; O let them bring me to Thy ho - ly hill. A - men.

MUSICAL AIDS TO WORSHIP

GLORY BE TO GOD ON HIGH 632

Before 500, A.D.
Gloria in excelsis Deo

Scottish Chant

1 Glory be to   God on   high: and on earth   peace, good will towards   men.
2 | We praise Thee, | wor- ship Thee: | we glorify Thee, | Thee for   Thy great   glory.
   | we bless Thee, we | | we give thanks to |

3 O Lord God, heaven - ly King: God the   Fa - ther Al - - mighty.
4 |O Lord, the only- | Je - sus Christ: |O Lord God, Lamb| Son   of the Father,
   | begotten Son | | of God, |

5 That takest away the   sins of the world: have mercy up - on   us.
6 Thou that takest away the   sins of the world: receive   our   prayer.
7 |Thou that sittest at the| God the   Father: have mercy up - on   us.
   | right hand of|

8 For Thou only   art   holy: Thou   on - ly art the Lord.
9 | Thou only, O | Ho - ly Ghost: |art most high| glory of God the Father. A - men.
   |Christ, with the| | in the|

MUSICAL AIDS TO WORSHIP

633 LET THE WORDS OF MY MOUTH

Psalm 19: 14

Adolph Baumbach, 1862

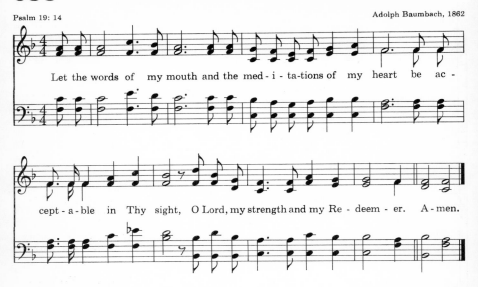

Let the words of my mouth and the med - i - ta-tions of my heart be ac -

cept - a - ble in Thy sight, O Lord, my strength and my Re - deem - er. A - men.

634 BLESS THOU THE GIFTS

CANONBURY L.M.

Samuel Longfellow, c. 1886

Arranged from Robert Schumann, 1839

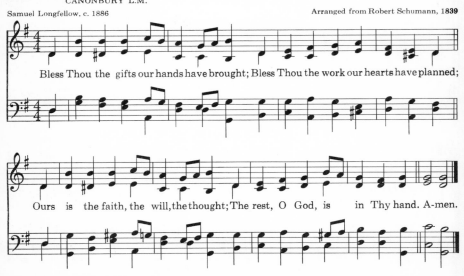

Bless Thou the gifts our hands have brought; Bless Thou the work our hearts have planned;

Ours is the faith, the will, the thought; The rest, O God, is in Thy hand. A-men.

MUSICAL AIDS TO WORSHIP

GRANT US, LORD, THE GRACE OF GIVING 635

STUTTGART 8.7.8.7.

C. F. Witt, 1715
Adapted by Henry John Gauntlett, 1861

Grant us, Lord, the grace of giv - ing, With a spir - it large and free,

That our-selves and all our liv - ing We may of - fer un - to Thee. A-men.

ALL THINGS COME OF THEE 636

I Chronicles 29: 14b

All things come of Thee, O Lord; and of Thine own have we giv - en Thee. A-men.

GREAT GOD, THOU GIVER OF ALL 637

RETREAT L.M.

James Skinner, d. 1881

Thomas Hastings, 1842

Great God, Thou giv - er of all good, Ac - cept our thanks and bless this food;

Grace, health, and strength to us af-ford, Through Je-sus Christ our ris - en Lord. A-men.

MUSICAL AIDS TO WORSHIP

638 PRAISE GOD FROM WHOM ALL BLESSINGS FLOW

OLD HUNDREDTH L.M.

Thomas Ken, 1709

Pseaumes octante trois . . . , Geneva, 1551

Praise God, from whom all bless-ings flow; Praise Him, all crea-tures here be - low;

Praise Him a-bove, ye heav'n-ly host; Praise Fa-ther, Son, and Ho - ly Ghost. A-men.

639 BE PRESENT AT OUR TABLE, LORD

OLD HUNDREDTH L.M.

Pseaumes octante trois . . . , Geneva, 1551
English form of final line

John Cennick, 1741

Be pres-ent at our ta - ble, Lord; Be here, and ev - ery - where a - dored;

Thy crea-tures bless, and grant that we May feast in par-a - dise with Thee. A-men.

MUSICAL AIDS TO WORSHIP   Other forms of Old Hundredth may be found at Numbers 2 and 3.

GLORY BE TO THE FATHER 640

Early Christian Doxology
Gloria Patri

From H. W. Greatorex' *Collection*, 1851

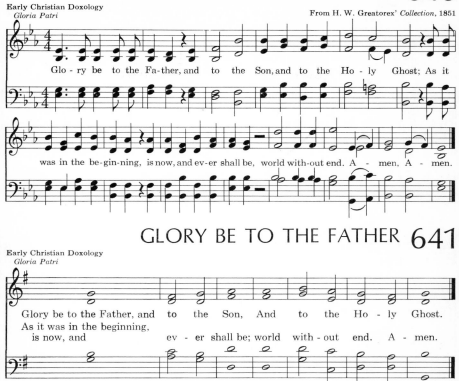

Glo - ry be to the Fa-ther, and to the Son, and to the Ho - ly Ghost; As it was in the be-gin-ning, is now, and ev-er shall be, world with-out end. A - men, A - men.

GLORY BE TO THE FATHER 641

Early Christian Doxology
Gloria Patri

Glory be to the Father, and to the Son, And to the Ho - ly Ghost.
As it was in the beginning,
is now, and ev - er shall be; world with - out end. A - men.

GLORY BE TO THE FATHER 642

Early Christian Doxology
Gloria Patri

Christopher Meineke, 1844

Glo - ry be to the Fa-ther, and to the Son, and to the Ho - ly Ghost; As it was in the be-gin-ning, is now, and ev- er shall be, world with-out end. A - men, A - men.

MUSICAL AIDS TO WORSHIP

643 CAST THY BURDEN UPON THE LORD

BIRMINGHAM (MENDELSSOHN)

Julius Schubring, b. 1806
Wirf dein Anliegen auf den Herrn
Tr. William Bartholomew, 1846

Felix Mendelssohn, 1846

Cast thy bur-den up - on the Lord, And He shall sus -
tain thee: He nev - er will suf - fer the
right - eous to fall; He is at thy right hand. Thy
mer - cy, Lord, is great, and far a - bove the heav'ns; Let
none be made a - sham - ed, that wait up - on Thee. A-men.

MUSICAL AIDS TO WORSHIP

CHRIST, WE DO ALL ADORE THEE 644

Adoramus Te Christe

Theodore Dubois, 1867

Christ, we do all a - dore Thee, And we do praise Thee for-ev - er, Christ, we do all a - dore Thee, And we do praise Thee for-ev - er, For on the ho - ly cross Thou hast the world from sin re - deem - ed. Christ, we do all a - dore Thee, And we do praise Thee for-ev - er. Christ, we do all a - dore Thee.

645 GOD BE IN MY HEAD

GOD BE IN MY HEAD

Book of Hours†, 1514

H. Walford Davies, 1910

God be in my head, and in my un-der-stand-ing;

God be in mine eyes and in my look-ing; God be in my mouth, and in my

speak - ing; God be in my heart, and in my think - ing;

God be at mine end, and at my de - part - ing.

MUSICAL AIDS TO WORSHIP

GRACE TO YOU AND PEACE 646

Romans 1:7

Alice Parker, 1962

Grace to you and peace from God the Fa - ther, and the Lord

Grace to you and peace from God the Fa - ther, and

Grace to you and peace from God the Fa -

Je - sus Christ, A - men.

the Lord Je - sus Christ, A - men.

ther, and the Lord Je - sus Christ, A - men.

MAY THE GRACE OF CHRIST 647

RINGE RECHT 8.7.8.7.

J. Thommen's *Erbaulicher Musicalischer Christen-Schatz*, 1745

John Newton, 1779

1 May the grace of Christ our Sav - ior, And the Fa-ther's bound-less love,
2 Thus may we a - bide in un - ion With each oth - er and the Lord,

With the Ho - ly Spir-it's fa - vor Rest up - on us from a - bove.
And pos - sess, in sweet com-mun-ion, Joys which earth can-not af - ford. A-men.

MUSICAL AIDS TO WORSHIP

648 DRESDEN AMEN

A - men, A - - men.

649 TWOFOLD AMEN

A - - men. A - men.

650 THREEFOLD AMEN

A - men, A-men, A - men.

651 THREEFOLD AMEN

A-men, A-men, A - - men.

652 FOURFOLD AMEN

John Stainer

A - men, A - men, A - - men, A - men.

A - men.

653 FOURFOLD AMEN

Robert G. Barrow, b. 1911

A - men,   A - - - men.

A - - - men, A - - - men, A - men, A - - - men.

A - - - men,   A - - men.

A - men, A - - - men.

Additional Worship Resources

Recently all churches have recognized a need for greater congregational participation in Christian worship. In many churches the only corporate expression has been the singing of hymns. If there is to be greater congregational involvement, materials must be available. This section of *The Mennonite Hymnal* is an attempt to meet that need. Materials are provided only for worship forms which can be used corporately by the congregation. Texts for other forms, such as calls to worship, pastoral prayers, etc., can be obtained elsewhere.

Scripture Readings

Scripture readings represent all portions of salvation history, from the song of Moses to the final songs of hope in the Book of Revelation. All readings are *units* of Scripture, not collections of verses from several chapters. Five English translations are represented, although most of the selections are from the *Revised Standard Version*. In selecting the translations to be used, each passage was studied for clarity of thought and for ease in group reading as well as accuracy of translation.

The format suggests that these readings can be read in three different ways: in unison, responsively, or antiphonally. For antiphonal passages the congregation will need to be divided into two groups for alternate reading. Where several suggestions are listed for one reading, they are given in order of preference, determined largely by the nature of the text. All readings can, of course, be in unison. Each worshiping group will need to decide how a Scripture passage is to be read. This choice will depend on the size of the group, the nature of the service, the preference of the worship leader, and other factors.

A topical index for Scripture readings has been incorporated in the Topical Index for Hymns. This encourages a close coordination of hymns and Scripture readings in worship services. Worship leaders may wish to develop their own topical index.

Affirmations of Faith

Four affirmations of faith are given to provide an opportunity for congregations to express unitedly and in summary form the essentials of Christian belief. These affirmations do not represent official documents of any church body; but they are, in a sense, the church's answer to the Word of God. No one statement covers the entire range of Christian doctrine. The Nicene Creed and the Apostles' Creed are confessions that were developed from the fourth to the eighth centuries. A contemporary Affirmation of Faith (No. 4) was created by several church leaders for *The Mennonite Hymnal* and was completed in 1967.

Every hymn that a congregation sings is, in a sense, an affirmation of faith. Scripture readings can also be used as confessions of faith.

Congregational Responses

Congregational responses offer opportunities for congregations to participate more actively in the many special services in the life of the church. Material given here is not the complete service, but can be included at the appropriate time.

Prayers

When congregations pray, they usually think about specific concerns at certain times and places. But there are also needs and conditions of a universal nature that find expression in the prayers of Christians everywhere. A need to confess, a desire to praise, a concern for the church and for the world—these and many more find expression in all congregations of Christian people. To enable churches to give corporate expression in prayer, several prayers from both ancient and contemporary sources are included. Scripture readings, such as No. 17 (Psalm 51) and No. 33 (Daniel 9), can also be used as prayers. Worship leaders may wish to supplement this collection with other prayers.

CONTENTS

Scripture Readings

654   Exodus 15:1-12, 15b-18

(Responsively or Antiphonally)

Then Moses and the people of Israel sang this song to the Lord, saying,

I will sing to the Lord, for he has triumphed gloriously; the horse and his rider he has thrown into the sea.

The Lord is my strength and my song, and he has become my salvation;

This is my God, and I will praise him, my father's God, and I will exalt him.

The Lord is a man of war; the Lord is his name.

Pharaoh's chariots and his host he cast into the sea; and his picked officers are sunk in the Red Sea.

The floods cover them; they went down into the depths like a stone.

Thy right hand, O Lord, glorious in power, thy right hand, O Lord, shatters the enemy.

In the greatness of thy majesty thou overthrowest thy adversaries; thou sendest forth thy fury, it consumes them like stubble.

At the blast of thy nostrils the waters piled up, the floods stood up in a heap; the deeps congealed in the heart of the sea.

The enemy said, "I will pursue, I will overtake, I will divide the spoil, my desire shall have its fill of them. I will draw my sword, my hand shall destroy them."

Thou didst blow with thy wind, the sea covered them; they sank as lead in the mighty waters.

Who is like thee, O Lord, among the gods? Who is like thee, majestic in holiness, terrible in glorious deeds, doing wonders?

Thou didst stretch out thy right hand, the earth swallowed them.

All the inhabitants of Canaan have melted away. Terror and dread fall upon them; because of the greatness of thy arm, they are as still as a stone,

Till thy people, O Lord, pass by, till the people pass by whom thou hast purchased.

Thou wilt bring them in, and plant them on thy own mountain, the place, O Lord, which thou hast made for thy abode, the sanctuary, O Lord, which thy hands have established.

The Lord will reign for ever and ever.

655   Exodus 20:2-17

(Antiphonally)

I am the Lord your God, who brought you out of the land of Egypt, out of the house of bondage.

You shall have no other gods before me.

You shall not make for yourself a graven image, or any likeness of anything that is in heaven above, or that is in the earth beneath, or that is in the water under the earth;

You shall not bow down to them or serve them; for I the Lord your God am a jealous God, visiting the iniquity of the fathers upon the children to the third and the fourth generation of those who hate me, but showing steadfast love to thousands of those who love me and keep my commandments.

You shall not take the name of the Lord your God in vain; for the Lord will not hold him guiltless who takes his name in vain.

Remember the sabbath day, to keep it holy. Six days you shall labor, and do all your work, but the seventh day is a sabbath to the Lord your God;

In it you shall not do any work, you, or your son, or your daughter, your manservant, or your maidservant, or your cattle, or the sojourner who is within your gates;

For in six days the Lord made heaven and earth, the sea, and all that is in them, and rested the seventh day; therefore the Lord blessed the sabbath day and hallowed it.

Honor your father and your mother, that your days may be long in the land which the Lord your God gives you.

You shall not kill.

You shall not commit adultery.

You shall not steal.

You shall not bear false witness against your neighbor.

You shall not covet your neighbor's house; you shall not covet your neighbor's wife, or his manservant, or his maidservant, or his ox, or his ass, or anything that is your neighbor's.

656 Deuteronomy 6:4-15
(Antiphonally)

(Unison)
Hear, O Israel: The Lord our God is one Lord; and you shall love the Lord your God with all your heart, and with all your soul, and with all your might.

(Antiphonally)
And these words which I command

you this day shall be upon your heart; and you shall teach them diligently to your children, and shall talk of them when you sit in your house, and when you walk by the way, and when you lie down, and when you rise.

And you shall bind them as a sign upon your hand, and they shall be as frontlets between your eyes. And you shall write them on the doorposts of your house and on your gates.

And when the Lord your God brings you into the land which he swore to your fathers, to Abraham, to Isaac, and to Jacob, to give you, with great and goodly cities, which you did not build, and houses full of all good things, which you did not fill, and cisterns hewn out, which you did not hew, and vineyards and olive trees, which you did not plant, and when you eat and are full,

Then take heed lest you forget the Lord, who brought you out of the land of Egypt, out of the house of bondage.

You shall fear the Lord your God; you shall serve him, and swear by his name.

You shall not go after other gods, of the gods of the peoples who are round about you; for the Lord your God in the midst of you is a jealous God; lest the anger of the Lord your God be kindled against you, and he destroy you from off the face of the earth.

657 2 Samuel 22:2-7, 17-25
(Responsively, Antiphonally, or Unison)
The Lord is my rock, and my fortress, and my deliverer, my God, my rock, in whom I take refuge,

My shield and the horn of my salvation, my stronghold and my refuge, my savior; thou savest me from violence.

I call upon the Lord, who is worthy to be praised, and I am saved from my enemies.

For the waves of death encompassed me, the torrents of perdition assailed me;

The cords of Sheol entangled me, the snares of death confronted me.

In my distress I called upon the Lord; to my God I called.

From his temple he heard my voice, and my cry came to his ears.

He reached from on high, he took me, he drew me out of many waters.

He delivered me from my strong enemy, from those who hated me; for they were too mighty for me.

They came upon me in the day of my calamity; but the Lord was my stay.

He brought me forth into a broad place; he delivered me, because he delighted in me.

The Lord rewarded me according to my righteousness; according to the cleanness of my hands he recompensed me.

For I have kept the ways of the Lord, and have not wickedly departed from my God.

For all his ordinances were before me, and from his statutes I did not turn aside.

I was blameless before him, and I kept myself from guilt.

Therefore the Lord has recompensed me according to my righteousness, according to my cleanness in his sight.

658   1 Chronicles 16:23-34
(Responsively, Antiphonally, or Unison)

Sing to the Lord, all the earth! Tell of his salvation from day to day.

Declare his glory among the nations, his marvelous works among all the peoples!

For great is the Lord, and greatly to be praised, and he is to be held in awe above all gods.

For all the gods of the peoples are idols; but the Lord made the heavens.

Honor and majesty are before him; strength and joy are in his place.

Ascribe to the Lord, O families of the peoples, ascribe to the Lord glory and strength!

Ascribe to the Lord the glory due his name; bring an offering, and come before him!

Worship the Lord in holy array; tremble before him, all the earth; yea, the world stands firm, never to be moved.

Let the heavens be glad, and let the earth rejoice, and let them say among the nations, "The Lord reigns!"

Let the sea roar, and all that fills it, let the field exult, and everything in it!

Then shall the trees of the wood sing for joy before the Lord, for he comes to judge the earth.

O give thanks to the Lord, for he is good; for his steadfast love endures for ever!

659   Job 28:12-15, 20-21, 23-28
(Antiphonally or Responsively)

But where shall wisdom be found? And where is the place of understanding?

Man does not know the way to it, and it is not found in the land of the living.

The deep says, "It is not in me," and the sea says, "It is not with me."

It cannot be gotten for gold, and silver cannot be weighed as its price.

Whence then comes wisdom? And where is the place of understanding?

It is hid from the eyes of all living, and concealed from the birds of the air.

God understands the way to it, and he knows its place.

For he looks to the ends of the earth, and sees everything under the heavens.

When he gave to the wind its weight, and meted out the waters by measure;

When he made a decree for the rain, and a way for the lightning of the thunder;

Then he saw it and declared it; he established it, and searched it out.

And he said to man, "Behold, the fear of the Lord, that is wisdom; and to depart from evil is understanding."

660 Psalm 1:1-6

(Antiphonally or Unison)

Blessed is the man who walks not in the counsel of the wicked,

Nor stands in the way of sinners, nor sits in the seat of scoffers;

But his delight is in the law of the Lord, and on his law he meditates day and night.

He is like a tree planted by streams of water, that yields its fruit in its

season, and its leaf does not wither.

In all that he does, he prospers.

The wicked are not so, but are like chaff which the wind drives away.

Therefore the wicked will not stand in the judgment, nor sinners in the congregation of the righteous;

For the Lord knows the way of the righteous, but the way of the wicked will perish.

661 Psalm 8:1-9

(Responsively, Antiphonally, or Unison)

O Lord, our Lord, how majestic is thy name in all the earth!

Thou whose glory above the heavens is chanted by the mouth of babes and infants, thou hast founded a bulwark because of thy foes, to still the enemy and the avenger.

When I look at thy heavens, the work of thy fingers, the moon and the stars which thou hast established;

What is man that thou art mindful of him, and the son of man that thou dost care for him?

Yet thou hast made him little less than God, and dost crown him with glory and honor.

Thou hast given him dominion over the works of thy hands; thou hast put all things under his feet,

All sheep and oxen, and also the beasts of the field, the birds of the air, and the fish of the sea, whatever passes along the paths of the sea.

O Lord, our Lord, how majestic is thy name in all the earth!

662 Psalm 19:1-14

(Responsively, Antiphonally, or Unison)

The heavens are telling the glory of God;

And the firmament proclaims his handiwork.

Day to day pours forth speech, and night to night declares knowledge.

There is no speech, nor are there words; their voice is not heard;

Yet their voice goes out through all the earth,

And their words to the end of the world.

In them he has set a tent for the sun which comes forth like a bridegroom leaving his chamber,

And like a strong man runs its course with joy.

Its rising is from the end of the heavens, and its circuit to the end of them;

And there is nothing hid from its heat.

The law of the Lord is perfect, reviving the soul;

The testimony of the Lord is sure, making wise the simple;

The precepts of the Lord are right, rejoicing the heart;

The commandment of the Lord is pure, enlightening the eyes;

The fear of the Lord is clean, enduring for ever;

The ordinances of the Lord are true, and righteous altogether.

More to be desired are they than gold, even much fine gold;

Sweeter also than honey and drippings of the honeycomb.

Moreover by them is thy servant warned;

In keeping them there is great reward.

But who can discern his errors?

Clear thou me from hidden faults.

Keep back thy servant also from presumptuous sins;

Let them not have dominion over me!

Then I shall be blameless, and innocent of great transgression.

Let the words of my mouth and the meditation of my heart be acceptable in thy sight, O Lord, my rock and my redeemer.

663 Psalm 23:1-6
(Unison)

The Lord is my shepherd; I shall not want. He maketh me to lie down in green pastures: he leadeth me beside the still waters. He restoreth my soul: he leadeth me in the paths of righteousness for his name's sake. Yea, though I walk through the valley of the shadow of death, I will fear no evil; for thou art with me; thy rod and thy staff they comfort me. Thou preparest a table before me in the presence of mine enemies: thou anointest my head with oil; my cup runneth over. Surely goodness and mercy shall follow me all the days of my life: and I will dwell in the house of the Lord for ever.

664 Psalm 24:1-10
(Responsively, Antiphonally, or Unison)

The earth is the Lord's and the fulness thereof, the world and those who dwell therein;

For he has founded it upon the seas, and established it upon the rivers.

Who shall ascend the hill of the Lord? And who shall stand in his holy place?

He who has clean hands and a pure heart, who does not lift up his soul to what is false, and does not swear deceitfully.

He will receive blessing from the Lord, and vindication from the God of his salvation.

Such is the generation of those who seek him, who seek the face of the God of Jacob.

Lift up your heads, O gates! and be lifted up, O ancient doors!

That the King of glory may come in.

Who is the King of glory?

The Lord, strong and mighty, the Lord, mighty in battle!

Lift up your heads, O gates! and be lifted up, O ancient doors!

That the King of glory may come in!

Who is this King of glory?

The Lord of hosts, he is the King of glory!

665   Psalm 27:1-5, 11-14
(Antiphonally or Unison)

The Lord is my light and my salvation; whom shall I fear?

The Lord is the stronghold of my life; of whom shall I be afraid?

When evildoers assail me, uttering slanders against me,

My adversaries and foes, they shall stumble and fall.

Though a host encamp against me, my heart shall not fear;

Though war arise against me, yet I will be confident.

One thing have I asked of the Lord, that will I seek after;

That I may dwell in the house of the Lord all the days of my life, to behold the beauty of the Lord, and to inquire in his temple.

For he will hide me in his shelter in the day of trouble;

He will conceal me under the cover of his tent, he will set me high upon a rock.

Teach me thy way, O Lord; and lead me on a level path because of my enemies.

Give me not up to the will of my adversaries; for false witnesses have risen against me, and they breathe out violence.

I believe that I shall see the goodness of the Lord in the land of the living!

Wait for the Lord; be strong, and let your heart take courage; yea, wait for the Lord!

666   Psalm 32:1-11
(Responsively, Antiphonally, or Unison)

Blessed is he whose transgression is forgiven, whose sin is covered.

Blessed is the man to whom the Lord imputes no iniquity, and in whose spirit there is no deceit.

When I declared not my sin, my body wasted away through my groaning all day long.

For day and night thy hand was heavy upon me; my strength was dried up as by the heat of summer.

I acknowledged my sin to thee, and I did not hide my iniquity; I said, "I will confess my transgressions to the Lord";

Then thou didst forgive the guilt of my sin.

Therefore let everyone who is godly offer prayer to thee;

At a time of distress, in the rush of great waters, they shall not reach him.

Thou art a hiding place for me, thou preservest me from trouble;

Thou dost encompass me with deliverance.

I will instruct you and teach you the way you should go; I will counsel you with my eye upon you.

Be not like a horse or a mule, without understanding, which must be curbed with bit and bridle, else it will not keep with you.

Many are the pangs of the wicked; but steadfast love surrounds him who trusts in the Lord.

Be glad in the Lord, and rejoice, O righteous, and shout for joy, all you upright in heart!

667 Psalm 34:1-10, 15-18
(Responsively, Antiphonally, or Unison)

I will bless the Lord at all times; his praise shall continually be in my mouth.

My soul makes its boast in the Lord; let the afflicted hear and be glad.

O magnify the Lord with me, and let us exalt his name together!

I sought the Lord, and he answered me, and delivered me from all my fears.

Look to him, and be radiant; so your faces shall never be ashamed.

This poor man cried, and the Lord heard him, and saved him out of all his troubles.

The angel of the Lord encamps around those who fear him, and delivers them.

O taste and see that the Lord is good! Happy is the man who takes refuge in him!

O fear the Lord, you his saints, for those who fear him have no want!

The young lions suffer want and hunger; but those who seek the Lord lack no good thing.

The eyes of the Lord are toward the righteous, and his ears toward their cry.

The face of the Lord is against evildoers, to cut off the remembrance of them from the earth.

When the righteous cry for help, the Lord hears, and delivers them out of all their troubles.

The Lord is near to the brokenhearted, and saves the crushed in spirit.

668 Psalm 42:1-11
(Responsively, Antiphonally, or Unison)

As a hart longs for flowing streams, so longs my soul for thee, O God.

My soul thirsts for God, for the living God.

When shall I come and behold the face of God?

My tears have been my food day and night, while men say to me continually, "Where is your God?"

These things I remember, as I pour out my soul:

How I went with the throng, and led them in procession to the house of God, with glad shouts and songs of thanksgiving, a multitude keeping festival.

Why are you cast down, O my soul, and why are you disquieted within me?

Hope in God; for I shall again praise him, my help and my God.

My soul is cast down within me, therefore I remember thee from the land of Jordan and of Hermon, from Mount Mizar.

Deep calls to deep at the thunder of thy cataracts; all thy waves and thy billows have gone over me.

By day the Lord commands his steadfast love;

And at night his song is with me, a prayer to the God of my life.

I say to God, my rock: "Why hast thou forgotten me? Why go I mourning because of the oppression of the enemy?"

As with a deadly wound in my body, my adversaries taunt me, while they say to me continually, "Where is your God?"

Why are you cast down, O my soul, and why are you disquieted within me?

Hope in God; for I shall again praise him, my help and my God.

669 Psalm 46:1-11

(Responsively, Antiphonally, or Unison)

God is our refuge and strength, a very present help in trouble.

Therefore we will not fear though the earth should change, though the mountains shake in the heart of the sea;

Though its waters roar and foam, though the mountains tremble with its tumult.

There is a river whose streams make glad the city of God, the holy habitation of the Most High.

God is in the midst of her, she shall not be moved; God will help her right early.

The nations rage, the kingdoms totter;

He utters his voice, the earth melts.

The Lord of hosts is with us; the God of Jacob is our refuge.

Come, behold the works of the Lord, how he has wrought desolations in the earth.

He makes wars cease to the end of the earth; he breaks the bow, and shatters the spear, he burns the chariots with fire!

"Be still, and know that I am God. I am exalted among the nations, I am exalted in the earth!"

The Lord of hosts is with us; the God of Jacob is our refuge.

670 Psalm 51:1-17

(Responsively, Antiphonally, or Unison)

Have mercy on me, O God, according to thy steadfast love; according to thy abundant mercy blot out my transgressions.

Wash me thoroughly from my iniquity, and cleanse me from my sin!

For I know my transgressions, and my sin is ever before me.

Against thee, thee only, have I sinned, and done that which is evil in thy sight, so that thou art justified in thy sentence and blameless in thy judgment.

Behold, I was brought forth in iniquity, and in sin did my mother conceive me.

Behold, thou desirest truth in the inward being; therefore teach me wisdom in my secret heart.

Purge me with hyssop, and I shall be clean; wash me, and I shall be whiter than snow.

Fill me with joy and gladness; let the bones which thou hast broken rejoice.

Hide thy face from my sins, and blot out all my iniquities.

Create in me a clean heart, O God, and put a new and right spirit within me.

Cast me not away from thy presence, and take not thy Holy Spirit from me.

Restore to me the joy of thy salvation, and uphold me with a willing spirit.

Then I will teach transgressors thy ways, and sinners will return to thee.

Deliver me from bloodguiltiness, O God, thou God of my salvation, and my tongue will sing aloud of thy deliverance.

O Lord, open thou my lips, and my mouth shall show forth thy praise.

For thou hast no delight in sacrifice; were I to give a burnt offering, thou wouldst not be pleased.

The sacrifice acceptable to God is a broken spirit;

A broken and contrite heart, O God, thou wilt not despise.

671 Psalm 84:1-12
(Responsively, Antiphonally, or Unison)

How lovely is thy dwelling place, O Lord of hosts!

My soul longs, yea, faints for the courts of the Lord; my heart and flesh sing for joy to the living God.

Even the sparrow finds a home, and the swallow a nest for herself, where she may lay her young, at thy altars, O Lord of hosts, my King and my God.

Blessed are those who dwell in thy house, ever singing thy praise!

Blessed are the men whose strength is in thee, in whose heart are the highways to Zion.

As they go through the valley of Baca they make it a place of springs; the early rain also covers it with pools.

They go from strength to strength; the God of gods will be seen in Zion.

O Lord God of hosts, hear my prayer; give ear, O God of Jacob!

Behold our shield, O God; look upon the face of thine anointed!

For a day in thy courts is better than a thousand elsewhere.

I would rather be a doorkeeper in the house of my God than dwell in the tents of wickedness.

For the Lord God is a sun and shield; he bestows favor and honor.

No good thing does the Lord withhold from those who walk uprightly.

O Lord of hosts, blessed is the man who trusts in thee!

672 Psalm 90:1-12
(Responsively, Antiphonally, or Unison)

Lord, thou hast been our dwelling place in all generations.

Before the mountains were brought forth, or ever thou hadst formed the earth and the world, from everlasting to everlasting thou art God.

Thou turnest man back to the dust, and sayest, "Turn back, O children of men!"

For a thousand years in thy sight are but as yesterday when it is past, or as a watch in the night.

Thou dost sweep men away; they are like a dream, like grass which is renewed in the morning:

In the morning it flourishes and is renewed; in the evening it fades and withers.

For we are consumed by thy anger; by thy wrath we are overwhelmed.

Thou hast set our iniquities before thee, our secret sins in the light of thy countenance.

For all our days pass away under thy wrath, our years come to an end like a sigh.

The years of our life are three-score and ten, or even by reason of strength fourscore; yet their span is but toil and trouble; they are soon gone, and we fly away.

Who considers the power of thy anger, and thy wrath according to the fear of thee?

So teach us to number our days that we may get a heart of wisdom.

673 Psalm 91:1-16

(Responsively, Antiphonally, or Unison)

He who dwells in the shelter of the Most High, who abides in the shadow of the Almighty, will say to the Lord, "My refuge and my fortress; my God, in whom I trust."

For he will deliver you from the snare of the fowler and from the deadly pestilence;

He will cover you with his pinions, and under his wings you will find refuge;

His faithfulness is a shield and buckler.

You will not fear the terror of the night,

Nor the arrow that flies by day,

Nor the pestilence that stalks in darkness,

Nor the destruction that wastes at noonday.

A thousand may fall at your side, ten thousand at your right hand; but it will not come near you.

You will only look with your eyes and see the recompense of the wicked.

Because you have made the Lord your refuge, the Most High your habitation, no evil shall befall you, no scourge come near your tent.

For he will give his angels charge of you to guard you in all your ways.

On their hands they will bear you up, lest you dash your foot against a stone.

You will tread on the lion and the adder, the young lion and the serpent you will trample under foot.

Because he cleaves to me in love, I will deliver him;

I will protect him, because he knows my name.

When he calls to me, I will answer him; I will be with him in trouble, I will rescue him and honor him.

With long life I will satisfy him, and show him my salvation.

674 Psalm 95:1-7a

(Responsively, Antiphonally, or Unison)

O come, let us sing to the Lord;

Let us make a joyful noise to the rock of our salvation!

Let us come into his presence with thanksgiving;

Let us make a joyful noise to him with songs of praise!

For the Lord is a great God,

And a great King above all gods.

In his hand are the depths of the earth;

The heights of the mountains are his also.

The sea is his, for he made it;

For his hands formed the dry land.

O come, let us worship and bow down, let us kneel before the Lord, our Maker!

For he is our God, and we are the people of his pasture, and the sheep of his hand.

675 Psalm 100:1-5

(Unison)

Make a joyful noise to the Lord, all the lands! Serve the Lord with gladness! Come into his presence with singing!

Know that the Lord is God! It is he that made us, and we are his; we are his people, and the sheep of his pasture.

Enter his gates with thanksgiving, and his courts with praise! Give thanks to him, bless his name!

For the Lord is good; his steadfast love endures for ever, and his faithfulness to all generations.

676 Psalm 103:1-22

(Responsively, Antiphonally, or Unison)

Bless the Lord, O my soul; and all that is within me, bless his holy name!

Bless the Lord, O my soul, and forget not all his benefits,

Who forgives all your iniquity,

Who heals all your diseases,

Who redeems your life from the Pit,

Who crowns you with steadfast love and mercy,

Who satisfies you with good as long as you live so that your youth is renewed like the eagle's.

The Lord works vindication and justice for all who are oppressed.

He made known his ways to Moses, his acts to the people of Israel.

The Lord is merciful and gracious, slow to anger and abounding in steadfast love.

He will not always chide, nor will he keep his anger for ever.

He does not deal with us according to our sins, nor requite us according to our iniquities.

For as the heavens are high above the earth, so great is his steadfast love toward those who fear him;

As far as the east is from the west, so far does he remove our transgressions from us.

As a father pities his children, so the Lord pities those who fear him.

For he knows our frame; he remembers that we are dust.

As for man, his days are like grass; he flourishes like a flower of the field;

For the wind passes over it, and it is gone, and its place knows it no more.

But the steadfast love of the Lord is from everlasting to everlasting upon those who fear him,

And his righteousness to children's children,

To those who keep his covenant and remember to do his commandments.

The Lord has established his throne in the heavens, and his kingdom rules over all.

Bless the Lord, O you his angels, you mighty ones who do his word, hearkening to the voice of his word!

Bless the Lord, all his hosts, his ministers that do his will!

Bless the Lord, all his works, in all places of his dominion.

Bless the Lord, O my soul!

677 Psalm 121:1-8
(Responsively, Antiphonally, or Unison)

I lift up my eyes to the hills. From whence does my help come?

My help comes from the Lord, who made heaven and earth.

He will not let your foot be moved, he who keeps you will not slumber.

Behold, he who keeps Israel will neither slumber nor sleep.

The Lord is your keeper; the Lord is your shade on your right hand.

The sun shall not smite you by day, nor the moon by night.

The Lord will keep you from all evil; he will keep your life.

The Lord will keep your going out and your coming in from this time forth and for evermore.

678 Psalm 136:1-26
(Responsively)

O give thanks to the Lord, for he is good,

For his steadfast love endures for ever.

O give thanks to the God of gods,

For his steadfast love endures for ever.

O give thanks to the Lord of lords,

For his steadfast love endures for ever;

To him who alone does great wonders,

For his steadfast love endures for ever;

To him who by understanding made the heavens,

For his steadfast love endures for ever;

To him who spread out the earth upon the waters,

For his steadfast love endures for ever;

To him who made the great lights,

For his steadfast love endures for ever;

The sun to rule over the day,

For his steadfast love endures for ever;

The moon and stars to rule over the night,

For his steadfast love endures for ever;

To him who smote the first-born of Egypt,

For his steadfast love endures for ever;

And brought Israel out from among them,

For his steadfast love endures for ever;

With a strong hand and an outstretched arm,

For his steadfast love endures for ever;

To him who divided the Red Sea in sunder,

For his steadfast love endures for ever;

And made Israel pass through the midst of it,

For his steadfast love endures for ever;

But overthrew Pharaoh and his host in the Red Sea,

For his steadfast love endures for ever;

To him who led his people through the wilderness,

For his steadfast love endures for ever;

To him who smote great kings,

For his steadfast love endures for ever;

And slew famous kings,

For his steadfast love endures for ever;

Sihon, king of the Amorites,

For his steadfast love endures for ever;

And Og, king of Bashan,

For his steadfast love endures for ever;

And gave their land as a heritage,

For his steadfast love endures for ever;

A heritage to Israel his servant,

For his steadfast love endures for ever.

It is he who remembered us in our low estate,

For his steadfast love endures for ever;

And rescued us from our foes,

For his steadfast love endures for ever;

He who gives food to all flesh,

For his steadfast love endures for ever.

O give thanks to the God of heaven,

For his steadfast love endures for ever.

679 Isaiah 9:2-7

(Unison)

The people who walked in darkness have seen a great light;

Those who dwelt in a land of deep darkness, on them has light shined.

Thou hast multiplied the nation, thou hast increased its joy;

They rejoice before thee as with joy at the harvest, as men rejoice when they divide the spoil.

For the yoke of his burden, and the staff for his shoulder, the rod of his oppressor, thou hast broken as on the day of Midian.

For every boot of the tramping warrior in battle tumult and every garment rolled in blood will be burned as fuel for the fire.

For to us a child is born, to us a son is given;

And the government will be upon his shoulder, and his name will be called "Wonderful Counselor, Mighty God, Everlasting Father, Prince of Peace."

Of the increase of his government and of peace there will be no end,

Upon the throne of David, and over his kingdom, to establish it, and to uphold it

With justice and with righteousness from this time forth and for evermore.

The zeal of the Lord of hosts will do this.

680

Isaiah 11:1-9

(Antiphonally or Responsively)

There shall come forth a shoot from the stump of Jesse,

And a branch shall grow out of his roots.

And the Spirit of the Lord shall rest upon him, the spirit of wisdom and understanding, the spirit of counsel and might, the spirit of knowledge and the fear of the Lord.

And his delight shall be in the fear of the Lord.

He shall not judge by what his eyes see, or decide by what his ears hear;

But with righteousness he shall judge the poor, and decide with equity for the meek of the earth;

And he shall smite the earth with the rod of his mouth, and with the breath of his lips he shall slay the wicked.

Righteousness shall be the girdle of his waist, and faithfulness the girdle of his loins.

The wolf shall dwell with the lamb, and the leopard shall lie down with the kid,

And the calf and the lion and the fatling together, and a little child shall lead them.

The cow and the bear shall feed; their young shall lie down together; and the lion shall eat straw like the ox.

The sucking child shall play over the hole of the asp, and the weaned child shall put his hand on the adder's den.

They shall not hurt or destroy in all my holy mountain;

For the earth shall be full of the knowledge of the Lord as the waters cover the sea.

681

Isaiah 40:1-11

(Unison or Antiphonally)

Comfort, comfort my people, says your God. Speak tenderly to Jerusalem, and cry to her that her warfare is ended, that her iniquity is pardoned, that she has received from the Lord's hand double for all her sins.

A voice cries:
"In the wilderness prepare the way of the Lord, make straight in the desert a highway for our God. Every valley shall be lifted up, and every mountain and hill be made low; the uneven ground shall become level, and the rough places a plain. And the glory of the Lord shall be revealed, and all flesh shall see it together, for the mouth of the Lord has spoken."

A voice says, "Cry!" And I said, "What shall I cry?" All flesh is grass, and all its beauty is like the flower of the field. The grass withers, the flower fades, when the breath of the Lord blows upon it; surely the people is grass. The grass withers, the flower fades; but the word of our God will stand for ever.

Get you up to a high mountain, O Zion, herald of good tidings, lift up your voice with strength, O Jerusalem, herald of good tidings, lift it up, fear not; say to the cities of Judah, "Behold your God!" Behold, the Lord God comes with might, and his arm rules for him; behold, his reward is with him, and his recompense before him. He will feed his flock like a shepherd, he will gather the lambs in his arms, he will carry them in his bosom, and gently lead those that are with young.

682 Isaiah 40:27-31

(Unison)

Why do you say, O Jacob, and speak, O Israel, "My way is hid from the Lord, and my right is disregarded by my God"? Have you not known? Have you not heard? The Lord is the everlasting God, the Creator of the ends of the earth. He does not faint or grow weary, his understanding is unsearchable. He gives power to the faint, and to him who has no might he increases strength. Even youths shall faint and be weary, and young men shall fall exhausted; but they who wait for the Lord shall renew their strength, they shall mount up with wings like eagles, they shall run and not be weary, they shall walk and not faint.

683 Isaiah 53:1-12

(Antiphonally)

Who has believed what we have heard? And to whom has the arm of the Lord been revealed?

For he grew up before him like a young plant, and like a root out of dry ground;

He had no form or comeliness that we should look at him, and no beauty that we should desire him.

He was despised and rejected by men; a man of sorrows, and acquainted with grief;

And as one from whom men hide their faces he was despised, and we esteemed him not.

Surely he has borne our griefs and carried our sorrows;

Yet we esteemed him stricken, smitten by God, and afflicted.

But he was wounded for our transgressions, he was bruised for our iniquities;

Upon him was the chastisement that made us whole, and with his stripes we are healed.

All we like sheep have gone astray; we have turned every one to his own way;

And the Lord has laid on him the iniquity of us all.

He was oppressed, and he was afflicted, yet he opened not his mouth;

Like a lamb that is led to the slaughter, and like a sheep that before its shearers is dumb, so he opened not his mouth.

By oppression and judgment he was taken away; and as for his generation, who considered that he was cut off out of the land of the living, stricken for the transgression of my people?

And they made his grave with the wicked and with a rich man in his death, although he had done no violence, and there was no deceit in his mouth.

Yet it was the will of the Lord to bruise him; he has put him to grief;

When he makes himself an offering for sin, he shall see his offspring, he shall prolong his days;

The will of the Lord shall prosper in his hand; he shall see the fruit of the travail of his soul and be satisfied;

By his knowledge shall the righteous one, my servant, make many to be accounted righteous; and he shall bear their iniquities.

Therefore I will divide him a portion with the great, and he shall divide the spoil with the strong;

Because he poured out his soul to death, and was numbered with the transgressors;

Yet he bore the sin of many, and made intercession for the transgressors.

684 Jeremiah 31:31-34
(Unison)

Behold, the days are coming, says the Lord, when I will make a new covenant with the house of Israel and the house of Judah, not like the covenant which I made with their fathers when I took them by the hand to bring them out of the land of Egypt, my covenant which they broke, though I was their husband, says the Lord. But this is the covenant which I will make with the house of Israel after those days, says the Lord: I will put my law within them, and I will write it upon their hearts; and I will be their God, and they shall be my people. And no longer shall each man teach his neighbor and each his brother, saying, "Know the Lord," for they shall all know me, from the least of them to the greatest, says the Lord; for I will forgive their iniquity, and I will remember their sin no more.

685 Lamentations 3:22-27, 31-42
(Antiphonally)

The steadfast love of the Lord never ceases, his mercies never come to an end; they are new every morning; great is thy faithfulness. "The Lord is my portion," says my soul, "therefore I will hope in him."

The Lord is good to those who wait for him, to the soul that seeks him. It is good that one should wait quietly for the salvation of the Lord. It is good for a man that he bear the yoke in his youth.

For the Lord will not cast off for ever, but, though he cause grief, he will have compassion according to the abundance of his steadfast love; for he does not willingly afflict or grieve the sons of men.

To crush under foot all the prisoners of the earth, to turn aside the right of a man in the presence of the Most High, to subvert a man in his cause, the Lord does not approve.

Who has commanded and it came to pass, unless the Lord has ordained it? Is it not from the mouth of the Most High that good and evil come? Why should a living man complain, a man, about the punishment of his sins?

Let us test and examine our ways, and return to the Lord! Let us lift up our hearts and hands to God in heaven: "We have transgressed and rebelled, and thou hast not forgiven."

686 Daniel 9:4b-7a, 8b-10, 12, 13, 15, 18, 19
(Unison)

O Lord, the great and terrible God, who keepest covenant and steadfast love with those who love him and keep his commandments,

(Unison or Antiphonal)

We have sinned and done wrong and acted wickedly and rebelled, turning aside from thy commandments and ordinances;

We have not listened to thy servants the prophets, who spoke in thy name to our kings, our princes, and our fathers, and to all the people of the land.

To thee, O Lord, belongs righteousness, but to us confusion of face, to our kings, to our princes, and to our fathers, because we have sinned against thee.

To the Lord our God belong mercy and forgiveness; because we have rebelled against him, and have not obeyed the voice of the Lord our God by following his laws, which he set before us by his servants the prophets.

He has confirmed his words, which he spoke against us and against our rulers who ruled us, by bringing upon us a great calamity.

As it is written in the law of Moses, all this calamity has come upon us, yet we have not entreated the favor of the Lord our God, turning from our iniquities and giving heed to thy truth.

And now, O Lord our God, who didst bring thy people out of the land of Egypt with a mighty hand, and hast made thee a name, as at this day, we have sinned, we have done wickedly.

O my God, incline thy ear and hear; open thy eyes and behold our desolations, and the city which is called by thy name; for we do not present our supplications before thee on the ground of our righteousness, but on the ground of thy great mercy.

(Unison)

O Lord, hear; O Lord, forgive; O Lord, give heed and act; delay not, for thy own sake, O my God, because thy city and thy people are called by thy name.

687
Micah 4:1-4
(Unison)

It shall come to pass in the latter days that the mountain of the house of the Lord

Shall be established as the highest of the mountains, and shall be raised up above the hills;

And peoples shall flow to it, and many nations shall come, and say:

"Come, let us go up to the mountain of the Lord, to the house of the God of Jacob;

That he may teach us his ways and we may walk in his paths."

For out of Zion shall go forth the law, and the word of the Lord from Jerusalem.

He shall judge between many peoples, and shall decide for strong nations afar off;

And they shall beat their swords into plowshares, and their spears into pruning hooks;

Nation shall not lift up sword against nation, neither shall they learn war any more;

But they shall sit every man under his vine and under his fig tree, and none shall make them afraid; for the mouth of the Lord of hosts has spoken.

688
Micah 6:1-8
(Antiphonally)

Hear what the Lord says: Arise, plead your case before the mountains, and let the hills hear your voice. Hear, you mountains, the controversy of the Lord, and you enduring foundations of the earth; for the Lord has a controversy with his people, and he will contend with Israel.

"O my people, what have I done to you? In what have I wearied you? Answer me! For I brought you up from the land of Egypt, and redeemed you from the house of bondage; and I sent before you Moses, Aaron, and Miriam. O my people, remember what Balak king of Moab devised, and what Balaam the son of Beor answered him, and what happened from Shittim to Gilgal, that you may know the saving acts of the Lord."

"With what shall I come before the Lord, and bow myself before God on high? Shall I come before him with burnt offerings, with calves a year old? Will the Lord be pleased with thousands of rams, with ten thousands of rivers of oil? Shall I give my first-born for my transgression, the fruit of my body for the sin of my soul?"

He has showed you, O man, what is good; and what does the Lord require of you but to do justice, and to love kindness, and to walk humbly with your God?

689 Matthew 6:1-18
(Antiphonally)

Beware of practicing your piety before men, in order to be seen by them; for then you will have no reward from your Father who is in heaven.

Thus, when you give alms, sound no trumpet before you, as the hypocrites do in the synagogues and in the streets, that they may be praised by men. Truly, I say to you, they have their reward. But when you give alms, do not let your left hand know what your right hand is doing, so that your alms may be in secret; and your Father who sees in secret will reward you.

And when you pray, you must not be like the hypocrites; for they love to stand and pray in the synagogues and at the street corners, that they may be seen by men. Truly, I say to you, they have their reward. But when you pray, go into your room and shut the door and pray to your Father who is in secret; and your Father who sees in secret will reward you.

And in praying do not heap up empty phrases as the Gentiles do; for they think that they will be heard for their many words. Do not be like them, for your Father knows what you need before you ask him. Pray then like this:

(Unison)
Our Father who art in heaven, Hallowed be thy name. Thy kingdom come, Thy will be done, On earth as it is in heaven. Give us this day our daily bread; And forgive us our debts, As we also have forgiven our debtors; And lead us not into temptation, But deliver us from evil.

For if you forgive men their trespasses, your heavenly Father also will forgive you; but if you do not forgive men their trespasses, neither will your Father forgive your trespasses.

And when you fast, do not look dismal, like the hypocrites, for they disfigure their faces that their fasting may be seen by men. Truly, I say to you, they have their reward. But when you fast, anoint your head and wash your face, that your fasting may not be seen by men but by your Father who is in secret; and your Father who sees in secret will reward you.

690 Matthew 6:25-33
(Antiphonally)

Therefore I bid you put away anxious thoughts about food and drink to keep you alive, and clothes to cover your body.

Surely life is more than food, the body more than clothes.

Look at the birds of the air; they do not sow and reap and store in barns, yet your heavenly Father feeds them. You are worth more than the birds!

Is there a man of you who by anxious thought can add a foot to his height? And why be anxious about clothes?

Consider how the lilies grow in the fields; they do not work, they do not spin; and yet, I tell you, even Solomon in all his splendour was not attired like one of these.

But if that is how God clothes the grass in the fields, which is there today, and tomorrow is thrown on the stove, will he not all the more clothe you? How little faith you have!

No, do not ask anxiously, "What are we to eat? What are we to drink? What shall we wear?"

All these are things for the heathen to run after, not for you, because your heavenly Father knows that you need them all.

Set your mind on God's kingdom and his justice before everything else, and all the rest will come to you as well.

So do not be anxious about tomorrow; tomorrow will look after itself. Each day has troubles enough of its own.

691 Matthew 13:31-33, 44-52
(Unison or Antiphonally)

Another parable he put before them, saying, "The kingdom of heaven is like a grain of mustard seed which a man took and sowed in his field; it is the smallest of all seeds, but when it has grown it is the greatest of shrubs and becomes a tree, so that the birds of the air come and make nests in its branches."

He told them another parable. "The kingdom of heaven is like leaven which a woman took and hid in three measures of meal, till it was all leavened."

"The kingdom of heaven is like treasure hidden in a field, which a man found and covered up; then in his joy he goes and sells all that he has and buys that field.

"Again, the kingdom of heaven is like a merchant in search of fine pearls, who, on finding one pearl of great value, went and sold all that he had and bought it.

"Again, the kingdom of heaven is like a net which was thrown into the sea and gathered fish of every kind; when it was full, men drew it ashore and sat down and sorted the good into vessels but threw away the bad. So it will be at the close of the age. The angels will come out and separate the evil from the righteous, and throw them into the furnace of fire; there men will weep and gnash their teeth.

"Have you understood all this?" They said to him, "Yes." And he said to them, "Therefore every scribe who has been trained for the kingdom of heaven is like a householder who brings out of his treasure what is new and what is old."

692 Matthew 18:10-22
(Antiphonally)

Never despise one of these little ones; I tell you, they have their guardian angels in heaven, who look continually on the face of my heavenly Father.

What do you think? Suppose a man has a hundred sheep. If one of them strays, does he not leave the other ninety-nine on the hillside and go in search of the one that strayed?

And if he should find it, I tell you this: he is more delighted over that sheep than over the ninety-nine that never strayed. In the same way, it is not your heavenly Father's will that one of these little ones should be lost.

If your brother commits a sin, go and take the matter up with him, strictly between yourselves, and if he listens to you, you have won your brother over.

If he will not listen, take one or two others with you, so that all facts may be duly established on the evidence of two or three witnesses.

If he refuses to listen to them, report the matter to the congregation; and if he will not listen even to the congregation, you must then treat him as you would a pagan or a tax-gatherer.

I tell you this: whatever you forbid on earth shall be forbidden in heaven, and whatever you allow on earth shall be allowed in heaven.

Again I tell you this: if two of you agree on earth about any request you have to make, that request will be granted by my heavenly Father. For where two or three have met together in my name, I am there among them.

693 Matthew 25:31-46
(Antiphonally)

When the Son of man comes in his glory, and all the angels with him, then he will sit on his glorious throne. Before him will be gathered all the nations, and he will separate them one from another as a shepherd separates the sheep from the goats, and he will place the sheep at his right hand, but the goats at the left.

Then the King will say to those at his right hand, "Come, O blessed of my Father, inherit the kingdom prepared for you from the founda-

tion of the world; for I was hungry and you gave me food, I was thirsty and you gave me drink, I was a stranger and you welcomed me, I was naked and you clothed me, I was sick and you visited me, I was in prison and you came to me."

Then the righteous will answer him, "Lord, when did we see thee hungry and feed thee, or thirsty and give thee drink? And when did we see thee a stranger and welcome thee, or naked and clothe thee? And when did we see thee sick or in prison and visit thee?"

And the King will answer them, "Truly, I say to you, as you did it to one of the least of these my brethren, you did it to me."

Then he will say to those at his left hand, "Depart from me, you cursed, into the eternal fire prepared for the devil and his angels; for I was hungry and you gave me no food, I was thirsty and you gave me no drink, I was a stranger and you did not welcome me, naked and you did not clothe me, sick and in prison and you did not visit me."

Then they also will answer, "Lord, when did we see thee hungry or thirsty or a stranger or naked or sick or in prison, and did not minister to thee?"

Then he will answer them, "Truly, I say to you, as you did it not to one of the least of these, you did it not to me."

And they will go away into eternal punishment, but the righteous into eternal life.

694 Mark 14:32-42
(Unison)

And they went to a place which was called Gethsemane; and he said to his disciples, "Sit here, while I pray." And he took with him Peter and James and John, and began to be greatly distressed and troubled. And he said to them, "My soul is very sorrowful, even to death; remain here, and watch." And going a little farther, he fell on the ground and prayed that, if it were possible, the hour might pass from him. And he said, "Abba, Father, all things are possible to thee; remove this cup from me; yet not what I will, but what thou wilt."

And he came and found them sleeping, and he said to Peter, "Simon, are you asleep? Could you not watch one hour? Watch and pray that you may not enter into temptation; the spirit indeed is willing, but the flesh is weak." And again he went away and prayed, saying the same words. And again he came and found them sleeping, for their eyes were very heavy; and they did not know what to answer him.

And he came the third time, and said to them, "Are you still sleeping and taking your rest? It is enough; the hour has come; the Son of man is betrayed into the hands of sinners. Rise, let us be going; see, my betrayer is at hand."

695 Luke 1:46b-55
(Unison)

My soul magnifies the Lord, and my spirit rejoices in God my Savior, for he has regarded the low estate of his handmaiden.

For behold, henceforth all generations will call me blessed; for he who is mighty has done great things for me, and holy is his name.

And his mercy is on those who fear him from generation to generation.

He has shown strength with his arm, he has scattered the proud in the imagination of their hearts, he has put down the mighty from their thrones, and exalted those of low degree; he has filled the hungry with good things, and the rich he has sent empty away.

He has helped his servant Israel, in remembrance of his mercy, as he spoke to our fathers, to Abraham and to his posterity for ever.

696 Luke 6:20b-36
(Antiphonally or Unison)

Blessed are you poor, for yours is the kingdom of God. Blessed are you that hunger now, for you shall be satisfied. Blessed are you that weep now, for you shall laugh. Blessed are you when men hate you, and when they exclude you and revile you, and cast out your name as evil, on account of the Son of man! Rejoice in that day, and leap for joy, for behold, your reward is great in heaven; for so their fathers did to the prophets.

But woe to you that are rich, for you have received your consolation. Woe to you that are full now, for you shall hunger. Woe to you that laugh now, for you shall mourn and weep. Woe to you, when all men speak well of you, for so their fathers did to the false prophets.

But I say to you that hear, Love your enemies, do good to those who hate you, bless those who curse you, pray for those who abuse you. To him who strikes you on the cheek, offer the other also; and from him who takes away your cloak do not withhold your coat as well. Give to every one who begs from you; and of him who takes away your goods do not ask them again. And as you wish that men would do to you, do so to them.

If you love those who love you, what credit is that to you? For even sinners love those who love them. And if you do good to those who do good to you, what credit is that to you? For even sinners do the same. And if you lend to those from whom you hope to receive, what credit is that to you? Even sinners lend to sinners, to receive as much again. But love your enemies, and do good, and lend, expecting nothing in return; and your reward will be great, and you will be sons of the Most High; for he is kind to the ungrateful and the selfish. Be merciful, even as your Father is merciful.

697 John 1:1-14
(Antiphonally)

In the beginning was the Word, and the Word was with God, and the Word was God. He was in the beginning with God; all things were made through him, and without him was not anything made that was made. In him was life, and the life was the light of men. The light shines in the darkness, and the darkness has not overcome it.

There was a man sent from God, whose name was John. He came for testimony, to bear witness to the light, that all might believe through him. He was not the light, but came to bear witness to the light.

The true light that enlightens every man was coming into the world. He was in the world, and the world was made through him, yet the world knew him not. He came to his own home, and his own people received him not.

But to all who received him, who believed in his name, he gave power to become children of God; who were born, not of blood nor of the will of the flesh nor of the will of man, but of God.

(Unison)
And the Word became flesh and dwelt among us, full of grace and truth; we have beheld his glory, glory as of the only Son from the Father.

698 John 3:3b-21
(Antiphonally or Unison)

"Truly, truly, I say to you, unless one is born anew, he cannot see the kingdom of God."

Nicodemus said to him, "How can a man be born when he is old? Can he enter a second time into his mother's womb and be born?"

Jesus answered, "Truly, truly, I say to you, unless one is born of water and the Spirit, he cannot enter the kingdom of God. That which is born of the flesh is flesh, and that which is born of the Spirit is spirit. Do not marvel that I said to you, 'You must be born anew.' The wind blows where it wills, and you hear the sound of it, but you do not know whence it comes or whither it goes; so it is with every one who is born of the Spirit."

Nicodemus said to him, "How can this be?"

Jesus answered him, "Are you a teacher of Israel, and yet you do not understand this? Truly, truly, I say to you, we-speak of what we know, and bear witness to what we have seen; but you do not receive our testimony. If I have told you earthly things and you do not believe, how can you believe if I tell you heavenly things? No one has ascended into heaven but he who descended from heaven, the Son of man. And as Moses lifted up the serpent in the wilderness, so must the Son of man be lifted up, that whoever believes in him may have eternal life."

For God so loved the world that he gave his only Son, that whoever believes in him should not perish but have eternal life. For God sent the Son into the world, not to condemn the world, but that the world might be saved through him.

He who believes in him is not condemned; he who does not believe is condemned already, because he has not believed in the name of the only Son of God. And this is the judgment, that the light has come into the world, and men loved darkness rather than light, because their deeds were evil.

For every one who does evil hates the light, and does not come to the light, lest his deeds should be exposed. But he who does what is true comes to the light, that it may be clearly seen that his deeds have been wrought in God.

699   John 6:35-40, 47-58
(Unison or Antiphonally)

Jesus said to them, "I am the bread of life; he who comes to me shall not hunger, and he who believes in me shall never thirst. But I said to you that you have seen me and yet do not believe.

All that the Father gives me will come to me; and him who comes to me I will not cast out. For I have come down from heaven, not to do my own will, but the will of him who sent me; and this is the will of him who sent me, that I should lose nothing of all that he has given me, but raise it up at the last day.

For this is the will of my Father, that every one who sees the Son and believes in him should have eternal life; and I will raise him up at the last day."

"Truly, truly, I say to you, he who believes has eternal life. I am the bread of life. Your fathers ate the manna in the wilderness, and they died. This is the bread which comes down from heaven, that a man may eat of it and not die.

I am the living bread which came down from heaven; if any one eats of this bread, he will live for ever; and the bread which I shall give for the life of the world is my flesh."

The Jews then disputed among themselves, saying, "How can this man give us his flesh to eat?"

So Jesus said to them, "Truly, truly, I say to you, unless you eat the flesh of the Son of man and drink his blood, you have no life in you; he who eats my flesh and drinks my blood has eternal life, and I will raise him up at the last day. For my flesh is food indeed, and my blood is drink indeed.

He who eats my flesh and drinks my blood abides in me, and I in him. As the living Father sent me, and I live because of the Father, so he who eats me will live because of me. This is the bread which came down from heaven, not such as the fathers ate and died; he who eats this bread will live for ever."

700   John 15:1-11
(Unison)

"I am the true vine, and my Father is the vinedresser. Every branch of mine that bears no fruit, he takes away, and every branch that does bear fruit he prunes, that it may bear more fruit. You are already made clean by the word which I have spoken to you.

"Abide in me, and I in you. As the branch cannot bear fruit by itself, unless it abides in the vine, neither can you, unless you abide in me. I am the vine, you are the branches. He who abides in me, and I in him, he it is that bears much fruit, for apart from me you can do nothing.

"If a man does not abide in me, he is cast forth as a branch and withers; and the branches are gathered, thrown into the fire and burned. If you abide in me, and my words abide in you, ask whatever you will, and it shall be done for you. By this my Father is glorified, that you bear much fruit, and so prove to be my disciples.

"As the Father has loved me, so have I loved you; abide in my love. If you keep my commandments, you will abide in my love, just as I have kept my Father's commandments and abide in his love. These things I have spoken to you, that my joy may be in you, and that your joy may be full."

701 John 17:3-6, 16-26

(Unison)

"And this is eternal life, that they know thee the only true God, and Jesus Christ whom thou hast sent. I glorified thee on earth, having accomplished the work which thou gavest me to do; and now, Father, glorify thou me in thy own presence with the glory which I had with thee before the world was made.

"I have manifested thy name to the men whom thou gavest me out of the world; thine they were, and thou gavest them to me, and they have kept thy word. They are not of the world, even as I am not of the world. Sanctify them in the truth;

thy word is truth. As thou didst send me into the world, so I have sent them into the world. And for their sake I consecrate myself, that they also may be consecrated in truth.

"I do not pray for these only, but also for those who believe in me through their word, that they may all be one; even as thou, Father, art in me, and I in thee, that they also may be in us, so that the world may believe that thou hast sent me. The glory which thou hast given me I have given to them, that they may be one even as we are one, I in them and thou in me, that they may become perfectly one, so that the world may know that thou hast sent me and hast loved them even as thou hast loved me.

"Father, I desire that they also, whom thou hast given me, may be with me where I am, to behold my glory which thou hast given me in thy love for me before the foundation of the world. O righteous Father, the world has not known thee, but I have known thee; and these know that thou hast sent me. I made known to them thy name, and I will make it known, that the love with which thou hast loved me may be in them, and I in them."

702 Romans 8:1-11

(Unison or Antiphonally)

There is therefore now no condemnation for those who are in Christ Jesus. For the law of the Spirit of life in Christ Jesus has set me free from the law of sin and death.

For God has done what the law, weakened by the flesh, could not do: sending his own Son in the likeness of sinful flesh and for sin, he condemned sin in the flesh, in order that the just requirement of the law might be fulfilled in us, who walk not according to the flesh but according to the Spirit.

For those who live according to the flesh set their minds on the things of the flesh, but those who live according to the Spirit set their minds on the things of the Spirit.

To set the mind on the flesh is death, but to set the mind on the Spirit is life and peace.

For the mind that is set on the flesh is hostile to God; it does not submit to God's law, indeed it cannot; and those who are in the flesh cannot please God.

But you are not in the flesh, you are in the Spirit, if the Spirit of God really dwells in you. Any one who does not have the Spirit of Christ does not belong to him.

But if Christ is in you, although your bodies are dead because of sin, your spirits are alive because of righteousness.

If the Spirit of him who raised Jesus from the dead dwells in you, he who raised Christ Jesus from the dead will give life to your mortal bodies also through his Spirit which dwells in you.

703 Romans 8:28-39

(Unison)

Moreover we know that to those who love God, who are called according to his plan, everything that happens fits into a pattern for good. God, in his foreknowledge, chose them to bear the family likeness of his Son, that he might be the eldest of a family of many brothers. He chose them long ago; when the time came he called them, he made them righteous in his sight and then lifted them to the splendor of life as his own sons.

(Unison or Antiphonally)
In face of all this, what is there left to say? If God is for us, who can be against us?

He that did not spare his own Son but gave him up for us all—can we not trust such a God to give us, with him, everything else that we can need?

Who dares accuse us now? The Judge himself has declared us free from sin. Who is in a position to condemn?

Only Christ, and Christ died for us, Christ rose for us, Christ reigns in power for us, Christ prays for us!

Can anything separate us from the love of Christ?

Can trouble, pain or persecution? Can lack of clothes and food, danger to life and limb, the threat of· force of arms?

Indeed some of us know the truth of that ancient text: For thy sake we are killed all the day long; We were accounted as sheep for the slaughter.

(Unison)

No, in all these things we win an overwhelming victory through him who has proved his love for us. I have become absolutely convinced that neither death nor life, neither messenger of Heaven nor monarch of earth, neither what happens today nor what happens tomorrow, neither a power from on high nor a power from below, nor anything else in God's whole world has any power to separate us from the love of God in Jesus Christ our Lord!

704 Romans 12:1, 2, 9-21

(Unison)

Therefore, my brothers, I implore you by God's mercy to offer your very selves to him: a living sacrifice, dedicated and fit for his acceptance, the worship offered by mind and heart. Adapt yourselves no longer to the pattern of this present world, but let your minds be remade and your whole nature thus transformed. Then you will be able to discern the will of God, and to know what is good, acceptable, and perfect.

(Unison or Antiphonally)

Love in all sincerity, loathing evil and clinging to the good. Let love for our brotherhood breed warmth of mutual affection. Give pride of place to one another in esteem.

With unflagging energy, in ardour of spirit, serve the Lord.

Let hope keep you joyful; in trouble stand firm; persist in prayer.

Contribute to the needs of God's people, and practise hospitality.

Call down blessings on your persecutors—blessings, not curses.

With the joyful be joyful, and mourn with the mourners.

Have equal regard for one another. Do not be haughty, but go about with humble folk. Do not keep thinking how wise you are.

Never pay back evil for evil. Let your aims be such as all men count honourable.

If possible, so far as it lies with you, live at peace with all men.

My dear friends, do not seek revenge, but leave a place for divine retribution; for there is a text which reads, 'Justice is mine, says the Lord, I will repay.'

But there is another text: 'If your enemy is hungry, feed him; if he is thirsty, give him a drink; by doing this you will heap live coals on his head.'

(Unison)
Do not let evil conquer you, but use good to defeat evil.

705   1 Corinthians 13:1-13

(Unison)

If I speak in the tongues of men and of angels, but have not love, I am a noisy gong or a clanging cymbal. And if I have prophetic powers, and understand all mysteries and all knowledge, and if I have all faith, so as to remove mountains, but have not love, I am nothing. If I give away all I have, and if I deliver my body to be burned, but have not love, I gain nothing.

Love is patient and kind; love is not jealous or boastful; it is not arrogant or rude. Love does not insist on its own way; it is not irritable or resentful; it does not rejoice at wrong, but rejoices in the right. Love bears all things, believes all things, hopes all things, endures all things.

Love never ends; as for prophecies, they will pass away; as for tongues, they will cease; as for knowledge, it will pass away. For our knowledge is imperfect and our prophecy is imperfect; but when the perfect comes, the imperfect will pass away. When I was a child, I spoke like a child, I thought like a child, I reasoned like a child; when I became a man, I gave up childish ways. For now we see in a mirror dimly, but then face to face. Now I know in part; then I shall understand fully, even as I have been fully understood. So faith, hope, love abide, these three; but the greatest of these is love.

706   1 Corinthians 15:20b-26, 51-58

(Responsively, Antiphonally, or Unison)
Christ has been raised from the dead, the first fruits of those who have fallen asleep.

For as by a man came death, by a man has come also the resurrection of the dead. For as in Adam all die, so also in Christ shall all be made alive. But each in his own order: Christ the first fruits, then at his coming those who belong to Christ.

Then comes the end, when he delivers the kingdom to God the Father after destroying every rule and every authority and power.

For he must reign until he has put all his enemies under his feet. The last enemy to be destroyed is death.

Lo! I tell you a mystery. We shall not all sleep, but we shall all be changed, in a moment, in the twinkling of an eye, at the last trumpet.

For the trumpet will sound, and the dead will be raised imperishable, and we shall be changed.

For this perishable nature must put on the imperishable, and this mortal nature must put on immortality. When the perishable puts on the imperishable, and the mortal puts on immortality, then shall come to pass the saying that is written:

"Death is swallowed up in victory." "O death, where is thy victory? O death, where is thy sting?"

The sting of death is sin, and the power of sin is the law. But thanks be to God, who gives us the victory through our Lord Jesus Christ.

Therefore, my beloved brethren, be steadfast, immovable, always abounding in the work of the Lord, knowing that in the Lord your labor is not in vain.

707   2 Corinthians 9:6b-15
(Antiphonally or Unison)

Sow bountifully, and you will reap bountifully. Each person should give

as he has decided for himself; there should be no reluctance, no sense of compulsion; God loves a cheerful giver.

And it is in God's power to provide you richly with every good gift; thus you will have ample means in yourselves to meet each and every situation, with enough and to spare for every good cause.

Scripture says of such a man: 'He has lavished his gifts on the needy, his benevolence stands fast for ever.'

Now he who provides seed for sowing and bread for food will provide the seed for you to sow; he will multiply it and swell the harvest of your benevolence, and you will always be rich enough to be generous.

Through our action such generosity will issue in thanksgiving to God, for as a piece of willing service this is not only a contribution towards the needs of God's people; more than that, it overflows in a flood of thanksgiving to God.

For through the proof which this affords, many will give honour to God when they see how humbly you obey him and how faithfully you confess the gospel of Christ; and will thank him for your liberal contribution to their need and to the general good.

And as they join in prayer on your behalf, their hearts will go out to you because of the richness of the grace which God has imparted to you.

(Unison)

Thanks be to God for his gift beyond words!

708   Philippians 2:1-11
(Unison)

Does your life in Christ make you

strong? Does his love comfort you? Do you have fellowship with the Spirit? Do you feel kindness and compassion for one another? I urge you, then, make me completely happy by having the same thoughts, sharing the same love, and being one in soul and mind. Don't do anything from selfish ambition, or from a cheap desire to boast; but be humble toward each other, never thinking you are better than others. And look out for each other's interests, not for just your own. The attitude you should have is the one that Christ Jesus had:

He always had the very nature of God,
But he did not think that by force he should try to become equal with God.
Instead, of his own free will he gave it all up,
And took the nature of a servant. He was born like man, he appeared in human likeness;
He was humble and walked the path of obedience to death—his death on the cross.
For this reason God raised him to the highest place above.
And gave him the name that is greater than any other name,
So that all beings in heaven, and on earth, and in the world below
Will fall on their knees,
In honor of the name of Jesus,
And all will openly proclaim that Jesus Christ is the Lord,
To the glory of God the Father.

709 Philippians 4:4-13

(Unison)

Rejoice in the Lord always; again I will say, Rejoice. Let all men know your forbearance. The Lord is at hand. Have no anxiety about anything, but in everything by prayer and supplication with thanksgiving let your requests be made known to God. And the peace of God, which passes all understanding, will keep your hearts and your minds in Christ Jesus.

Finally, brethren, whatever is true, whatever is honorable, whatever is just, whatever is pure, whatever is lovely, whatever is gracious, if there is any excellence, if there is anything worthy of praise, think about these things. What you have learned and received and heard and seen in me, do; and the God of peace will be with you.

I rejoice in the Lord greatly that now at length you have revived your concern for me; you were indeed concerned for me, but you had no opportunity. Not that I complain of want; for I have learned, in whatever state I am, to be content. I know how to be abased, and I know how to abound; in any and all circumstances I have learned the secret of facing plenty and hunger, abundance and want. I can do all things in him who strengthens me.

710 Colossians 3:1-17

(Antiphonally, Responsively, or Unison)

If then you have been raised with Christ, seek the things that are above, were Christ is, seated at the right hand of God.

Set your minds on things that are above, not on things that are on earth.

For you have died, and your life is hid with Christ in God.

When Christ who is our life appears, then you also will appear with him in glory.

Put to death therefore what is earthly in you: immorality, impurity, passion, evil desire, and covetousness, which is idolatry.

On account of these the wrath of God is coming.

In these you once walked, when you lived in them.

But now put them all away: anger, wrath, malice, slander, and foul talk from your mouth.

Do not lie to one another, seeing that you have put off the old nature with its practices and have put on the new nature, which is being renewed in knowledge after the image of its creator.

Here there cannot be Greek and Jew, circumcised and uncircumcised, barbarian, Scythian, slave, free man, but Christ is all, and in all.

Put on then, as God's chosen ones, holy and beloved, compassion, kindness, lowliness, meekness, and patience, forbearing one another and, if one has a complaint against another, forgiving each other; as the Lord has forgiven you, so you also must forgive.

And above all these put on love, which binds everything together in perfect harmony.

And let the peace of Christ rule in your hearts, to which indeed you were called in the one body. And be thankful.

Let the word of Christ dwell in you richly, as you teach and admonish one another in all wisdom, and as you sing psalms and hymns and spiritual songs with thankfulness in your hearts to God.

(Unison)

And whatever you do, in word or deed, do everything in the name of the Lord Jesus, giving thanks to God the Father through him.

711 1 Thessalonians 4:13-18
(Unison)

But we would not have you ignorant, brethren, concerning those who are asleep, that you may not grieve as others do who have no hope. For since we believe that Jesus died and rose again, even so, through Jesus, God will bring with him those who have fallen asleep. For this we declare to you by the word of the Lord, that we who are alive, who are left until the coming of the Lord, shall not precede those who have fallen asleep.

For the Lord himself will descend from heaven with a cry of command, with the archangel's call, and with the sound of the trumpet of God. And the dead in Christ will rise first; then we who are alive, who are left, shall be caught up together with them in the clouds to meet the Lord in the air; and so we shall always be with the Lord. Therefore comfort one another with these words.

712 1 Timothy 6:7-12, 17-19
(Unison)

We brought nothing into the world, because when we leave it we cannot take anything with us either, but if we have food and covering we may rest content. Those who want to be rich fall into temptations and snares and many foolish harmful desires which plunge men into ruin and perdition. The love of money is the root of all evil things, and there are some who in reaching for it have wandered from the faith and spiked themselves on many thorny griefs.

But you, man of God, must shun all this, and pursue justice, piety, fidelity, love, fortitude, and gentleness. Run the great race of faith and take hold of eternal life. For to this you were called; and you confessed your faith nobly before many witnesses.

Instruct those who are rich in this world's goods not to be proud, and not to fix their hopes on so uncertain a thing as money, but upon God, who endows us richly with all things to enjoy. Tell them to hoard a wealth of noble actions by doing good, to be ready to give away and to share, and so acquire a treasure which will form a good foundation for the future. Thus they will grasp the life which is life indeed.

713 Hebrews 11:1-6, 13-16, 39, 40; 12:1, 2

(Antiphonally)

Now faith is the assurance of things hoped for, the conviction of things not seen. For by it the men of old received divine approval.

By faith we understand that the world was created by the word of God, so that what is seen was made out of things which do not appear.

By faith Abel offered to God a more acceptable sacrifice than Cain, through which he received approval as righteous, God bearing witness by accepting his gifts; he died, but through his faith he is still speaking.

By faith Enoch was taken up so that he should not see death; and he was not found, because God had taken him. Now before he was taken he was attested as having pleased God.

And without faith it is impossible to please him. For whoever would draw near to God must believe that he exists and that he rewards those who seek him.

These all died in faith, not having received what was promised, but having seen it and greeted it from afar, and having acknowledged

that they were strangers and exiles on the earth.

For people who speak thus make it clear that they are seeking a homeland. If they had been thinking of that land from which they had gone out, they would have had opportunity to return. But as it is, they desire a better country, that is, a heavenly one.

Therefore God is not ashamed to be called their God, for he has prepared for them a city.

And all these, though well attested by their faith, did not receive what was promised, since God had foreseen something better for us, that apart from us they should not be made perfect.

(Unison)

Therefore, since we are surrounded by so great a cloud of witnesses, let us also lay aside every weight, and sin which clings so closely, and let us run with perseverance the race that is set before us, looking to Jesus the pioneer and perfecter of our faith, who for the joy that was set before him endured the cross, despising the shame, and is seated at the right hand of the throne of God.

714 James 1:12-27

(Unison)

Blessed is the man who endures trial, for when he has stood the test he will receive the crown of life which God has promised to those who love him. Let no one say when he is tempted, "I am tempted by God"; for God cannot be tempted with evil and he himself tempts no one; but each person is tempted when he is lured and enticed by his own desire. Then desire when it has conceived gives birth to sin; and sin when it is full-grown brings forth death.

Do not be deceived, my beloved brethren. Every good endowment and every perfect gift is from above, coming down from the Father of lights with whom there is no variation or shadow due to change. Of his own will he brought us forth by the word of truth that we should be a kind of first fruits of his creatures.

Know this, my beloved brethren. Let every man be quick to hear, slow to speak, slow to anger, for the anger of man does not work the righteousness of God. Therefore put away all filthiness and rank growth of wickedness and receive with meekness the implanted word, which is able to save your souls.

But be doers of the word, and not hearers only, deceiving yourselves. For if any one is a hearer of the word and not a doer, he is like a man who observes his natural face in a mirror; for he observes himself and goes away and at once forgets what he was like. But he who looks into the perfect law, the law of liberty, and perseveres, being no hearer that forgets but a doer that acts, he shall be blessed in his doing.

If any one thinks he is religious, and does not bridle his tongue but deceives his heart, this man's religion is vain. Religion that is pure and undefiled before God and the Father is this: to visit orphans and widows in their affliction, and to keep oneself unstained from the world.

715   1 John 1:1—2:2

(Antiphonally)

It was there from the beginning; we have heard it; we have seen it with our own eyes; we looked upon it, and felt it with our own hands; and it is of this we tell. Our theme is the word of life.

This life was made visible; we have seen it and bear our testimony; we here declare to you the eternal life which dwelt with the Father and was made visible to us. What we have seen and heard we declare to you, so that you and we together may share in a common life, that life which we share with the Father and his Son Jesus Christ. And we write this in order that the joy of us all may be complete.

Here is the message we heard from him and pass on to you: that God is light, and in him there is no darkness at all.

If we claim to be sharing in his life while we walk in the dark, our words and our lives are a lie;

But if we walk in the light as he himself is in the light, then we share together a common life, and we are being cleansed from every sin by the blood of Jesus his Son.

If we claim to be sinless, we are self-deceived and strangers to the truth.

If we confess our sins, he is just, and may be trusted to forgive our sins and cleanse us from every kind of wrong;

But if we say we have committed no sin, we make him out to be a liar, and then his word has no place in us.

My children, in writing thus to you my purpose is that you should not commit sin.

But should anyone commit a sin, we have one to plead our cause with the Father, Jesus Christ, and he is just.

(Unison)

He is himself the remedy for the defilement of our sins, not our sins only but the sins of all the world.

716

1 John 4:7-21

(Unison)

Beloved, let us love one another; for love is of God, and he who loves is born of God and knows God. He who does not love does not know God; for God is love. In this the love of God was made manifest among us, that God sent his only Son into the world, so that we might live through him. In this is love, not that we loved God but that he loved us and sent his Son to be the expiation for our sins. Beloved, if God so loved us, we also ought to love one another. No man has ever seen God; if we love one another, God abides in us and his love is perfected in us.

By this we know that we abide in him and he in us, because he has given us of his own Spirit. And we have seen and testify that the Father has sent his Son as the Savior of the world. Whoever confesses that Jesus is the Son of God, God abides in him, and he in God. So we know and believe the love God has for us.

God is love, and he who abides in love abides in God, and God abides in him. In this is love perfected with us, that we may have confidence for the day of judgment, because as he is so are we in this world. There is no fear in love, but perfect love casts out fear. For fear has to do with punishment, and he who fears is not perfected in love. We love, because he first loved us. If any one says, "I love God," and hates his brother, he is a liar; for he who does not love his brother whom he has seen, cannot love God whom he has not seen. And this commandment we have from him, that he who loves God should love his brother also.

717

Revelation 5:1-14

(Antiphonally)

And I saw in the right hand of him who was seated on the throne a scroll written within and on the back, sealed with seven seals; and I saw a strong angel proclaiming with a loud voice, "Who is worthy to open the scroll and break its seals?"

And no one in heaven or on earth or under the earth was able to open the scroll or to look into it, and I wept much that no one was found worthy to open the scroll or to look into it.

Then one of the elders said to me, "Weep not; lo, the Lion of the tribe of Judah, the Root of David, has conquered, so that he can open the scroll and its seven seals."

And between the throne and the four living creatures and among the elders, I saw a Lamb standing, as though it had been slain, with seven horns and with seven eyes, which are the seven spirits of God sent out into all the earth; and he went and took the scroll from the right hand of him who was seated on the throne.

And when he had taken the scroll, the four living creatures and the twenty-four elders fell down before the Lamb, each holding a harp, and with golden bowls full of incense, which are the prayers of the saints; and they sang a new song, saying,

"Worthy art thou to take the scroll and to open its seals, for thou wast slain and by thy blood didst ransom men for God from every tribe and tongue and people and nation, and hast made them a kingdom and priests to our God, and they shall reign on earth."

Then I looked, and I heard around

the throne and the living creatures and the elders the voice of many angels, numbering myriads of myriads and thousands of thousands, saying with a loud voice, "Worthy is the Lamb who was slain, to receive power and wealth and wisdom and might and honor and glory and blessing!"

And I heard every creature in heaven and on earth and under the earth and in the sea, and all therein, saying, "To him who sits upon the throne and to the Lamb be blessing and honor and glory and might for ever and ever!" And the four living creatures said, "Amen!" and the elders fell down and worshiped.

718   Revelation 7:9-17

(Unison)

After this I looked, and behold, a great multitude which no man could number, from every nation, from all tribes and peoples and tongues, standing before the throne and before the Lamb, clothed in white robes, with palm branches in their hands, and crying out with a loud voice, "Salvation belongs to our God who sits upon the throne, and to the Lamb!"

And all the angels stood round the throne and round the elders and the four living creatures, and they fell on their faces before the throne and worshiped God, saying, "Amen! Blessing and glory and wisdom and thanksgiving and honor and power and might be to our God for ever and ever! Amen."

Then one of the elders addressed me, saying, "Who are these, clothed in white robes, and whence have they come?" I said to him, "Sir, you know." And he said to me, "These are they who have come out of the great tribulation; they have washed their robes and made them white in the blood of the Lamb.

"Therefore are they before the throne of God, and serve him day and night within his temple; and he who sits upon the throne will shelter them with his presence. They shall hunger no more, neither thirst any more; the sun shall not strike them, nor any scorching heat. For the Lamb in the midst of the throne will be their shepherd, and he will guide them to springs of living water; and God will wipe away every tear from their eyes."

719   Revelation 21:1-4; 22:1-5

(Unison)

Then I saw a new heaven and a new earth; for the first heaven and the first earth had passed away, and the sea was no more. And I saw the holy city, new Jerusalem, coming down out of heaven from God, prepared as a bride adorned for her husband; and I heard a great voice from the throne saying,

"Behold, the dwelling of God is with men. He will dwell with them, and they shall be his people, and God himself will be with them; he will wipe away every tear from their eyes, and death shall be no more, neither shall there be mourning nor crying nor pain any more, for the former things have passed away."

Then he showed me the river of the water of life, bright as crystal, flowing from the throne of God and of the Lamb through the middle of the street of the city; also, on either side of the river, the tree of life with its twelve kinds of fruit, yielding its fruit each month; and the leaves of the tree were for the healing of the nations.

There shall no more be anything accursed, but the throne of God and of the Lamb shall be in it, and his servants shall worship him; they shall see his face, and his name shall be on their foreheads. And night shall be no more; they need no light of lamp or sun, for the Lord God will be their light, and they shall reign for ever and ever.

Affirmations of Faith

720 An Affirmation of Faith from the Writings of John

We believe that God is Spirit, and they that worship Him must worship Him in spirit and in truth.

That God is Light, and that if we walk in the light, as He is in the light, we have fellowship one with another.

That God is Love, and that every one that loves is born of God and knows God.

We believe that Jesus Christ is the Son of God, and that God has given to us eternal life, and this life is in His Son.

That He is the Resurrection and the Life, and that whoever believes on Him, though he were dead, yet shall he live.

We believe that the Holy Spirit has come and convinces the world of sin, and of righteousness, and of judgment; that He guides us into all truth.

We believe that we are children of God, and that He has given us of His Spirit.

We believe that if we confess our sins He is faithful and just to forgive us our sins, and to cleanse us from all unrighteousness.

We believe that the world passes away and the lust thereof, but he that does the will of God abides forever.

721 The Apostles' Creed

I believe in God the Father Almighty, maker of heaven and earth: and in Jesus Christ His only Son our Lord, who was conceived by the Holy Spirit, born of the Virgin Mary, suffered under Pontius Pilate, was crucified, dead, and buried. He descended into hell;* the third day He arose again from the dead. He ascended into heaven, and sitteth on the right hand of God the Father Almighty; from thence He shall come to judge the quick and the dead. I believe in the Holy Spirit; the holy catholic** church; the communion of saints; the forgiveness of sins; the resurrection of the body; and the life everlasting.   Amen.

*"Hades," meaning realm of the dead.
**Meaning "universal."

722 The Nicene Creed

I believe in one God the Father Almighty, maker of heaven and earth, and of all things visible and invisible: and in one Lord Jesus Christ, the only-begotten Son of God, begotten of His Father before all worlds, God of God, Light of Light, very God of very God, begotten, not made, being of one substance with the Father, by whom all things were made: who for us men and for our salvation came down from heaven, and was incarnate by the Holy Spirit of the Virgin Mary, and was made man, and was crucified also for us under Pontius Pilate. He suffered and was buried, and the third day

He rose again according to the Scriptures, and ascended into heaven, and sitteth on the right hand of the Father. And He shall come again with glory to judge both the quick and the dead: whose kingdom shall have no end. And I believe in the Holy Spirit, the Lord and giver of life, who proceedeth from the Father and the Son, who with the Father and the Son together is worshiped and glorified, who spoke by the prophets. And I believe in one catholic* and apostolic church; I acknowledge one baptism for the remission of sins, and I look for the resurrection of the dead, and the life of the world to come. Amen.

*Meaning "universal."

723 An Affirmation of Faith *(Contemporary)*

We believe in Jesus Christ the Lord,
    Who was promised to the people of Israel,
    Who came in the flesh to dwell among us,
    Who announced the coming of the rule of God,
    Who gathered disciples and taught them,
    Who died on the cross to free us from sin,
    Who rose from the dead to give us life and hope,
    Who reigns in heaven at the right hand of God,
    Who comes to judge and bring justice to victory.

We believe in God His Father,
    Who raised Him from the dead,
    Who created and sustains the universe,
    Who acts to deliver His people in times of need,
    Who desires all men everywhere to be saved,
    Who rules over the destinies of men and nations,
    Who continues to love men even when they reject Him.

We believe in the Holy Spirit,
    Who is the form of God present in the church,
    Who moves men to faith and obedience,
    Who is the guarantee of our deliverance,
    Who leads us to find God's will in the Word,
    Who assists those whom He renews in prayer,
    Who guides us in discernment,
    Who impels us to act together.

We believe God has made us His people,
    To invite others to follow Christ,
    To encourage one another to deeper commitment,
    To proclaim forgiveness of sins and hope,
    To reconcile men to God through word and deed,
    To bear witness to the power of love over hate,
    To proclaim Jesus the Lord over all,
    To meet the daily tasks of life with purpose,
    To suffer joyfully for the cause of right,
        To the ends of the earth,
        To the end of the age,
        To the praise of His glory. Amen.

Congregational Responses

724 Response to Baptism (No. 1)

Congregation: As we now receive you into the fellowship of Christ's body, the church, we pledge that we will uphold and strengthen you in the Christian life, and that we will endeavor to grow together in the knowledge of Christ, that we may advance His kingdom throughout the world.

725 Response to Baptism (No. 2)

Congregation: As we now receive you into the fellowship of the church, we make a covenant with you as we renew our own covenant with our Lord:
To bear one another's burdens,
To share mutually in the forgiving or the retaining of our sins,
To share in the abundance of this world's goods,
To assist each other in times of need,
To share our joys and our sorrows,
And in all things to work for the common good,
Thus manifesting God's presence among us to His glory. As we unite with each other now, may we all be joined with Christ our Lord.

726 A Pledge of Faith and Love *(In preparation for the Lord's Supper)*

In token of the faith which binds us to God and of the love in which we are united,

We join in voicing our trust in God as our Father, in Christ as our Savior and Lord, and in the Holy Spirit as our Divine Strengthener.

We acknowledge our inclination to sin, both in what we do and in what we leave undone.

We ask for divine forgiveness for all our failure to glorify our Father, and we pledge ourselves to forsake and disown all conduct and attitudes which are unworthy of Christ.

We declare our love for the church, our belief in her principles, and our desire to practice them in all of life.

We pledge to the church our support in prayers, counsels, and gifts, so that she might become stronger in both her inward life and her outward witness.

We will strive by God's grace to remove from our lives all unlove, and cause of disharmony, so that our mutual love may lead men to know true discipleship.

We engage to watch over one another with Christian discernment, to counsel those who are weak, to seek in meekness to restore any who fall.

We will give ourselves to self-examination in preparation for the Lord's Supper, so that the Lord's table may be honored, and that we who gather around it may, by faith, eat and drink richly of Christ.

(A Prayer)

O God, who searchest the thoughts and triest the hearts of all men, enable us to prepare ourselves to approach Thy table; cleanse us from all unlove, that being pure in heart, we may without fear of condemnation commune in the body and blood of our Lord. Amen.

727 On Reception of New Members

Minister: These persons now presented to you, have witnessed to their faith in Jesus Christ, and offer themselves as companions in our obedience to Christ. It is our privilege and joy to welcome them into our family of faith.

Congregation: Your expressed faith and Christian intention compels us to renew our own covenant with Christ. In your coming to us, we are newly summoned to become a community in which the wholeness of Christ is realized.

We freely receive you, even as Christ has received us. We open ourselves to fellowship with you in worship, study, service, and discipline. We commit ourselves to watch over you and one another with a heart of concern and caring. We pledge our willingness to offer and to receive forgiveness in the redeemed community. We joyfully accept you as partners, both in the care of our spiritual family, and in our mission to the world.

728 To the Newly Married

Congregation: With joy we identify with you in this high moment of commitment and covenant. The vows you have taken compel us to weigh the purity of our love and to strengthen the relationships of our homes. We pledge that, as you follow Christ, we will join you in seeking to apprehend Him as our true life, and in serving Him by our love.

We offer our prayers that your lives may become increasingly rich in understanding, in common loyalties, and in useful vocation. We thank God for the home you now establish, and anticipate its strength, influence, and support of the church in its mission.

729 At the Dedication of Children

Congregation: You have offered your child to the strong and tender providence of God, and to the nurture of the church. We accept with humility of spirit and seriousness of purpose our responsibility for the spiritual well-being of this child. By our example and our words, we will support your parental role, in disposing this child to respond to the fullness that is in Christ. We earnestly pray that the life and witness of each of us will make your task both joyful and fruitful.

730 On Installation or Ordination of a Minister

Congregation: The charge to you becomes a charge to all of us, for we are all members one of another. As you exercise your gifts in equipping God's people for their work of ministering, we also will exercise our Spirit-given gifts. They are His to use even as your gifts are at His disposal. In common vocation with you as servants, we pledge to you our ungrudging support that you might freely exercise the ministries of leadership committed to you. Our material gifts, our prayers, our counsel, and our encouragement will be freely shared to support you. We are fellow servants, and seek to have you and ourselves realize the true fulfillment of the people of God. We earnestly desire that for us and for all whom you will serve, you will be a "good minister of Jesus Christ."

731 Statement of Restoration

Congregation: In your confession of failure to fulfill your Christian commitment, we are involved with you. We have failed to provide the supporting community which keeps the conscience alert, and the will strong to resist temptation. Forgive us for our failure to surround you with sufficient resources to draw you from the mastery of sin. We assure you that we are now, and will be, a forgiving community in which you are loved, accepted, and encouraged. We promise to be a caring, healing fellowship, forgetting the past in our continuing quest of following Christ. Having been freely pardoned ourselves, and having received your confession, we declare you forgiven in the name and for the sake of Christ. We therefore commend you to the strength and guardianship of the Holy Spirit.

732 In Commissioning Workers

Minister: God gives His people many gifts, all of which are useful in building His church. He calls all of us to serve in the ministry of reconciliation. Each of us thus participates in the servanthood of each. Of this vocation we are again reminded as these representatives leave us for service assignments elsewhere. Their task becomes our task. We, therefore, join in this commissioning charge.

Congregation: As God's Spirit calls and the church commissions, the servants of Christ are scattered in places of need throughout the world. We accept your service as an extension of this congregation, and pledge our support in ways which will make your ministry effective. We join with you in affirming the priority of Christ's kingdom. We urge you to consider your assignment as God's occasion to work through you in ministering to human need. We pray that you may be given a deep love for those whom you will serve. May Christ express Himself through you in word and deed. Our prayers will constantly support you while you are absent from us.

733 A Benediction *(For Congregational Use in Unison)*

Congregation: May the grace of Christ which daily renews our lives, and the love of God which enables us to love all men, and the fellowship of the Holy Spirit which unites us in one body, make us keen to discern and prompt to obey the complete will of God until we meet again, through Jesus Christ our Lord. Amen.

Prayers

734

Our God, how great You are! On the first day of the week we commemorate
Your creation of the world and all that is in it.
Thank You for the light which wakes us morning by morning
and for that greater light which shines in Jesus Christ.

Our God, how great You are! On the first day of the week You raised
Jesus from the dead.
Raise us with Him to a new quality of faith and life.

Our God, how great You are! Again on the first day of the week
You sent Your Spirit on Your disciples.
Do not deprive us of Your Spirit,
but renew Him in us day by day. Amen.

735

Lord, You are our God.
We want to realize how much we depend upon You.
You have not only given us life,
    You have made us able to think about its meaning
    And to choose and work for what is good.
In the world much is confusing;
    Many voices strive to be heard.
Yet we have Your word to guide us,
    The life and teaching of Your Son,
    The example of many faithful Christians.
We have known Your hand holding us fast,
    Your steps marking out the way for us:
    We long to know You still.
Your presence transforms even the darker times:
    With You we need not be afraid.
Nothing can separate us from Your love.
Draw out from us such an answering love
    That in our time of testing we may not fall away. Amen.

736

Come, O Holy Spirit.
Come as Holy Fire and burn in us,
Come as Holy Wind and cleanse us within,
Come as Holy Light and lead us in the darkness,
Come as Holy Truth and dispel our ignorance,
Come as Holy Power and enable our weakness,
Come as Holy Life and dwell in us.

Convict us, convert us, consecrate us until we are set free from the service of ourselves to be Thy servants to the world.

O Holy God, place us humbly at the feet of Thy Son Jesus Christ, that looking steadfastly up unto Him we may both learn and receive from Him those things that belong to the world's true peace and salvation and do Thou make us such faithful interpreters of His life that our fellowmen may return unto Thee and be saved through the same Jesus Christ our Lord. Amen.

737 Thanksgiving Prayers

Lord Jesus Christ, our great High Priest, merciful and faithful, we are glad that You were made like us, that You passed through the test of suffering, that You were made perfect through suffering.

Humbly and joyfully we thank You for offering Yourself to God as the perfect sacrifice, to cleanse our consciences and make us fit to serve God.

We thank You that by dying You broke the power of death, and that You live to intercede on our behalf.

Grant our request that today and throughout our lives we may approach God through You with confidence, and hold fast to the faith we profess. Amen.

738

Thou, O Lord, art the giver of every good and perfect gift. Thou hast called us to the adventure of life, sustained us by Thy providence, chastened us by Thy discipline, and redeemed us by Thy love.

We thank Thee for life with its mystery and wonder, its friendships and activities, its splendor and satisfactions.

We thank Thee for food, raiment, shelter, and all the material benefits of Thy providence.

We thank Thee for burdens which increase our strength, for hindrances that turn our steps away from evil, and for all discipline that brings us closer to Thee.

We thank Thee for the divine light that shone in the face of Jesus, the divine spirit that showed in His teachings, and the divine love that made Him obedient unto death, even the death of the cross.

Our tribute of praise we offer in the name of our Savior. Amen.

739 Prayers of Confession

We confess to You, Lord, what we are: we are not the people we like others to think we are; we are afraid to admit even to ourselves what lies in the depths of our souls. But we do not want to hide our true selves from You. We believe that You know us as we are, and yet You love us. Help us not to shrink from self-knowledge; teach us to respect ourselves for Your sake; give us the courage to put our trust in Your guiding and power.

We also confess to You, Lord, the unrest of the world, to which we contribute and in which we share. Forgive us that so many of us are indifferent to the needs of our fellowmen.

Forgive our reliance on weapons of terror, our discrimination against people of different race, and our preoccupation with material standards. And forgive us Christians for being so unsure of our good news and so unready to tell it.

Raise us out of the paralysis of guilt into the freedom and energy of forgiven people. And for those who through long habit find forgiveness hard to accept, we ask You to break their bondage and set them free. Through Jesus Christ our Lord. Amen.

740

Almighty and most merciful God, we acknowledge and confess that we have sinned against Thee in thought and word and deed, that we have not loved Thee with all our heart and soul, with all our mind and strength, and that we have not loved our neighbor as ourselves.

We beseech Thee, O God, to be forgiving to what we have been, to help us to amend what we are, and by Thy mercy to direct what we shall be, so that the love of goodness may ever be first in our hearts, that we may always walk in Thy commandments and ordinances blameless, and follow unto our life's end in the steps of Jesus Christ our Lord. Amen.

741   **Supplication and Intercession**

Lord, make me an instrument of Thy peace.
    Where there is hatred, let me sow love;
    Where there is injury, pardon;
    Where there is doubt, faith;
    Where there is despair, hope;
    Where there is darkness, light;
    Where there is sadness, joy.
O Divine Master, grant that I may not so much seek
    To be consoled, as to console;
    To be understood, as to understand;
    To be loved, as to love.
For it is in giving that we receive;
It is in pardoning that we are pardoned;
It is in dying that we are born to eternal life.

742

Lord Jesus, when You have drawn all men to Yourself, there will be peace on earth.

When we try to get things for ourselves, and have things our own way, we fight and push, and are angry and cruel, and everything is made less happy than it was meant to be, and Your kingdom does not come.

So give us Your Spirit, to make us people who build Your kingdom, not people who pull it down.

Help us to want things Your way, not our way.

Take our strength and our energy, and help us to put all we have into the struggle for Your goodness and Your truth.

Yours be the power and the victory for ever and ever. Amen.

743

O Thou who rulest the world from end to end and from everlasting to everlasting, make us to know that Thou art God and that in Thee alone is our hope.

Grant us grace to repent of our sins and to yield our wills to Thine, that Thou mayest forgive all our iniquities and heal all our diseases and redeem our lives from destruction.

Bring us more and more into fellowship with Thee, O God of peace, that we may have peace within our hearts and that Thou, O Lord, mayest work through us to give peace to the world; through Jesus Christ our Lord. Amen.

744

Lord God, the story of Your love for us makes us realize that there are many others as well as ourselves who need Your help and Your grace. So we bring our prayers to You:
For those who suffer pain;
For those whose minds are disturbed, or have never matured;
For those who have not had the opportunity to realize their potentialities;
For those who are satisfied with something less than the life for which they were made;
For those who know their guilt, their shallowness, their need, but who do not know of Jesus;
For those who know that they must shortly die;
For those who cannot wait to die.
Lord God, Your Son has taken all our sufferings upon Himself and has transformed them.
Help us, who offer these prayers, to take the sufferings of others upon ourselves, and so, by Your grace, become the agents of Your transforming love.
Through Jesus Christ our Lord. Amen.

745

Thou Father of our Lord Jesus Christ, who is head of the church, give us grace to lay to heart the great dangers we are in by our unhappy divisions. Take away all hatred and prejudice, and whatsoever else may hinder us from godly union and concord, that as there is but one body, and one spirit, and one hope of our calling, one Lord, one faith, one baptism, one God and Father of us all, so we may henceforth be all of one heart, and of one soul, united in one holy bond of truth and peace, of faith and charity, and may with one mind and one mouth glorify Thee, through Jesus Christ our Lord. Amen.

746

O Lord, we know not what to ask of Thee.
Thou alone knowest what are our true needs.
Thou lovest us more than we ourselves know how to love.
Help us to see our real needs which are concealed from us.
We dare not ask either a cross or consolation.
We can only wait on Thee. Our hearts are open unto Thee.
    Visit and help us, for Thy great mercy's sake.
    Strike us and heal us.
    Cast us down and raise us up.
We worship in silence Thy holy will and Thine inscrutable ways.
We offer ourselves as a sacrifice unto Thee.
We put all our trust in Thee.
We have no other desire than to fulfill Thy will.
    Teach us how to pray.
    Pray Thou Thyself in us. Amen.

747

O Master, lover of mankind, kindle within our hearts the clear light of Thy divine knowledge, and open the eyes of our understanding, that we may understand the preaching of Thy gospel: graft in us also the fear of Thy blessed commandments, that having trodden underfoot all fleshly lusts, and thinking and doing always such things as please Thee, we may continue in a spiritual manner of life.

For Thou art the light, O Christ our God, both of our souls and bodies, and we give glory to Thee, together with Thine unbegotten Father, and Thy most holy and gracious and life-giving Spirit, now and for ever and world without end. Amen.

748

Heavenly Father, give us Your Holy Spirit that He may enable us to make known to You our needs by our prayers and supplications; that He Himself may intercede for us with groanings which cannot be uttered, sanctifying us and keeping our hearts, our thoughts, and our desires; and that in these days particularly, He will grant us to know ourselves and to manifest to the world Your light in Jesus Christ, Your Son, our Lord, who lives and reigns with You in the unity of the Holy Spirit, one God, now and always and unto ages of ages. Amen.

749   **Offering**

Father, we give back to You in thankfulness what You have given to us in Your kindness. We acknowledge that the world and its resources are not ours but Yours, and that You have put us in charge as Your trustees. Help us to exercise responsibly the authority You give us in Your world.

Let Jesus Your Son be the pattern for all our dealings with one another, and with the rest of creation. He is truth: so help us to take our quest for truth seriously, whether in the research laboratories, or in the dialectic of philosophy and politics. He is life: so give us reverence for life, whether on the poultry farms or on the roads.

Yet with His care give us also His joy in life. With His compassion give us also His strength. So that in everything He may be everything to us. Praise and victory be to Him from all, and in all, for ever and ever. Amen.

750
Closing

Father, as we go to our homes and our work this coming week, we ask You to send the Holy Spirit into our lives.

Open our ears—To hear what You are saying to us in the things that happen to us and in the people we meet.
Open our eyes—To see the needs of the people round us.
Open our hands—To do our work well. To help when help is needed.
Open our lips—To tell others the good news of Jesus and bring comfort, happiness, and laughter to other people.
Open our minds—To discover new truth about You and the world.
Open our hearts—To love You and our fellowmen as You have loved us in Jesus.

To Him, with You our Father and the Holy Spirit, one God, all honor and praise shall be given now and for ever. Amen.

751

Lord Jesus, Word of the Father, spoken in mercy and power to mankind, may all power serve You, all mercy follow Your lead.

Word of pity, let men find in You an example to inspire them without daunting them, and a love to reassure them without smothering them.

Word of life, let men find in You the key to all the riddles of existence, and the door to an eternal hope.

Word of command, may we go now, refreshed by Your presence, and put Your plans into action and Your energy to good use.

For Your name's sake. Amen.

752

Lord God, You have come near to us and shown us something of Your patience, something of Your sympathy, something of Your love.

Give us, Lord, as we go about our life in the world, patience when men are indifferent to Your claims, sympathy for the needs of all Your creatures, a love which reflects Your forgiving love for men.

Through Jesus Christ our Lord. Amen.

Topical Index of Worship Resources

TOPICAL INDEX OF WORSHIP RESOURCES

Acknowledgments

With sincere gratefulness and deep appreciation the publishers wish to acknowledge all persons, publishers, and trustees of estates for permission to use the copyrighted matter in this *Hymnal*. Numerous correspondents were especially helpful in providing addresses difficult to locate and in giving information on copyright material. To these, too, we wish to express our gratitude. Every effort was made to locate and write to copyright owners for permissions. If we have inadvertently omitted securing permission or have used material which we had thought to be in public domain, you will be doing the publishers a favor by giving them the correct information. Proper acknowledgment can then be made in future editions.

THE HYMNS

9. Music from *Gesangbuch der Mennoniten* by permission of Faith and Life Press. International copyright, 1965.
10. Music by permission of Verein zur Herausgabe des Gesangbuches der Evangelisch-Reformierten Kirchen der Deutschsprachigen Schweiz.
13. Words by permission of J. Curwen & Sons, Ltd.
17. Harmonization from *Songs of Syon*, Schott & Co., London; by permission of J. Meredith Tatton, copyright owner.
20. Translation by permission of Lester Hostetler. Music from *Gesangbuch der Mennoniten* by permission of Faith and Life Press. International copyright, 1965.
22. Music by permission of Public Trustee Office, London.
23. Words from the *Scottish Metrical Psalter* by Nichol Grieve by permission of T. & T. Clark, Edinburgh.
24, 26. Music from *Gesangbuch der Mennoniten* by permission of Faith and Life Press. International copyright, 1965.
28. Music by permission of Public Trustee Office, London.
31. Music from *Gesangbuch der Mennoniten* by permission of Faith and Life Press. International copyright, 1965.
33. Words and music copyright 1941 by Eden Publishing House. Used by permission.
38. Music by permission of Verein zur Herausgabe des Gesangbuches der Evangelisch-Reformierten Kirchen der Deutschsprachigen Schweiz.
40. Translation by permission of Marion Wenger. Music from *Gesangbuch der Mennoniten*. International copyright, 1965.
51. Words by permission of J. Curwen & Sons, Ltd. Music from *The English Hymnal* by permission of Oxford University Press. Arrangement altered with permission.
52. Words by permission of J. Curwen & Sons, Ltd.
55. Words and music from the *EACC Hymnal*. Copyright by Christian Audio Visual Center, Tokyo.
59. Music from *Gesangbuch der Mennoniten* by permission of Faith and Life Press. International copyright, 1965.
60. Music from Layriz from *Eine Sammlung der gangbarsten Chorale der evang.-Lutherischen Kirchen.*
62. Words by permission of Lord Brooke of Cumnor, Hampstead, England.
68. Words from *The Mennonite Hymnary* by permission of the Board of Publication of the General Conference of the Mennonite Church of North America. Music from *Gesangbuch der Mennoniten* by permission of Faith and Life Press. International copyright, 1965.
71. Music from *The English Hymnal* by permission of Oxford University Press.
73. Melody by permission of the original publisher, Breitkopf and Hartel, Wiesbaden. Arrangement of music copyright 1933, 1961, by Presbyterian Board of Education. Used by permission.
76. Music copyright by Mary B. Rowlands. Used by permission.
77. Music by permission of Verein zur Herausgabe des Gesangbuches der Evangelisch-Reformierten Kirchen der Deutschsprachigen Schweiz.
82. Words from the *Scottish Metrical Psalter* by Nichol Grieve by permission of T. & T. Clark, Edinburgh.
88. Words by permission of Robert B. Y. Scott. Music

by permission of James Hopkirk.
92. Music by permission of The Church Pension Fund.
94. Music from *Enlarged Songs of Praise* by permission of Oxford University Press.
115. Music from *The BBC Hymn Book* by permission of Oxford University Press.
116. Translation by permission of Martin L. Seltz. Music from *Gesangbuch der Mennoniten* by permission of Faith and Life Press. International copyright, 1965.
118. Music from the *Service Book and Hymnal* (Lutheran) by permission of the Commission on the Liturgy and the Hymnal.
119. Words and music from the *Hymnal for Colleges and Schools* by permission of Yale University Press.
124. Words and music from the *Service Book and Hymnal* (Lutheran) by permission of the Commission on the Liturgy and the Hymnal.
131. Words for stanza 3 from the *Service Book and Hymnal* (Lutheran) by permission of the Commission on the Liturgy and the Hymnal. Words for stanzas 1 and 2 by permission of G. Schirmer, Inc., New York and E. C. Shirmer Music Co., Boston.
134. Music altered from Layriz by permission from *Eine Sammlung der gangbarsten Chorale der evang.-Lutherischen Kirchen.*
141. Music from the *Service Book and Hymnal* (Lutheran) by permission of the Commission on the Liturgy and the Hymnal.
145. Words copyright 1927 by Calvin W. Laufer; renewed 1955 by E. B. Laufer; from *Hymns for Junior Worship*. Used by permission.
153. Music from the *Service Book and Hymnal* (Lutheran) by permission of the Commission on the Liturgy and the Hymnal.
158. Words copyright. From *The Yattendon Hymnal* by permission of Oxford University Press. Stanza 3 omitted with permission.
163. Harmony by permission of Alice Parker.
172. Words from the *Service Book and Hymnal* (Lutheran) by permission of the Commission on the Liturgy and the Hymnal. The tune is copyright and reprinted by permission of the executors of the late Dr. John Ireland.
173. Music by permission of Verein zur Herausgabe des Gesangbuches der Evangelisch-Reformierten Kirchen der Deutschsprachigen Schweiz.
175. Music from *Choralbuch zum Einheitsgesangbuch* by permission of Gutersloher Verlagshaus Gerd Mohn, Gutersloh, Germany.
180. Words from *Cantate Domino*. By permission of the Word Student Christian Federation, Geneva.
182. Words and music from the *Service Book and Hymnal* (Lutheran) by permission of the Commission on the Liturgy and the Hymnal.
196. Words from *Hymns of the Russian Church* by permission of Oxford University Press.
198. Words from *Enlarged Songs of Praise* by permission of Oxford University Press.
200. Words by permission of Independent Press, Ltd., London.
204. Words and music from *The Hymnbook* of the Mennonite Brethren Church of Canada.
205. Words from *The Common Service Book of the United Lutheran Church of America*. Used by permission. Music by permission of Verein zur Herausgabe des Gesangbuches der Evangelisch-Reformierten Kirchen der Deutschsprachigen Schweiz.

207. Music by permission of Alice Parker.
209. Translation copyright, 1953, by Frank W. Price. Used by permission. Music by permission of The United Church of Christ in Japan, Tokyo.
210. Music from *The English Hymnal* by permission of Oxford University Press.
211. Words copyright. From *The Yattendon Hymnal* by permission of Oxford University Press. Stanzas 3 and 5 omitted with permission. Music from the *Hymnal for Colleges and Schools* by permission of Yale University Press.
212. Words from the *Service Book and Hymnal* (Lutheran) by permission of the Commission on the Liturgy and the Hymnal. Music by permission of Verein zur Herausgabe des Gesangbuches der Evangelisch-Reformierten Kirchen der Deutschsprachigen Schweiz.
218. Words and music from the *Service Book and Hymnal* (Lutheran) by permission of the Commission on the Liturgy and the Hymnal.
223. Music from *Gesangbuch der Mennoniten* by permission of Faith and Life Press. International copyright, 1965.
224. Words from *Enlarged Songs of Praise* by permission of Oxford University Press. Music from *Gesangbuch der Mennoniten* by permission of Faith and Life Press. International copyright, 1965.
228. Music by permission of J. Harold Moyer.
231. Music from *The English Hymnal* by permission of Oxford University Press.
232. Music from the *Church Hymnal.* Copyright 1927 by the Mennonite Publishing House.
235. Words from the *Service Book and Hymnal* (Lutheran) by permission of the Commission on the Liturgy and the Hymnal. Music by permission of Verein zur Herausgabe des Gesangbuches der Evangelisch-Reformierten Kirchen der Deutschsprachigen Schweiz.
247. Words by permission of Walter Russell Bowie.
250. Music from Layriz from *Eine Sammlung der gangbarsten Chorale der evang.-Lutherischen Kirchen.*
252. Music from *Revised Church Hymnary* by permission of Oxford University Press.
253. Words from the *Service Book and Hymnal* (Lutheran) by permission of the Commission on the Liturgy and the Hymnal. Tune copyright reprinted by permission of the Executors of the late Professor David Evans.
255. Words copyright and used by permission of Bryn A. Rees.
256. Music from the *Hymnal for Colleges and Schools* by permission of Yale University Press.
264. Music by permission of Verein zur Herausgabe des Gesangbuches der Evangelisch-Reformierten Kirchen der Deutschsprachigen Schweiz.
274. Words by permission of Houghton Mifflin Co. Music copyright. Used by permission of the Psalms and Hymns Trust.
278. Words from the *Scottish Metrical Psalter* by Nichol Grieve by permission of T. & T. Clark, Edinburgh.
281. Music by permission of Novello & Co., Ltd.
286. Words from the *Service Book and Hymnal* (Lutheran) by permission of the Commission on the Liturgy and the Hymnal.
291. Words copyright. From *The Yattendon Hymnal* by permission of Oxford University Press.
295. Words from *Eleven Ecumenical Hymns,* copyright 1954 by The Hymn Society of America. Used by permission.
297. Music by permission of The Church Pension Fund.
299. Words by permission of Ernest Merrill.
300. Words from *The Poem Book of the Gael* by permission of the literary estate of the editor, Eleanor Hull, and Chatto and Windus, Ltd., London. Music from *Enlarged Songs of Praise* by permission of Oxford University Press. Harmonization altered by permission.
304. Words from *Enlarged Songs of Praise* and music from *The English Hymnal,* both by permission of Oxford University Press.
308. Words from *The Lutheran Hymnal,* copyright 1941. Reprinted by permission of Concordia Publishing House.
309. Words copyright by Harry Webb Farrington and used by permission of The Hymn Society of America.
311. Music under international copyright of Mrs. Dilys Webb through Mechanical-Copyright Protection Society, Ltd., and reproduced by permission of the legal representatives of the composer who reserve all rights therein.
312. Words © Copyright 1960, Broadman Press. All rights reserved. International copyright secured. Used by permission.
319. Music from *Gesangbuch der Mennoniten* by permission of Faith and Life Press. International copyright, 1965.
323. Words from *The English Hymnal* by permission of Oxford University Press. Music by permission of The Church Pension Fund.
329. Translation by permission of Joanna S. Andres.
335. Words and music from the *Service Book and Hymnal* (Lutheran) by permission of the Commission on the Liturgy and the Hymnal.
338. Words and music from *The Hymnbook* of the Mennonite Brethren Church of Canada.
339. Translation copyright, 1953, by Frank W. Price. Used by permission. Music from *Hymns of Universal Praise.* Copyright 1965 by Bliss Wiant. Used by permission.
341. Music by permission of Verein zur Herausgabe des Gesangbuches der Evangelisch-Reformierten Kirchen der Deutschsprachigen Schweiz.
344. Translation by permission of David Augsburger.
352. Words and music from *Hymnal for Colleges and Schools* by permission of Yale University Press.
353. Music by permission of J. Randall Zercher.
359. Words by permission of Oxford University Press.
360. Words from *Fourteen New Rural Hymns,* copyright 1955 by The Hymn Society of America. Used by permission.
361. Music from *The English Hymnal* by permission of Oxford University Press.
362. Words and music from the *Pilgrim Hymnal.* Copyright 1958, The Pilgrim Press. Used by permission.
363. Words from *Ten Stewardship Hymns,* copyright 1961 by The Hymn Society of America. Used by permission. Music from *The BBC Hymn Book* by permission of Oxford University Press.
365. Music by permission of Verein zur Herausgabe des Gesangbuches der Evangelisch-Reformierten Kirchen der Deutschsprachigen Schweiz.
367. Words by permission of Oxford University Press. Music by permission of Independent Press, Ltd., London.
377. Words and music by permission of The United Church of Christ in Japan, Tokyo. Base stave added by permission.
384. Words by permission of Ernest A. Payne. Music from Layriz from *Eine Sammlung der gangbarsten Chorale der evang.-Lutherischen Kirchen.*
386. Translation by permission of Walter Klaassen.
387. Words by permission of Theo. Oxenham.
391. Music by permission of Verein zur Herausgabe des Gesangbuches der Evangelisch-Reformierten Kirchen der Deutschsprachigen Schweiz.
395. Music from *The English Hymnal* by permission of Oxford University Press.
396. Music from Layriz from *Eine Sammlung der gangbarsten Chorale der evang.-Lutherischen Kirchen.*
403. Words from *Enlarged Songs of Praise* by permission of Oxford University Press.
404. Music by permission of The Church Pension Fund.
406. Words and music from the *Service Book and Hymnal* (Lutheran) by permission of the Commission on the Liturgy and the Hymnal.
414. Words by permission of Philip E. Gregory.
415. Music from Layriz from *Eine Sammlung der gangbarsten Chorale der evang.-Lutherischen Kirchen.*
417. Words and music from *The Lutheran Hymnal,* copyright 1941. Reprinted by permission of Concordia Publishing House.
420. Words from the *Service Book and Hymnal* (Lutheran) by permission of the Commission on the Liturgy and the Hymnal.
425. Music by permission of Independent Press, Ltd., London.
426. Words and music copyright 1941 by Eden Publishing House. Used by permission.

427. Music by permission of Independent Press, Ltd., London.
433. Words from *The Toiling of Felix and Other Poems* by Henry van Dyke. Charles Scribner's Sons (1900). Music from *The BBC Hymn Book* by permission of Oxford University Press.
434. Words by permission of Harry Emerson Fosdick. Music under international copyright of Mrs. Dilys Webb through Mechanical-Copyright Protection Society, Ltd., and reproduced by permission of the legal representatives of the composer who reserve all rights therein.
435. Music by permission of the Proprietors of *Hymns Ancient and Modern*.
438. Words and music from *Life Songs II*. Copyright 1938 by Mennonite Publishing House.
441. Words by permission of Ernest Merrill and *The Presbyterian Outlook*.
445. Music by permission of Schott & Co., Ltd., London.
446, 447. Words by permission of Oxford University Press.
449. Words by permission of Theo. Oxenham.
450. Words by permission of Walter Russell Bowie. Music from *Hymnal for Colleges and Schools* by permission of Yale University Press.
452. Music by permission of Oxford University Press.
453. Words by permission of Elispeth Dunkerley.
455. Words by permission of The American Peace Society.
457. Words and music by permission of Oxford University Press. Arrangement altered with permission.
459. Words by permission of S. Ralph Harlow.
462. Words by permission of Albert Frederick Bayly. Music from *Songs of Praise* (1925) by permission of Oxford University Press. Arrangement altered with permission.
466. Words and music from the *Service Book and Hymnal* (Lutheran) by permission of the Commission on the Liturgy and the Hymnal.
467. Words by permission of the National Sunday School Union. Music from *A Student's Hymnal* by permission of Oxford University Press.
468. Words copyright. By permission of the Methodist Youth Department. Music by permission of Kenneth G. Finlay.
469. Words by permission of Albert Frederick Bayly. Music by permission of Kenneth G. Finlay.
470. Words copyright 1946 by the Westminster Press; from *Hymns for Primary Worship*. Used by permission.
471. Words for stanzas 1, 2, and 3 from *Youth Hymnary* by permission of Faith and Life Press. Copyright 1956. Words for stanza 4 and refrain from *The Hymnbook* of the Mennonite Brethren Church of Canada.
476. Words from *Songs of Praise for Boys and Girls* by permission of Oxford University Press.
479. Words and music from the *Church Hymnal*. Copyright 1927 by Mennonite Publishing House.
480. Words from *The English Hymnal* by permission of Oxford University Press. Music from *Hymnal for Colleges and Schools* by permission of Yale University Press.
484. Words and music from the *Service Book and Hymnal* (Lutheran) by permission of the Commission on the Liturgy and the Hymnal.
486. Music from *Gesangbuch der Mennoniten* by permission of Faith and Life Press. International copyright, 1965.
487, 489. Words copyright. From *The Yattendon Hymnal* by permission of Oxford University Press.
497. Words and music from *The Hymnbook* of the Mennonite Brethren Church of Canada.
498. Words by permission of Frank W. Price. Music from *Hymns of Universal Praise*. Copyright 1965 by Bliss Wiant. Used by permission.
503. Music from *The English Hymnal* by permission of Oxford University Press. Arrangement altered with permission.
511. Music from Layriz from *Eine Sammlung der gangbarsten Chorale der evang.-Lutherischen Kirchen*.
513. Music from *The English Hymnal* by permission of Oxford University Press.
520. Music from *The Church Choir Book*; setting by

Healy William. Reprinted by permission of Concordia Publishing House.
523. Words and music from the *Service Book and Hymnal* (Lutheran) by permission of the Commission on the Liturgy and the Hymnal.
534. Words and music copyright, 1923. Renewal, 1951, by W. M. Runyan. Assigned to Hope Publishing Co. All rights reserved. Used by permission.
535. Copyright 1955 by Manna Music, Inc., Hollywood, Calif. International copyright secured. All rights reserved. Used by permission.
538. Words and music copyright 1917. Renewed 1945 by Nazarene Publishing House. Used by permission.
541. Words and music copyright, 1910. Renewal, 1938, by A. P. Towner. Assigned to Hope Publishing Co. All rights reserved. Used by permission.
545. Words and music copyright 1942 by Broadman Press. Used by permission.
548. Words and music from *The Hymnbook* of the Mennonite Brethren Church of Canada.
584. Words and music by permission of Carl Fischer, Inc., New York.
595. Music by permission of Oxford University Press.
597. German words and music from *Harvard University Hymn Book* by permission of Harvard University Press. English words from *Hymnal for Colleges and Schools* by permission of Yale University Press.
603. Words copyright 1928, renewed 1956 by Board of Christian Education of the Presbyterian Church in the U.S.A.; from *The Hymnal;* used by permission. Music copyright. From *The Yattendon Hymnal* by permission of Oxford University Press.
604. Words copyright. From *The Yattendon Hymnal* by permission of Oxford University Press. Music from *Hymnal for Colleges and Schools* by permission of Yale University Press.
605. Words by permission of Major E. Ainger and S.P.C.K. Music from *Enlarged Songs of Praise* by permission of Oxford University Press.
609. Words for first stanza from the *Service Book and Hymnal* (Lutheran) by permission of the Commission on the Liturgy and the Hymnal.
610. Music from Layriz from *Eine Sammlung der gangbarsten Chorale der evang.-Lutherischen Kirchen*.
612. Words from *The Lutheran Hymnal*, copyright 1941. Reprinted by permission of Concordia Publishing House.
614. Words by permission of A. R. Mowbray & Co., Ltd., London. Harmony by permission of Alice Parker.
615. Words and music from the *Service Book and Hymnal* (Lutheran) by permission of the Commission on the Liturgy and the Hymnal.
616. Words from *Five New Hymns on the City*, copyright 1954 by The Hymn Society of America. Used by permission. Original hymn tune: "City of God" by Daniel Moe. Reprinted from ACL 1193, "O Jesus Christ to Thee May Hymns be Rising." Copyright 1957. By permission of Augsburg Publishing House, Minneapolis, Minn., copyright owners.
617, 618. Words and music by permission of The Grail, London.
619. Music from *Hymnal for Colleges and Schools* by permission of Yale University Press.
626. Music by permission of J. Harold Moyer.
630. Words and music by permission of the Brethren Press.
645. Music from *The Clarendon Hymnbook* by permission of the Trustees of the late Sir Walford Davies.
646. Music by permission of Alice Parker.
653. Music from *Pilgrim Hymnal*. Copyright, 1958, The Pilgrim Press. Used by permission.
The following material is covered by the publisher's copyright:
Translations and Words: 40, 284, 344, 386.
Altered Words: 158, 211.
Music and Harmonizations: 163, 207, 228, 273, 353, 615, 626, 64b.
Altered Music: 51, 134, 300, 377, 457, 462, 503.

ADDITIONAL WORSHIP RESOURCES

654-662, 664-689, 691, 693-702, 705, 706, 709-711, 713, 714, 716-719. These readings are from the *Revised Standard Version* of the Bible. Copyrighted 1946 and 1952. Used by permission.

663. From the *King James Version* of the Bible.

690, 692, 704, 707, 712, 715. From *The New English Bible.* © the Delegates of the Oxford University Press and the Syndics of the Cambridge University Press 1961. Used by permission.

703. From *The New Testament in Modern English.* © J. B. Phillips, 1958. Used by permission of The Macmillan Company. Changes in the text of verses 32 and 33 by permission of J. B. Phillips.

708. From *Good News for Modern Man* copyright © 1966 by American Bible Society. Used by permission.

720. From *Book of Common Worship* by Bishop Wilbur P. Thirkield and Dr. Oliver Huckle. Copyright, 1932, by E. P. Dutton & Co., Inc. Renewal, © 1960 by Gilbert H. Thirkield. Reprinted by permission of the publishers.

723. By Committee on Worship Aids for *The Mennonite Hymnal*, 1967.

725. Patterned after the baptismal vows made at an Anabaptist congregation in Strasbourg in 1557.

726-733. By John H. Mosemann, 1967.

734, 735, 737, 739, 744, 749-752. From *Contemporary Prayers for Public Worship* by Caryl Micklem. Copyright 1967 by Wm. B. Eerdmans Publishing Co. Used by permission.

738. From *Prayers for Christian Service* by Carl A. Glover. Copyright © 1959 by Abingdon Press. Used by permission.

740. From the book *Devotional Services* by Rev. John Hunter, DD. Reprinted by permission of the publishers, E. P. Dutton & Co., Inc.

741. From St. Francis of Assisi.

743. From *A Book of Pastoral Prayers* by Ernest Fremont Tittle. Copyright 1951 by Pierce and Smith (Abingdon Press). Used by permission.

745. From the *Book of Common Worship*, Eden Publishing House. Used by permission.

746. From *A Manual of Eastern Orthodox Prayers.* Published by the S.P.C.K. for the Fellowship of St. Alban and St. Regius. Used by permission.

747. From *The Orthodox Liturgy*, Published by the S.P.C.K. for the Fellowship of St. Alban and St. Regius. Used by permission.

Index of Authors, Translators, and Sources

Index of Composers, Arrangers, and Sources

Metrical Index of Tunes

SHORT METER
S.M. 6.6.8.6.

SHORT METER
with Refrain

SHORT METER DOUBLE
S.M.D. 6.6.8.6. D.

COMMON METER
C.M. 8.6.8.6.

COMMON METER
with Refrain

COMMON METER DOUBLE
C.M.D. 8.6.8.6. D.

COMMON METER DOUBLE
with Refrain

LONG METER
L.M. 8.8.8.8.

Alphabetical Index of Tunes

Index of Scriptural Allusions

Topical Index

Cry out with joy, 618
Eternal Father, 37
Father, we praise, 480
Glory be to God, 632
Glory be to the Father, 640, 641, 642
Holy, holy, holy, 5
Holy God, we praise, 1
Jehovah, let me now, 8
Jesus, with Thy church, 379
Jerusalem the golden, 416
Joy dawned again, 181
Lift up your heads, 120
Lord Jesus Christ, 91
My God, accept my, 399
Now praise we Christ, 598
O Christ, our hope, 288
O gladsome light, 489
O love that casts out, 287
O perfect love, 412
Of the Father's love, 92
Praise God from whom, 638
Praise, O praise, 518
Rejoice, ye pure, 277
Sing, my tongue, 404
The God of Abraham, 11
Thou, whose almighty, 429

TRUST
Scripture Readings, 663, 665, 666, 669, 671, 673, 682, 690

All the way my Savior, 573
As pants the hart, 285
As the hart, 284
Be not dismayed, 574
Be still, my soul, 73
Come, come, ye saints, 312
Father, whate'er, 336
God is my light, 85
God moves, 80
God of our life, 603
Great God, we sing, 508
How lovely are Thy, 393
If thou but suffer, 314
I love Thy kingdom, 380
I waited for the Lord, 302
Jesus, keep me near, 560
Lord, all my heart, 608
Lord of the worlds, 392
My hope is built, 558
O God of love, O King, 454
O Lord of life, 418
Peace, perfect peace, 271
Take Thou my hand, 318
Teach me the measure, 315
Thy way, not mine, 341
What God hath done, 77
When we walk, 577

TRUTH
Scripture Readings, 670, 701

Before Jehovah's aweful, 48
Eternal One, 313
God the omnipotent, 86
I love Thy kingdom, 380
Lead us, O Father, 317
O wonderful, wonderful, 587
O Word of God, 219
Send out Thy light, 631
Teach me Thy truth, 438
The heavens declare, 220

UNITY
(See CHURCH: Unity of)

VICTORY
(See also Conflict and Victory, 321-332)
Scripture Readings, 659, 669, 673, 703, 706, 717

A safe stronghold, 597
Alleluia! the strife, 183
Am I a soldier, 348
Awake, my soul, 110
Christ has for sin, 562
Christ is arisen, 612
Encamped along, 589
For all the saints, 395
Forty days and forty, 144
God is working, 605
Hail the day, 185
Heart and mind, 362
I will sing, 554
If ye then with Christ, 564
Jerusalem the golden, 416
Lead on, O King, 443
Look, ye saints, 186
Low in the grave, 567
O where are kings, 378
Onward, Christian, 591
Peace, perfect peace, 271
Rejoice, the Lord is, 184
Ride on, ride on, 156
Rise, glorious, 188
Sing, my tongue, 404
Stand up, stand up, 592
The day of resurrection, 174
The head that once, 189
The Savior died, 268
Thine is the glory, 180
This is the day, 499
Wake the song, 199
We have heard a joyful, 594
We welcome glad Easter, 474

VISION
Be Thou my vision, 300
God of our life, 603
Not always, 153
O holy city, 450

WAITING FOR GOD
Scripture Readings, 665, 682, 685

WALKING WITH GOD
Scripture Readings, 663, 677, 715

Come, we that love, 529
Forth in Thy name, 430, 432
I love the Lord, 617
In heavenly love, 252
O for a closer walk, 305
O happy day, 398
O Master, let me walk, 440
So let our lips, 327
The Lord's my Shepherd, 67
To Thy temple I repair, 390
Walk in the light, 282
When we walk, 577

WARNING
Scripture Readings, 655, 662

A charge to keep, 350, 351
Come with thy sins, 548
O wherefore do, 202
The Lord is King, 204
This body in the grave, 417

WATCHFULNESS
Scripture Reading, 694

A charge to keep, 350, 351
Am I a soldier, 348
Awake, my soul, 485
It may be at morn, 570
My soul, be on thy, 321
Rejoice, all ye, 194
The bridegroom soon, 195
Wake, awake, for night, 118

WATCH-NIGHT HYMNS
(See also Old and New Year, 508-511)
God is working, 605

WEDDING HYMNS
(See MARRIAGE HYMNS)

WHIT SUNDAY
(See HOLY SPIRIT)

WINTER
Great is Thy, 534
'Tis winter now, 512

WISDOM
Scripture Reading, 659

WITNESSING
(See also Evangelism and Missions, 419-429)

Scripture Readings, 670, 691, 697, 712, 716
Faith of our fathers, 262
Heart with loving, 386
I love to tell, 593
Jesus, from whom all, 372
Lord, speak to me, 389
O Master of the loving, 145
Savior, Thy dying, 355
Spread, still spread, 224
Take my life, 358

WORD OF GOD
(See BIBLE)
Scripture Readings, 655, 681, 686, 697, 713, 714

WORLD FRIENDSHIP AND PEACE
(See also PEACE—AMONG MEN)
Hope of the world, 295

WORSHIP AND PRAISE
Scripture Readings, 658, 664, 665, 671, 674, 675, 688, 689, 692, 708, 717, 718, 719

YOUTH, HYMNS FOR
All creatures, 51, 52
Away in a manger, 472
Be Thou my vision, 300
Come, Thou Almighty, 4
Day is dying, 493
Dear Lord and Father, 274
Fairest Lord Jesus, 97
Faith of our fathers, 262
Hark! the herald, 135
Heralds of Christ, 420
Holy, holy, holy, 5
How firm a foundation, 260
In the cross of Christ, 169
Jesus shall reign, 203
Joyful, joyful, 13
Joy to the world, 122
Just as I am, 354
O little town, 133
O young and fearless, 459
Rejoice, ye pure, 277
The church's one, 375
This is my Father's, 49
When morning gilds, 107

ZEAL
A charge to keep, 350, 351
Awake, my soul, 332
Christ, of all my, 286
Jesus merciful, 339
My soul, be on thy, 321
O God, Thou faithful, 352
Rise up, O men of God, 441
Strive aright, 328

Index of First Lines